The Sense of the Sixties

The Sense of the Sixties

Edited by

EDWARD QUINN
City College of the City University of New York

and

PAUL J. DOLAN
State University of New York at Stony Brook

New York THE FREE PRESS

First Printing

THE MAGNIFICENT SEVEN

For

*Deirdre, Colin, David, Jennifer,
Peter, John, and Paul II*

Preface

This is a book of readings with a difference. It is aimed at a specific audience—the audience for whom the Korean war is an historical event learned about in school. The writing is for here and now; the selections are all from the Sixties and they are all relevant. Our purpose is to show students their world interpreted in a variety of prose styles which they might emulate. Journalists and parajournalists, political leaders and scientists, novelists and critics, the writers included and the subjects with which they are concerned combine, both to make writing come alive and to give some perspectives, some angles of vision, on the world the students have inherited.

Although all the selections are from the Sixties, the book cannot cover the whole decade as we have come to know it. The relative complexity of our world is probably no greater than any other, but we learn so much more about it so quickly that it is more complicated for those living in it. The population explosion, the information explosion, the profusion of media and messages have made it impossible to present a unified or even representative sample of the age's thoughts, aspirations and preoccupations. What we have gathered are some of the quanta of contemporary experience.

You will very quickly become aware of areas of concern we have missed. Since our vision is not unlimited, this awareness is all to the good, and we welcome your additions and corrections. The selections should arouse your students enough to make them want to find out more about a given topic than we have provided. Since the topics are central to their world, we are all in trouble if they don't respond.

Most of the topics with which we deal have been of concern for some time. God and the Negro, War and Science have been with us for a long time. Each of these had, however, a special new definition, a new immediacy in the Sixties. One section is uniquely part of the Sixties. It relates to the question a journalist once asked: "How can you tell your children what it was like to be alive when John Kennedy was a man and not an airport?"

In preparing the book, we have had in mind, more than anything else, a new generation of students. Our feeling is that the new students and the teachers of these students are better served by prose that speaks to them directly. We further think that they will think more about good prose and how it is made by being caught up in good prose that is relevant. All good prose is relevant, but the topics and selections that follow have, we think, an immediacy that should save some time in engaging students in thinking and in determining the quality of their thought.

The book is specifically addressed to those Americans, born after World War II, now flooding the colleges, the generation of rising expectations that has crowded the universities. Others have been concerned with getting them classroom seats and dormitory beds. Our concern is with reminding them of something else. They must, as do the writers here, carry on the great human responsibility—the articulation of their experience. Our hope is that the selections will give impetus and provide models for the articulation which they, in their turn, must attempt.

Edward Quinn
Paul J. Dolan

Contents

The Sense of the Sixties

1
The Sense of the Sixties

In the sixth decade of the twentieth century America entered its middle age, and discovered its youth. The Fifties had been a period in which the key word had been *security*, personal and corporate, internal and external. The young people appeared intent only on being absorbed into the comfortable, well-regulated life of their elders. They were dubbed, appropriately enough, "The Silent Generation."

Quite suddenly, or so it seemed, the silence was broken. A new president was elected who represented, more than anything else, youth. He spoke of a new generation and of new frontiers, and the nation responded. Older people stopped looking at younger ones as a necessary evil they might either ignore or overindulge but never take seriously. And the young people themselves began to develop a sense of their own identity and with it a radically critical attitude about the society that their elders had created. They dissented, they dropped out, they said "No"—and the reverberations of that No are still being heard.

Some of these objections are presented with striking effectiveness in the opening selection, from Paul Goodman's *Growing Up Absurd,* a book that was itself one of the major testaments of the new spirit. Many of the general problems treated by Goodman were contributing factors to that particular incident that has come to symbolize the attitude of the youth of the Sixties, the so-called revolution at Berkeley. The conditions that precipitated the Berkeley incident and some of its implications are explored from contrasting viewpoints by Michael Miller and Lewis Feuer.

But Berkeley was only one expression of youthful activism in the Sixties. Civil rights, pacifism, political commitment, and the demand for social justice were some of the others. The result of this activity was the creation of a new political style described by Michael Harrington as "mystical militancy," and by Staughton Lynd as "participatory democracy." Taken together they define better than anything else the aspirations of a profoundly revolutionary spirit.

I

PAUL GOODMAN

1.

Growing up as a human being, a "human nature" assimilates a culture, just as other animals grow up in strength and habits in the environments that are for them, and that complete their natures. Present-day sociologists and anthropologists don't talk much about this process, and not in this way. Among the most competent writers, there is not much mention of "human na-

Growing Up Absurd—
"Human Nature" and the Organized System

ture." Their diffidence makes scientific sense, for everything we observe, and even more important, our way of observing it, is already culture and a pattern of culture. What is the sense of mentioning "human nature" if we can never observe it? The old-fashioned naïve thought, that primitive races or children are more natural, is discounted. And the classical anthropological question, What is Man?—"how like an angel, this quintessence of dust!"—is not now asked by anthropologists. Instead, they commence with a chapter on Physical Anthropology and then forget the whole topic and go on to Culture.

On this view, growing up is sometimes treated as if it were acculturation, the process of giving up one culture for another, the way a tribe of Indians takes on the culture of the whites; so the wild Babies give up their "individualistic" mores and ideology, e.g., selfishness or magic thinking or omnipotence, and join the tribe of Society; they are "socialized." More frequently, however, the matter is left vague: we start with a *tabula rasa* and end up with "socialized" and cultured. ("Becoming cultured" and "being adjusted to the social group" are taken almost as synonymous.) Either way, it follows that you can teach people anything; you can adapt them to anything if you use the right techniques of "socializing" or "communicating." The essence of "human nature" is to be pretty indefinitely malleable. "Man," as

C. Wright Mills suggests, is what suits a particular type of society in a particular historical stage.

This fateful idea, invented from time to time by philosophers, seems finally to be empirically evident in the most recent decades. For instance, in our highly organized system of machine production and its corresponding social relations, the practice is, by "vocational guidance," to fit people wherever they are needed in the productive system; and whenever the products of the system need to be used up, the practice is, by advertising, to get people to consume them. This works. There is a man for every job and not many are left over, and the shelves are almost always cleared. Again, in the highly organized political industrial systems of Germany, Russia, and now China, it has been possible in a short time to condition great masses to perform as desired. Social scientists observe that these are the facts, and they also devise theories and techniques to produce more facts like them, for the social scientists too are part of the highly organized systems.

2

Astonishingly different, however, is the opinion of experts who deal with human facts in a more raw, less highly processed, state. Those who have to cope with people in small groups rather than statistically, attending to *them* rather than to some systematic goal—parents and teachers, physicians and psychotherapists, policemen and wardens of jails, shop foremen and grievance committees—these experts are likely to hold stubbornly that there is a "human nature." You can't teach people some things or change them in some ways, and if you persist, you're in for trouble. Contrariwise, if you *don't* provide them with certain things, they'll fill the gaps with eccentric substitutes.

This is immediately evident when something goes wrong; for instance, when a child can't learn to read because he has not yet developed the muscular accommodation of his eyes; if you persist, he withdraws or becomes tricky. Such a case is clear-cut (it is "physical"). But the more important cases have the following form: the child *does* take on the cultural habit, e.g., early toilet training, and indeed the whole corresponding pattern of culture,

but there is a diminishing of force, grace, discrimination, intellect, feeling, in specific behaviors or even in his total behavior.
He may become too obedient and lacking in initiative, or im-
practically careful and squeamish; he may develop "psychoso-
matic" ailments like constipation. Let me give an instance even
earlier in life: an infant nurtured in an institution without a
particular nurse attending him during the first six months does
not seem to develop abnormally; but if during the end of the
first year and for some time thereafter he is not given personal
care, he will later be in some ways emotionally cold and un-
reachable—either some function has failed to develop, or he has
already blocked it out as too frustrated and painful. In such
examples, the loss of force, grace, and feeling seems to be evidence that somehow the acquired cultural habits do not draw on
unimpeded outgoing energy, they are against the grain, they do
not fit the child's needs or appetites; *therefore* they have been
ill adapted and not assimilated.

That is, on this view we do not need to be able to say what
"human nature" *is* in order to be able to say that some training
is "against human nature" and you persist in it at peril. Teachers
and psychologists who deal practically with growing up and the
blocks to growing up may never mention the word "human
nature" (indeed, they are better off without too many a priori
ideas), but they cling stubbornly to the presumption that at
every stage there is a developing potentiality *not* yet cultured,
and yet not blank, and that makes possible the taking on of
culture. We must draw "it" out, offer "it" opportunities, not
violate "it" except for unavoidable reasons. What "it" is, is not
definite. It is what, when appealed to in the right circumstances,
gives behavior that has force, grace, discrimination, intellect,
feeling. This vagueness is of course quite sufficient for education, for education is an art. A good teacher feels his way, looking for response.

3

The concept of "human nature" has had a varied political
history in modern times. If we trace it, we can see the present
disagreement developing.

In the eighteenth century, the Age of Reason and the early Romantic Movement, the emphasis was on "*human* nature," referring to man's naturally sympathetic sentiments, his communicative faculties, and unalienable dignity. (Immanuel Kant immortally thought up a philosophy to make these cohere.) Now this human nature was powerfully enlisted in revolutionary struggles against courts and classes, poverty and humiliation, and it began to invent progressive education. Human nature unmistakably demanded liberty, equality, and fraternity—and every man a philosopher and poet.

As an heir of the French Revolution, Karl Marx kept much of this concept. Sympathy recurred as solidarity. Dignity and intellect were perhaps still in the future. But he found an important new essential: man is a maker, he must use his productive nature or be miserable. This too involved a revolutionary program, to give back to man his tools.

During the course of the nineteenth century, however, "human nature" came to be associated with conservative and even reactionary politics. The later Romantics were historical minded and found man naturally traditional and not to be uprooted. A few decades later, narrow interpretations of Darwin were being used to support capitalist enterprise; and racial and somatic theories were used to advance imperial and elite interests. (The emphasis was now on "*nature*"; the humanity became dubious.) It was during this later period that the social scientists began to be diffident about "human nature"; for, politically, they wanted fundamental social changes, different from those indicated by the "natural" theory of the survival of the fittest; and, scientifically, it was evident that many anthropological facts were being called natural which were overwhelmingly cultural. Most of the social scientists began to lay all their stress on political organization, to bring about reform. Nevertheless, scientifically trained anarchists like Kropotkin insisted that "human nature"—which had now become mutual-aiding, knightly, and craftsmanlike—was still on the side of revolution.

In our own century, especially since the Twenties and Thirties, the social scientists have found another reason for diffidence: it seems to them that "human nature" implies "not social" and refers to something prior to society, belonging to an isolated individual. They have felt that too much importance has been assigned to Individual Psychology (they were reacting to Freud) and this has stood in the way of organizing people for political reform. It is on this view, finally, that growing up is now interpreted as a process of socializing some rather indefinite kind of animal, and "socializing" is used as a synonym for teaching him the culture.

4

Let us now proceed more carefully, for we are approaching our present plight. *Is* "being socialized," no matter what the society, the same as growing up and assimilating human culture? The society to which one is socialized would have to be a remarkably finished product.

There are here three distinct concepts, which sometimes seem the same but sometimes very different: (1) society as the relations of human social animals, (2) the human culture carried by society, and (3) a particular society, like ours, formed by its pattern of culture and institutions, and to which its members are socialized or adjusted.

In ordinary, static circumstances, and especially when a dominant system in a society is riding high (as the organized system is with us), socializing to that society seems to provide all valuable culture. But *as soon as we think of a fundamental social change*, we begin to say that people are being adjusted, "socialized," to a very limited kind of human society; and our notion of "human culture" at once broadens out to include ancient, exotic, and even primitive models as superior to the conventional standards (as, e.g., our disaffected groups lay store by the Japanese or the Samoans and Trobriand Islanders). Then at once "human nature" is again invoked to prove the necessity of change, for "human nature" has been thwarted or insulted by the dominant system. "Man" can no *longer* be defined as what suits the dominant system, when the dominant system apparently does not suit men.

I think many social scientists have been making an error in logic. Certainly only society is the carrier of culture (it is not inborn). But it does not follow that socialized and cultured are synonymous. What follows, rather, is that, since culture is so overwhelmingly evident in observing mankind, social properties must be of the essence of original "human nature," and indeed that the "isolated individual" is a product of culture.

This, of course, was just the line that Freud really took. Far from having an Individual Psychology, he tended to exaggerate the social nature of the baby by reading into it preformed traits of his own society. From the earliest infancy, imitation and emulation, love, striving to communicate, rivalry, exclusiveness and jealousy, punishment, introjected authority, identification, growing up on a model, finding safety in conforming—these were among the conflicting elementary functions of the "human nature" that must grow into culture. And Freud, with magnificent originality, tried to show that by their very conflict they made it possible to assimilate culture; only such a social animal *could* become cultured. Every step of education was the resolution of a difficult social conflict.

As might have been expected, from this hectic theory of human nature were drawn the most various political implications. Some, in the interests of community and sex reform, have wanted fundamental social changes, like Ferenczi and Reich. Others, to save religion, have been ultratraditionalist, like Jung or Laforgue. The run of orthodox psychoanalytic practice has been quietist, as the social scientists claimed. But the most surprising implication has been drawn by the social scientists themselves, when they finally got around to making use of modern psychology: they have found in it techniques for harmoniously belonging to the organized system of society!

A curious thing has occurred. Unlike the majority of their predecessors for a century and a half, most of our contemporary social scientists are not interested in fundamental social change. To them, we have apparently reached the summit of institutional progress, and it only remains for the sociologists and applied-anthropologists to mop up the corners and iron out the kinks. Social scientists are not attracted to the conflictful core of Freud's theory of human nature; a more optimistic theory, like Reich's, is paid no attention at all. But they have hit on the theory I mentioned at the beginning: that you can adapt people to anything, if you use the right techniques. Our social scientists have become so accustomed to the highly organized and by-and-large smoothly running society that they have begun to think that "social animal" means "harmoniously belonging." They do not like to think that fighting and dissenting are proper social functions, nor that rebelling or initiating fundamental change is a social function. Rather, if something does not run smoothly, they say it has been improperly socialized; there has been a failure in communication. The animal part is rarely mentioned at all; if it proves annoying, it too has been inadequately socialized.

5

Nevertheless, we see groups of boys and young men disaffected from the dominant society. The young men are Angry and Beat. The boys are Juvenile Delinquents. These groups are not small, and they will grow larger. Certainly they are suffering. Demonstrably they are not getting enough out of our wealth and civilization. They are not growing up to full capacity. They are failing to assimilate much of the culture. As was predictable, most of the authorities and all of the public spokesmen explain it by saying there has been a failure of socialization. They say that background conditions have interrupted socialization and must be improved. And, not enough effort has been made to guarantee belonging, there must be better bait or punishment.

But perhaps there has *not* been a failure of communication. Perhaps the social message has been communicated clearly to the young men and is unacceptable.

In this book I shall therefore take the opposite tack and ask, "Socialization to what? to what dominant society and available culture?" And if this question is asked, we must at once ask the other question, "Is the harmonious organization to which the young are inadequately socialized, perhaps against human nature, or not worthy of human nature, and *therefore* there is difficulty in growing up?" If this is so, the disaffection of the young is profound and it will not be finally remediable by better techniques of socializing. Instead, there will have to be changes in our society and its culture, so as to meet the appetites and capacities of human nature, in order to grow up.

This brings me to another proposition about growing up, and

perhaps the main theme of this book. *Growth, like any ongoing function, requires adequate objects in the environment* to meet the needs and capacities of the growing child, boy, youth, and young man, until he can better choose and make his own environment. It is not a "psychological" question of poor influences and bad attitudes, but an objective question of real opportunities for worth-while experience. It makes no difference whether the growth is normal or distorted, only real objects will finish the experience. (Even in the psychotherapy of adults one finds that many a stubborn symptom vanishes if there is a real change in the vocational and sexual opportunities, so that the symptom is no longer needed.) It is here that the theory of belonging and socializing breaks down miserably. For it can be shown—I intend to show—that with all the harmonious belonging and all the tidying up of background conditions that you please, our abundant society is at present simply deficient in many of the most elementary objective opportunities and worth-while goals that could make growing up possible. It is lacking in enough man's work. It is lacking in honest public speech, and people are not taken seriously. It is lacking in the opportunity to be useful. It thwarts aptitude and creates stupidity. It corrupts ingenuous patriotism. It corrupts the fine arts. It shackles science. It dampens animal ardor. It discourages the religious convictions of Justification and Vocation and it dims the sense that there is a Creation. It has no Honor. It has no Community.

Just look at that list. There is nothing in it that is surprising, in either the small letters or the capitals. I have nothing subtle or novel to say in this book; these are the things that *everybody* knows. And nevertheless the Governor of New York says, "We must give these young men a sense of belonging."

Thwarted, or starved, in the important objects proper to young capacities, the boys and young men naturally find or invent deviant objects for themselves; this is the beautiful shaping power of our human nature. Their choices and inventions are rarely charming, usually stupid, and often disastrous; we cannot expect average kids to deviate with genius. But on the other hand, the young men who conform to the dominant society become for the most part apathetic, disappointed, cynical, and wasted.

(I say the "young men and boys" rather than the "young people" because the problems I want to discuss in this book belong primarily, in our society, to the boys: how to be useful and make something of oneself. A girl does not *have* to, she is not expected to, "make something" of herself. Her career does not have to be self-justifying, for she will have children, which is absolutely self-justifying, like any other natural or creative act. With this background, it is less important, for instance, what job an average young woman works at till she is married. The quest for the glamour job is given at least a little substance by its relation to a "better" marriage. Correspondingly, our "youth troubles" are boys' troubles—female delinquency is sexual: "incorrigibility" and unmarried pregnancy. Yet as every woman knows, these problems are intensely interesting to women, for if the boys do not grow to be men, where shall the women find men? If the husband is running the rat race of the organized system, there is not much father for the children.)

6

This essay is on "Youth Problems." But the reader will find, perhaps to his surprise, that I shall make little distinction in value between talking about middle-class youths being groomed for ten-thousand-dollar "slots" in business and Madison Avenue, or underprivileged hoodlums fatalistically hurrying to a reformatory; or between hard-working young fathers and idle Beats with beards. For the salient thing is the sameness among them, the waste of humanity. In our society, bright lively children, with the potentiality for knowledge, noble ideals, honest effort, and some kind of worth-while achievement, are transformed into useless and cynical bipeds, or decent young men trapped or early resigned, whether in or out of the organized system. My purpose is a simple one: to show how it is desperately hard these days for an average child to grow up to be a man, for our present organized system of society does not want men. They are not safe. They do not suit.

Our public officials are now much concerned about the "waste of human resources." Dr. Conant, the former president of Harvard, has surveyed the high schools. But our officials are not serious, and Dr. Conant's report is superficial. For the big causes of stupidity, of lack of initiative and lack of honorable incentive, are glaring; yet they do not intend to notice or remedy these big causes. (This very avoidance of the real issues on the part of our public officials is, indeed, one of the big causes.) Our society cannot have it both ways: to maintain a conformist and ignoble system and to have skillful and spirited men to man that system with.

7

It is not my purpose in this essay to outline a better world. But I think it requires no deep wisdom or astonishing imagination to know what we need, and in a later chapter of this book I shall even list some points of a rough program. The prevalent sentiment that it is infinitely impractical to follow the suggestions of common reason, is not sound. If it is impractical, it is because some people don't want to, and the rest of us don't want to enough.

For instance, there is a persistent presumption among our liberal statesmen that the old radical-liberal program has been importantly achieved, and that therefore there is no familiar major proposal practical to remedy admittedly crying ills. This is a false presumption. Throughout the nineteenth and twentieth centuries, the radical-liberal program was continually compromised, curtailed, sometimes realized in form without content, sometimes swept under the rug and heard of no more. I shall later list more than twenty fundamental liberal demands that have gone unfulfilled which would still be live and salutary issues today if anybody wanted to push them. This has occurred, and keeps occurring, by the mutual accommodation of both "liberals" and "conservatives" in the interests of creating our present coalition of semimonopolies, trade unions, government, Madison Avenue, etc. (including a large bloc of outlaw gangsters); thriving on maximum profits and full employment; but without regard for utility, quality, rational productivity, personal freedom, independent enterprise, human scale, manly vocation, or genuine culture. It is in this accommodation that our politicians survive, but it does not make for statesmanship.

Even so mild a critic as Henry Steele Commager, in the *New York Times*, judges that we have had only three reputable statesmen in fifty years, the last of whom died fifteen years ago. While one may not agree with his number and examples, there is no doubt that we have been living in a political limbo.

Naturally this unnatural system has generated its own troubles, whether we think of the unlivable communities, the collapse of public ethics, or the problems of youth. I shall try to show in this essay that these ills are by no means inherent in modern technological or ecological conditions, nor in the American Constitution as such. But they have followed precisely from the betrayal and neglect of the old radical-liberal program and other changes proposed to keep up with the advancing technology, the growth of population, and the revolution in morals. Important reforms did not occur when they were ripe, and we have inherited the consequences: a wilderness of unfinished situations, unequal developments and inconsistent standards, as well as new business. And now, sometimes the remedy must be stoically to go back and carry *through* the old programs (as we are having to do with racial integration), e.g., finally to insist on stringent master-planning of cities and conserving of resources, or on really limiting monopolies. Sometimes we must make changes to catch up—e.g., to make the laws more consistent with the sexual revolution, or to make the expenditure on public goods more commensurate with the geometrically increasing complications of a more crowded population. And sometimes, finally, we have to invent really new devices—e.g., how to make the industrial technology humanly important for its workmen, how to use leisure nobly, or even how, in a rich society, to be decently poor if one so chooses.

This book is not about these great subjects. But they hover in the background of the great subject that it is about. For it is impossible for the average boy to grow up and use the remarkable capacities that are in every boy, unless the world is for him and makes sense. And a society makes sense when it understands that its chief wealth *is* these capacities.

MICHAEL HARRINGTON

When I became a radical in 1948 (the last year of the politics of the Thirties), it was taken for granted (on the Left) that the Fourth of July was really a front for the four hundred families. In part, this was a heritage of European socialist theory, in part a legacy of the American experience of a Depression which had demystified so many clichés. One did not get angry that the

The Mystical Militants

powers-that-be lied and cheated and manipulated. That, after all, was their function in life, just as it was the task of the Left to create a society which would not need to corrupt its avowed values.

The young radicals of today, it seems to me, did not start with this inherited cynicism. They came to teen-age during the American celebration of the Eisenhower years and were, for the most part, not really conscious until after both Korea and McCarthyism. They seemed to have believed what they were told about freedom, equality, justice, world peace and the like. They became activists in order to affirm these traditional values with regard to some ethical cause: defending civil liberties against HUAC, picketing for the life of Caryl Chessman, demanding an end to nuclear testing, fighting for civil rights. The shock generated by the society's duplicity in this or that single issue then opened their eyes to larger, and even more systematic, injustices.

It is, I suspect, this unique Fifties-Sixties experience which gives the New Left its distinctive flavor: a sense of outrage, of having been betrayed by all the father-figures, which derives from an original innocence. And it is also the source of the young radicals' insistence on sincerity and community. They begin, not with an image of the future which was received, in one way or another, from Europe and involves theory and history, but from a sense of the immediate contradiction between democratic posturing and the undemocratic reality. They descend from the Abolitionists and Wobblies, not from Marx.

This intense, even painful, consciousness of American hy-

From *The New Republic*, 154 (Feb. 19, 1966), 20–22. Reprinted with the permission of *The New Republic*.

pocrisy has led the young radicals to people who do not, or cannot, play the national rhetorical game: the left-outs, the outcasts. And it has involved them in a contradiction between mysticism and militancy.

In the iconography of the Thirties, the proletarian was a figure of incipient power and a Puritan sense of duty. The *lumpen* proletarian was despised because he did not belong to a conscious class, because he floated; and he was feared as a potential shock trooper of fascism. By the Fifties, much of the old élan had left the labor movement and, with an overwhelming majority of the people satisfied with Eisenhower, there did not seem to be much of a political perspective for insurgency. At this point a cultural rebellion took place among young people. It was expressed among the Beats who contracted out of the system; it informed Norman Mailer's vision of the white man who aspired to the cool and the hip which white society provoked in the Negro.

As disestablishmentarians, the young radicals continue this tradition of the Fifties. They identify precisely with the *lumpen*, the powerless, the maimed, the poor, the criminal, the junkie. And there is a mystical element in this commitment which has nothing to do with politics. By going into the slum, they are doing penance for the sins of affluence; by sharing the life of those who are so impoverished that they are uncorrupted, values are affirmed. It is honest and moral and anti-hypocritical to be on the margin of society *whether the community organization works or not.* Indeed, there is a fear of "success," a suspicion that it would mean the integration of the oppressed into the corruption of the oppressors.

But, on the other hand, the New Leftists are not Fifties Beats (and, by the way, I do not use the term Beat pejoratively). They are angry militants who see the poor as a new force in America, perhaps even as a substitute for the proletariat that failed. So Stokely Carmichael, one of the best of the breed, insists that the Mississippi and Alabama sharecroppers can choose for themselves. He understands that ultimately, to paraphrase an old labor song, no one can abolish poverty for you, you've got to abolish it yourself. And from this point of view, it does make quite a bit of difference whether the community organizing campaign works or not.

An analogy from the Thirties might illuminate the political

hope that is here asserted by the young radicals. In 1932 or 1933, many polite Americans believed that if you gave a worker a bathtub, he would put coal in it. And the skilled AFL members thought it preposterous that mass production machine operators could form *their own* union. On paper, the right to organize was proclaimed by the Wagner Act. In fact, it took at least five tumultuous years of picketing, striking and sitting-in before the CIO turned the brave words into something of a reality. Similarly in 1964, America declared war on poverty; and most of the well-bred citizenry did not intend by that to have field hands and janitors speaking up for themselves; and the young radicals, who have this knack of taking America's promises seriously, sought a surge from below to give meaning to the phrasemaking on high. But, as I think the New Left realizes, this analogy is faulty in part. The mass production workers were, just as radical theory had said, forced by the conditions of their existence (thousands of men assembled at one miserable place with common problems and interests) into a solidarity which became the basis of union organization. The poor, as Tom Hayden noted in his *New Republic* contribution, are not grouped into incipient communities. A slum street fragments and atomizes people; the two largest groups of the poor, the young and the old, have little to do with one another; and even if they could get together, the poor are still a minority of the society. Therefore it is going to take even more creativity to help the outcasts into their own than it did to build industrial unionism.

What Hope for the Poor?

For a number of reasons the New Leftists shied away, until quite recently, from thinking through the problems posed by their own militancy. For one thing, they are indeed "American" in the empirical, activist, anti-theoretical sense of the word. For another, they rejected the scholasticism of some of the traditional Left formulae (as well as the genuine profundity of the Left's intellectual heritage) and they were imbued with the spirit of the civil rights movement of the early Sixties where the willingness to go to jail was more important than political abstractions. This winter there have been signs that the young radicals are moving into a phase of discussion and debate (at a Christmas vacation meeting at the University of Illinois, the SDS militants discussed political strategy, ideology, Communism, the role of women in the movement, etc.). And this is necessary if the conflict of mysticism and militancy is to be resolved. For if the poor are seen as Dostoevskian peasants whose beauty is their suffering, then politics and the inevitable alliances with others is a contamination; but if they are to be a social force, then coalition is a necessity.

The New Leftists regard the welfare state, rather than the economic royalists, as the incarnation of the status quo. This is an almost inevitable result of trying to look at America with the eyes of the poor. It is very right—and it is a dangerous half-truth.

The welfare state developed in the Thirties was created by, and for, the "middle third" of American society: the liberal middle class and the organized workers. The poor were, and still are, those who were left behind in the Depression because of bad geographical, occupational or political luck: migrants, farm workers, full-time laborers at poverty jobs, racial and ethnic minorities which came into the economic mainstream at the time of the computer rather than of the assembly line. In addition, the poor include all those who have suffered from a *relative deterioration* in various social insurance and income maintenance programs (social security, unemployment compensation, etc.).

The visible enemies of the poor are not the captains of industry but the landlords, shopkeepers and, often enough, the agents of the welfare state. For the welfare state is, of course, ill-financed and bureaucratic, and this distorts the good intentions of many of the fine people who work for it and it reinforces the vices of the bad. So for the poor the welfare state means a humiliating dependence and fear, and requires a constant, cunning, battle against authority. The young radicals attempt to articulate these fierce resentments which they discovered in the slums, and the experience does not leave them in a mood for sociological nicety. The welfare state is, they say, a fraud. And the liberals, who actually boast of having created this monster in the name of humane values are therefore the worst hypocrites.

In formulating this attitude, it is not simply that the New Leftists overlook some history, which youth always does, but that they ignore some *relevant* history. The welfare state did not come out of the Thirties as a result of a liberal plot to manipulate the dispossessed. It was created over the violent resistance of most men of property and wealth, and its creation required a major upheaval on the part of the workers, from the bottom up. Business did not begin its conversion to welfare statism until the World War II discovery that a federal agency staffed by corporation executives was not exactly a class enemy of the rich; and its final conversion to "tax cut" Keynesianism waited upon the persuasiveness of Lyndon B. Johnson. There was, and is, a very real element of buying off the restless natives in business acceptance of welfarism.

The relevance of this history is that the current welfare state consensus is not quite so homogeneous as the President and some New Leftists sometimes think. For the apparent agreement conceals the latent conflict between the sophisticated conservatives on the one hand, and the liberal-labor-civil rights forces on the other. One can rightly accuse the liberal welfarists of having been too nostalgically proud of *their* upheaval to understand the terrible urgency of more change now as seen from the bottom of society. But it is something else again to *equate* all present supporters of the welfare state with one another.

Acting Out a Morality Play

And here I think I come to my most serious criticism of the New Radicals: that they sometimes expect the poor to act out the moral values of the middle-class radical who has come to the slum.

I find, for instance, a genuine poignancy in Tom Hayden's realization that a coalition of the outcasts will not really be able to change the society and that radicalism can only give itself up to, and become part of, "the energy kept restless and active under the clamps of paralyzed imperial society. Radicalism then would go beyond the concepts of optimism and pessimism as guides to work, finding itself in working despite odds. Its realism and sanity would be grounded in nothing more than the ability to face whatever comes."

This attitude is a logical deduction from theory that all the welfare staters, from Henry Ford to Walter Reuther if you will, are the same kind of manipulative bureaucrats. For if everybody but the poor and outcast are "them," then "we" must inevitably lose, for by definition "we" are not strong enough to transform a fraud and scandal supported by 60 or 70 percent of the society.

The conscious and committed radical can find his solace in such a vision; most of the poor, I suspect, cannot. Indeed, one of the things that has made the poor so inarticulate, so unorganized, so hopeless, is precisely the conviction that they can't win. Are they now to be told stoically to treasure their misery which, though permanent, is at least not corrupted by the hypocrisy of affluence? That will be cold comfort. And it will not move them to action, but rather reinforce them in their passivity.

The danger is that the poor will thus be assigned roles as abstractions in the morality plays of the disenchanted middle class. To fight this possibility, the New Leftists must come up with a strategy which offers real hope to the other America. And this means making a more sophisticated analysis of the coalition which supports the welfare state.

For the liberal wing of this consensus certainly did not start with the intention to build a manipulative bureaucracy, and it maintains values which *could* provide a basis for transforming the present structure. If the social-change movements of the previous generation must be shaken up by the poor, they must be shaken up in order to be made allies. To do this requires an intensification of the efforts to organize the slums and ghettos and backwoods as an independent political force. But if there is to be honest hope, that organization must be thought of as the catalyst of a new political majority in the United States, and not as a doomed last stand of noble savages.

There is reason to hope that these new directions will be taken. An incredibly American generation in our midst has become radical by taking the house platitudes seriously. Its hatred of hypocrisy and its identification with the outcasts are magnificent; its empiricism and its middle-class mysticism are sometimes troubling. Now that New Leftists are becoming more reflective, their anger and their activism should become even more effective, their radicalism that much deeper and more profound.

MICHAEL VINCENT MILLER

I

Nearly everyone who has tried to account for the recent uprising on the Berkeley campus has drawn a picture of students struggling for identity in a vast, impersonal educational and research factory run by IBM cards, remote professors subsidized by federal funds, and administrators with the temperaments of corporation executives. This analysis has the curious effect of

The Student State of Mind

making University of California President Clark Kerr the prophet of the student revolution against his administration. Kerr's description of the bureaucratized "multiversity," set forth in his Godkin lectures at Harvard in 1963, has even been converted into an ideology of justification for the revolt by its leadership.

There is more than a grain of truth in this account. The students were waging war against absurdities and hypocrisies that seem endemic to modern bureaucracy. And no doubt some form of pervasive alienation drove numerous students into the fray. But however plausible it may be, the multiversity analysis portrays the landscape of the Berkeley rebellion without sufficient color or contour. The student assault upon the attempt of Berkeley deans to control their tiny strip of land at Bancroft and Telegraph Avenues marshalled support from students and faculty on a scale unprecedented at American universities. Freshmen whose minds had never been violated by a political thought, as well as hardened politicoes, became caught up in direct action in-fighting with the authorities. But all shades of motivation were functioning here, and alienation is only part of the story. Perhaps student supporters of the revolt could be lumped under three rough categories:

Some students derive gratification and a sense of meaning from their involvement in politics. They are the ones who have fought in the student movement on several fronts—against HUAC and capital punishment, for peace and civil rights. Rather

From *Dissent*, 12 (Spring, 1965), 176–183. Reprinted with permission of *Dissent*.

than feeling that school has nothing to give them, they get good educations because they have found a way of making knowledge relevant, by immersing it in the social present. By and large, these seem to me among the least alienated students on campus, at least from themselves. But they did feel that alienation threatened when they saw the administration attempt to sever the connection between school and society.

Another segment of the student body constitutes, more or less, a community of self-pity. It is made up mostly of older undergrads and a few beginning graduate students who have sulked through their years at Berkeley in a pose of militant sensitivity. These students tend to be bright and talented, yet feel themselves edging ever closer to a failure of self-realization. They like to see themselves as misunderstood and unable to communicate —and not only with professors; they have bittersweet histories of brief and tragic love affairs to relate. Now and then, they may leave school for New York or Europe on the hunt for significance, but they usually wend their way back to Berkeley.

Perhaps such students are a little too quick to blame their stifled creativity on the system, or their inability to find love on the structure of modern society. Their politics border on melodrama. They are the specialists in alienation.

My impression is that the revolt drew its leaders and its most vocal and committed supporters mainly from these two groups. With the final group, the vast mass of sympathizers who signed petitions, swelled the ranks of sit-ins, or went on strike, alienation is not so much the issue, although many are undoubtedly uneasy about the university's size and red-tape procedures. What enraged them was the realization that the administration was being overbearing and unfair by suddenly trying to chop the guts out of student politics, which are as much a part of Berkeley as its tradition of Nobel prize winners in science. And they feared that apparently arbitrary restriction on freedom in one area might quickly lead to similar infringements in others.

II

Many features of the impersonal machine exist at other large universities like Harvard, Columbia, or U.C.L.A., which is itself part of the west coast multiversity. Yet Berkeley is probably the only campus in the country where students could transform a general mood of restlessness and resentment into an effective political weapon against their administration. One of the most striking characteristics of the revolt was its interplay of spontaneity and efficient organization. When negotiations between students and deans over the original administration ban on political activity broke down, a few student organizations set up booths in protest. The administration threatened disciplinary action and subsequently suspended eight student leaders. Almost instantaneously a full-scale student movement was afoot with its organizers, orators, heroes ready to commit themselves to action, even martyrs.

Clearly a movement of such magnitude and sophistication could not have been born overnight—as Free Speech Movement virtually was—without experienced tacticians to create it, in addition to widespread unrest to nourish it.

Students interested in tactics and ideology hang out on the Terrace, an elevated outdoor cafeteria in the student union complex with a touch of Left Bank atmosphere. The Terrace was already humming with discussion of the recent ban on politics last September 30, when five students who had manned political tables in defiance of the administration ruling were summoned to appear at a dean's office that afternoon. A couple of hours before this eventful appointment, a leading opponent of the ban stood near the Sather Gate entrance to campus and shouted at students coming off the Terrace, "All right, all you Terrace intellectuals, here's your chance finally to *do* something!" In this manner, he recruited many of the several hundred students who appeared later at the dean's office along with the five to protest the impending suspensions.

Those students who paused on their way to class from the Terrace are part of an important—by now even traditional—subculture of the Berkeley student body. A melting pot of campus intellectuals, aesthetes, and politicoes, it includes a lot of the "non-students" who have unjustly been used as a scapegoat by opponents of the FSM (most non-students involved in FSM activities are temporarily out of school, very recent graduates, university employees, or students' wives). Any afternoon in the week this crowd is found lounging between classes on the Terrace or in Telegraph Avenue's two coffee-houses arrayed in styles from classic beat to classic Harris tweed. Admittedly, its ranks contain a quota of the hipsters and revolutionary zealots concerned with little but the right names and phrases, the devotees of the latest chemical highs, the lunatic fringe of the avantgarde. But here also are a surprisingly large proportion of the most intellectually serious and morally alert students on campus, fellowship holders as well as veterans of the Mississippi wars. And sometimes the lines are extremely difficult to draw.

The bright and serious students in this group are the ones who demand the most from the university. They get good grades, although they often feel cynical about the system. Many of them are genuinely more concerned with putting knowledge of the past to work in the present than regurgitating it on a final. In a sense they are always putting administrators on the spot, because they believe that the educational process should provide a continuum between ideas and social and political action. For instance, when these students sit in for Negro rights in San Francisco or go off to register Negro voters in Mississippi, they are convinced that they are only carrying out a literal application of the democratic ideals they are supposed to memorize in the classroom. Such behavior unnerves the administration, which has to soothe the ruffled feelings of taxpayers and their representatives who grow anxious about the threats their sons and daughters are posing to the Established order.

III

The overall cast of Berkeley campus politics is distinctly to the left of center, despite a sprinkling of moderate Republicans and Goldwaterites. In general, the student political framework is flexible, communal, non-ideological. Of course there is plenty of organizational room for left-wing ideological temperaments in YSA, YPSL, the DuBois Club, and other groups. But Slate, the unaffiliated Berkeley political organization, has always been an issue-oriented and action-oriented group, a collectivity of political independents and various shades of socialists who came together to work on specific issues.

Political enthusiasm with an emphasis on action pervades the cultural habits of Berkeley student intellectuals to an extraordinary degree. This shows up even in their choice of entertainment. For instance, Bogart's films are among the most popular attractions at movie theaters around Berkeley just as they are in Cambridge, Massachusetts. At Harvard, the Bogart rage is mainly a cult of style. I have even heard of Harvard students parading through the Yard in early 1940's trench coats and snap-brim hats picked up in second-hand clothing stores. But the Berkeley film audience, though it digs the Bogie style, also tends to regard his films as ideological morality plays, in which Bogart, the lonewolf private eye or soldier of fortune, risks his neck for his principles and eventually wins out over the fumbling, insensitive bureaucratic cops or military officers.

To understand the explosive nature of the administration's restriction on campus politics, one must bear in mind that political activities have become in the last few years a primary means of personal expression and social contact for numerous students. Because of its size and setup, the University of California does, after all, have some of the impersonal features of a modern metropolis. Students have had to build their own sense of community, and bonds formed in fighting for causes supply a powerful way of filling this need. When the administration suddenly barred all meaningful political activity from campus—recruiting members, soliciting funds, advocating action—it created a situation that threatened partially to rupture these bonds.

IV

Two features peculiar to the Berkeley campus have played an essential part in determining the recent drift of student politics. In the first place, there is a running controversy between students, faculty, and administration about the nature of the university. Everything is forever being revised, from methods of registration and length of terms (about to be changed from semesters to quarters) to styles of architecture and, of course, rules governing student political behavior. Like the state itself the University of California still feels new, a little rootless, unsure of the boundaries between itself and outside social forces.

It is not surprising that Cal students feel they should have a say in shaping the university's image, their own role, even the society around them.

Secondly, the university is constantly buffeted by currents of animosity from the surrounding world. This puts students on the defensive and the administration under pressure. The campus atmosphere is modern and cosmopolitan; for several years now Berkeley has attracted urban youngsters who in previous times might have gone to the University of Chicago or C.C.N.Y. But the campus is enclosed by a typical conservative California town —and the two tend to grate on each other. Elderly Berkeley landladies often seem to loathe and fear the emancipated habits of students from whom they earn their bread and butter. Certain city councilmen cry out about once a week for investigations into student activities, both moral and political. Furthermore, Cal is a public school in a state the government of which contains a powerful minority on the right. A number of conservative state legislators make a habit of tossing bills in the hopper that promise to chop off large amounts of university budget unless the administration undertake purges of controversial students and faculty members.

Part of the local press is only too happy to abet the friction between the university and California taxpayers. For this purpose, Red-baiting and beatnik-baiting are favorite devices. Every now and then, the Berkeley *Gazette* prints a column of "campus news" written by ladies with three names who express profound shock over rumors of female students walking around campus in their bare feet. San Francisco *Chronicle* columnist Lucius Beebe, a self-styled connoisseur of expensive restaurants and rugged individualism, frequently launches attacks in atrocious polysyllabic rhetoric on the unwashed hordes of "Red Square in Berkeley" or "Kremlin West," as he alternately terms the school. One can imagine the attitude of William Knowland's paper, the Oakland *Tribune*.

V

During the height of the campus struggle, some newspaper reports, national magazine articles (including the liberal press on occasion), and statements by university administrators accused the FSM of being dupes for Castroite and Maoist agitators. Of course this is so much garbage; neither Peking- nor Havana-brand Communism had anything to do with FSM methods or goals. However, a few student activists do like to praise the revolutionary deeds of Castro and Mao Tse-tung. There are several aspects to this admiration, and one should put them in perspective and not simply write off these students.

Though most student offspring of thirties' radicals are wary of Communism, a few gravitate toward a doctrinaire left position, and for them Mao and Castro are the ideological replacements for Lenin and Stalin. Some do not love Castro and Mao as much as they detest Batista and Chiang Kai-shek. Behind their praise lies a critique of American society; an intuition that perhaps America has played an underhanded game in its treatment of the Cuban and Chinese Revolutions; that democratic ideals too often do not seem to extend beyond the borders of the U.S. if that far.

Another factor is that extolling of Castro and Mao, in the minds of a few, confers special avant-garde status that goes along with being tuned into the most far-out, especially if banned, films and the newest and most unconventional poetry. Castro's bearded revolutionary swagger with its touch of the *bandito,* Mao's militant anti-bourgeois posture and championing of underdog countries make these figures into culture heroes that conjure up a sense of the forbidden, the experimental, the provocative.

Finally, nearly all radicals are fascinated to some degree with two men who—whether for better or worse—have so completely transformed their societies.

VI

Nothing is gained from regarding the Berkeley uprising as a Freudian clash of sons against the fathers, as some commentators (fathers) have suggested. There is, of course, a sense in which the events at Berkeley involve a battle between generations. Students against administrators obviously means youth against its elders. Generational conflict, however, is so ancient and archetypal a social mechanism—certainly it functions in almost every revolution, political or artistic—that it affords little insight into the campus turmoil. It is far more important to realize that the revolt was the latest and most explicit confrontation at Berkeley between two antagonistic political styles.

Let us look at the Berkeley administrator's style as viewed by the students. From the time they began trying to negotiate the administration ban on politics, students came up against constant buck-passing responsibility for decisions. They were shuttled back and forth between a battery of deans and obscure committees. What the students found behind all this were not corrupt villains who wished them ill, but rather nervous modern liberals dressed out as bureaucrats.

To many students, there is something ineffectual and a little slippery about the new liberal-bureaucrat with his tools of mediation and compromise. He reminds them too closely of Peter Sellers playing the U.S. President in *Dr. Strangelove*, who tries unsuccessfully to juggle forces in a society gone mad; or of Major Major Major, the squadron commander in *Catch-22*, who signs his daily allotment of papers but leaps out his office window whenever anyone shows up with a problem.

Furthermore, the more militant students regard modern liberalism as a whole with something less than pleasure. They feel it is somehow implicated, if only by default, in the heritage of nightmares that compose recent history: Auschwitz, Hiroshima, the Cold War, McCarthy. They consider liberalism far too cumbersome an instrument for altering evils like the nuclear stalemate, U.S. support for tyrannical rule in foreign lands, the exclusion of the Negro from his fair share of society's rewards.

The Berkeley student activist has fashioned a style of political action out of materials borrowed from the South in order to make himself a gadfly in the hide of the local liberal Establishment. When all else fails, he resorts to impoliteness. He refuses to go through proper channels when they lead nowhere and turns his back on the decorum of committees when all the real issues have already been quietly tabled. Impoliteness, politicized, is civil disobedience.

The experience of these students is that it takes radical action on their part to get the liberals in motion. Last spring a huge number of Berkeley and other northern California college students helped stage sit-ins in a fight for equal employment opportunities for Negroes at a major hotel and several automobile dealers in San Francisco. Eventually agreements were hammered out between the Hotel Owners' Association, the auto dealers, a commission appointed by San Francisco's liberal Mayor John Shelley, and NAACP and CORE. Meanwhile, several hundred students had been arrested; many ended up paying fines and being put on probation. But they considered the outcome their victory. Similarly, 814 FSM supporters were carted off to jail before Berkeley's mostly liberal faculty came out in force to affirm the movement's goals.

VII

Students at Berkeley say that incredible changes have occurred on campus as a result of the struggle, which the FSM for the moment appears to have won. Everyone speaks of an authentic, campus-wide feeling of community in the air; of professors and students greeting each other by first names; of innumerable plans cropping up to give students more control over course content and professors over student discipline; of traditional divisions between campus cliques—bohemians, "dormies," even fraternity and sorority types—having been bridged. Will this state of affairs endure? Or are the victors only basking in the warm afterglow of revolutionary solidarity?

LEWIS S. FEUER

American colleges and universities are wondering whether they are entering an era of basic change in the relations between students and their professors. The rules of student life are probably going to be greatly liberalized; militant undergraduates, viewing themselves not without reason as an "exploited class," will ask for more than an advisory role in the formation of

The Risk Is Juvenocracy

courses and curriculums. A new mode of student self-government, which extends both the duties and rights of self-discipline, is long overdue. At the same time there is a growing concern that the demands for students' "rights" may take on the character of ideological pressures on the university and pose a threat to its fundamental work as the bearer and transmitter of the heritage of science and learning. An "ideological university" has ceased to be a community of free-minded scholars.

The college halls echo today with calls for a "student bill of rights" as a safeguard against the presumed tyrannies of administrators and professors. Students are asking for a role in the appointment and promotion of professors; they want also to govern themselves, enact their own rules of discipline, be their own judges, and abolish the vestigial rules in dormitories which make for restrictions in personal life. They want to participate in the design of curriculums. On top of it all, the new student restlessness goes hand in hand with the emergence after more than twenty years of a political student movement. Yet these are essentially two independent developments, which for accidental reasons have merged in some institutions.

Students have periodically rebelled against university administrators and faculties. In fact, one of the functions of the university has unwittingly been to provide the students with surrogate fathers against whom they can rebel. It makes life that much easier for the fathers at home.

From *The New York Times Magazine*, September 18, 1966, 56–64, © 1966 by The New York Times Company. Reprinted by permission.

Our present crisis is not the worst we have had. Actually, the stormiest era in the history of American colleges was from about 1880 to 1895, when strikes, demonstrations, violence and resignations erupted at Dartmouth, Union, Bowdoin, Wesleyan, Amherst, Middlebury. In 1883, for instance, "the greatest rebellion in Bowdoin's history" saw the outbreak of several riots against its military president, Maj. Gen. Joshua Chamberlain. Eleven sophomores had been expelled for involvement in a hazing incident; thereupon almost the entire studentry went on strike, and the General resigned. At Union College in 1888, the entire student body demonstrated behind a drum corps in Schenectady's main street; undaunted by a snowstorm, they demanded the appointment of a new president. They had their own candidate, a professor who had led them in their fight against the previous incumbent, and they got their man. Students and professors in this era held public "trials" of their presidents; Dartmouth and Hamilton were among those which saw such proceedings.

The history of student movements tells some strange stories. Not the least strange was that of the student leader in Amherst's great rebellion of 1894. He was Harlan Fiske Stone, later Chief Justice of the United States Supreme Court, and his trusted aides are said to have been Dwight Morrow and possibly Calvin Coolidge! Harlan was the mastermind behind the "Gates Rebellion," named for the unfortunate Amherst president against whom it was directed. As one reads the story now, one wonders at the passion which it aroused. Pres. Merrill Edwards Gates had expelled a student who intercepted a letter from the college to his father, telling of the boy's unexcused absences. The students felt that the president's summary judgment violated the principle of Amherst self-government. Indeed, what has characterized many student uprisings is the feeling that their elders are not giving them "due process of law."

At any rate, such was the argument of Harlan Stone, chairman of the senior class committee, as he presented the student's case. Behind the legal technicalities, however, was an accumulated hatred and suspicion. The Amherst students felt their president was an egotistical, narrow-minded fundamentalist. Many years later, the Chief Justice still recalled with anger that his college president had tried to humiliate him publicly; President Gates, he said, did not know how to appeal to "the manly and generous instinct of young men."

Underlying college revolts of this time was a discontent with the patriarchal powers of the president and the evangelical character of the curriculum and college rules. It is noteworthy that before he had come to Amherst Harlan Stone had already been expelled from Massachusetts Agricultural College where he had led a revolt against compulsory chapel: as the hymn singing and Scriptural reading came to a close, all the students at a signal had leaped up and rushed for the exit en masse. On the stairway, young Harlan engaged in a physical altercation with the chaplain: "I turned and grabbed him and shook him until his teeth rattled. I continued shaking him till I suddenly discovered who he was!" Harlan, 17½ years old, in revolt against the stern Puritan discipline he knew at home, thus warred against the evangelical manifestation of the principle of *in loco parentis*.

Two years ago Berkeley's chief student leader bit a policeman in the left thigh under similarly hectic circumstances. Those who take comfort from the notion that history repeats itself will hope that a Chief Justice's wisdom may yet emerge from the incendiary manifestoes of Berkeley's student leader.

There was a great difference, however, between the college rebels of the eighteen-nineties and those of 1964–66. The earlier rebels, for all their physical militancy, were not "alienated" from their society; their rebellion merged with no political movement, and they never cast their demands in ideological terms. Harlan Stone as a student was chairman of the Amherst Republican Town Committee; when Calvin Coolidge marched in 1892, it was with a torchlight procession of the college Republican Club. No students went to demonstrate with Coxey's Army or the Pullman strikers. What is distinctive of the New Student Unrest is the merger of its demands with an over-all political criticism, even rejection, of our society.

Perhaps the most far-reaching of the new student demands is the desire to participate in the appointment and promotion of professors. Various plans for student consultation have been proposed. At the University of Washington, the students' organ-

ization published an exhaustive survey and evaluation with
grades of the entire faculty. The City College in New York plans
to have evaluations of its teachers by the student body at large.

Would student participation in the selection of faculty improve the character of the teaching? Curiously, the movement
to grade and evaluate professors comes at the very time when
many students are seeking a relaxation of their own grading
system. Students complain of the never-ending competitive tension over grades distorts the spontaneity of their study, makes
them into examination-feedback machines, and poisons their
personal relations with teachers. Therefore, young teachers especially ask why they should be placed under the additional strain
of knowing that their classes will be called upon to vote on their
retention. The young instructor hitherto, they say, has been
haunted by the warning: "Publish or perish!" Will he now face
an even more potent admonition: "Be popular or be purged"?

Most important, there can be little doubt that student participation in the selection of faculties today will lead to a deeper rift
within colleges along political lines. Those teachers who wish to
play it safe will try to win the good favor of the dominant
opinion-making student political group. Where the political right
wing is dominant, young instructors will experience reactionary
pressures; where the left wing is dominant, they will feel the
force of radical criteria from their activist students.

In 1919, it was the student political right wing that was
dominant at Harvard College, and these students made life as
miserable as they could for a young instructor in political science, Harold J. Laski, who 26 years later became chairman of
the British Labour party. At that time, there was great anger
against radicals; anarchists had taken to planting bombs, and
the Government retaliated with large-scale arrests and raids.
Then the Boston police went on strike for higher wages and
recognition of their union.

Laski, 26 years old, incensed the Harvard community by his
outspoken sympathy with the strikers. Thereupon the Harvard
Lampoon on Jan. 16, 1920, devoted a whole issue to what was
probably the most savage personal attack ever made by students
on a teachar in an American university. Laski was depicted as

Prof. Moses Smartelikoff, Laski de Lenin, and Ivan Itchykoff, Bolshevik and seducer of Radcliffe girls:

> Stop a moment, let us warn you,
>   Nature's freak,
> That we loathe you and we scorn you,
>   Bolshevik!
>
> The moral, O ye masters, is, without a doubt,
> "Stop infection early: kick the first one out!"

Evidently Harvard students, had they been polled in 1920, would have been ready to follow the advice of the "Laski Lampoon." As it was, Laski was deeply hurt, and told his friend, Supreme Court Justice Holmes, how he longed for clearer skies. Shortly afterward, he accepted a post at the London School of Economics. "Many men deliberately adopt reactionary views to secure promotion," he later wrote. But if that were true in the Harvard of 1920, the opposite was much more the case in 1966.

At Berkeley, for instance, during the last six semesters, Slate, the left-wing student political party, has sold many thousands of its "Supplement to the General Catalogue" which, it claims, is based on representative student polls. According to the Director of Admissions, when Slate praised a class, its enrollment jumped by as many as 200 students. Take, for instance, several of Slate's analyses of September, 1965:

"Mr. Ross is a terribly dull, insincere professor who should be avoided at all costs." . . . "Mr. Cheit is an entertaining lecturer, but not a challenging one. He presents a liberal apology for capitalism." Professor Aikin, it conceded, was "an excellent teacher of constitutional law," but because he had failed students who missed their examination in order to picket, the "rating of him as a human being would be much lower." These are three cases the like of which would probably become all too common if student participation in appointments became real. Student parties would vie with each other to promote advocates of their respective political orthodoxies.

The facts in the foregoing examples were that Arthur Ross, as mediator between the student activists and the administration, had offended some of the militants; Professor Ross has since assumed the duties of United States Commissioner of Labor

Statistics. Earl Cheit, now vice chancellor, likewise had run afoul of the student activists for his moderate positions on the University Interim Rules Committee. The student evaluators with their terminology "liberal apology" had gone a long way in substituting ideology for science. A professor of classics, sympathetic with their policies but outraged by their anti-intellectualism, was shunted aside when he persistently asked to see the questionnaires on which their judgments were based.

Probably what colleges and universities need is not more formal controls of students and faculties (as if of two parties warring against each other) but a greater recognition of the obligations of a community of scholars. There are many human situations in which informal controls are far better than formal ones. It would be unwise, for instance, to have patients' councils reporting officially on physicians, or clients' councils on lawyers, or parishioners on their ministers. These relationships are already subject to great strain, and demand the utmost confidence and trust.

Among students, the word-of-mouth, informal impressions of teachers which are transmitted from one class to another are a far more reliable aid than would be the votes of a Student Committee for Faculty Appointments. Over the years the academic profession has managed to build a respect for criteria of professional competence and freedom. Student "participatory democracy" would open the way for the "ideological university" in which academic freedom would be regarded as an outmoded idea, as at the University of Havana.

At the same time there is an unsolved problem in the whole character of the teacher-student relationship in the modern university. A minority of students crave to be disciples to a master, for they are seekers, in the old religious sense, after a way of life, and the agnostic presupposition of the modern university, which proposes no philosophy, is one they find unsatisfying. A teacher, unlike a master, aims to impart only a sense of objective analysis and the study of a "field." The last professor of philosophy in an American college who was widely renowned as a master to disciples insofar as he exerted an immense influence in shaping the characters of his pupils was Charles Edward Garman of Amherst; curiously, he was not an original thinker or scholar, and his type is perforce becoming extinct in the process of educational evolution.

Consequently, a minority of students are turning to shadow faculties on the outskirts of the universities where a variety of people, usually without academic credentials, offer courses in which they provide answers as well as questions. In these so-called "free universities," existentialists without portfolio preach their doctrine, anarchists tell of Kropotkin and assail the System, aging believers renew their faith in Soviet Communism, angry graduate students denounce the poverty of the social sciences, philosophical activists expound nonviolence.

In Berkeley the year before the Uprising, a middle-aged Socialist librarian ran an evening school, with a course entitled "Ten Revolutions That Shook the World"—five evenings, or two revolutions an evening—all for a tuition fee of $1. The revolutionary experience was held up as somehow the culminating moment in human life. About 100 students attended; the next year as graduates of the revolutionary academy they were trying to make the Eleventh Revolution at Berkeley, and to savor their philosophy in action. Occasionally shadow schools have asked that their masters be appointed to the regular university staffs. One admirer of the Soviets has published articles in the campus newspaper stating that the university will be politically liberated only when persons like himself have been appointed as professors.

Actually it would be well worthwhile for the Government or the foundations to undertake the financing of bona fide experimental colleges in which precisely such shadow faculties could be assembled. To be sure, the era of experimental colleges seems past; Black Mountain College and Commonwealth College are gone; in the Vermont hills, one or two still hold on. Generally their results have been sad: disciples and masters with their messianic intolerance have engaged in the kind of strife in which almost all utopias have ended. Nevertheless, these efforts deserve encouragement.

In the past, almost every religious and political movement has led to the creation of a new educational institution. Today, however, existentialist, neo-Marxist, neo-pacifist and neo-anarchist schools have not arisen; the exigencies of professionalization and financing make them nearly impossible. The principal value of the experimental colleges is that they provide their participants the full opportunity to test (and perhaps refute) their theories of student self-government, anarchy, the end of examinations, the abolition of dormitory rules, sexual promiscuity, the study of life rather than books. Almost always, the rebels, enacting their rebellion, find the results of the experiment negative, and they return, a year or two later, older and wiser, to the time-honored methods of study and discipline. A minority in each successive generation, however, hears the call to find the way to utopia.

Some years back I visited a neighboring experimental college several times, and talked with its students. Then later, I heard they had begun a movement to have me brought to lecture once a week. This puzzled me because I did not share their philosophy, and was then teaching at a most conventional university. They then explained that they were so tired of teachers entering into their personal lives and trying to influence them emotionally that they would appreciate one teacher who would be more impersonal and concerned with his subject. The attempt to overcome all alienation and achieve the organic community usually ends with the rediscovery of the bourgeois right to privacy. The would-be master is too often a "psychological imperialist" who feels an emotional need to impose his own flaws on his disciples.

The new student bodies are reaching for new forms of association and self-government. The old fraternities and sororities are in decline, and are having trouble filling their ranks. When these secret societies were founded more than a century ago, they aroused great battles in the universities. At Michigan in 1849 a "Society War" broke out when several regents of the Anti-Masonic party, tried to ban the fraternities. A professor of moral philosophy found that Michigan students had secretly built a cabin in the forest; that was the subversive origin of the first fraternity house in American history. A third of the student body was suspended as the faculty denounced the "monster power, which lays its hand upon every college faculty in our country," and fosters debauchery, drunkenness and disorder.

Time mellowed both fraternities and faculties. Now students demand the sale of contraceptives in university stores and the virtual abolition of dormitory rules. They demand an end to the ancient schoolmaster's legal mandate *in loco parentis*. When the college pleads that the students' own parents wish some rules to be observed, the students reply, as one girl did in The Swarthmore Phoenix, that they doubt "whether the attitude of parents ought to be a major consideration in shaping college policy"; the college, they say, should mold itself in the image it considers best without trying to please the applicants' parents.

Certainly the trend to make the students responsible for their own discipline will continue in American universities. At the City University in New York, for instance, a judiciary, principally composed of students, has long handled the customary cases of indiscipline and cheating. A. H. Raskin, now assistant editor of the editorial page of The New York Times, and I both thought 35 years ago that we made better judges than did our faculty-colleagues.

At the same time, if the university removes itself from the *in loco parentis* role, it has to do so consistently. It must not try to be the all-permissive parent giving the student the benefit of its blessing for the student's explorations in a new morality or immorality. The university cannot allow a set of rules or non-rules which indicate that it puts its moral sanction on what must remain the student's own decision. And where rules seem to involve endorsement of the student's decisions to violate the social norms in sexual life, the university cannot accept the role of a revolutionary parent.

The college can never remove itself altogether from the unpopular parental role, and rebellious students themselves seem to waver between demanding that the college cease to exercise a parental role altogether or become rather a more progressive, intimate and permissive parent. The real parents meanwhile are often pleased to see the students fight these issues out with the colleges rather than with themselves.

No matter how much responsible student self-government emerges, it still remains true that a modern university cannot be a republic of equals. It is an institution which tries to transmit the accumulated knowledge, wisdom, doubts and uncertainties of the past's scholars, artists and scientists and to impart to the student a sense of probity and evidence so that he can carry on the unfinished work of civilization. It is based on one essential presupposition—that knowledge and wisdom are cross-generational, that the elders have something to transmit. This can be carried to an extreme of gerontocracy, where the elder generation thinks in its pride it has exhausted all experience. Far more real today, however, it is the risk of "juvenocracy," which strikes at the whole of wisdom.

For some time after Students for a Democratic Society in 1962 coined the term "participatory democracy," it was received with more humor than respect by civil rights workers in the South. The concept has become important this past winter, for two reasons. First, a number of SDS leaders have left college and are seeking to apply the idea in Northern ghettoes. Second, many

The New Radicals and "Participatory Democracy"

members of the staff of the Student Nonviolent Coordinating Committee have begun to look beyond voter registration to what SDS, in its Port Huron Statement, called its

> two central aims: that the individual share in those social decisions determining the quality and direction of his life; that society be organized to encourage independence in men and provide the media for their common participation.

A new style of work, fusing politics and direct action into radical community organization, is emerging in both SDS and SNCC.

Those in SNCC most interested in the SDS concept as a guide to their own work in the South are mainly stationed in Mississippi. This adds significance to their sense of the future, for Mississippi has been the place where the emphasis on voter registration, dominant in SNCC since 1961, has been most fruitfully developed. Why should activists who have just finished so successfully founding the Mississippi Freedom Democratic Party now find themselves questioning conventional politics as a desirable agency for social change?

One could see the new emphasis growing in Mississippi last summer. Bob Parris, personally, has always intensely distrusted leaders who prevent the growth of a capacity for responsibility in others: he is famous for sitting in the back of meetings, avoiding speeches, and when obliged to speak standing in his place and asking questions. His is the philosophy of the anarchist leader in the Spanish Civil War who, discovered at the rear of

---

From *Dissent,* 12 (Summer, 1965), 324–333. Reprinted with permission of *Dissent.*

a long lunch line and reminded of his importance to the revo-
tion, answered, "This is the revolution." As "freedom registration" went on in Mississippi last summer, SNCC staff workers
and volunteers at many places in the state began to ask questions, in the spirit of Parris' concern, about the process of political organization they were engineering.

It was necessary, for example, to hold precinct meetings of
the FDP so as to duplicate fully the steps through which the
regular Democratic Party selected delegates to the Atlantic City
convention. Such meetings, with perhaps ten to fifty persons in
attendance, were something quite different from the mass meetings at which charismatic orators harangue an audience on the
eve of direct action. The Southern mass meeting is modeled on
a church service. The minister, or his functional substitute, the
civil rights worker, remains firmly in control despite the vocal
participation of the congregation; decisions made in advance by
a small group are translated to the rank and file in an emotional
setting. The FDP precinct meeting appeared to offer a setting in
which members of the rank and file could be drawn into the
expression of their ideas, in which the anguished back-and-forth
of decision-making familiar to SNCC staff could become the experience of the Negro masses too, in which the distinction between rank and file and leaders could be broken down. Should
not the precinct meetings be continued for other purposes? some
asked. Others began to experiment with block meetings and
ward meetings, conversations outside the church in a neighbor's
living room, at which thinking began about local problems, programs, candidates.

Meantime the Freedom School component of the Mississippi
Summer Project offered something of a model to those working
in voter registration and pondering new approaches to the political process. In the schools 2,500 Mississippi Negro youngsters
miraculously found voice, in poems, in plays, in newspapers, in
the honest asking of questions about their society. Early in
August each of the Freedom Schools sent delegates to a Freedom
School Convention. The delegates brought with them political
programs hammered out in every school in response to the challenge: If you could elect a Mayor, or a state legislator, or a
Senator, what would you want him to do? By the second day of

the convention the delegates were confidently rejecting adult participation in their workshops or plenary sessions. The convention, and the atmosphere of free and intimate discussion from which the convention was precipitated, left seeds in the minds of participants.

Then came Atlantic City. However successful the FDP challenge may have seemed to television viewers, for those who were there the experience was traumatic. Clearly, starkly, the result of an enormous months-and-years-long labor of preparation, the Negro people of Mississippi themselves brought to the attention of the nation their political exclusion. As seen by their SNCC collaborators, what they received was a piece of public relations, the offer of a deal which would not add to their power. Hardened SNCC veterans wept. Bitterness at those national civil rights personalities who urged acceptance of the compromise on grounds of political expediency—Martin Luther King, Bayard Rustin, Joseph Rauh, as well as Walter Reuther and other erstwhile allies—was indescribable. Three months later Bob Parris told a New York audience: They told us to be responsible because the destiny of America was in our hands. We learned that it is not in our hands. We will pursue our own goals, and let the chips fall where they may.

Surely for Bob Parris and for others in SNCC the trauma of Atlantic City brought to the surface, not only a growing awareness of the positive possibilities of participatory politics, but also certain ambiguities imbedded in the FDP challenge from the start. The challenge as a strategy had not been created by the Negro people of Mississippi, but by a handful of leaders. The strategy required the demonstration that the FDP was more loyal to the national platform of the Democratic Party, and to President Johnson personally, than the regular Democrats of the state. It led to a focus of attention on Washington which, no matter how one sought to involve local people by delegations to the Capitol, enfeebled civil rights activity at the grass roots. Precisely as the FDP succeeded, it began to develop a hierarchy of its own. Seeking to escape from issue-less politics and charismatic leaders, the FDP in its own work emphasized personalities —that is, the seating of individual challengers—rather than program. In each of these ways the institutional thrust of the FDP as it developed ran counter to the new notions about people and politics which the summer had also produced.

The old politics and the new confronted each other once again in Selma. SNCC was the first civil rights group on the ground there. This winter, in step with the new thinking in the organization, it began to develop ward meetings and a youth group in which local Negroes could learn to manage their own destinies. Then, by agreement with SNCC but nonetheless traumatically for the SNCC workers in Selma, Dr. King's Southern Christian Leadership Conference moved in. SCLC's focus was the passage of national legislation, not the political maturing of persons in the Alabama Black Belt. Ward meetings, stimulated at first by the new activity, stopped as the pattern of demonstration intensified and each evening had its mass meeting as each morning had its march. SNCC had seen that pattern before, notably in Albany, Ga., where SNCC workers Charles Sherrod and Cordell Reagan had been displaced by Dr. King and his assistants and the upshot, for the people of Albany, had been disillusion, a great weight of court costs, and bitterness on the part of local whites.

Concerned that the obstacles to voting be torn down but concerned also that institutional progress go hand-in-hand with a quickening of the people's capacity for self-direction, SNCC could only experience Selma with mixed feelings and considerable frustration. The "march" of March 9, when Dr. King led people to a confrontation he knew would not occur and then accused the police of bad faith for exposing his hypocrisy, must have seemed to those in SNCC a symbolic summation of much that had gone before.

The concern to involve plain people in the decisions which affect their lives crops out elsewhere in SNCC's activity this winter. An educational conference in Mississippi in November threw away a prepared agenda to encourage open-ended discussion among the participants. A fear, muted last summer, lest masses of white volunteers inhibit Southern Negroes from developing their own leaders, led to scaling-down of the Black Belt project planned for summer 1965. Meeting in Atlanta in February SNCC planned instead to organize "people's conferences" in states of the Deep South, at which new Freedom Democratic parties, directed from the beginning by local leaders, could take root.

Also in February 1965 indigenous leaders drawn from SDS ghetto projects in the North met at Cleveland with some Negroes activated by SNCC work in the South. In SDS as in SNCC workers seek to apply the participatory philosophy to their own organizations, asking that central offices be abolished, leaders rotated, and executive committees curbed by general staff meetings. In both groups, the elite of the New Left, the theory and practice of participatory democracy grow.

I

What is the strategy of social change implicit in the concept of participatory democracy? What is its relation to older philosophies of the Left: socialism, nonviolence, anarchism? As one distant from the scene I offer the following observations diffidently, in the hope that they will [draw] comment from "participatory democrats," North and South.

One aspect of participatory democracy is the idea of parallel structures. The FDP is a parallel political party, prompted by the conclusion that registration of Negroes in the regular Democratic party of Mississippi is presently impossible. Freedom Schools were parallel schools, although delegates to the Freedom School Convention decided they would return to the public schools and seek to transform them rather than continue into the winter a parallel school system. In the North, neighborhood unions organized by SDS represent parallel antipoverty agencies, challenging the legitimacy of the top-down middle-class "community organizations" sponsored by urban renewal and antipoverty administrators.

The intent of these structures is still unclear, even to those involved in organizing them. There is a spectrum of possibilities. At one end of the spectrum is the concept of using parallel institutions to transform their Establishment counterparts. Thus it would follow that when Mississippi Negroes *can* register and vote, the FDP would wither away. At the spectrum's other end is the conviction that in an America whose Establishment is inherently and inevitably hostile, existing institutions cannot be transformed, participation will always mean cooptation and merely token successes, hence parallel institutions must survive and grow into an anti-Establishment network, a new society.

For the moment participatory democracy cherishes the practice of parallelism as a way of saying No to organized America, and of initiating the unorganized into the experience of self-government. The SNCC or SDS worker does not build a parallel institution to impose an ideology on it. He views himself as a catalyst, helping to create an environment which will help the local people to decide what they want. Recognizing himself as a part of the society's sickness, the organizer inclines to regard the unorganized poor as purer than himself. There is an unstated assumption that the poor, when they find voice, will produce a truer, sounder radicalism than any which alienated intellectuals might prescribe. In the meantime the very existence of the parallel institution is felt to be a healthier and more genuine experience than any available alternative. It seems better to sit in the back of the room in silent protest against the bureaucrats up front than to seek to elect a man to join the executive committee.

In form, parallelism suggests a kinship between participatory democracy and Trotsky's conception of the Soviets as a "dual power," or Gandhi's concern to preserve the Indian village community. But thus far the new movement does not feel itself a part of either the Marxist or anarcho-pacifist traditions. What is most clear at the moment is the call reminiscent of the Radical Reformation to "come out of Babylon." Let the teacher leave the university and teach in Freedom Schools; let the reporter quit his job on a metropolitan daily and start a community newspaper; generally, let the intellectual make insurgency a full-time rather than a part-time occupation. As the Russian radical movement grew from Tolstoyism and the Narodnik's concern to dress simply, speak truth, and "go to the people," so participatory democracy at this point speaks most clearly to the middle-class man, daring him to forsake powerlessness and act.

I for one believe that participatory democracy, even thus vaguely conceived, offers a growing point far more alive than conventional coalition politics. At the same time, it is incumbent upon new radicals to explain how they propose to answer the problems which conventional politics purports to solve. How will participatory democracy feed and clothe the poor, as well as stimulate and involve them? If voting is a snare and a delusion, what is not? Unless in time these questions can be answered participatory democracy could become a subtle, even if heroic, form of self-indulgence.

Employment appears to be the Achilles heel of parallelism. From time to time SNCC workers have sought to organize producers and consumers cooperatives, and the leather-working business in Haywood and Fayette counties, Tennessee, has had considerable success. The thriving toy business of the Society of Brothers (Bruderhof) proves that even in the age of monopoly a small cooperative enterprise can survive. But one cannot imagine such economic beginnings becoming, like the free cities of the Middle Ages, the "germ of a new society within the womb of the old." In Mississippi the movement has hardly been able to provide for Negroes fired as a result of civil rights activity, let alone address itself to the larger problem of cotton-picking machinery and the displacement of farm labor; and what provision there has been has come, not through the creation of a new economic base, but from charity.

It would seem, therefore, that in the area of economics participatory democracy cannot provide a full alternative to established institutions except by capturing and transforming them. By pressure it can democratize the distribution of income, as SDS does in boring-from-below against antipoverty programs, as SNCC does in demanding the participation of Negroes in local committees sponsored by the Department of Agriculture. Perhaps, like Dolci in Italy, radical community organizers can use symbolic direct action to dramatize the need for that massive public works program which the March on Washington called for (and then forgot). Thus Noel Day proposes using money collected from rent strikes to employ unemployed youngsters at a $2.00 an hour wage to repair substandard housing. But can we not agree that participatory democracy, understood as a movement building new institutions side-by-side with the old, cannot provide bread and land? Failure to face this problem realistically

will result in the poor turning for help to those who can provide
it at least in part, and the cooptation of protest movements by
the Establishment.

A similar perspective is suggested by turning to the theorists
of existential radicalism in other countries. Let us use the term
"socialism" to designate the movement for a planned publicly-
owned economy which, in Europe as America, preceded the
newer radicalism of "participatory democracy." If one examines
carefully the formulations of the latter tendency in Europe (and
I believe much the same thing would appear from a scrutiny of
Africa), one finds it articulated as a partner in dialogue with
socialism, as a humane affirmation constantly necessary to correct (but not to supplant entirely) bureaucratic institutions and
political action. Thus in Silone's *Bread and Wine* the protagonist,
like Thoreau, asserts that the social action needed above all is
individual lives displaying morality and truth. But Silone adds:

> He had not forgotten that the social question is not a moral
> one and is not resolved by purely moral means. He knew
> that in the last resort the relations established among men
> are dictated by necessity and not by good will or bad. Moral
> preaching did not suffice to change them. But there came a
> moment when certain social relations revealed themselves
> as outworn and harmful. Morality then condemned what
> had already been condemned by history.

This is a formulation which has not yet created an impassable
gulf between itself and Marxism. Silone's statement could be
rendered, more woodenly to be sure, as an assertion that when
"objective" conditions are "ripe" for change, the "subjective factor" becomes all-important.

To much the same effect, Martin Buber in *Paths in Utopia*
takes public ownership as a matter of course, arguing that the
critical question is: "what sort of Socialism is it to be?" The
relation between centralization and decentralization, between
bureaucracy and community is, says Buber,

> a problem which cannot be approached in principle, but,
> like everything to do with the relationship between idea and
> reality, only with great spiritual tact, with the constant and
> tireless weighing and measuring of the right proportion be-
> tween them.

This is to say of popular participation much what Howard Zinn has insisted regarding nonviolence, that to ignore its limitations invites hypocrisy and, ultimately, a tendency for it to turn into its opposite.

Even Camus—so far as I can judge the strongest intellectual influence on the thinking of Bob Parris—does not quite turn his back on the Marxist "logic of history." Rather, he writes in "Neither Victims Nor Executioners":

> Since these forces are working themselves out and since it is inevitable that they continue to do so, there is no reason why some of us should not take on the job of keeping alive through the apocalyptic historical vista that stretches before us, a modest thoughtfulness which, without pretending to solve everything, will constantly be prepared to give some human meaning to everyday life.

Others of us, then, will continue to address ourselves to structural changes, to socialism. In the words of the Port Huron Statement, "a truly 'public sector' must be established," and the new left should include socialists "for their sense of thoroughgoing reforms in the system."

II

In itself, however, this formulation papers over a difference rather than resolving it. What could be more sterile than a movement with two predefined wings, a left one and a right one (we could argue endlessly about which was which)? If "some of us" were committed to one traditional concept and others of us to another, would it not be another version of coalition politics, frustrating and dead?

Some common ground, some underlying vision needs to be articulated which genuinely unites socialism and "participatory democracy," which challenges each to transcend itself. Here one strikes out into unexplored territory which can only be adequately clarified by experience. A helpful starting point may be the concept of "community." "Politics," affirms the Port Huron Statement, "has the function of bringing people out of isolation and into community." And A. J. Muste writes, correctly I think, of the civil rights movement:

No one can have a fairly close contact with the civil rights movement and the people in it, including the young people, without feeling that, in spite of all contrary appearances and even realities in the movement, deep near its center is this aspiration for a blessed community and the faith that this is what they are working for and already in a sense realizing now.

Community was what one Freedom School teacher meant who wrote to me: "The summer project presented itself to us as a potentially life-endangering situation, and so we all worked our fears out together, which gave coherence to our group. We had temporarily put aside our human fears and were accepting a responsibility which was ours and we were doing it together."

Lest this seem maudlin utopianism, let us begin with the most hard-headed meaning of community to a new radical movement: the political. How can one build a political campaign, or a polit-ical party, without sacrificing the shared intimacy experienced in a direct action "project"? If it be true that both peace and civil rights activists must turn toward politics to cope with the economic problems which confront their movements, can it be done without losing the spiritual exaltation of the direct action years?

I think a clue here is to begin to think of politics as administra-tion. Political representation was devised as a mechanism to obtain consent for taxation. It is an institutional process pecul-iarly appropriate to an economy in which production is in private hands, and the state takes money from the citizen to spend it on a separate category of public activities. In a communal economy —by which I simply mean an economy wherein men share the fruits of their labor in the spirit of a family—many functions, now centralized in private hands, would be centralized in the hands of the government; but also, many functions now locally privatized would at once become neighborly responsibilities. Consider urban renewal. If land were publicly owned and build-ing a public function, slum clearance could really become a process in which the people of a site participated at each stage. Nation- and city-wide considerations would enter in, of course: but much that now happens in public and private offices on upper floors could then be left to the collective discretion of neighborhood meetings.

In centering its attention on grass roots participation in urban renewal and antipoverty programs, rather than on running candidates, SDS appears instinctively to recognize the communal opportunities of public economic administration. As more and more candidates begin to run for public office on a movement platform, so also new forms of direct action will be improvised to democratize administration; and as regional and national coordination takes form in the one area, so will it in the other, too. Thus entrance into politics need *not* mean an abandonment of direct action demonstration, nor of its spirit.

In conversation after the recent March on Washington, Bob Parris suggested two specific ways in which an elected "freedom candidate" could keep himself from being absorbed by conventional politics. First, if an MFDP candidate were elected to the Mississippi legislature he could act as a representative of *all* the Negroes of Mississippi rather than of a particular locality. Second, an elected candidate could simply decline to "take his seat" in a legislature and remain in his constituency as a symbol of identification with their concerns.

The local project can grow from protest into administration; if necessary it could also be the building block for resistance to more extreme forms of repression, for protest against Fascism. Like a biological cell it can take many forms, responding in a variety of appropriate ways to alternate stimuli from the environment.

But for this to be so it becomes necessary to think of a project from the beginning, not merely as a tool for social change, but as a community. The community is made up both of people from the neighborhood and of staff persons who, on a long-term basis, so far as they can, become part of the neighborhood. The spirit of a community, as opposed to an organization, is not, We are together to accomplish this or that end, but, We are together to face together whatever life brings.

The experience of Utopian or "intentional" communities suggests certain ground rules which all groups seeking to live as brothers should consider. One is: It is important to be honest with each other, to carry grievances directly to those concerned rather than to third parties. Another is: The spiritual unity of the group is more important than any external accomplishment, and time must be taken to discover and restore that unity even at the cost of short-run tangible failures.

If indeed, as Marxism affirms, mankind will one day enter a realm of freedom that will permit men to guide their behavior by more humane and immediate criteria than the minimum and maximum demands of political programs, the work of transition can begin now. The need for structural change (socialism) should neither be ignored nor overemphasized. Provided we do not deceive ourselves as to the bleakness of our society's prospects for hopeful change or the catastrophic dangers of nuclear war and domestic totalitarianism, perhaps it is not unreasonable to look for a more firm and definite strategy to develop as the collective experience of the movement unfolds.

Peculiarly difficult, I think, will be the coming-together of "staff" and "neighborhood" persons on questions of foreign policy. This was a problem which confronted the Freedom Democratic Party, obliged by its strategy to support a President just then escalating the war in Vietnam. Tentatively it would seem that staff must be honest about such questions; and surely the ideological framework of brotherhood and community should make it easier to be so than one simply oriented to pragmatic goals.

In sum, then, participatory democracy seems to be driving toward the "live-in," the building of a brotherly way of life even in the jaws of Leviathan. It is conscientious objection not just to war, but to the whole fabric of a dehumanized society. It is civil disobedience not just by individuals, but, hopefully, by broad masses of alienated Americans. Like the conscientious objector, however, the participatory democrat has unfinished business with the question: Is what's intended a moral gesture only, or a determined attempt to transform the American power structure?

Oh, deep in my heart, I do believe we shall overcome, someday.

—FREEDOM SONG

Give flowers to the rebels failed.

—ANARCHIST POEM

A prophetic minority creates each generation's legend. In the
1920's it was the expatriate quest for personal expression. In
the 1930's it was radical social action. In the 1940's it was the
heroism of the trenches. In the 1950's it was the cultivation of
the private self. Now, halfway through the decade, it is once
again the ideal of social action that is *defining a generation*.

A Prophetic Minority: The Future

By this I mean specifically that in fifteen years Bob Dylan's
poems will be taught in college classrooms, that Paul Booth,
Julian Bond, and Stokely Carmichael will be the leaders of adult
protest movements, that the Beatles movies will be revived in art
houses, and that Tom Hayden, Norman Fruchter, Robb Burlage,
Mario Savio, Dick Flacks, Bob Parris, and Carl Oglesby will be
major social critics. But I also mean to emphasize that the New
Left has, and always will have, only a fraction of the whole
truth, just as the Freudians, the Symbolists, Marxists and the
Impressionists possessed only a fragment of the truth. But it is
the fragment glimpsed by this generation.

The legend of the 1930's turned to ashes in Washington,
Moscow, and Madrid before the decade was over. It is entirely
possible that the New Left can meet such a tragic end as well.
The possibility of political fissures exists in any movement. This
one could split over tactics like the Bolsheviks or Mensheviks, or
over morality like Sartre and Camus. Black nationalism may yet
poison it, and unfocused activism may exhaust it. But I doubt
it.

In the immediate future, the impulse to rebel will continue to grow among marginal groups like students, Negroes, migrant farm workers, intellectuals, and white-collar workers. This will happen because the generators of dissent—war, bureaucracy, guilt-producing affluence, racism, hypocrisy, moral rot—are enduring in the fabric of American society. If the Vietnam war is settled, there will be another one in Thailand, or Angola, or Peru. If Bobby Baker is jailed, there will be another fast buck politician exposed. If the killers of Goodman, Chaney, and Schwerner are convicted, there will be other atrocities in the South.

All this means that the New Left—and the other sections of the society in motion—will grow and become even more uncomfortably radical. My own hunch is that SDS will be the chief repository of this radical mood, that SNCC's time has passed, its gifts taken without adequate acknowledgment. I also suspect the Hereditary Left will not grow much, because it is too weighted down with the moral bankruptcy of Communism, and because it misses completely this generation's indictment of impersonal bureaucracies and the existential void of the middle class. Primarily, the New Left will become increasingly the umbrella under which indigenous, decentralized movements will grow. Grass-roots insurgencies, such as the grape strike in California, Berkeley's Vietnam Day Committee, the NCUP project in Newark, the Lowndes County Freedom Organization in Alabama, Dick Gregory's campaign for mayor of Chicago, independent community committees against the war in Vietnam, and campus protests against the draft like those at Chicago and CCNY, are the shadows of the future. National organizations are not the style of anarchists and improvisers.

Beneath this nation's gleaming surface of computers, Hilton hotels, and super-highways, there are latent volcanoes of violence. These volcanoes have erupted tragically in Birmingham, Mississippi, and Dallas in 1963; in Harlem and Rochester in 1964; in Watts and Selma in 1965; and in Watts and in Mississippi again in 1966. Riot and assassination are symptoms of the disease in our society below the Disneyland façade. The New Radicals will rub these hidden sores until they bleed, or until the Great Society begins to heal the one in five who are poor, and the millions who are voteless, powerless, victimized, and mad.

But two yawning pitfalls stretch out before the New Left, diluting the chances of its growth. One is the rising tide of domestic McCarthyism, which is paralleling the escalation of the war in Vietnam. The other is the culture's spongelike genius for either absorbing or merchandising all dissent.

If the Great Society becomes preoccupied by a narrow choice between "guns and butter," then it will become impossible even to hold up the alternate vision of "bread and roses." Already some social welfare and anti-poverty programs are not being funded, and New York's reform Congressman, William F. Ryan, has quipped, "Johnson is asking us to choose between guns and oleo."

There has always been a latent anti-intellectual strain to the American character, as Richard Hofstadter documented in his Pulitzer Prize-winning book, *Anti-intellectualism in American Life*. The country's repudiation of Adlai Stevenson and the upsurge of McCarthyism in the 1950's were the latest expression of attitudes that go back to the Alien and Sedition Acts and the Salem witch trials. Now, as the Vietnam war grows more bloody, the stalemate more frustrating, there seems to be a resurgence of paranoid know-nothing sentiment throughout the country. My fear is that if the war drags on, and there are 400,000 American troops in Vietnam at the start of 1967, then all of America will begin to close down, just as the nation turned in on itself during the Korean war, or as France became repressive during the last stages of its seven-year conflict with Algeria. If this happens, then all bets are off on the future of the New Left. Its elite will be drafted, its organizations pilloried and red-baited, its idealism shattered, its mentality turned underground.

The first smell of this new McCarthyism is already in the air, burning the nostrils and poisoning the lungs.

In October of 1965 Congress enacted a law that made the burning of a draft card punishable by five years in jail and a five-thousand-dollar fine. A few weeks later, Attorney General Katzenbach announced the Justice Department was investigating SDS. In January of 1966 the Georgia state legislature refused to seat the democratically elected Julian Bond because of his opposition to the Vietnam war. In February, Congressman Olin E. Teague of Texas introduced legislation making all anti-war protests illegal; he characterized the demonstrators as "beatnik types and pseudo-intellectuals." A few days later the Michigan state legislature adopted a resolution banning Communists from speaking on campuses in the state. On March 3rd, the Justice Department petitioned the Subversive Activities Control Board to order the Du Bois Clubs to register as a Communist-front organization. Within forty-eight hours the clubs' national headquarters was blown up, and its members beaten up on a Brooklyn street, and then arrested by police. On March 26th, anti-war marches in Oklahoma City and Boston were broken up by hooligans, and in New York, twenty thousand marchers were pelted with rotten eggs, and assailed by the *Daily News* as "dupes of the communists." On March 31st, four young draft-card burners were savagely beaten on the steps of a Boston courthouse by a mob of teen-agers, while police looked on, and newsreel photographers jostled each other for close-ups of the pummeling. On April 8th the VDC headquarters in Berkeley was bombed. On May 15th a crazed gunman killed a member of the YSA in Detroit. On June 5th, a sniper waiting in ambush shot James Meredith near Hernando, Mississippi.

The other pitfall blocking the path of the New Left is the culture's skill at amiably absorbing all manner of rebels and turning them into celebrities. To be a radical in America today is like trying to punch your way out of a cage made of marshmallow. Every thrust at the jugular draws not blood, but sweet success; every hack at the roots draws not retaliation, but fame and affluence. The culture's insatiable thirst for novelty and titillation insured LeRoi Jones television interviews, Norman Mailer million-dollar royalties, and Paul Goodman fat paychecks as a government consultant. Yesterday's underground becomes today's vaudeville and tomorrow's cliché. If the draft, superpatriots, and the Justice Department don't wreck the New Left, masscult may kill it with kindness and then deposit its carcass in the cemetery of celebrities, alongside of Baby Jane Holzer, Liberace, and Jack Kerouac.

Already there are signs that the middle class enjoys being flogged by the New Radicals, while ignoring their criticisms and ideas. Magazines like *Esquire, Mademoiselle,* and *Playboy* have printed glowing accounts of the New Left. Publishing houses have handed out thousands of dollars to the New Radicals for books they know will indict America root and branch—but will return a handsome profit. Government agencies like the Peace Corps and the Office of Economic Opportunity have offered several of the most gifted members of the New Left lucrative jobs.

This paradox of radical ideas creating celebrities can be an insidious process. It is hard to nurse your anger if you're getting two thousand dollars to spill it out on national television. And it is hard to think creatively, or to organize effectively, if you are deluged with a stream of speaking engagements, interviews, and symposia. The danger of becoming performers subsidized to goose a decadent middle class is a real one for the New Left.

Directly toward these twin pitfalls—the escalating war in Vietnam and an endlessly absorptive culture—the New Radicals will march, just as they marched into Mississippi, Sproul Hall, and the urban slums of the North. They will continue to challenge the gods because they are cursed with the passion of Ahab and the innocence of Billy Budd. And because no one else is doing the marching.

The New Radicalism began with a request for a cup of coffee. In six years it has become a new way of looking at the world and a vision of a new kind of politics. It has given a whole generation what William James called "the moral equivalent of war."

To demand any more of this generation is to deny the responsibility of the last one—and the possibility of the next.

2

The Legacy

The three pieces in this section, from the living John Kennedy, from the funeral that was the central event of its decade, and the last expressing one kind of memory that will linger, do not solve the problem Pete Hamill once posed: "How do you tell your children what it was like to be alive when John Kennedy was a man and not an airport?" but they are part of our legacy.

America can never again be as it was before John Kennedy became President. Because of his style and program, wit and irony, and a vision, a generation of Americans came, after January 20th, 1961, to see themselves and their country differently. This new generation of Americans will in one way or another continue the tasks and emulate the style. This is the public part of his legacy. The private each keeps for himself.

JOHN F. KENNEDY

We observe today not a victory of party but a celebration of freedom, symbolizing an end as well as a beginning, signifying renewal as well as change. For I have sworn before you and Almighty God the same solemn oath our forebears prescribed nearly a century and three-quarters ago.

The world is very different now. For man holds in his mortal

Inaugural Address

hands the power to abolish all forms of human poverty and all forms of human life. And yet the same revolutionary belief for which our forebears fought is still at issue around the globe, the belief that the rights of man come not from the generosity of the state but from the hand of God.

We dare not forget today that we are the heirs of that first revolution. Let the word go forth from this time and place, to friend and foe alike, that the torch has been passed to a new generation of Americans, born in this century, tempered by war, disciplined by a hard and bitter peace, proud of our ancient heritage, and unwilling to witness or permit the slow undoing of those human rights to which this nation has always been committed, and to which we are committed today at home and around the world.

Let every nation know, whether it wishes us well or ill, that we shall pay any price, bear any burden, meet any hardship, support any friend, oppose any foe to assure the survival and the success of liberty.

This much we pledge—and more.

To those old allies whose cultural and spiritual origins we share, we pledge the loyalty of faithful friends. United, there is little we cannot do in a host of cooperative ventures. Divided, there is little we can do, for we dare not meet a powerful challenge at odds and split asunder.

To those new states whom we welcome to the ranks of the free, we pledge our word that one form of colonial control shall not have passed away merely to be replaced by a far more iron tyranny. We shall not always expect to find them supporting our view. But we shall always hope to find them strongly supporting their own freedom, and to remember that, in the past, those who foolishly sought power by riding the back of the tiger ended up inside.

To those peoples in the huts and villages of half the globe struggling to break the bonds of mass misery, we pledge our best efforts to help them help themselves, for whatever period is required, not because the Communists may be doing it, not because we seek their votes, but because it is right. If a free society cannot help the many who are poor, it cannot save the few who are rich.

To our sister republics south of our border, we offer a special pledge: to convert our good words into good deeds, in a new alliance for progress, to assist free men and free governments in casting off the chains of poverty. But this peaceful revolution of hope cannot become the prey of hostile powers. Let all our neighbors know that we shall join with them to oppose aggression or subversion anywhere in the Americas. And let every other power know that this hemisphere intends to remain the master of its own house.

To that world assembly of sovereign states, the United Nations, our last best hope in an age where the instruments of war have far outpaced the instruments of peace, we renew our pledge of support: to prevent it from becoming merely a forum for invective, to strengthen its shield of the new and the weak, and to enlarge the area in which its writ may run.

Finally, to those nations who would make themselves our adversary, we offer not a pledge but a request: that both sides begin anew the quest for peace, before the dark powers of destruction unleashed by science engulf all humanity in planned or accidental sclf-destruction.

We dare not tempt them with weakness. For only when our arms are sufficient beyond doubt can we be certain beyond doubt that they will never be employed.

But neither can two great and powerful groups of nations take comfort from our present course—both sides overburdened by the cost of modern weapons, both rightly alarmed by the steady spread of the deadly atom, yet both racing to alter that uncertain balance of terror that stays the hand of mankind's final war.

So let us begin anew, remembering on both sides that civility is not a sign of weakness, and sincerity is always subject to proof. Let us never negotiate out of fear, but let us never fear to negotiate.

Let both sides explore what problems unite us instead of belaboring those problems which divide us.

Let both sides, for the first time, formulate serious and precise proposals for the inspection and control of arms, and bring the absolute power to destroy other nations under the absolute control of all nations.

Let both sides seek to invoke the wonders of science instead of its terrors. Together let us explore the stars, conquer the deserts, eradicate disease, tap the ocean depths and encourage the arts and commerce.

Let both sides unite to heed in all corners of the earth the command of Isaiah to "undo the heavy burdens . . . [and] let the oppressed go free."

And if a beachhead of cooperation may push back the jungle of suspicion, let both sides join in creating a new endeavor, not a new balance of power, but a new world of law, where the strong are just and the weak secure and the peace preserved.

All this will not be finished in the first one hundred days. Nor will it be finished in the first one thousand days, nor in the life of this Administration, nor even perhaps in our lifetime on this planet. But let us begin.

In your hands, my fellow citizens, more than mine, will rest the final success or failure of our course. Since this country was founded, each generation of Americans has been summoned to give testimony to its national loyalty. The graves of young Americans who answered the call to service surround the globe.

Now the trumpet summons us again—not as a call to bear arms, though arms we need; not as a call to battle, though embattled we are; but a call to bear the burden of a long twilight struggle, year in and year out, "rejoicing in hope, patient in tribulation," a struggle against the common enemies of man: tyranny, poverty, disease and war itself.

Can we forge against these enemies a grand and global alliance, North and South, East and West, that can assure a more fruitful life for all mankind? Will you join in that historic effort?

In the long history of the world, only a few generations have been granted the role of defending freedom in its hour of maximum danger. I do not shrink from this responsibility; I welcome it. I do not believe that any of us would exchange places with any other people or any other generation. The energy, the faith, the devotion which we bring to this endeavor will light our country and all who serve it, and the glow from that fire can truly light the world.

And so, my fellow Americans, ask not what your country can do for you; ask what you can do for your country.

My fellow citizens of the world, ask not what America will do for you, but what together we can do for the freedom of man.

Finally, whether you are citizens of America or citizens of the world, ask of us here the same high standards of strength and sacrifice which we ask of you. With a good conscience our only sure reward, with history the final judge of our deeds, let us go forth to lead the land we love, asking His blessing and His help, but knowing that here on earth God's work must truly be our own.

MURRAY KEMPTON AND
JAMES RIDGEWAY

> "Robert Frost wrote 50 years ago, 'nothing is true except as a man or men adhere to it—to live for it, to spend themselves on it, to die for it.' We need this spirit even more than money or institutions or agreements."
> —*John F. Kennedy, November 18, 1963*

By Saturday night, even the television seemed worn out by attempt and failure and ceased to comment and gave over to a succession of photographs of the columns and the windows and the corners of the White House and of the shadows of the great Lincoln head in Springfield and to a voice reciting "Oh, Captain, My Captain." It is to be, then, the grand style. But the ship has

Romans

not weathered every storm; Mr. Kennedy is not Abraham Lincoln; not because he is more or less, but because he is a remembered physical presence and Mr. Lincoln an image of the plastic arts. One's own time is personal, not historical. Just how long will it be before many of us will want to read a book about the day Mr. Kennedy was shot?

The news of the President's assassination was given by a taxi driver to three gentlemen as they left a hotel on Arlington Street in Boston. They turned right around and hurried back inside to attend to their investments. Packed with students and businessmen a shuttle plane from Boston to Washington waited for permission to take off when the captain came on the intercom: "Folks, up here on the flight deck we've been listening to the news and the President is dead." There was only time to hear one woman say, "How dreadful" before three men went back to discussing plan specifications. A college student reading *Agamemnon* paid no visible attention. One of his notes read, "love-in-hate." The plane took off, the stewardess collected the money and started to serve drinks. Then the captain was back again. They

From *The New Republic*, 149 (Dec. 7, 1963), 9–11. Reprinted by permission of *The New Republic*, copyright 1963, Harrison-Blaine of New Jersey, Inc.

had been listening to more news, that is trying to listen to news because their real job was to hear flight control. There had been a gun battle in Dallas; a patrolman was killed; the police had taken a man in a movie theater. Vice President Johnson was now the President. The talk of business went on through this, and stopped only when the captain again interrupted to say that the new President had been sworn in aboard an aircraft. A few laughed.

They ask too much of us when they ask us to act up to the grand style. We are not an emotionally affluent people. And yet some of us always complained that Mr. Kennedy did not seem quite emotionally committed enough. But now someone remembered with special affection a moment late in the 1960 campaign. Mr. Kennedy was in a motorcade and the Democratic governor who was with him said how wonderful it was to feel the love with which these crowds pressed forward to feel the touch of their candidate. "Oh, dry up," Mr. Kennedy said. It seemed now somehow a special grace in him that he used only the real in emotion and abstained from fabricating the expected. He had too much respect for the grand style to counterfeit it; how much truer to him might we have been if we had come down in scale and if the many of us who must have remembered the lines from *Cymbeline* had thought them proper to speak

> "Fear no more the heat of the sun
>   Nor the furious winter's rages.
> Thou thy worldly task hast done
>   Home art thou and ta'en thy wages.
> Golden lads and girls all must
>   As chimney sweepers come to dust."

Cymbeline is a Roman play. The Kennedys are a Roman family; America seems only a Roman crowd. For us alone in it, there is only a terrible irritation with God and with self and with every other face that is left.

Friday night caught most of the President's Cabinet away from the city. All that could be collected from his official establishment came to Andrews Air Force base to meet the dead man come back from Dallas.

Everything mechanical intruded as it would intrude all weekend. The lights were vagrant, savage and aimless; the planes came and went on distracting irrelevant missions. The face of Undersecretary of Commerce Roosevelt seemed the ruin of his father's. Every uncared-for lank of Senator Dirksen's hair, every fold under every chin seemed for the moment our own fault.

For we had lost in the instant the hope of beginning again. Reason might argue that the sense of a new start was already gone. The main story in the morning's *Washington Post* had detailed the exculpations of a Congressman who had made a 1,000 percent profit from the stock of a company which had enjoyed his good offices with the Internal Revenue Service. The very Senate which dissipated in shock at the news from Texas had just before been waspishly disputing the privileges and emoluments of elective office. For weeks it had been hard to remember anyone in Washington talking about anything except who was getting what from whom. Mr. Kennedy seemed to be wasting in his city and to be nourished only by the great crowds in the countryside. The films from Dallas, painful as they were, reinforced the feeling that he was his old self only away from Washington. It could be argued then that we would see a time when we recognized that all that promise had been an illusion; but you need only look at hope lain dead to know how easy it is to look forward to regret. It had been less than three years since Mr. Kennedy had announced that a new generation was taking up the torch; now old General de Gaulle and old Mr. Mikoyan were coming to see the young man buried.

The great red and white plane of the President of the United States came to Andrews at last bearing all the transition in one horrid large economy-size package. There was a portable yellow elevator to bring Mrs. Kennedy and Attorney-General Kennedy down with a casket that looked like a ship's chest. Half of Lyndon Johnson could be seen waiting in the open door behind them. Mrs. Kennedy's weeds as a widow had to be what some said was a strawberry and some said was a raspberry-colored campaign suit. Everything mechanical that did not intrude functioned badly; the elevator seemed to stall; Mrs. Kennedy tried a door of the ambulance, which did not work, and the Attorney-General, with a deliberation unbroken as hers was, found one which did and she was gone at last, the high Roman figure that she would be all weekend.

So Mr. Johnson came on, tall as ever but wearing the glasses which his image of himself has always thought unsuitable to state occasions, emptied by his misfortune of all his vanity, small and large, and of almost everything else. His lips seemed wet, his chin uncertain; there was a fear that he might be a man who would cry in public and who there was enough his better to blame him? He said something into the microphones that was identifiable only as being hoarse, broken and undeservedly apologetic, and then his new household gathered around him. And the eye as cruel to everyone else as the heart was cruel to self, focused and saw only the hearing aid of an Undersecretary. The next morning, Mr. Johnson had repaired his interior and left off resenting himself, as all of us had better do if we are to get about our business.

As the people waited the passing of the cortege on Sunday some of them squabbled over who was to stand on the step ladder and shoot the first pictures and at what speed and at what lens opening. A mother trying to tune up a transistor radio said to a pouting child, "I want you to understand one thing. This is very important to me." Amidst the people came a teenager with a portable tape recorder. He stuck out a microphone and said, "Sir, on this day of national mourning how do you feel?" Coming away from the Capitol after viewing the bier, a man with a camera slung over his head, said to another man with a camera, "Did you get any good pictures?"

One sat in the Senate press room away from the rotunda on Sunday night and read a wire service report on the tributes paid to the patriotism of Jack Ruby by the master of ceremonies of Mr. Ruby's strip parlor. There was a story about the good fortune of the Dallas citizen who had been in at the death with his movie camera and had sold the films to *Life* for $40,000. The National Football League had played its full Sunday schedule; every seat in Yankee Stadium was filled with mourners. One thought with respect—it was not possible to be grateful to anyone—of Randall Jarrell for having known enough soon enough to have written a book and called it *A Sad Heart at the Supermarket*.

Then a man spoke up and said:

"She came in with the children this afternoon when the rotunda was first opened and she was standing and waiting and the kid looked up at the dome and began to walk around, and she bent over and touched him and he looked up and she straightened her shoulders to show him how to stand at attention, and he did it for about ten seconds. You know, I wish it was a dynasty and the kid was taking over and she was the regent."

Monday was sunny and for those to whom life is a picture, the Capitol was the best and largest color television screen anyone could hope for. A boy sat on his father's shoulders and his father told him to use the Number One setting. The band began "Hail to the Chief," the boy raised his camera and instructed his father not to move. Behind them a woman put a child on her shoulders; the child must have tickled her because she kept laughing, comfortably, and this pleasant distraction continued until the coffin could be detected from its flag to be coming out and she left off and pointed her finger and said with undiminished gaiety, "See, there he is." One left and walked past a girl clutching a paperback. Then suddenly there was one man kneeling with his hands over his eyes and his hat on the sidewalk, and it was impossible not to stop and put a hand upon his shoulder and not to begin to hope that a chain might be put together again.

In front of St. Matthew's the crowd was quieter. The bands and the soldiers went by, the pipers last; and then, like thunder, there was Mrs. Kennedy with the Senator on one side and the Attorney-General on the other and ramrods up their spines. And behind them, the powers and potentates of the earth; the Kennedys were marching with all of Madame Tussaud's in their train, as though Charles de Gaulle had been created a Marshal of France and Haile Selassie I the Lion of Judah only for this last concentrated moment. The powers and potentates waited; Mrs. Kennedy, for the moment made flesh again, gathered her children. Cardinal Cushing came down, under his mitre, looking, to his credit, a trifle irritated with God; we could be grateful for the Catholics and grateful to them for providing one Cardinal who looked like a Prince of the Church.

And the children in their sunny pale blue coats began walking with their mother up the stairs, the little boy stumbling only at the vestibule and then they were gone. We had lived awhile with old Romans; now the doors were closing and we must make do with ourselves.

TOM WICKER

Shortly after President Kennedy was shot, the following inscription appeared on a plaque in one of the private bedrooms of the White House:

> In this room Abraham Lincoln slept during his occupancy of the White House as President of the United States, March 4, 1861–April 13, 1865.
> In this room lived John Fitzgerald Kennedy with his wife Jacqueline Kennedy during the two years, ten months and two days he was President of the United States, January 20, 1961–November 22, 1963.

Kennedy Without Tears

Before many years pass, that deliberate linkage of two Presidents, that notice chiseled upon history by Jacqueline Kennedy, may seem as inevitable as the Washington Monument. Already, airports and spaceports and river bridges and a cultural center have been named for her husband. Books about him, even phonograph records, are at flood tide and *Profiles in Courage* has returned to the top of The New York *Times* best-seller list. It is almost as if he had never called businessmen sons of bitches, sent the troops to Ole Miss, the refugees to the Bay of Pigs, or kicked the budget sky-high.

Six months after his death, John F. Kennedy is certain to take his place in American lore as one of those sure-sell heroes out of whose face or words or monuments a souvenir dealer can turn a steady buck. There he soon will stand, perhaps in our lifetime—cold stone or heartless bronze, immortal as Jefferson, revered as Lincoln, bloodless as Washington. One can imagine the graven words on his pedestal:

> Ask not what your country can do for you. Ask what you can do for your country.

What his country inevitably will do for John Kennedy seems a curious fate for the vitality and intensity, the wry and derisive

From *Esquire*, 61 (June, 1964), 108 ff. Copyright © 1964 by Tom Wicker. Reprinted by permission of Paul R. Reynolds, Inc., 599 Fifth Avenue, New York, N.Y. 10017.

style of the man who was the Thirty-fifth President of the United States. His wit surely would have seared the notion of John F. Kennedy International Airport, much less Cape Kennedy—for this was the man who once told the great-great-grandson of John Adams, "It is a pleasure to live in your family's old house, and we hope that you will come by and see us."

One suspects the Eternal Flame might have embarrassed him as much as the Navy did that brilliant Pacific day last June when the strutting admirals put him literally on a flag-draped pedestal aboard an aircraft carrier while the band played *Hail to the Chief* and the jets screamed overhead on taxpayers' money; one of his favorite quips, after all, was that he had gone from Lieutenant J.G. to Commander-in-Chief without any qualifications at all.

I can almost hear that amused Boston voice inquiring, as he once did after reading a favorable Gallup Poll, where all those people who admired him so much were when Congress turned down his school bill in 1961. Staring from Valhalla at himself cast in stone in the middle of some downtown Washington traffic circle, he might well whisper to earthly passersby what he once told 12,000 Democrats in Harrisburg, Pennsylvania:

"I will introduce myself. I am Teddy Kennedy's brother."

And when children rise reverently in some future Fourth of July pageant to recite the chiastic prose of the Kennedy Inaugural Address—the stirring words that raced so many pulses among that "new generation of Americans" to which he appealed —some may recall instead the same rhythm, the same rhetoric, but different words and a more subtle imagination at work:

"We observe tonight not a celebration of freedom but a victory of party, for we have sworn to pay off the same party debt our forebears ran up nearly a year and three months ago. Our deficit will not be paid off in the next hundred days, nor will it be paid off in the first one thousand days, nor in the life of this Administration. Nor, perhaps, even in our lifetime on this planet. But let us begin—remembering that generosity is not a sign of weakness and that ambassadors are always subject to Senate confirmation. For if the Democratic party cannot be helped by the many who are poor, it cannot be saved by the few who are rich. So let us begin."

Now a politician who could laugh at a parody of his noblest speech—let alone make it himself, as Kennedy did the foregoing —obviously was something more intricate in life than the mere sum of the virtues symbolized by the Eternal Flame: purity, steadfastness, warmth, light. A President delighted by the political caricature of Everett McKinley Dirksen, but impatient with the solemn earnestness of Chester Bowles obviously had a wide streak of Honey Fitz down his spine; yet that same President, confronted with an adulatory mob of hundreds of thousands of cheering Europeans, could not bring himself to respond with more than a halfhearted jab of the arm from the chest—something like a halfback straight-arming a tackler, apologetically. And lest it be imagined that he was merely unemotional, remember that it was the crowd's transmitted frenzy that led Kennedy to make the inspiring but not very wise cry: *Ich bin ein Berliner!*

In the early days of Kennedy's New Frontier (there was bound to be something roguish about a man who could bring the Ivy Leaguers—and himself—to Washington with a slogan that evoked echoes of the Wild West, which appalled most of them), I thought Richard Nixon was perhaps a more interesting *man* than Kennedy. I thought Nixon was, as Conrad wrote of Lord Jim, "one of us." But Kennedy, I thought then, for all his charm and fire and eloquence, was a straightforward political man, who listened to his own rhetoric, contrived his "image" in the comforting faith that a statesman had to get elected before he could do anyone any good, and believed sincerely that his causes were not only right but actually offered solutions to human problems. I thought Kennedy had what Senator Eugene McCarthy called the perfect political mentality—that of a football coach, combining the will to win with the belief that the game is important.

Now, I think that what Kennedy really had of that mentality was a rather peculiar form of the will to win. He wanted power, all right, but something more; "This ability," he once said, "to do things well, and to do them with precision and with modesty, attracts us all." It was a theme to which he often returned—the pursuit of excellence. And as the probability of his political canonization turns toward certainty, and the sad calcification of his humanity into stone and bronze continues, there is not much football coach in the man Kennedy who recalls himself to me most strongly.

If that human Kennedy still seems to me to have been altogether too detached and too controlled to have been, as were Nixon and Lord Jim, "one of us," with all those fascinating hesitancies and inadequacies and torments out of which literature is made, nevertheless he *was* a man "of few days and full of trouble," and for all I know he may even have played "such fantastic tricks before high heaven as to make the angels weep." But the statues will tell us nothing of that.

Not many of them, for instance, will bear inscriptions drawn from his wit—that derisive, barbed, spontaneous wit, just short of mordant, that played so steadily through his speeches and recurred in such stable patterns of wording and attitude that it strikes me in retrospect as the true expression of a point of view, of a way of thinking not subject to time or circumstance or conditions.

It is astonishing, in retrospect, how constantly and boldly this Irish Catholic President, this young man so publicly committed to things like patriotism and public affairs, lampooned politicians, politics, notions, men, systems, myths, himself, even his church. When *The Wall Street Journal* criticized Nixon, Kennedy said, it was like *"L'Osservatore Romano* criticizing the Pope." And Speaker John McCormack denies that Kennedy called him "Archbishop"; "He called me 'Cardinal,' " McCormack recalls.

When the Vatican implied some criticism of Kennedy's campaign efforts to prove himself free of papal influence, Kennedy said ruefully to a pair of reporters: "Now I understand why Henry the Eighth set up his own church."

He and McKinley were the only Presidents ever to address the National Association of Manufacturers, Kennedy told that august body, so "I suppose that President McKinley and I are the only two that are regarded as fiscally sound enough to be qualified." And to the $100-a-plate guests at a glittering political occasion, he confessed: "I could say I am deeply touched, but not as deeply touched as you have been in coming to this luncheon."

Not even the Kennedy family was spared its scion's irreverence. To a dinner of the Alfred E. Smith Foundation during the 1960 campaign, he remarked:

"I had announced earlier this year that if successful I would not consider campaign contributions as a substitute for experience in appointing ambassadors. Ever since I made that statement I have not received one single cent from my father."

Everyone remembers his remark, upon appointing Bob Kennedy Attorney General, that his brother might as well get a little experience before having to practice law; not so many heard him late one night at a Boston dinner last fall when he paid similar respects to the youthful Edward M. Kennedy:

"My last campaign may be coming up very shortly," he said, "but Teddy is around and, therefore, these dinners can go on indefinitely."

The Kennedy wit was so pronounced and so identifiable that it could be reproduced with near exactitude by Ted Sorensen, his speech writer. A deadly serious man, Sorensen's few recorded public jokes include one perfect specimen of Kennedy-style wit.

"There will be a meeting this afternoon of representatives from Baltimore, Atlantic City, San Francisco, Philadelphia, Chicago and other cities interested in holding the 1964 national convention," he said in a mock announcement to a Democratic party gathering. "The meeting will be held in Mayor Daley's room."

In order to laugh—as the Democrats did—one had to know of course that Richard Daley was mayor of Chicago and one of the most powerful figures in the Democratic party—and that the competition for the convention was cutthroat. But Sorensen, as Kennedy always did, had turned his derision precisely to his audience and the circumstances. The target was the situation— Daley's power, the party's foibles, the audience's pretensions. But whatever the situation, the *point of view* remained constant in Kennedy-style wit; it was the point of view that marked the man.

That point of view, as these few examples show, was a blending of amiable irreverence into a faintly resigned tolerance. It was a point of view that did not expect too much of human beings, even of its possessor; even less did it count heavily upon the wisdom or majesty of politicians; and often enough the political process itself was seen with frank disrespect. Perhaps a British M.P., but no American politician in memory except John Kennedy, would have been capable of the devastating "endorsement" of Senator George Smathers that the President delivered at a fund-raising dinner in Miami Beach:

"I actually came down here tonight to pay a debt of obligation to an old friend and faithful adviser. He and I came to the Eightieth Congress together and have been associated for many years, and I regard him as one of my most valuable counselors in moments of great personal and public difficulty.

"In 1952, when I was thinking about running for the United States Senate, I went to the then Senator Smathers and said, 'George, what do you think?'

"He said, 'Don't do it. Can't win. Bad year.'

"In 1956, I was at the Democratic convention, and I said—I didn't know whether I would run for Vice President or not, so I said, 'George, what do you think?'

"'This is it. They need a young man. It's your chance.' So I ran—and lost.

"And in 1960, I was wondering whether I ought to run in the West Virginia primary. 'Don't do it. That state you can't possibly carry.'

"And actually, the only time I really got nervous about the whole matter at the Democratic Convention of 1960 was just before the balloting and George came up and he said, 'I think it looks pretty good for you.' "

The audience was already in stitches, but Kennedy had saved the real barb of his wit to the last, for an astonishing punch line in which Smathers appears not only as a target but as part of an apparatus—the Presidency and its problems—that was in itself somewhat ridiculous in its pretensions:

"It will encourage you to know [Kennedy said] that every Tuesday morning . . . we have breakfast together and he advises with me—Cuba, anything else, Laos, Berlin, anything—George comes right out there and gives his views and I listen very carefully."

Nor did he stop with such small targets as Smathers. Composing a birthday telegram to his touchy Vice President, Lyndon Johnson, he once told a reporter, was like "drafting a state document."

When Prime Minister Lester B. Pearson of Canada arrived at Hyannis Port in the Spring of 1963, his reputation as a baseball expert had preceded him. The resident White House baseball nut was Dave Powers, an Irishman of jovial mien who could sing *Bill Bailey Won't You Please Come Home* with marvelous vigah at the drop of a Scotch and soda. After a chilly Cape Cod dinner, Pearson followed Kennedy into seclusion, only to find it shattered by a summons to Powers.

"Dave," the President said, "test him out."

Whereupon Powers put the Prime Minister through an exhaustive baseball catechism, while the President rocked silently in his rocking chair, puffing on a cigar inscrutably, either measuring his man or enjoying the incongruous match—or both. Back and forth flowed the batting averages, managers' names, World Series statistics, and other diamond esoterica, until finally it was Dave Powers, not Mike Pearson, who tripped on some southpaw's 1926 earned run average.

"He'll do," Kennedy said then, with some satisfaction. After which he and Pearson hit it off famously and jointly equipped Canada with nuclear warheads.

Probably the finest piece of work Kennedy did in his eight generally lackluster years in the Senate was his leadership of the fight against reform of the electoral college in 1956. He argued brilliantly for the system as it was and still is. His side prevailed for a number of sound reasons, but not least because Kennedy succeeded in convincing enough Senators that, as he put it, "Falkland's definition of conservatism is quite appropriate— 'When it is not necessary to change, it is necessary not to change.'"

That might almost have been Lord Melbourne speaking: *If it was not absolutely necessary, it was the foolishest thing ever done,* Melbourne said of a Parliamentary act. Indeed, Melbourne may have been in Kennedy's mind; for in the course of that brutal exposure of all his habits and persuasions to which Amer-

icans subject their President, it was to become known that his
favorite book was David Cecil's *Melbourne.*

Probably no monument of the future will record that fact; yet
it ought to give biographers pause. If the Kennedy campaign of
1960 meant anything, in terms of the man who waged it, it
ought to have meant that Kennedy was a man who aimed to set
the country right, who saw no reason it couldn't be done, who
intended to let nothing stand in the way of doing it. The President who took office that cold day in January, 1961, saying, "let
us begin," seemed to promise that the nation's problems could
be solved if only enough brains and vigor and determination and
money were applied to them.

Why would such a man enjoy reading of Melbourne, who believed government, in fact most human effort, was futile; who
counseled, *When in doubt do nothing;* who said of a proposal to
reform the English municipal councils, *We have got on tolerably
well with the councils for five hundred years; we may contrive to
go on with them for another few years or so;* and who thought
the most damaging part of reform was that it aroused extravagant hopes that government and society—even men—might
actually be improved.

But perhaps Kennedy was never quite the man the 1960 campaign suggested—just as Melbourne was not quite the fogy a
few random quotations might suggest. Melbourne, in fact, as his
biographer pictures him, was a man of immense charm and wit,
great learning, considerable understanding of human nature,
and remarkable courage in going his way—attributes that might
be aspired to by any man. Certainly Kennedy possessed some of
them and there is evidence to suggest that he shared to some
extent Melbourne's skepticism about political and other human
efforts at improving the condition of man.

The Kennedy wit certainly implies that he did. So did his remarks on a famous television interview in December of 1962,
when he reviewed his first two years in office.

"There is a limitation upon the ability of the United States to
solve these problems," he said. ". . . there is a limitation, in
other words, upon the power of the United States to bring about
solutions. . . . The responsibilities placed on the United States

are greater than I imagined them to be and there are greater limitations upon our ability to bring about a favorable result than I had imagined them to be. . . . It is much easier to make the speeches than it is finally to make the judgments. . . ."

And it might have been Melbourne speaking again when he said of his efforts to roll back steel prices: "There is no sense in raising hell and then not being successful. There is no sense in putting the office of the Presidency on the line on an issue and then being defeated."

A few months later, I asked Kennedy at a news conference if he would comment on what I said was a feeling in the country that his Administration seemed "to have lost its momentum and to be slowing down and to be moving on the defensive."

"There is a rhythm to a personal and national and international life and it flows and ebbs," Kennedy replied. He even conceded— sounding not unlike Melbourne on the Reform Laws— that "Some of our difficulties in Europe have come because the military threat in Europe is less than it has been in the past. In other words, whatever successes we may have had in reducing that military threat to Europe brought with it in its wake other problems. . . ."

Later, Ted Sorensen was to publish a book that in its essence was a discussion of the limitations upon a President—the reasons why, as Kennedy wrote in a foreword, "Every President must endure a gap between *what he would like and what is possible"* (the italics are mine). Once again Sorensen had caught the spirit of his chief and reproduced it; politics was not after all simply a matter of brains and vigor and determination, or even money. Its events, life itself, flowed also from the contrary nature of men, the blind turns of chance, the inertia of custom. And in that same foreword Kennedy quoted Franklin Roosevelt as saying:

> Lincoln was a sad man because he couldn't get it all at once. And nobody can.

On a more personal level, some who knew Kennedy well sensed something deeper than skepticism in him, though he was a private man who did not much reveal himself even to men who worked with him for years. He was absolutely fearless about airplanes, for instance, flying anywhere, at any time, in any weather in which he could get aloft, sleeping through anything, scarcely seeming aware that he was off the ground. Yet four persons in his family—his brother, his sister, Ethel Kennedy's parents—had died in aircraft accidents.

Kennedy sometimes discussed the possibility that he would be assassinated with members of his staff. They would be anxious to explain the details of security precautions to him, to show him that it was unlikely it could happen. "If someone is going to kill me," he would say, "they're going to kill me."

And one of those who was close to him believes that Kennedy bothered little about what he was going to do with all those years that presumably would be on his hands when he emerged from the White House at age fifty-one (assuming he won two terms).

"It didn't really concern him," the aide recalls. "He never thought he was going to live to be an old man anyway."

Yet he had his imperatives. A man owed something to the public service. He had to be a patriot. He ought to be physically fit and courageous. (Good war records received special consideration on the New Frontier, and Dave Powers remembers that Kennedy once learned by heart the citation for a medal that had been awarded to General Douglas MacArthur.) A man's job was to act, not talk—to begin, to take the first step in a journey of a thousand miles.

Kennedy has been compared to Franklin Roosevelt and he liked to pose in front of an F.D.R. portrait. In fact, some of his qualities more nearly recall Theodore Roosevelt, the apostle of the big stick, the strenuous life and the bully pulpit. Like T.R., for instance, Kennedy fancied himself in the role of national taste maker—Roosevelt picked up Edward Arlington Robinson and Kennedy adopted Robert Frost. Roosevelt let his rather rigid literary ideas get about and the Kennedys thought they ought to provide White House examples—Casals, Shakespeare and opera in the East Room—for the cultural uplift of the nation. Yet, after an American opera group had sung a scene from *The Magic Flute* in English, after a dinner for the President of India, Kennedy could confess to a group of guests: "I think they ought to sing it in the original language. It doesn't sound right any other way."

There is not much doubt that Kennedy's publicized delight in Ian Fleming's spoof-spy novels doubled Fleming's sales, although there has been no big run on Cecil's *Melbourne*. He kept green, graceful, Lafayette Square in Washington from disappearing into the capital's Great Stone Face. One of his last interests was in a plan to redeem Pennsylvania Avenue from army-surplus stores, cheap steak houses and bumbling federal architects. But it was as if art and culture were in the National Interest, like the test-ban treaty and Project Mercury; and if Kennedy was an avid reader of history, he did not seem to suffer from a great personal involvement in drama, music, art. The movies shown in the White House screening room were often the commonplace of Hollywood, and, except in the East Room, Kennedy's favorite music was more nearly Sinatra than Schönberg. As President, his first venture to Broadway took him to the slick musical, *How to Succeed in Business Without Really Trying*. Once, when he had a group of newspapermen in his house at Palm Beach, I stole a look at a stack of recordings; the one on top was a Chubby Checker twist collection.

But the imperatives of taking part, of public service, seemed, like those that moved Teddy Roosevelt, to be genuine and even profound. To the Touchdown Club of New York, he quoted with obvious approval the rather fervent view of T.R. on the matter:

"The credit belongs to the man who is actually in the arena—whose face is marred by dust and sweat and blood . . . a leader who knows the great enthusiasms, the great devotions—and spends himself in a worthy cause—who at best if he wins knows the thrills of high achievement—and if he fails at least fails while daring greatly—so that his place shall never be with those cold and timid souls who know neither victory nor defeat."

Many times, he voiced a similar sentiment in his own words. Oddly, the man of detachment, of cool wit and ironic view, preached the "long twilight struggle" in which the most certain thing was that there would be "neither victory nor defeat." Yet, the man of commitment, of action, rejected with robustious Teddy the "cold and timid souls" who had no blood and dust upon their faces. And another quotation he liked to throw at university audiences was the rhetorical question of George William Curtis of Massachusetts:

"Would you have counted him a friend of ancient Greece who quietly discussed the theory of patriotism on that hot summer day through whose hopeless and immortal hours Leonidas and the three hundred stood at Thermopylae for liberty? Was John Milton to conjugate Greek verbs in his library when the liberty of Englishmen was imperiled?"

To the students of George Washington University, Kennedy gave his own answer: "No, quite obviously, the duty of the educated man or woman, the duty of the scholar, is to give his objective sense, his sense of liberty to the maintenance of our society at the critical time."

But in the next breath he was telling the story of someone who went to Harvard years ago and "asked for President Lowell. They said, 'He's in Washington, seeing Mr. Taft.' I know that some other day, when they are asking for the President of your university, they will say that he is over at the White House seeing Mr. Kennedy. They understood at Harvard, and you understand here, the relative importance of a university president and a President of the United States."

If that was a joke, it did not come from one who often gave up "his objective sense, and his sense of liberty." Honey Fitz would sing *Sweet Adeline* until his tonsils gave out, but his grandson was never known to wear a funny hat in public. It may seem a small point, but John Kennedy maintained it literally to his dying day. On November 22, in Fort Worth, he went through the Texas ritual of being presented a cowboy hat—but steadfastly resisted the pleas of two thousand Texans that he put it on.

"Come to Washington Monday and I'll put it on for you in the White House," he joked. But even in that comparative privacy, had he reached it, he would not have worn that hat. The man of detachment had yielded himself enough; he would make his little pushing gesture at the crowds, but he would not wave his arms exuberantly above his head like Eisenhower, or thump his chest like Theodore Roosevelt.

So, despite their similarities, he was radically different from the ebullient T.R. Restraint was his style, not arm-waving. There was nothing detached, nothing ironic, about Roosevelt, who could say and believe it that in the White House "my teaching has been plain morality." Kennedy would never claim more than that he hoped he was a "responsible President"; he would not often speak on television because he believed people would tire of him and stop listening.

Sometimes it seemed, he even thought of politics, the Presidency itself, as a sporting proposition. Kennedy never tired of exhorting college students to prepare themselves for the public service, but he was seldom stuffy about it. He did not propose, he told the University of North Carolina student body, to adopt "from the Belgian constitution a provision giving three votes instead of one to college graduates—at least not until more Democrats go to college."

As the campaign of 1960 wore on, the atmosphere around the candidate sometimes seemed almost like one of those parlor games the Kennedys played so often. "Tell me a delegate and I'll tell you who he's for," Kennedy would say to members of his staff, in his best Twenty Questions manner. "Give me a state and I'll give you the delegate breakdown."   The election was so close it inhibited Kennedy; he would point out how closely divided was the country at every opportunity. Yet, he could compare his own disputed election to the plight of a Notre Dame football team that had won a game by means some thought illegal. "And we're not going to give it back," he told the National Football Foundation.

Kennedy disliked the solemn ideologues and myopic Babbitts who crowd American political life—Senator Karl Mundt of South Dakota, for instance—but he delighted in the skillful shenanigans of some who took the game of politics less seriously—even, in some cases, when the voters and taxpayers were taken too. With obvious relish, he once described the operations of the raffish but highly effective Senator Warren Magnuson of Washington as follows:

> "He speaks in the Senate so quietly that few can hear him. He looks down at his desk—he comes into the Senate late in the afternoon—he is very hesitant about interrupting other members of the Senate—when he rises to speak, most members of the Senate have left—he sends his messages up to

the Senate and everyone says, 'What is it?' And Senator
Magnuson says, 'It's nothing important.' And Grand Coulee
Dam is built."

The night before he died, Kennedy spoke in tribute to Representative Albert Thomas in Houston, Texas. Not the least of
Thomas' achievements over the years had been the enrichment
of Houston with federal investments; his most recent coup had
been the somewhat controversial establishment there of the
Manned Spacecraft Center. Kennedy recounted a bit floridly
how Thomas had helped put the United States in a position to
fire into space the largest booster rocket bearing the largest "payroll" in history. As the audience laughed, Kennedy hastily cor-
rected the word to "payload."

That slip might have embarrassed most politicians, but it
obviously struck Kennedy as funny. "It will be the largest payroll, too," he added, grinning, "and who should know that better
than Houston. We put a little of it right in here." Wasn't that
what made the wheels go round?

Kennedy laughed out loud when he heard that Everett Dirksen
had said that one of his early economic measures would have
"all the impact of a snowflake on the bosom of the Potomac."
He once carried a letter from de Gaulle around the White House,
pointing out its elegances to his staff. It mattered not who won
or lost, but how they played the game.

Even the selection of winners of the Medal of Freedom, a sort
of royal honors list Mrs. Kennedy and the President invented,
was not free in Kennedy's mind from the sporting balance of
politics—you scratch mine and I'll scratch yours. When the
painter Andrew Wyeth was selected, Kennedy—who had put
up an early argument for Ben Shahn—decreed: "Next year,
we'll have to go abstract."

One night on his plane, returning to Washington from a
speech in Trenton, he talked about his love of boating with
a group of us, and confided: "I'd really like to have that yacht
Eisenhower laid up in Philadephia [the old *Williamsburg*]. But
he said he did it for economy reasons and if I took it out of moth-
balls now they'd never let me hear the end of it." That was how
the game was played; all you could do was grin and bear it, and
play the game yourself.

Thus, John Kennedy in his pursuit of excellence, his commitment to active service, spent a great deal of his short life playing and thinking politics—running and angling for office, first; pushing political solutions to social and economic problems, second. But that is not necessarily the same thing as being profoundly involved in politics; it is not the same thing as a belief in solutions or the efficacy of politics. Kennedy seemed sometimes to think of himself as taking the first steps he so often urged upon the country and the world; he would use politics, he would propose a program, not with much hope for either, but to raise a question, start someone thinking, to bring a matter into whatever light there was.

One Saturday morning in 1963 in Los Angeles he appeared at the Hollywood Palladium to address a Democratic women's breakfast; it was the only time I ever heard *Hail to the Chief* played with a twist beat. He was supposed to make "brief remarks"; instead, he plunged in his familiar machine-gun delivery into a half hour of Democratic party evangelism so impassioned and so portentous of phrase that some of my colleagues wrote that he had "kicked off his 1964 campaign." I was so stirred by the speech that I phoned The *Times* to hold space for the full text of it. It was a "major address," I assured my editors.

When the transcript came spinning from the White House mimeograph an hour later, I thumbed through it in search of those memorable phrases, those ringing pledges, those grand calls to battle, that had rung through the Palladium. I have that transcript before me now and it confirms my disillusionment; there was nothing there, nothing but rhetoric and delivery. We had seen a performance in which J.F.K had been playing the game unusually well.

In 1962, Kennedy proposed a Cabinet-level Department of Urban Affairs. Robert C. Weaver, the Administration's housing chief, was to be its Secretary—the first Negro to sit in any President's Cabinet. The proposal was hailed as a political masterstroke. Who could vote, in effect, against Weaver except the Southerners? And who cared about them?

In any event, a great many members of Congress voted against the proposal and it became one of Kennedy's most embarrassing defeats. Not long afterward, I asked him how it had happened.

He took a cigar out of his mouth and answered bluntly: "I played it too cute. It was so obvious it made them mad." In short, he had played the game poorly. I think he often did.

He could go before a captive audience of Democratic old people in Madison Square Garden and shed crocodile tears in behalf of his medical-care plan—and look as political and as uncomfortable as he was. Before an audience in Miami Beach from which he had little further to gain, the A.F.L.-C.I.O., he was so palpably bored, his speech was so blatantly routine and uninspired, that men of more objective political judgment might have booed him from the platform. He went into General Eisenhower's home county during the 1962 campaign and delivered a speech so demogogic and so extravagant in its claims for Democratic virtue and Republican sloth that even the General was enraged and promptly proceeded to emerge from retirement to campaign against him—a development that might have been politically important had not the Cuban crisis changed the whole picture in October. On his Western trip in the Fall of 1963—his last extended tour in the country—Kennedy looked and felt so out of place talking about conservation and nature and wildlife that the reporters following him gave him the nickname "Smokey the Bear"; it was reported by Pierre Salinger at Jackson Lake Lodge that the President actually had seen a moose from the window of his room.

Shortly after Kennedy's death, Carroll Kilpatrick and I visited J. Frank Dobie at the University of Texas and asked him what was the difference in Kennedy and Lyndon Johnson. Mr. Dobie knew Johnson well; he knew Kennedy only as most Americans knew him—as a voice on the radio, a face on the screen, a presence in the land. "Johnson is concerned with means," Mr. Dobie said at once, as if the contrast was obvious. "Kennedy was interested in ends."

A generality, perhaps, but near enough to truth to *ring* true. Kennedy played the game as a political man had to, sometimes brilliantly, often with boredom and ineptitude. But it was not then that he stirred us. Even his memorable campaign of 1960, the finest exercise of his strictly political life, was not politics-as-usual; it was outside the ordinary rules, for Kennedy was a Roman Catholic, an inexperienced younger man, something of an intellectual, who put little trust in traditional politicians, and relied instead upon his own men, his own techniques, his own personality.

Perhaps he had to move beyond the rules, get out of the game, before he really involved himself—and therefore involved other men. His trip to Europe in 1963 exhilarated him, for instance; he knew he had broken through the traditional wall of diplomatic niceties, spoken above the heads of politicians and governments, and he believed a new generation of Europeans had responded. At his death, his tax bill was mired in Congress, but its mere presentation may yet be the longest step toward lifting American economic policy out of the twin ruts of ignorance and cliché. His civil-rights bill was fumbled and botched, but he was the first American President to recognize in the outpouring of events a "moral crisis" in race relations. The long shadow of de Gaulle darkened his European policy, but he had proclaimed on both sides of the Atlantic a commitment to the interdependence of two continents. Nobody could say there would be no nuclear war, but he had taken the "first step" of the test-ban treaty.

That is what haunts me about Kennedy—not just that he was a man of certain admirable visions, but that he had the kind of mind that could entertain vision, the kind of outlook that could put in perspective the gambits and maneuvers of the moment, see truly the futility of most means, the uncertain glory of most ends. Surely he was one of those men "educated in the liberal traditions, willing to take the long look, undisturbed by prejudices and slogans of the moment, who attempt to make an honest judgment on difficult events"; surely he tried to be one of those, to borrow his words again, who could "distinguish the real from the illusory, the long-range from the temporary, the significant from the petty. . . ."

And that is the real irony of John F. Kennedy's coming immortality. For when James Reston asked him in the Summer of 1961, during a long afternoon's talk at Hyannis Port, what kind of a world it was he had in mind, what vision he had of the future, John Kennedy—President of the United States for a half a year, perpetrator of the Bay of Pigs, not long home from his "somber" meeting with Khrushchev in Vienna—could reply: "I haven't had time to think about that yet."

It is the classic story of the liberal man in politics. *I claim not to have controlled events*, Lincoln said, *but confess plainly that events have controlled me.* And perhaps it is symbolized in a compelling picture of Kennedy that comes to us from one of Washington's most imposing men.

It is a glimpse from the Cuban missile crisis of October, 1962, a period of great tension at the White House as throughout the world. The personage and the President were alone in Kennedy's oval office, discussing what in New Frontier jargon were known as "the options"; that month, the options were pretty grim.

Kennedy rose from his rocking chair, leaving his visitor seated on a sofa. The President went across his office to the French doors that opened on the terrace of the West Executive Wing. Beyond the terrace lay the famous Rose Garden, redesigned like almost everything else about the White House by the elegant stylists who had come to live there. But at its end still towered the famous magnolia planted by Andrew Jackson.

Kennedy stood for a long time, silent, gazing at the garden and the magnolia, his hands behind his back, the burden of decision almost visible on his shoulders. "Well," he said at last, "I guess this is the week I earn my salary."

The detached thinker had been brought to bay by the necessities of the moment. That questing mind with its sensitivity to the complexity of things, to the illusory nature of answers and solutions, had come to the moment of black vs. white. That derisive and worldly wit was stilled in the sheer responsibility of choice. Action and events had overtaken contemplation and vision, and Kennedy shared the plight of Melbourne: *I am afraid the question of the Irish Church can neither be avoided or postponed. It must therefore be attempted to be solved.* And for Kennedy, that fall, humanity itself was the question.

So with his football coach's will to win, with his passion for "the ability to do things well," Kennedy had had his dreams and realized them. But I believe he stood on the sidelines, too, even while the game was going on, measuring his performance, wryly remarking upon it, not much impressed, not much deluded. Perhaps he knew all along that events would control, action overwhelm, means fail to reach ends. "There stands the decision," he wrote, "and there stands the President." Sooner or later, they would be as one.

The decisions he made, the slogans he spoke—let them be carved on the monuments. But for me his epitaph is inscribed on Dave Powers' silver beer mug, that John Kennedy gave him for his birthday last year. It reads:

> There are three things which are real:
> God, human folly and laughter.
> The first two are beyond our comprehension
> So we must do what we can with the third.

No one at the White House knew the source of those lines. I can find the words in no book of quotations. The Library of Congress has not been able to discover who wrote them. But I think I know.

3

The Scene

In the chill California dawn teenagers on a beach stare blankly at the ocean and silently wax their surf boards. On the Upper West Side of Manhattan a coterie of intellectuals earnestly debates a burning question: Who is more perfectly the embodiment of the American dream, Batman or Daddy Warbucks? In a small village in West Africa a young American from New Hampshire shows a group of natives the principles of modern agriculture. In a fraternity house of a large university in the midwest, a twenty-year-old student prepares to take a trip—his ticket is a small cube of sugar.

These hypothetical events are all aspects of a phenomenon that has come to be called, inaccurately, The Scene. The term is inaccurate because it suggests something fixed, not changing, a place rather than an event, space rather than time. The idea of The Scene is probably more precisely conveyed by bringing it together with another term coined in the Sixties, *happening*. "The Scene is what's happening." The formula characterizes the style and texture of the social life of the Sixties. Its disruption of normal English syntax is a reflection of the disrupted sense of reality to which it refers.

Surfing, "Camp," drugs, the Peace Corps, the sexual revolution represent radically different responses to that disruption, just as the essays printed here represent radically different styles and perspectives. However, despite their differences, these fragments all combine to convey some sense of the multiplicity, fragmentation and excitement of contemporary life.

SUSAN SONTAG

Many things in the world have not been named; and many things, even if they have been named, have never been described. One of these is the sensibility—unmistakably modern, a variant of sophistication but hardly identical with it—that goes by the cult name of "Camp."

A sensibility (as distinct from an idea) is one of the hardest

Notes on "Camp"

things to talk about; but there are special reasons why Camp, in particular, has never been discussed. It is not a natural mode of sensibility, if there be any such. Indeed the essence of Camp is its love of the unnatural: of artifice and exaggeration. And Camp is esoteric—something of a private code, a badge of identity even, among small urban cliques. Apart from a lazy two-page sketch in Christopher Isherwood's novel *The World in the Evening* (1954), it has hardly broken into print. To talk about Camp is therefore to betray it. If the betrayal can be defended, it will be for the edification it provides, or the dignity of the conflict it resolves. For myself, I plead the goal of self-edification, and the goad of a sharp conflict in my own sensibility. I am strongly drawn to Camp, and almost as strongly offended by it. That is why I want to talk about it, and why I can. For no one who wholeheartedly shares in a given sensibility can analyze it; he can only, whatever his intention, exhibit it. To name a sensibility, to draw its contours and to recount its history, requires a deep sympathy modified by revulsion.

Though I am speaking about sensibility only—and about a sensibility that, among other things, converts the serious into the frivolous—these are grave matters. Most people think of sensibility or taste as the realm of purely subjective preferences, those mysterious attractions, mainly sensual, that have not been brought under the sovereignty of reason. They *allow* that considerations of taste play a part in their reactions to people and to works of art. But this attitude is naïve. And even worse. To

From *Against Interpretation* by Susan Sontag, by permission of Farrar, Straus & Giroux, Inc. Copyright © 1964 by Susan Sontag. The article first appeared in *Partisan Review* (Fall, 1964).

patronize the faculty of taste is to patronize oneself. For taste governs every free—as opposed to rote—human response. Nothing is more decisive. There is taste in people, visual taste, taste in emotion—and there is taste in acts, taste in morality. Intelligence, as well, is really a kind of taste: taste in ideas. (One of the facts to be reckoned with is that taste tends to develop very unevenly. It's rare that the same person has good visual taste *and* good taste in people *and* taste in ideas.)

Taste has no system and no proofs. But there is something like a logic of taste: the consistent sensibility which underlies and gives rise to a certain taste. A sensibility is almost, but not quite, ineffable. Any sensibility which can be crammed into the mold of a system, or handled with the rough tools of proof, is no longer a sensibility at all. It has hardened into an idea. . . .

To snare a sensibility in words, especially one that is alive and powerful,* one must be tentative and nimble. The form of jottings, rather than an essay (with its claim to a linear, consecutive argument), seemed more appropriate for getting down something of this particular fugitive sensibility. It's embarrassing to be solemn and treatise-like about Camp. One runs the risk of having, oneself, produced a very inferior piece of Camp.

These notes are for Oscar Wilde.

"One should either be a work of art, or wear a work of art."
        —*Phrases & Philosophies for the Use of the Young*

1. To start very generally: Camp is a certain mode of aestheticism. It is *one* way of seeing the world as an aesthetic phenomenon. That way, the way of Camp, is not in terms of beauty, but in terms of the degree of artifice, of stylization.

2. To emphasize style is to slight content, or to introduce an attitude which is neutral with respect to content. It goes without saying that the Camp sensibility is disengaged, depoliticized— or at least apolitical.

* The sensibility of an era is not only its most decisive, but also its most perishable, aspect. One may capture the ideas (intellectual history) and the behavior (social history) of an epoch without ever touching upon the sensibility or taste which informed those ideas, that behavior. Rare are those historical studies—like Huizinga on the late Middle Ages, Febvre on 16th century France—which do tell us something about the sensibility of the period.

3. Not only is there a Camp vision, a Camp way of looking at things. Camp is as well a quality discoverable in objects and the behavior of persons. There are "campy" movies, clothes, furniture, popular songs, novels, people, buildings. . . . This distinction is important. True, the Camp eye has the power to transform experience. But not everything can be seen as Camp. It's not *all* in the eye of the beholder.

4. Random examples of items which are part of the canon of Camp:

Zuleika Dobson
Tiffany lamps
Scopitone films
The Brown Derby restaurant on Sunset Boulevard in LA
The Enquirer, headlines and stories
Aubrey Beardsley drawings
Swan Lake
Bellini's operas
Visconti's direction of *Salome* and *'Tis Pity She's a Whore*
certain turn-of-the-century picture postcards
Schoedsack's *King Kong*
the Cuban pop singer La Lupe
Lynn Ward's novel in woodcuts, *God's Man*
the old Flash Gordon comics
women's clothes of the twenties (feather boas, fringed and
     beaded dresses, etc.)
the novels of Ronald Firbank and Ivy Compton-Burnett
stag movies seen without lust

5. Camp taste has an affinity for certain arts rather than others. Clothes, furniture, all the elements of visual décor, for instance, make up a large part of Camp. For Camp art is often decorative art, emphasizing texture, sensuous surface, and style at the expense of content. Concert music, though, because it is contentless, is rarely Camp. It offers no opportunity, say, for a contrast between silly or extravagant content and rich form. . . . Sometimes whole art forms become saturated with Camp. Classical ballet, opera, movies have seemed so for a long time. In the last two years, popular music (post rock-'n'-roll, what the French call *yé yé*) has been annexed. And movie criticism (like lists of "The 10 Best Bad Movies I Have Seen") is probably the greatest popularizer of Camp taste today, because most people still go to the movies in a high-spirited and unpretentious way.

6. There is a sense in which it is correct to say: "It's too good to be Camp." Or "too important," not marginal enough. (More on this later.) Thus, the personality and many of the works of Jean Cocteau are Camp, but not those of André Gide; the operas of Richard Strauss, but not those of Wagner; concoctions of Tin Pan Alley and Liverpool, but not jazz. Many examples of Camp are things which, from a "serious" point of view, are either bad art or kitsch. Not all, though. Not only is Camp not necessarily bad art, but some art which can be approached as Camp (example: the major films of Louis Feuillade) merits the most serious admiration and study.

"The more we study Art, the less we care for Nature."
                                                —*The Decay of Lying*

7. All Camp objects, and persons, contain a large element of artifice. Nothing in nature can be campy. . . . Rural Camp is still man-made, and most campy objects are urban. (Yet, they often have a serenity—or a naïveté—which is the equivalent of pastoral. A great deal of Camp suggests Empson's phrase, "urban pastoral.")

8. Camp is a vision of the world in terms of style—but a particular kind of style. It is the love of the exaggerated, the "off," of things-being-what-they-are-not. The best example is in Art Nouveau, the most typical and fully developed Camp style. Art Nouveau objects, typically, convert one thing into something else: the lighting fixtures in the form of flowering plants, the living room which is really a grotto. A remarkable example: the Paris Métro entrances designed by Hector Guimard in the late 1890s in the shape of cast-iron orchid stalks.

9. As a taste in persons, Camp responds particularly to the markedly attenuated and to the strongly exaggerated. The androgyne is certainly one of the great images of Camp sensibility. Examples: the swooning, slim, sinuous figures of pre-Raphaelite painting and poetry; the thin, flowing, sexless bodies in Art Nouveau prints and posters, presented in relief on lamps and ash-trays; the haunting androgynous vacancy behind the perfect beauty of Greta Garbo. Here, Camp taste draws on a mostly unacknowledged truth of taste: the most refined form of sexual attractiveness (as well as the most refined form of sexual

pleasure) consists in going against the grain of one's sex. What is most beautiful in virile men is something feminine; what is most beautiful in feminine women is something masculine. . . . Allied to the Camp taste for the androgynous is something that seems quite different but isn't: a relish for the exaggeration of sexual characteristics and personality mannerisms. For obvious reasons, the best examples that can be cited are movie stars. The corny flamboyant femaleness of Jayne Mansfield, Gina Lollobrigida, Jane Russell, Virginia Mayo; the exaggerated he-man-ness of Steve Reeves, Victor Mature. The great stylists of temperament and mannerism, like Bette Davis, Barbara Stanwyck, Tallulah Bankhead, Edwige Feuillière.

10. Camp sees everything in quotation marks. It's not a lamp, but a "lamp"; not a woman, but a "woman." To perceive Camp in objects and persons is to understand Being-as-Playing-a-Role. It is the farthest extension, in sensibility, of the metaphor of life as theater.

11. Camp is the triumph of the epicene style. (The convertibility of "man" and "woman," "person" and "thing.") But all style, that is, artifice, is, ultimately, epicene. Life is not stylish. Neither is nature.

12. The question isn't, "Why travesty, impersonation, theatricality?" The question is, rather, "When does travesty, impersonation, theatricality acquire the special flavor of Camp?" Why is the atmosphere of Shakespeare's comedies (*As You Like It,* etc.) not epicene, while that of *Der Rosenkavalier* is?

13. The dividing line seems to fall in the 18th century; there the origins of Camp taste are to be found (Gothic novels, Chinoiserie, caricature, artificial ruins, and so forth.) But the relation to nature was quite different then. In the 18th century, people of taste either patronized nature (Strawberry Hill) or attempted to remake it into something artificial (Versailles). They also indefatigably patronized the past. Today's Camp taste effaces nature, or else contradicts it outright. And the relation of Camp taste to the past is extremely sentimental.

14. A pocket history of Camp might, of course, begin farther back—with the mannerist artists like Pontormo, Rosso, and Caravaggio, or the extraordinarily theatrical painting of Georges de La Tour, or Euphuism (Lyly, etc.) in literature. Still, the

soundest starting point seems to be the late 17th and early 18th century, because of that period's extraordinary feeling for artifice, for surface, for symmetry; its taste for the picturesque and the thrilling, its elegant conventions for representing instant feeling and the total presence of character—the epigram and the rhymed couplet (in words), the flourish (in gesture and in music). The late 17th and early 18th century is the great period of Camp: Pope, Congreve, Walpole, etc., but not Swift; *les précieux* in France; the rococo churches of Munich; Pergolesi. Somewhat later: much of Mozart. But in the 19th century, what had been distributed throughout all of high culture now becomes a special taste; it takes on overtones of the acute, the esoteric, the perverse. Confining the story to England alone, we see Camp continuing wanly through 19th century aestheticism (Burne-Jones, Pater, Ruskin, Tennyson), emerging full-blown with the Art Nouveau movement in the visual and decorative arts, and finding its conscious ideologists in such "wits" as Wilde and Firbank.

15. Of course, to say all these things are Camp is not to argue they are simply that. A full analysis of Art Nouveau, for instance, would scarcely equate it with Camp. But such an analysis cannot ignore what in Art Nouveau allows it to be experienced as Camp. Art Nouveau is full of "content," even of a political-moral sort; it was a revolutionary movement in the arts, spurred on by a utopian vision (somewhere between William Morris and the Bauhaus group) of an organic politics and taste. Yet there is also a feature of the Art Nouveau objects which suggests a disengaged, unserious, "aesthete's" vision. This tells us something important about Art Nouveau—and about what the lens of Camp, which blocks out content, is.

16. Thus, the Camp sensibility is one that is alive to a double sense in which some things can be taken. But this is not the familiar split-level construction of a literal meaning, on the one hand, and a symbolic meaning, on the other. It is the difference, rather, between the thing as meaning something, anything, and the thing as pure artifice.

17. This comes out clearly in the vulgar use of the word Camp as a verb, "to camp," something that people do. To camp is a mode of seduction—one which employs flamboyant mannerisms

susceptible of a double interpretation; gestures full of duplicity, with a witty meaning for cognoscenti and another, more impersonal, for outsiders. Equally and by extension, when the word becomes a noun, when a person or a thing is "a camp," a duplicity is involved. Behind the "straight" public sense in which something can be taken, one has found a private zany experience of the thing.

> "To be natural is such a very difficult pose to keep up."
> —*An Ideal Husband*

18. One must distinguish between naïve and deliberate Camp. Pure Camp is always naïve. Camp which knows itself to be Camp ("camping") is usually less satisfying.

19. The pure examples of Camp are unintentional; they are dead serious. The Art Nouveau craftsman who makes a lamp with a snake coiled around it is not kidding, nor is he trying to be charming. He is saying, in all earnestness: Voilà! the Orient! Genuine Camp—for instance, the numbers devised for the Warner Brothers musicals of the early thirties (*42nd Street; The Golddiggers of 1933; . . . of 1935; . . . of 1937;* etc.) by Busby Berkeley—does not *mean* to be funny. Camping—say, the plays of Noël Coward—does. It seems unlikely that much of the traditional opera repertoire could be such satisfying Camp if the melodramatic absurdities of most opera plots had not been taken seriously by their composers. One doesn't need to know the artist's private intentions. The work tells all. (Compare a typical 19th century opera with Samuel Barber's *Vanessa,* a piece of manufactured, calculated Camp, and the difference is clear.)

20. Probably, intending to be campy is always harmful. The perfection of *Trouble in Paradise* and *The Maltese Falcon,* among the greatest Camp movies ever made, comes from the effortless smooth way in which tone is maintained. This is not so with such famous would-be Camp films of the fifties as *All About Eve* and *Beat the Devil.* These more recent movies have their fine moments, but the first is so slick and the second so hysterical; they want so badly to be campy that they're continually losing the beat. . . . Perhaps, though, it is not so much a question of the unintended effect versus the conscious intention,

as of the delicate relation between parody and self-parody in Camp. The films of Hitchcock are a showcase for this problem. When self-parody lacks ebullience but instead reveals (even sporadically) a contempt for one's themes and one's materials —as in *To Catch a Thief, Rear Window, North by Northwest*— the results are forced and heavy-handed, rarely Camp. Successful Camp—a movie like Carné's *Drôle de Drame;* the film performances of Mae West and Edward Everett Horton; portions of the Goon Show—even when it reveals self-parody, reeks of self-love.

21. So, again, Camp rests on innocence. That means Camp discloses innocence, but also, when it can, corrupts it. Objects, being objects, don't change when they are singled out by the Camp vision. Persons, however, respond to their audiences. Persons begin "camping": Mae West, Bea Lillie, La Lupe, Tallulah Bankhead in *Lifeboat*, Bette Davis in *All About Eve*. (Persons can even be induced to camp without their knowing it. Consider the way Fellini got Anita Ekberg to parody herself in *La Dolce Vita.*)

22. Considered a little less strictly, Camp is either completely naïve or else wholly conscious (when one plays at being campy). An example of the latter: Wilde's epigrams themselves.

> "It's absurd to divide people into good and bad. People are either charming or tedious."
>
> *—Lady Windemere's Fan*

23. In naïve, or pure, Camp, the essential element is seriousness, a seriousness that fails. Of course, not all seriousness that fails can be redeemed as Camp. Only that which has the proper mixture of the exaggerated, the fantastic, the passionate, and the naïve.

24. When something is just bad (rather than Camp), it's often because it is too mediocre in its ambition. The artist hasn't attempted to do anything really outlandish. ("It's too much," "It's too fantastic," "It's not to be believed," are standard phrases of Camp enthusiasm.)

25. The hallmark of Camp is the spirit of extravagance. Camp is a woman walking around in a dress made of three million feathers. Camp is the paintings of Carlo Crivelli, with their real

jewels and *trompe-l'oeil* insects and cracks in the masonry. Camp is the outrageous aestheticism of Sternberg's six American movies with Dietrich, all six, but especially the last, *The Devil Is a Woman.* . . . In Camp there is often something *démesuré* in the quality of the ambition, not only in the style of the work itself. Gaudí's lurid and beautiful buildings in Barcelona are Camp not only because of their style but because they reveal— most notably in the Cathedral of the Sagrada Familia—the ambition on the part of one man to do what it takes a generation, a whole culture to accomplish.

26. Camp is art that proposes itself seriously, but cannot be taken altogether seriously because it is "too much." *Titus Andronicus* and *Strange Interlude* are almost Camp, or could be played as Camp. The public manner and rhetoric of de Gaulle, often, are pure Camp.

27. A work can come close to Camp, but not make it, because it succeeds. Eisenstein's films are seldom Camp because, despite all exaggeration, they do succeed (dramatically) without surplus. If they were a little more "off," they could be great Camp— particularly *Ivan the Terrible I & II.* The same for Blake's drawings and paintings, weird and mannered as they are. They aren't Camp; though Art Nouveau, influenced by Blake, is.

What is extravagant in an inconsistent or an unpassionate way is not Camp. Neither can anything be Camp that does not seem to spring from an irrepressible, a virtually uncontrolled sensibility. Without passion, one gets pseudo-Camp—what is merely decorative, safe, in a word, chic. On the barren edge of Camp lie a number of attractive things: the sleek fantasies of Dali, the haute couture preciosity of Albicocco's *The Girl with the Golden Eyes.* But the two things—Camp and preciosity— must not be confused.

28. Again, Camp is the attempt to do something extraordinary. But extraordinary in the sense, often, of being special, glamorous. (The curved line, the extravagant gesture.) Not extraordinary merely in the sense of effort. Ripley's Believe-It-Or-Not items are rarely campy. These items, either natural oddities (the two-headed rooster, the eggplant in the shape of a cross) or else the products of immense labor (the man who walked from here to China on his hands, the woman who en-

graved the New Testament on the head of a pin), lack the visual reward—the glamour, the theatricality—that marks off certain extravagances as Camp.

29. The reason a movie like *On the Beach,* books like *Winesburg, Ohio* and *For Whom the Bell Tolls* are bad to the point of being laughable, but not bad to the point of being enjoyable, is that they are too dogged and pretentious. They lack fantasy. There is Camp in such bad movies as *The Prodigal* and *Samson and Delilah,* the series of Italian color spectacles featuring the super-hero Maciste, numerous Japanese science fiction films (*Rodan, The Mysterians, The H-Man*) because, in their relative unpretentiousness and vulgarity, they are more extreme and irresponsible in their fantasy—and therefore touching and quite enjoyable.

30. Of course, the canon of Camp can change. Time has a great deal to do with it. Time may enhance what seems simply dogged or lacking in fantasy now because we are too close to it, because it resembles too closely our own everyday fantasies, the fantastic nature of which we don't perceive. We are better able to enjoy a fantasy as fantasy when it is not our own.

31. This is why so many of the objects prized by Camp taste are old-fashioned, out-of-date, *démodé.* It's not a love of the old as such. It's simply that the process of aging or deterioration provides the necessary detachment—or arouses a necessary sympathy. When the theme is important, and contemporary, the failure of a work of art may make us indignant. Time can change that. Time liberates the work of art from moral relevance, delivering it over to the Camp sensibility. . . . Another effect: time contracts the sphere of banality. (Banality is, strictly speaking, always a category of the contemporary.) What was banal can, with the passage of time, become fantastic. Many people who listen with delight to the style of Rudy Vallee revived by the English pop group, The Temperance Seven, would have been driven up the wall by Rudy Vallee in his heyday.

Thus, things are campy, not when they become old—but when we become less involved in them, and can enjoy, instead of be frustrated by, the failure of the attempt. But the effect of time is unpredictable. Maybe "Method" Acting (James Dean, Rod Steiger, Warren Beatty) will seem as Camp some day as Ruby

Keeler's does now—or as Sarah Bernhardt's does, in the films she made at the end of her career. And maybe not.

32. Camp is the glorification of "character." The statement is of no importance—except, of course, to the person (Loie Fuller, Gaudí, Cecil B. De Mille, Crivelli, de Gaulle, etc.) who makes it. What the Camp eye appreciates is the unity, the force of the person. In every move the aging Martha Graham makes she's being Martha Graham, etc., etc. . . . This is clear in the case of the great serious idol of Camp taste, Greta Garbo. Garbo's incompetence (at the least, lack of depth) as an *actress* enhances her beauty. She's always herself.

33. What Camp taste responds to is "instant character" (this is, of course, very 18th century); and, conversely, what it is not stirred by is the sense of the development of character. Character is understood as a state of continual incandescence—a person being one, very intense thing. This attitude toward character is a key element of the theatricalization of experience embodied in the Camp sensibility. And it helps account for the fact that opera and ballet are experienced as such rich treasures of Camp, for neither of these forms can easily do justice to the complexity of human nature. Wherever there is development of character, Camp is reduced. Among operas, for example, *La Traviata* (which has some small development of character) is less campy than *Il Trovatore* (which has none).

> "Life is too important a thing ever to talk seriously about it."
> —Vera, or The Nihilists

34. Camp taste turns its back on the good-bad axis of ordinary aesthetic judgment. Camp doesn't reverse things. It doesn't argue that the good is bad, or the bad is good. What it does is to offer for art (and life) a different—a supplementary—set of standards.

35. Ordinarily we value a work of art because of the seriousness and dignity of what it achieves. We value it because it succeeds—in being what it is and, presumably, in fulfilling the intention that lies behind it. We assume a proper, that is to say, straightforward relation between intention and performance. By such standards, we appraise *The Iliad*, Aristophanes' plays, The Art of the Fugue, *Middlemarch*, the paintings of Rembrandt,

Chartres, the poetry of Donne, *The Divine Comedy*, Beethoven's
quartets, and—among people—Socrates, Jesus, St. Francis,
Napoleon, Savonarola. In short, the pantheon of high culture:
truth, beauty, and seriousness.

36. But there are other creative sensibilities besides the seriousness (both tragic and comic) of high culture and of the high
style of evaluating people. And one cheats oneself, as a human
being, if one has *respect* only for the style of high culture, whatever else one may do or feel on the sly.

For instance, there is the kind of seriousness whose trademark
is anguish, cruelty, derangement. Here we do accept a disparity
between intention and result. I am speaking, obviously, of a
style of personal existence as well as of a style in art; but the
examples had best come from art. Think of Bosch, Sade, Rim-
baud, Jarry, Kafka, Artaud, think of most of the important works
of art of the 20th century, that is, art whose goal is not that of
creating harmonies but of overstraining the medium and introducing more and more violent, and unresolvable, subject-matter.
This sensibility also insists on the principle that an *oeuvre* in the
old sense (again, in art, but also in life) is not possible. Only
"fragments" are possible. . . . Clearly, different standards apply
here than to traditional high culture. Something is good not
because it is achieved, but because another kind of truth about
the human situation, another experience of what it is to be
human—in short, another valid sensibility—is being revealed.

And third among the great creative sensibilities is Camp: the
sensibility of failed seriousness, of the theatricalization of experience. Camp refuses both the harmonies of traditional seriousness, and the risks of fully identifying with extreme states
of feeling.

37. The first sensibility, that of high culture, is basically
moralistic. The second sensibility, that of extreme states of
feeling, represented in much contemporary "avant-garde" art,
gains power by a tension between moral and aesthetic passion.
The third, Camp, is wholly aesthetic.

38. Camp is the consistently aesthetic experience of the world.
It incarnates a victory of "style" over "content," "aesthetics" over
"morality," of irony over tragedy.

39. Camp and tragedy are antitheses. There is seriousness in
Camp (seriousness in the degree of the artist's involvement)
and, often, pathos. The excruciating is also one of the tonalities
of Camp; it is the quality of excruciation in much of Henry
James (for instance, *The Europeans, The Awkward Age, The
Wings of the Dove*) that is responsible for the large element of
Camp in his writings. But there is never, never tragedy.

40. Style is everything. Genet's ideas, for instance, are very
Camp. Genet's statement that "the only criterion of an act is its
elegance" * is virtually interchangeable, as a statement, with
Wilde's "in matters of great importance, the vital element is not
sincerity, but style." But what counts, finally, is the style in which
ideas are held. The ideas about morality and politics in, say,
Lady Windemere's Fan and in *Major Barbara* are Camp, but
not just because of the nature of the ideas themselves. It is
those ideas, held in a special playful way. The Camp ideas in
Our Lady of the Flowers are maintained too grimly, and the
writing itself is too successfully elevated and serious, for Genet's
books to be Camp.

41. The whole point of Camp is to dethrone the serious. Camp
is playful, anti-serious. More precisely, Camp involves a new,
more complex relation to "the serious." One can be serious about
the frivolous, frivolous about the serious.

42. One is drawn to Camp when one realizes that "sincerity"
is not enough. Sincerity can be simple philistinism, intellectual
narrowness.

43. The traditional means for going beyond straight seriousness—irony, satire—seem feeble today, inadequate to the
culturally oversaturated medium in which contemporary sensibility is schooled. Camp introduces a new standard: artifice
as an ideal, theatricality.

44. Camp proposes a comic vision of the world. But not a
bitter or polemical comedy. If tragedy is an experience of hyper-
involvement, comedy is an experience of underinvolvement, of
detachment.

---

* Sartre's gloss on this in *Saint Genet* is: "Elegance is the quality
of conduct which transforms the greatest amount of being into appearing."

"I adore simple pleasures, they are the last refuge of the complex."

—*A Woman of No Importance*

45. Detachment is the prerogative of an elite; and as the dandy is the 19th century's surrogate for the aristocrat in matters of culture, so Camp is the modern dandyism. Camp is the answer to the problem: how to be a dandy in the age of mass culture.

46. The dandy was overbred. His posture was disdain, or else *ennui*. He sought rare sensations, undefiled by mass appreciation. (Models: Des Esseintes in Huysmans' *À Rebours*, *Marius the Epicurean*, Valéry's *Monsieur Teste*.) He was dedicated to "good taste."

The connoisseur of Camp has found more ingenious pleasures. Not in Latin poetry and rare wines and velvet jackets, but in the coarsest, commonest pleasures, in the arts of the masses. Mere use does not defile the objects of his pleasure, since he learns to possess them in a rare way. Camp—Dandyism in the age of mass culture—makes no distinction between the unique object and the mass-produced object. Camp taste transcends the nausea of the replica.

47. Wilde himself is a transitional figure. The man who, when he first came to London, sported a velvet beret, lace shirts, velveteen knee-breeches and black silk stockings, could never depart too far in his life from the pleasures of the old-style dandy; this conservatism is reflected in *The Picture of Dorian Gray*. But many of his attitudes suggest something more modern. It was Wilde who formulated an important element of the Camp sensibility—the equivalence of all objects—when he announced his intention of "living up" to his blue-and-white china, or declared that a door-knob could be as admirable as a painting. When he proclaimed the importance of the necktie, the boutonniere, the chair, Wilde was anticipating the democratic *esprit* of Camp.

48. The old-style dandy hated vulgarity. The new-style dandy, the lover of Camp, appreciates vulgarity. Where the dandy would be continually offended or bored, the connoisseur of Camp is continually amused, delighted. The dandy held a perfumed handkerchief to his nostrils and was liable to swoon; the connoisseur

of Camp sniffs the stink and prides himself on his strong nerves.

49. It is a feat, of course. A feat goaded on, in the last analysis, by the threat of boredom. The relation between boredom and Camp taste cannot be overestimated. Camp taste is by its nature possible only in affluent societies, in societies or circles capable of experiencing the psychopathology of affluence.

> "What is abnormal in Life stands in normal relations to Art. It is the only thing in Life that stands in normal relations to Art."
> —*A Few Maxims for the Instruction of the Over-Educated*

50. Aristocracy is a position vis-à-vis culture (as well as vis-à-vis power), and the history of Camp taste is part of the history of snob taste. But since no authentic aristocrats in the old sense exist today to sponsor special tastes, who is the bearer of this taste? Answer: an improvised self-elected class, mainly homosexuals, who constitute themselves as aristocrats of taste.

51. The peculiar relation between Camp taste and homosexuality has to be explained. While it's not true that Camp taste is homosexual taste, there is no doubt a peculiar affinity and overlap. Not all liberals are Jews, but Jews have shown a peculiar affinity for liberal and reformist causes. So, not all homosexuals have Camp taste. But homosexuals, by and large, constitute the vanguard—and the most articulate audience—of Camp. (The analogy is not frivolously chosen. Jews and homosexuals are the outstanding creative minorities in contemporary urban culture. Creative, that is, in the truest sense: they are creators of sensibilities. The two pioneering forces of modern sensibility are Jewish moral seriousness and homosexual aestheticism and irony.)

52. The reason for the flourishing of the aristocratic posture among homosexuals also seems to parallel the Jewish case. For every sensibility is self-serving to the group that promotes it. Jewish liberalism is a gesture of self-legitimization. So is Camp taste, which definitely has something propagandistic about it. Needless to say, the propaganda operates in exactly the opposite direction. The Jews pinned their hopes for integrating into

modern society on promoting the moral sense. Homosexuals
have pinned their integration into society on promoting the
aesthetic sense. Camp is a solvent of morality. It neutralizes
moral indignation, sponsors playfulness.

53. Nevertheless, even though homosexuals have been its vanguard, Camp taste is much more than homosexual taste. Obviously, its metaphor of life as theater is peculiarly suited as a
justification and projection of a certain aspect of the situation
of homosexuals. (The Camp insistence on not being "serious,"
on playing, also connects with the homosexual's desire to remain
youthful.) Yet one feels that if homosexuals hadn't more or less
invented Camp, someone else would. For the aristocratic posture
with relation to culture cannot die, though it may persist only in
increasingly arbitrary and ingenious ways. Camp is (to repeat)
the relation to style in a time in which the adoption of style—
as such—has become altogether questionable. (In the modern
era, each new style, unless frankly anachronistic, has come on
the scene as an antistyle.)

"One must have a heart of stone to read the death of Little
Nell without laughing."
                                                    —*In conversation*

54. The experiences of Camp are based on the great discovery
that the sensibility of high culture has no monopoly upon refine-
ment. Camp asserts that good taste is not simply good taste; that
there exists, indeed, a good taste of bad taste. (Genet talks about
this in *Our Lady of the Flowers.*) The discovery of the good
taste of bad taste can be very liberating. The man who insists on
high and serious pleasures is depriving himself of pleasure; he
continually restricts what he can enjoy; in the constant exercise
of his good taste he will eventually price himself out of the market, so to speak. Here Camp taste supervenes upon good taste as
a daring and witty hedonism. It makes the man of good taste
cheerful, where before he ran the risk of being chronically
frustrated. It is good for the digestion.

55. Camp taste is, above all, a mode of enjoyment, of appreciation—not judgment. Camp is generous. It wants to enjoy. It
only seems like malice, cynicism. (Or, if it is cynicism, it's not
a ruthless but a sweet cynicism.) Camp taste doesn't propose

that it is in bad taste to be serious; it doesn't sneer at someone who succeeds in being seriously dramatic. What it does is to find the success in certain passionate failures.

56. Camp taste is a kind of love, love for human nature. It relishes, rather than judges, the little triumphs and awkward intensities of "character.". . . Camp taste identifies with what it is enjoying. People who share this sensibility are not laughing at the thing they label as "a camp," they're enjoying it. Camp is a *tender* feeling.

(Here, one may compare Camp with much of Pop Art, which —when it is not just Camp—embodies an attitude that is related, but still very different. Pop Art is more flat and more dry, more serious, more detached, ultimately nihilistic.)

57. Camp taste nourishes itself on the love that has gone into certain objects and personal styles. The absence of this love is the reason why such kitsch items as *Peyton Place* (the book) and the Tishman Building aren't Camp.

58. The ultimate Camp statement: it's good *because* it's awful. . . . Of course, one can't always say that. Only under certain conditions, those which I've tried to sketch in these notes.

Our boys never hair out. The black panther has black feet. Black feet on the crumbling black panther, Pan-thuh. Mee-dah. Pam Stacy, 16 years old, a cute girl here in La Jolla, California, with a pair of orange bell-bottom hip-huggers on, sits on a step about four steps down the stairway to the beach and she can see a pair of revolting black feet without lifting her head. So she says it out loud, "The black panther."

The Pump House Gang

Somebody farther down the stairs, one of the boys with the *major* hair and khaki shorts, says, "The black feet of the black panther."

"Mee-dah," says another kid. This happens to be the cry of a, well, *underground* society known as the Mac Meda Destruction Company.

"The pan-thuh."

"The poon-thuh."

All these kids, 17 of them, members of the Pump House crowd, are lollygagging around the stairs down to Windansea Beach, La Jolla, California, about 11 A.M., and they all look at the black feet, which are a woman's pair of black street shoes, out of which stick a pair of old veiny white ankles, which lead up like a senile cone to a fudge of tallowy, edematous flesh, her thighs, squeezing out of her bathing suit, with old faded yellow bruises on them, which she probably got from running eight feet to catch a bus or something. She is standing with her old work-a-hubby, who has on *san*dals: you know, a pair of navy-blue anklet socks and these sandals with big, wide, new-smelling tan straps going this way and that, *for keeps*. Man, they look like orthopedic sandals, if one can imagine that. Obviously, these people come from Tucson or Albuquerque or one of those hincty adobe towns. All these hincty, crumbling black feet come to La Jolla-by-the-sea

---

from the adobe towns for the weekend. They even drive in cars all full of thermos bottles and mayonnaisey sandwiches and some kind of latticework wooden-back support for the old crock who drives and Venetian blinds on the back window.

"The black panther."

"Pan-thuh."

"Poon-thuh."

"Mee-dah."

Nobody says it to the two old crocks directly. God, they must be practically 50 years old. Naturally, they're carrying every piece of garbage imaginable: the folding aluminum chairs, the newspapers, the lending-library book with the clear plastic wrapper on it, the sunglasses, the sun ointment, about a vat of goo—

It is a Mexican standoff. In a Mexican standoff, both parties narrow their eyes and glare but nobody throws a punch. Of course, nobody in the Pump House crowd would ever even jostle these people or say anything right to them; they are too cool for that.

Everybody in the Pump House crowd looks over, even Tom Coleman, who is a cool person. Tom Coleman, 16 years old, got thrown out of his garage last night. He is sitting up on top of the railing, near the stairs, up over the beach, with his legs apart. Some nice long willowy girl in yellow slacks is standing on the sidewalk but leaning into him with her arms around his body, just resting. Neale Jones, 16, a boy with great lank perfect surfer's hair, is standing nearby with a Band-aid on his upper lip, where the sun has burnt it raw. Little Vicki Ballard is up on the sidewalk. Her older sister, Liz, is down the stairs by the pump house itself, a concrete block, 15 feet high, full of machinery for the La Jolla water system. Liz is wearing her great "Liz" styles, a hulking rabbit-fur vest and black-leather boots over her Levis, even though it is about 85 out here and the sun is plugged in up there like God's own dentist lamp and the Pacific is heaving in with some fair-to-middling surf. Kit Tilden is lollygagging around, and Tom Jones, Connie Carter, Roger Johnson, Sharon Sandquist, Mary Beth White, Rupert Fellows, Glenn Jackson, Dan Watson from San Diego, they are all out here, and everybody takes a look at the panthers.

The old guy, one means, you know, he must be practically 50 years old, he says to his wife, "Come on, let's go farther up," and he takes her by her fat upper arm as if to wheel her around and aim her away from here.

But she says, "No! We have just as much right to be here as they do."

"That's *not the point*—"

"Are you going to—"

"*Mrs. Roberts*," the work-a-day hubby says, calling his own wife by her official married name, as if to say she took a vow once and his word is law, even if he is not testing it with the blonde kids here—"farther up, *Mrs. Roberts*."

They start to walk up the sidewalk, but one kid won't move his feet, and, oh, god, her work-a-hubby breaks into a terrible shaking Jello smile as she steps over them, as if to say, Excuse me, sir, I don't mean to make trouble, please, and don't you and your colleagues rise up and jump me, screaming *Gotcha*—

Mee-dah!

But exactly! This beach *is* verboten for people practically 50 years old. This is a segregated beach. They can look down on Windansea Beach and see nothing but lean tan kids. It is posted "no swimming" (for safety reasons), meaning surfing only. In effect, it is segregated by age. From Los Angeles on down the California coast, this is an era of age segregation. People have always tended to segregate themselves by age, teenagers hanging around with teenagers, old people with old people, like the old men who sit on the benches up near the Bronx Zoo and smoke black cigars. But before, age segregation has gone on within a larger community. Sooner or later during the day everybody has melted back into the old community network that embraces practically everyone, all ages.

But in California today surfers, not to mention rock and roll kids and the hot-rodders or Hair Boys, named for their fanciful pompadours—all sorts of sets of kids—they don't merely hang around together. They establish whole little societies for themselves. In some cases they live with one another for months at a time. The "Sunset Strip" on Sunset Boulevard used to be a kind of Times Square for Hollywood hot dogs of all ages, anyone who wanted to promenade in his version of the high life. Today "The

Strip" is almost completely the preserve of kids from about 16 to 25. It is lined with go-go clubs. One of them, a place called It's Boss, is set up for people 16 to 25 and won't let in anybody over 25, and there are some terrible I'm-dying-a-thousand-deaths scenes when a girl comes up with her boyfriend and the guy at the door at It's Boss doesn't think she looks under 25 and tells her she will have to produce some identification proving she is young enough to come in here and live The Strip kind of life and—she's *had* it, because she can't get up the I.D. and nothing in the world is going to make a woman look stupider than to stand around trying to argue *I'm younger than I look, I'm younger than I look.* So she practically shrivels up like a Peruvian shrunken head in front of her boyfriend and he trundles her off, looking for some place you can get an old doll like this into. One of the few remaining clubs for "older people," curiously, is the Playboy Club. There are apartment houses for people 20 to 30 only, such as the Sheri Plaza in Hollywood and the E'Questre Inn in Burbank. There are whole suburban housing developments, mostly private developments, where only people over 45 or 50 can buy a house. Whole towns, meantime, have become identified as "young": Venice, Newport Beach, Balboa—or "old": Pasadena, Riverside, Coronado Island.

. . . . That is what makes it so weird when all these black pan-thuhs come around to pick up "surfing styles," like the clothing manufacturers. They don't know what any of it means. It's like archeologists discovering hieroglyphics or something, and they say, god, that's neat—Egypt!—but they don't know what the hell it is. They don't know anything about . . . *The Life.* It's great to think of a lot of old emphysematous pan-thuhs in the Garment District in New York City struggling in off the street against a gummy 15-mile-an-hour wind full of soot and coffee-brown snow and gasping in the elevator to clear their old nicotine-phlegm tubes on the way upstairs to make out the invoices on a lot of surfer stuff for 1966, the big nylon windbreakers with the wide, white horizontal competition stripes, nylon swimming trunks with competition stripes, bell-bottom slacks for girls, the big hairy sleeveless jackets, vests, the blue "tennies," meaning tennis shoes, and the . . . *look,* the Major Hair, all this long lank blonde hair, the plain face kind of tanned and bleached out at the same time, but with big eyes. It all starts in a few places, a few strategic groups, the Pump House gang being one of them, and then it moves up the beach, to places like Newport Beach and as far up as Malibu.

Well, actually there is a kind of back-and-forth thing with some of the older guys, the old heroes of surfing, like Bruce Brown, John Severson, Hobie Alter and Phil Edwards. Bruce Brown will do one of those incredible surfing movies and he is out in the surf himself filming Phil Edwards coming down a 20-footer in Hawaii, and Phil has on a pair of nylon swimming trunks, which he has had made in Hawaii, because they dry out fast—and it is like a grapevine. Everybody's got to have a pair of nylon swimming trunks, and then the manufacturers move in, and everybody's making nylon swimming trunks, boxer trunk style, and pretty soon every kid in Utica, N. Y., is buying a pair of them, with the competition stripe and the whole thing, and they never heard of Phil Edwards. So it works back and forth— but so what? Phil Edwards is part of it. He may be an old guy, he is 27 years old, but he and Bruce Brown, who is even older, 29, and John Severson, 31, and Hobie Alter, 28, never haired out to the square world even though they make thousands. Hair refers to courage. A guy who "has a lot of hair" is courageous; a guy who "hairs out" is yellow.

Bruce Brown and Severson and Alter are known as the "surfing millionaires." They are not millionaires, actually, but they must be among the top businessmen south of Los Angeles. Brown grossed something around $500,000 in 1965 and he has only about three people working for him. He goes out on a surfboard with a camera encased in a plastic shell and takes his own movies and edits them himself and goes around showing them himself and narrating them at places like the Santa Monica Civic Auditorium, where 24,000 came in eight days once, at $1.50 a person, and all he has to pay is for developing the film and hiring the hall. John Severson has the big surfing magazine, *Surfer*. Hobie Alter is the biggest surfboard manufacturer, all hand-made boards. He made 5000 boards in 1965 at $140 a board. He also designed the "Hobie" skate boards and gets 25 cents for every one sold. He grossed between $900,000 and $1 million in 1964.

God, if only everybody could grow up like these guys and know
that crossing the horror dividing line, 25 years old, won't be the
end of everything. One means, keep on living *The Life* and not
get sucked into the ticky-tacky life with some insurance sales-
man sitting forward in your stuffed chair on your wall-to-wall
telling you that life is like a football game and you sit there and
take that stuff. The hell with that! Bruce Brown has the money
and *The Life*. He has a great house on a cliff about 60 feet above
the beach at Dana Point. He is married and has two children,
but it is not that hubby-mommy you're-breaking-my-gourd scene.
His office is only two blocks from his house and he doesn't even
have to go on the streets to get there. He gets on his Triumph
scrambling motorcycle and cuts straight across a couple of
vacant lots and one can see him . . . *bounding* to work over the
vacant lots. The Triumph hits ruts and hummocks and things
and Bruce Brown bounces into the air with the motor—
thragggggh—moaning away, and when he gets to the curbing
in front of his office, he just leans back and pulls up the front
wheel and hops it and gets off and walks into the office barefooted. *Barefooted;* why not? He wears the same things now that
he did when he was doing nothing but surfing. He has on a
faded gray sweatshirt with the sleeves cut off just above the
elbows and a pair of faded corduroys. His hair is the lightest corn
yellow imaginable, towheaded, practically white, from the sun.
Even his eyes seem to be bleached. He has a rain-barrel old-
apple-tree Tom-Sawyer little-boy roughneck look about him, like
Bobby Kennedy.

Sometimes he carries on his business right there at the house.
He has a dugout room built into the side of the cliff, about 15
feet down from the level of the house. It is like a big pale green
box set into the side of the cliff, and inside is a kind of uphol-
stered bench or settee you can lie down on if you want to and
look out at the Pacific. The surf is crashing like a maniac on the
rocks down below. He has a telephone in there. Sometimes it will
ring, and Bruce Brown says hello, and the surf is crashing away
down below, roaring like mad, and the guy on the other end,
maybe one of the TV networks calling from New York or some
movie hair-out from Los Angeles, says:

"What is all that noise? It sounds like you're sitting out in the
surf."

"That's right," says Bruce Brown, "I have my desk out on the beach now. It's nice out here."

The guy on the other end doesn't know what to think. He is another Mr. Efficiency who just got back from bloating his colon up at a three-hour executive lunch somewhere and now he is Mr.-Big-Time-Let's-Get-This-Show-on-the-Road.

"On the beach?"

"Yeah. It's cooler down here. And it's good for you, but it's not so great for the desk. You know what I have now? A warped leg."

"A warped leg?"

"Yeah, and this is an $800 desk."

Those nutball California kids—and he will still be muttering that five days after Bruce Brown delivers his film, on time, and Mr. Efficiency is still going through memo thickets or heaving his way into the bar car to Darien—in the very moment that Bruce Brown and Hobie Alter are both on their motorcycles out on the vacant lot in Dana Point. Hobie Alter left his surf board plant about two in the afternoon because the wind was up and it would be good catamaranning and he wanted to go out and see how far he could tip his new catamaran without going over, and he did tip it over, about half a mile out in high swells and it was hell getting the thing right side up again. But he did, and he got back in time to go scrambling on the lot with Bruce Brown. They are out there, roaring over the ruts, bouncing up in the air, and every now and then they roar up the embankment so they can . . . fly, going up in the air about six feet off the ground as they come up off the embankment—*thraaagggggh*—all these people in the houses around there come to the door and look out. These two . . . nuts are at it again. Well, they can only fool around there for 20 minutes, because that is about how long it takes the cops to get there if anybody gets burned up enough and calls, and what efficient business magnate wants to get hauled off by the Dana Point cops for scrambling on his motorcycle in a vacant lot.

Bruce Brown has it figured out so no one in the whole rubber-bloated black pan-thuh world can trap him, though. He bought a forest in the Sierras. There is nothing on it but trees. His own wilds: no house, no nothing, just Bruce Brown's forest. Beautiful things happen up there. One day, right after he bought it, he was on the edge of his forest, where the road comes into it, and one of these big rancher king motheroos with the broad belly and the $70 lisle Safari shirt comes tooling up in a Pontiac convertible with a funnel of dust pouring out behind. He gravels it to a great flashy stop and yells:

"Hey! You!"

Of course, what he sees is some towheaded barefooted kid in a torn-off sweatshirt fooling around the edge of the road.

"Hey! You!"

"Yeah?" says Bruce Brown.

"Don't you know this is private property?"

"Yeah," says Bruce Brown.

"Well, then, why don't you get yourself off it?"

"Because it's mine, it's my private property," says Bruce Brown. "Now you get *your*self off it."

And Safari gets a few rays from that old appletree rain-barrel don't-cross-that-line look and doesn't say anything and roars off, slipping gravel, the dumb crumbling pan-thuh.

But . . . perfect! It is like, one means, you know, poetic justice for all the nights Bruce Brown slept out on the beach at San Onofre and such places in the old surfing days and would wake up with some old crock's black feet standing beside his head and some phlegmy black rubber voice saying:

"All right, kid, don't you know this is private property?"

And he would prop his head up and out there would be the Pacific Ocean, a kind of shadowy magenta-mauve, and one thing, *that* was nobody's private property—

But how many Bruce Browns can there be? There is a built-in trouble with age segregation. Eventually one *does* reach the horror age of 25, the horror dividing line. Surfing and the surfing life have been going big since 1958, and already there are kids who—well, who aren't kids anymore, they are pushing 30, and they are stagnating on the beach. Pretty soon the California littoral will be littered with these guys, stroked out on the beach like beached white whales, and girls, too, who can't give up the mystique, the mysterioso mystique, Oh Mighty Hulking Sea, who can't *conceive* of living any other life. It is pathetic when they are edged out of groups like the Pump House gang. Already there are some guys who hang around with the older crowd around the

Shack who are stagnating on the beach. Some of the older guys, like Gary Wickham, who is 24, are still in *The Life*, they still have it, but even Gary Wickham will be 25 one day and then 26 and then. . . . and then even pan-thuh age. Is one really going to be pan-thuh age one day? Watch those black feet go. And Tom Coleman still snuggles with Yellow Slacks, and Liz still roosts moodily in her rabbit fur at the bottom of the Pump House and Pam still sits on the steps contemplating the mysterioso mysteries of Pump House ascension and John and Artie still bob, tiny pink porcelain shells, way out there waiting for godsown bitchen *set,* and godsown sun is still turned on like a dentist's lamp and so far—

—the panthers scrape on up the sidewalk. They are at just about the point Leonard Anderson and Donna Blanchard got that day, December 6, 1964, when Leonard said, Pipe it, and fired two shots, one at her and one at himself. Leonard was 18 and Donna was 21—21!—god, for a girl in the Pump House gang that is almost the horror line right there. But it was all so mysterioso. Leonard was just lying down on the beach at the foot of the Pump House, near the stairs, just talking to John K. Weldon down there, and then Donna appeared at the top of the stairs and Leonard got up and went up the stairs to meet her, and they didn't say anything, they weren't *angry* over anything, they never had been, although the police said they had, they just turned and went a few feet down the sidewalk, away from the Pump House and—blam blam!—these two shots. Leonard fell dead on the sidewalk and Donna died that afternoon in Scripps Memorial Hospital. Nobody knew what to think. But one thing it seemed like—well, it seemed like Donna and Leonard thought they had lived *The Life* as far as it would go and now it was running out. All that was left to do was—but that is an *insane* idea. It can't be like that, *The Life* can't run out, people can't change all that much just because godsown chronometer runs on and the body packing starts deteriorating and the fudgy tallow shows up at the thighs where they squeeze out of the bathing suit—

Tom, boy! John, boy! Gary, boy! Neale, boy! Artie, boy! Pam, Liz, Vicki, Jackie Haddad! After all this—just a pair of bitchen black panther bunions inching down the sidewalk away from the old Pump House stairs?

Oscar Wilde is said to have observed that America really was discovered by a dozen people before Columbus, but it was always successfully hushed up. I am tempted to feel that way about the Peace Corps; the idea of a national effort of this type had been proposed many times in past years. But in 1960 and 1961 for the first time the idea was joined with the power and the desire to

The Peace Corps

implement it. On November 2, 1960, Senator John F. Kennedy proposed a "peace corps" in a campaign speech at the Cow Palace in San Francisco. Thirty thousand Americans wrote immediately to support the idea; thousands volunteered to join.

The early days of the Peace Corps were like the campaign days of 1960, but with no election in sight. My colleagues were volunteer workers and a few key officials loaned from other agencies. "I use not only all the brains I have, but all I can borrow," Woodrow Wilson said. So did we. Letters cascaded in from all over the country in what one writer described as "paper tornadoes at the Peace Corps." The elevators to our original two-room office disgorged constant sorties of interested persons, newspaper reporters, porters, job seekers, academic figures and generous citizens offering advice. Everywhere, it seemed, were cameras, coils of cable and commentators with questions.

An organization, we know, gains life through hard decisions, so we hammered out basic policies in long, detailed discussions in which we sought to face up to the practical problems and reach specific solutions before we actually started operations. We knew that a few wrong judgments in the early hours of a new organization's life, especially a controversial government agency, can completely thwart its purposes—even as a margin of error of a thousandth of an inch in the launching of a rocket can send it thousands of miles off course. And we knew the Peace Corps would have only one chance to work. As with the parachute jumper, the chute had to open the first time. We knew, too, that a thousand suspicious eyes were peering over our shoulders.

Some were the eyes of friendly critics, but many belonged to unfriendly skeptics. The youthfulness of the new Administration,
particularly the President, enhanced the risk; an older leadership
would have had greater immunity from charges of "sopho-
morism."

Even the choice of a name took on serious overtones. The
phrase "Peace Corps" was used in the original San Francisco
speech, but many of our advisers disliked it. "Peace," they
claimed, was a word the Communists had preempted, and
"Corps" carried undesirable military connotations. We did not
want a name contrived out of initials which a public relations
firm might have devised; nor did we want to restrict participation in the program by calling it a "Youth Corps." What we did
want was a name which the public at large could grasp emotionally as well as intellectually. Whatever name we did choose,
we would give it content by our acts and programs. We wanted
it, also, to reflect the seriousness of our objectives. We studied
dozens of other names and finally came back to the original.
Peace is the fundamental goal of our times. We believed the
Peace Corps could contribute to its attainment, for while armaments can deter war, only men can create peace.

The ambitiousness of the name, of course, was only one reason
for early skepticism about the Peace Corps. Fears were voiced
that it might be a "second children's crusade." I was astonished
that a nation so young had become so suspicious of its youth. We
had forgotten that Thomas Jefferson drafted the Declaration of
Independence at age 33. Forgotten also was the fact that more
than half of the world's population is under 26, the age of the
average Peace Corps Volunteer. Sixteen of the nations in Africa
have heads of state under 45; five have leaders in their thirties.

Of course, youthful enthusiasm and noble purposes were not
enough. They had to be combined with hard-headed pragmatism
and realistic administration. In the early days of the Peace
Corps we were looking for a formula for practical idealism. The
formula worked out by experience has "the sweet smell of success" today, but it was far less clear two years ago.

Would enough qualified Americans be willing to serve? Even
if they started, would they be able to continue on the job despite
frustration, dysentery and boredom? Could Americans survive

overseas without special foods and privileges, special housing, automobiles, television and air conditioners? Many Americans thought not. The Washington correspondent of the respected *Times of India* agreed with them in these words:

> When you have ascertained a felt local need, you would need to find an American who can exactly help in meeting it. This implies not only the wherewithal (or what you inelegantly call the "know how") but also a psychological affinity with a strange new people who may be illiterate and yet not lack Wisdom, who may live in hovels and yet dwell in spiritual splendor, who may be poor in worldly wealth and yet enjoy a wealth of intangibles and a capacity to be happy. Would an American young man be in tune with this world he has never experienced before? I doubt it. . . .
>
> One also wonders whether American young men and tender young girls, reared in air-conditioned houses at a constant temperature, knowing little about the severities of nature (except when they pop in and out of cars or buses) will be able to suffer the Indian summer smilingly and, if they go into an Indian village, whether they will be able to sleep on unsprung beds under the canopy of the bejeweled sky or indoors in mud huts, without writing home about it.

At a time when many were saying that Americans had gone soft and were interested mainly in security, pensions and suburbia, the Peace Corps could have been timorous. Possible ways of hedging against an anticipated shortage of applicants could have included low qualification standards, generous inducements to service, cautious programming, a period of duty shorter than two years, an enforced period of enlistment such as the "hitch" in the armed forces, or draft exemption for volunteer service in the Peace Corps. We deliberately chose the risk rather than the hedge in each case and created an obstacle course. The applicant could remove himself any time he realized his motive was less than a true desire for service. This method of self-selection has by now saved us from compounded difficulties abroad.

Our optimism about sufficient recruits was justified. More than 50,000 Americans have applied for the Peace Corps. In the first three months of this year, more Americans applied for the Peace Corps than were drafted for military service. This happened notwithstanding the fact that young men who volunteer for the Peace Corps are liable to service on their return.

Selection was made rigorous. The process was fashioned to include a searchingly thorough application form, placement tests to measure useful skills, language aptitude exams, six to twelve reference inquiries, a suitability investigation and systematic observation of performance during the training program of approximately ten weeks. We invite about one in six applicants to enter training, and about five out of six trainees are finally selected for overseas service.

We debated hotly the question of age, and whether or not older people should be eligible. We listened to proposals for an age limit in the thirties and then in the sixties and finally decided to set no upper age limit at all. Our oldest volunteer today happens to be 76, and we have more grandparents than teenagers in the Peace Corps. Some older volunteers have turned out to be rigid and cantankerous in adapting to a standard of living *their* parents took for granted, but the majority of them make a lot of us in the New Frontier look like stodgy old settlers.

From the beginning we decided that effective volunteers abroad would need systematic administrative support and direction. Leaders of several developing nations, eager to have the assistance of trained manpower, warned against repeating the experiences of other highly motivated volunteer workers who had failed abroad for lack of cohesive leadership. A good program would need good people—not only as Peace Corps Volunteers but as Peace Corps staff members abroad. There was no counterpart in the U. S. Government of civilian leaders serving abroad on a volunteer basis. There was no precedent for what these men would have to do in programming, logistics and personal support for the volunteers in their charge. We needed the ablest of leaders in each position. Could we attract them even though we did not offer post differentials, cost-of-living allowances, commissary or diplomatic privileges?

Fortunately, the answer has been a continuing "yes." The Peace Corps has attracted intelligent and dedicated men to all positions on its overseas team. Ironically, the same critics who once complained that we would unleash hordes of uninstructed adolescents on the world are now complaining that we spend substantial sums to provide instruction and adequate direction.

Some of my colleagues proposed that Peace Corps Volunteers

act as technical helpers to I.C.A. technicians, "extra hands" for the more experienced older men. Peace Corps practice has moved in another direction. A natural distinction between the A.I.D. adviser at a high level in government and the Peace Corps Volunteer making his contribution as a "doer" or "worker" at the grass roots soon became apparent. It also became clear that the Peace Corps Volunteer had a new and perhaps unique contribution to make as a person who entered fully into host-country life and institutions, with a host-country national working beside him, and another directing his work. This feature of the Peace Corps contributed substantially to its early support abroad.

Discussion of the possibility that the Peace Corps might be affiliated with the I.C.A. led into the question of its relationship to U. S. political and information establishments overseas. The Peace Corps in Washington is responsible to the Secretary of State. Volunteers and staff abroad are responsible to the American Ambassador. Nevertheless, the Peace Corps maintains a distinction between its functions and those of Embassies, A.I.D. and U.S.I.A. offices. There was a design to this which Secretary Rusk has aptly described: "The Peace Corps is not an instrument *of* foreign policy, because to make it so would rob it of its contribution *to* foreign policy." Peace Corps Volunteers are not trained diplomats; they are not propagandists; they are not technical experts. They represent our society by what they are, what they do and the spirit in which they do it. They steer clear of intelligence activity and stay out of local politics. Our strict adherence to these principles has been a crucial factor in the decision of politically uncommitted countries to invite American volunteers into their midst, into their homes and even into their classrooms and schoolyards to teach future generations of national leaders. In an era of sabotage and espionage, intelligence and counter-intelligence, the Peace Corps and its volunteers have earned a priceless yet simple renown: they are trustworthy.

Another contested issue in the early days of the Peace Corps concerned private organizations and universities. We were advised by many to make grants to these institutions, then to leave recruitment, selection, training and overseas programming in their hands. That road would have led to an organization operating very much like the National Science Foundation. For better or worse, the Peace Corps chose not to become a grant-making organization and those decisions which give character to our operations—selection, training, programming, field leadership and so on—are still in our possession.

Nevertheless, the involvement of private organizations and universities has been crucial to the Peace Corps' success. America is a pluralistic society and the Peace Corps expresses its diversity abroad by demonstrating that the public and private sectors can work coöperatively and effectively. We consciously seek contracts with private organizations, colleges and universities to administer our programs. We gain the advantage of expert knowledge, long experience, tested working relationships and often even private material resources. For example, CARE has contributed more than $100,000 worth of equipment to the Peace Corps in Colombia. Initially, there was suspicion by some of these agencies that the Peace Corps, with the resources of the United States taxpayer behind it, would preëmpt their own work abroad. Suspicion has turned into understanding, however, as the United States Government, through the Peace Corps, has facilitated the work of private organizations and has focused new attention on the needs and opportunities for service abroad.

In our "talent search" we went to government, academic life, business, the bar, the medical profession and every other walk of life where leadership was available. We deliberately recruited as many Negroes and representatives of other minority groups as possible for jobs in every echelon. We knew that Negroes would not ordinarily apply for high-level policy jobs, so we decided to seek them out. Today 7.4 percent of our higher echelon positions are filled by Negroes as compared to .8 percent for other government agencies in similar grades; 24 percent of our other positions are filled by Negroes, compared to a figure for government agencies in general of 5.5 percent.

How big should the Peace Corps be? Everyone was asking this question and everyone had an answer. Advice ranged from 500 to 1,000,000. There were strong voices raised in support of "tentative pilot projects," looking to a Peace Corps of less than 1,000. However, Warren W. Wiggins, an experienced foreign-aid expert, took a broader view. He pointed out that ultra-cautious programming might produce prohibitive per capita costs, fail even to engage the attention of responsible foreign officials (let alone have an impact) and fail to attract the necessary American talent and commitment. Furthermore, when the need was insatiable why should we try to meet it with a pittance?

There were also arguments in those early days about "saturation" of the foreign country, either in terms of jobs or the psychological impact of the American presence. I have since noticed that the same arguments made about a 500–1,000 man program in 1961 were also made about our plans to expand to 5,000 volunteers (March 1963), to 10,000 volunteers (March 1964) and to 13,000 (September 1964). I am not suggesting that the Peace Corps should continue to grow indefinitely. But I am proposing that much time and energy are wasted in theoretical musings, introspections and worries about the future. Peace Corps Volunteers are a new type of overseas American. Who is to say now how many of them will be welcome abroad next year, or in the next decade? Our country and our times have had plenty of experience with programs that were too little, too late.

The question of the health of the volunteers concerned us from the beginning. The Peace Corps represents the largest group of Americans who have ever tried to live abroad "up country." Even in World War II our troops were generally in organized units where safe food and water could be provided and medical care was at hand. This would not be the case for the Peace Corps. And an incapacitated volunteer would probably be worse than no volunteer at all. How could we reduce the risks to a rational level? The Surgeon General studied the problem at our request. We then worked out a solution by which preventive health measures are provided by public health doctors assigned to the Peace Corps, while much of the actual medical care is handled by doctors of the host country. Of the first 117 volunteers returned to the United States, only 20 came back for medical reasons (21 returned for compassionate reasons, 71 failed to adjust to overseas living and 5 died or were killed in accidents). Our medical division's work is already showing up in the pages of scientific and medical journals. As an example, we recently decided to use large injections of gamma globulin as a preventive for hepatitis, which has presented one of the worst health problems for Americans overseas. Since then, there has not been a single case of infectious hepatitis reported among those who received the large injection in time.

Many of the original doubts and criticisms of the Peace Corps have not materialized. On the other hand, substantive problems have emerged which were little discussed or expected two years ago. One of the most difficult is the provision of adequate language training. This was foreseen, but most observers thought that the exotic languages such as Thai, Urdu, Bengali and Twi would give us our main problem, while Spanish and French speakers could be easily recruited or quickly trained. The opposite has been true. The first volunteers who arrived in Thailand in January 1962 made a great impression with what observers described as "fluent" Thai. As the volunteers were the first to point out, their Thai was not actually fluent, but their modest achievement was tremendously appreciated. Since then, of course, a large proportion of the volunteers there have become truly fluent.

On the other hand, a considerable number of volunteers going to Latin America and to French Africa have been criticized for their mediocre language fluency. Expectations are high in these countries and halting Spanish or French is not enough. We have learned that America contains rather few French-speaking bus mechanics, Spanish-speaking hydrologists or math-science teachers who can exegete theorems in a Latin American classroom. Can we devise more effective and intensive language training, particularly for farmers, craftsmen, construction foremen, well drillers and other Americans who never before have needed a second language? Should we take skilled people and teach them languages, or take people with language abilities and teach them skills?

We still need more volunteers, especially those who combine motivation and special skills. The person with a ready motivation for Peace Corps service tends to be the liberal arts student in college, the social scientist, the person with "human relations" interests. The developing countries need and want a great many Americans with this background, but they also want engineers, agronomists, lathe operators and geologists. We cannot make our maximum contribution if we turn down requests for skills which we have difficulty finding. There are presently 61 engineers in the Peace Corps, 30 geologists and 236 nurses, respectable numbers considering the ready availability of generously paying jobs in the domestic economy. But requests still far outnumber the supply.

Other industrialized countries may soon supplement our efforts by providing volunteers to developing countries with languages and skills we lack. The motivation to serve is not distinctively American, and half a dozen industrialized nations have established equivalents of the Peace Corps within the past few months. These programs grew out of an International Conference on Human Skills organized by the Peace Corps and held in Puerto Rico last October. The 43 countries represented at the meeting voted unanimously to establish an International Peace Corps Secretariat to help spread the concept of voluntarism as a tool of economic and social transformation. The response to this initiative is a reflection of the innate vitality of the Peace Corps idea.

We face increasingly difficult choices as we grow. Should we concentrate in the future on the countries where we now have programs and resist expanding to new areas? We are already committed to programs in 47 nations. Should we favor a program where there are relatively stable social conditions, good organization and effective leadership? Or should we take greater risks and commit our resources in a more fluid and disorganized situation, usually in a poorer country, where the Peace Corps might make a crucial difference or find a great opportunity? Where should we draw the line between adequate material support to the volunteers and the perils of providing them with too many material goods? Where is the equilibrium between safeguarding the volunteer's health and morale and protecting the Peace Corps' declared purpose that he should live as does his co-worker in the host country, without special luxury or advantage?

When is a particular program completed? In Nigeria the answer is relatively easy. That country's coördinated educational development plan projects a need for 815 foreign teachers in 1965, 640 in 1966, 215 in 1968 and none in 1970. By then enough Nigerians will have been trained to fill their own classrooms. Progress may not follow so fine a plan, but the Peace Corps can look ahead to a day when its academic, teaching work in Nigeria will be done.

The answer is not so simple in Colombia, where volunteers are working on community development in 92 rural towns. There is no lack of change and progress: the Colombian Government has trebled its own commitment of resources and staff to this progressive community development program. Scores of individual communities have already learned how to organize to transform their future. When volunteer John Arango organized the first town meeting in Cutaru almost two years ago, for example, not one soul showed up. Twenty months later almost every citizen turns out for these meetings. The townsmen have changed an old jail into a health clinic; they have drained the nearby swamps; they have rebuilt wharves on the river; they have cleared stumps out of the channel to make it navigable; and they are now building the first 18 of 72 do-it-yourself houses designed by the volunteer.

John Arango's Colombian co-worker is equally responsible for the results in Cutaru. In community development, particularly, the ability of the host organization to provide able counterparts is crucial to a program's success. I might also mention that host countries have in every case made voluntary contributions to the Peace Corps programs. In Africa alone, they have supported the program to the value of $2,500,000. During and after the Puerto Rico conference, three countries in Latin America announced plans to establish home-grown Peace Corps organizations; when implemented these will help solve the shortage of counterparts. We believe North American and Latin American volunteers will complement one another and increase the total effectiveness.

The first "replacement group" in the Peace Corps is about to complete training for service in Colombia. Should we send these volunteers to fill the shoes of their predecessors in the villages which are now moving ahead, albeit shakily? Or should we send the volunteers to new communities where nothing has been done? We know that more is needed than two years of work by a North American and his Colombian co-workers to effect self-perpetuating change. On the other hand, we do not want the

volunteer to become a crutch in a community's life. Some of the
new volunteers in Colombia will, therefore, try to follow through
with their predecessor's work, but others will take on villages
where no American has served. In the meantime we are planning to study what happens in those towns where volunteers are
not replaced.

Earlier I mentioned there has been a change in the nature of
comment and criticism about the Peace Corps. In the beginning,
the doubters worried about the callowness of youth and the ability of mortals to make any good idea work. The more recent
criticism is more sophisticated and more substantive. Eric Sevareid recently observed: "While the Corps has something to do
with spot benefits in a few isolated places, whether in sanitizing
drinking water or building culverts, its work has, and can have,
very little to do with the fundamental investments, reorganizations and reforms upon which the true and long-term economic
development of backward countries depends." Mr. Sevareid acknowledges that "giving frustrated American youth a sense of
mission and adding to our supply of comprehension of other
societies fatten the credit side of the ledger." He adds: "If fringe
benefits were all the Corps' originators had in mind, then this
should be made clear to the country." I do not agree with him
that the second and third purposes of the Peace Corps Act—
representing America abroad in the best sense and giving Americans an opportunity to learn about other societies—are "fringe
benefits." Fulton Freeman, the United States Ambassador in
Colombia, believes the whole Peace Corps program could be
justified by its creation of a new American resource in the volunteers who are acquiring language skills and intensive understanding of a foreign society. Former volunteers will be entering
government service (150 have already applied to join U.S.I.A.),
United Nations agencies, academic life, international business
concerns and a host of other institutions which carry on the
business of the United States throughout the world. Others will
return to their homes, capable of exerting an enlightened influence in the communities where they settle. Many trite euphe-
misms of the ignorant and ready panaceas of the uninformed
will clash immediately with the harsh facts that volunteers have
learned to live with abroad.

Is the second purpose of the Peace Corps Act—to be a good representative of our society—a "fringe benefit"? Peace Corps Volunteers are reaching the people of foreign countries on an individual basis at a different level from the influence of most Americans abroad. The Peace Corps Volunteer lives under local laws, buys his supplies at local stores and makes his friends among local people. He leaves to the diplomat and the technicians the complex tools which are peculiarly their own while he sets out to work in the local environment as he finds it.

I am not suggesting that life for the volunteer is always hard. A visiting Ghanaian said: "The Peace Corps teachers in my country don't live so badly. After all, they live as well as we do." I agree that this is not so bad; nor is our objective discomfort for discomfort's sake, but rather a willingness to share the life of another people, to accept sacrifice when sacrifice is necessary and to show that material privilege has not become the central and indispensable ingredient in an American's life. It is interesting to note that the happiest volunteers are usually those with the most difficult living conditions.

Although I disagree with Mr. Sevareid's emphasis in dismissing two of the three purposes of the Peace Corps Act as "fringe benefits," he does get to the heart of an important question when he compares the direct economic impact of the Peace Corps to fundamental investments, reorganizations and economic development. The Peace Corps' contribution has been less in direct economic development than in social development—health, education, construction and community organization. We are convinced that economic development directly depends on social development. In his valedictory report this past April as head of the Economic Commission for Latin America, Raul Prebisch observed that there are *not* "grounds for expecting that economic development will take place first and be followed in the natural course of events by social development. Both social and economic development must be achieved in measures that require the exercise of rational and deliberate action. . . . There can be no speed-up in economic development without a change in the social structure." While they have their differences, Theodore W. Schultz and J. Kenneth Galbraith have no disagreement on the essential role of social development in economic progress. In contrast, some who argue from the European-North American experience overlook the vital need for social development which had already been substantially achieved in the countries of the Atlantic community. This is the basic difference between the problem of the Marshall Plan, which was concerned with economic reconstruction in societies with abundant social resources, and the problem of forced-draft economic development in much of Asia, Africa and Latin America.

Notwithstanding the Peace Corps' primary emphasis on social development, volunteers are making a direct economic contribution in a variety of situations. They are helping to organize farmers' coöperatives in Chile, Ecuador and Pakistan; credit unions and savings and loan associations in Latin America; demonstration farms in the Near East. A group of volunteers in the Punjab sparked the creation of a poultry industry of some economic significance (using ground termite mounds for protein feed). These are "grass roots" projects. More of them will someday cause us to look back and wonder why it took so long to discover that people—human hands and enthusiasms—are an essential part of the relationship of mutual assistance which we must establish with our neighbors abroad.

The Peace Corps is not a "foreign aid" agency. Two of the three purposes of the Peace Corps as defined in the Act deal with understanding, not economic assistance. Moreover, our financial investment is in the volunteer who brings his skills and knowledge home with him. Seventy-five percent of the Peace Corps' appropriated funds enters the economy of the United States; of the remaining 25 percent, more than half (57 percent) is spent on American citizens, the Peace Corps Volunteers themselves.

A Jamaican radio commentator recently asserted that "a great distance between people is the best creator of good will. Jumble people up together on a sort of temporary basis of gratitude on one side and condescension on the other, and you'll have everyone at each other's throat in no time." If I believed this were inevitable, regardless of the attitude, preparation and mode of life of volunteers, I would advocate disbanding the Peace Corps —as well as most other programs overseas. But I have greater faith in the universality of men's aspirations and of men's ability to respect each other when they know each other. It is the American who lives abroad in isolation and the thoughtless tourist who create distrust and dislike.

I believe the Peace Corps is also having more impact than we may realize on our own society and among our own people. To take an example of the Peace Corps' impact on an institution, the President of the State University of Iowa, Virgil M. Hancher, recently observed:

> The Peace Corps project (training Volunteers for Indonesia) is already having salutary effects upon this University, and these seem likely to be residual. The members of our faculty are having to come together across disciplines. They are having to think through old problems of education freshly and to tackle new ones. Along with the trainees, they are learning—learning how to teach languages in the new method, how to teach new languages, how to teach area studies better, and how to adapt old and test new methods. The project is deepening the international dimension of the State University of Iowa. This international dimension is being shared, in various ways, with the people of the state, the eastern area in particular.

American schools and students may soon benefit from the Peace Corps' initiative in another fashion. Two countries, Ghana and Argentina, have expressed interest in making the Peace Corps a two-way street by sending volunteer teachers of special competence to interested American high schools or colleges. Ghana would provide experts in African history and Argentina teachers of Spanish. Other countries may follow suit.

Our own Peace Corps Volunteers are being changed in other ways in the acquisition of languages and expertise. They will be coming home more mature, with a new outlook toward life and work. Like many other Americans, I have wondered whether our contemporary society, with its emphasis on the organizational man and the easy life, can continue to produce the self-reliance, initiative and independence that we consider to be part of our heritage. We have been in danger of losing ourselves among the motorized toothbrushes, tranquilizers and television commercials. Will Durant once observed that nations are born stoic and die epicurean; we have been in danger of this happening to us. The Peace Corps is truly a new frontier in the sense that it provides the challenge to self-reliance and independent action which the vanished frontier once provided on our own continent. Sharing in the progress of other countries helps us to rediscover ourselves at home.

The influence of the Peace Corps idea might be described as a series of widening circles, like the expanding rings from a stone thrown into a pond. The inner, most sharply defined circle represents the immediate effect of the program—accomplishments abroad in social and economic development, skills, knowledge, understanding, institution-building, a framework for coöperative effort with private organizations, research and experiment in "overseas Americanship," language training and improvements in health.

The second ring moving outward on the water might be the Peace Corps' influence on our society, on institutions and people, on the creation of a new sense of participation in world events, an influence on the national sense of purpose, self-reliance and an expanded concept of volunteer service in time of peace.

There is still a wider circle and, being farthest from the splash, the hardest to make out clearly. Perhaps I can explain it by describing the relationships I see between the Peace Corps and our American Revolution. The Revolution placed on our citizens the responsibility for reordering their own social structure. It was a triumph over the idea that man is incompetent or incapable of shaping his destiny. It was our declaration of the irresistible strength of a universal idea connected with human dignity, hope, compassion and freedom. The idea was not simply American, of course, but arose from a confluence of history, geography and the genius of a resolute few at Philadelphia.

We still have our vision, but our society has been drifting away from the world's majority: the young and raw, the colored, the hungry and the oppressed. The Peace Corps is helping to put us again where we belong. It is our newest hope for rejoining the majority of the world without at the same time betraying our cultural, historic, political and spiritual ancestors and allies. As Pablo Casals, the renowned cellist and democrat, said of the Peace Corps last year: "This is new, and it is also very old. We have come from the tyranny of the enormous, awesome, discordant machine, back to a realization that the beginning and the end are man—that it is man who is important, not the machine, and that it is man who accounts for growth, not just dollars and factories. Above all, that it is man who is the object of all our efforts."

PAUL VELDE

Why is it that making paper lace is the occupation of only children and the insane? The end product is often a thing of beauty, quite out of proportion to the simple process of making it. Fold a sheet of paper crosswise and diagonally several times, then cut a few notches into the edges. Nip off one of the corners. The fascination with paper lace lies in the surprise of the design

Psychedelics:
You Can't Bring the Universe Home

as it unfolds to all appearances bearing no relation to the few original incisions. A crude wedge unfolds into a subtle snowflake pattern; a tiny nick opens spaces many times its size. To guess the final design would involve a feat of the imagination, with all the folds seen in their relation to each other and to the incisions. In much the same fashion, the psychedelic experience is an unfolding of a puzzle of freakish and often beautiful dimensions.

Time is elastic. A lifetime can be compressed into a split second, or a split second can break into a number of facets that may be explored for hours. The experience is comparable to refolding the paper lace and unfolding it again. Space is plastic. It folds in on itself, so that it is entirely conceivable to be in two places at one time. Conversely, planes and tangents may flatten out as in cubist painting and miles be trudged without leaving a small room.

Lost in Folds

The emotions are equally unpredictable, and seem to constitute a multi-faceted dimension all their own. The terror of being very tiny and lost in the folds of the sheet of paper as somebody is cutting into it with scissors is not difficult to imagine. But more is involved. The peculiar flavor of the terror depends on the outlook: whether the blades are missing by diabolically narrow margins or seem to be striking at random. Fate and chance merge; the odds against being struck are the same dodging or standing still. At such moments panic is always near, perhaps a flickering eyelash; yet it soon is apparent that nothing can be done.

The puzzle also unties itself. To be able to look at the lace pattern and see at a glance all the complexity devolve into the unity of the few original incisions can produce a range of emotions: pleasure, wonder, contentment, gratitude. Like fate and chance, unity and multiplicity become aspects of the same thing: through the emotions all four become aspects of each other.

Nothing is new about these perceptions as such. They have all been attained through various paths of normal cognition. Their outlines are retailed in college philosophy lectures and the better science courses. Thus, while it is nice to cover so much material in an eight-hour LSD session, the most interesting thing about psychedelics is what they tell us about how we sense things. The distinction between how we sense and what we sense is as difficult—and ultimately as impossible—to make as the old distinction between form and content; an understanding of one is necessary for an understanding of the other. For the most part, descriptions of psychedelic experiences have placed the emphasis on what is seen, consequently telling us very little about the experience itself.

Hollow Leg

We learn particularly little about the dangers (psychological) of the psychedelic experience when it is described with this emphasis, though the description is true enough. The risk, as people who have taken psychedelics often explain, lies primarily in the seeing. In their minds the risk is minimized inasmuch as what is seen under psychedelics is believed to be experienced anyway in daily life, though on an unconscious level. The unconscious is seen as a sort of hollow leg continually collecting the junk of sense experience which has been either consciously or unconsciously repressed. This material remains active, however, as part of the environment of the body below consciousness. The psychedelic experience, in this view, only makes us aware of this activity as part of the environment in which we function, like it or not. The assumption is that a normally healthy person, i.e., one who copes with daily life, has the resources needed to adjust to the psychedelic experience. The only result, what is felt by the fingers is transmitted to the brain in a whole state. A spongy, rubbery, slippery moist substance: a leaf. What is seen is curves, angles, colors, surfaces, not objects.

In itself this would not be exceptional. Everybody would like to feel more, have a more sensitive eye, be more aware generally. Certain psychic states are known to be more conducive to various sense experience, and people go to a good deal of trouble to induce such states in themselves. Most often these are states of relaxation or high excitement, produced either by environment or chemicals. Eating dinner outdoors on the patio, having a drink before going to the theatre, attending a political rally, are common strategies by which we open the pores. If the drugs merely provided the necessary openness by which we could feel the world around us more, there would be nothing exceptional about them.

Another Ladder

But this presumes that what we ordinarily recognize and describe as sense experience is a rung on an ever-ascending ladder. The degree to which psychedelics open the senses, however, suggests there is another ladder, or at least a different self and a different world to be learned. How things feel when the mind receives sensations unimpeded is exceptional because it excepts all of our previous notions, beginning with who we are. Not only does an orange taste more like an orange than ever before, but it can be tasted with the hand. The fingers can feel not only the skin, but through the skin and juices to the seeds. By a process of sense focusing, various parts of the body can be heard functioning, either individually or in unison; parts of the part can be sensed, down through the cells to the atoms, arriving finally at a perception of pure energy.

The experience of this can justifiably inspire awe, but fear is a close neighbor to awe and fright is always a possibility under psychedelics. The sound of one's own body, which the moment before suggested the well-ordered harmony of a water mill, can devolve into an internal agony of cries and piercing screams. The sight of the churning veins and bloody undersurface of the hand, sights normally blocked out, can seem repulsive. But once noticed, the grotesque is quick to be exaggerated. The hand may grow to enormous size. Or, if the skeletal structure is disturbing, it may shrivel to a death's hand. The imagination is in an extremely suggestible state, and what is imagined is immediately sensed as actually present. If an object is feared, it is promptly transformed into a projection of the fear. Other fears originating in the subconscious seem to surface for no apparent reason and occasionally project mental images. Often the projections are quite funny in a banal way. A fear of death may produce a B-movie caricature of a funeral, complete with spangled wreath and comic-strip sobs.

Cosmic Humor

Change, the emotions, and the imagination are at the heart of what is experienced under psychedelics. For example, a person notices that his shirt front is undulating with his own breathing. It seems more like a second skin than something separate and inanimate. At the thought of death, however, the sensuous rolling motion stops and the material becomes crisp and flattened out, like a pressed flower. But the realization that he has just imagined his corpus as a pressed flower can prick the solemnity of the moment, turning a quiet weeping into a gross snicker. The point of cosmic humor seems to be that the joke is always on oneself.

The absorbing thing about all this is to figure out how it happens. It is worth repeating that only by discovering how we sense can we begin to learn what it is that we see and feel and hear. And this brings us to the fundamental psychedelic perception, that the distinction between the self and the outside world is at best arbitrary and unimportant. From time to time in the experience the distinction evaporates completely. This is accompanied by a curious feeling of nakedness. Yet, contrary to what one might suppose, the sense of self is not lost, and during certain periods it can become very acute. These periods occur when the body is most aware of its environment. This is easily related to ordinary experience. To lie naked on a very rough surface, grass for instance, is to become very aware of both the grass, sharp and flexible, and one's skin, warm from the prickling sensation. One is aware of the skin's reaction. Soon, however, as the contact continues, it becomes difficult to tell which is the effect of the grass and which are one's reactions.

Self Is Environment

For the moment, the grass and the skin have entered a relationship, and distinctions between effect and reaction become arbitrary, if not impossible to make. The union disintegrates the separation between self and environment; the self is its environment. Put another way, friction generates heat which produces fusion. Visually the psychedelic world consists of curves, straight lines, grains, colors, all in dynamic relationships. A small node or swelling on a tree trunk, against the upward sweep of the tree, creates lines of tension. The psychedelic eye focuses on the field of tension, the visual manifestation of the energy flow at that point in the environment. The eye is "tuned in." Optical illusions are similarly created by plays on lines or on foreground and background colors. Is the painting red on blue or blue on red? The eye plays with both possibilities until gradually it is reacting primarily to the tension between the alternatives and its own vibrations. The eye is tuned in on the energy of the painting. The sensations and reactions in the psychedelic experience are correspondingly so strong, the relationships so intense, that the distinction between body and environment, self and world, is nonexistent.

Presumably this sense of union between self and the world could be merely an illusion. But we still would not know why direct sense experience of an environment produces such strong reactions from the body. These reactions are not an illusion. And if this effect of environment on the body occurs when we are in a normal state, but below the level of consciousness where it is creating reasons that the mind knows not, the question of illusion becomes moot. The body is then revealed as a field of energy operating in a larger field of energy and totally open to its currents. But where does this leave the self that we are still conscious of? As mentioned earlier, one of the paradoxes of sense experience is that as it increases the body becomes more aware of itself. This tells us something about both the self and the ego that is created to protect and further the self's interest.

Rough Moments

By now everybody who has heard of psychedelics knows there are such things as "bad trips." Even the best trips can have bad or rough moments. These are times of fear; sometimes the fear is felt for no apparent reason, at other times the fear is produced, or at least accompanied, by grotesque or bizarre phenomena. Being lost in the folds of the paper lace would be such an experience. Whatever the initial cause of the fear, the imagination usually supplies, in the form of fear projections, further material for the fear to feed upon. Thus, a feedback process is begun in which the person is trapped in an ever narrowing circle of intensity. He is aware of only his fear.

Once the person realizes he is trapped, he either panics, which is rare (somebody outside the experience is usually able to assure him), or he gives up. If he gives up, the fear goes away, but only to be replaced by another fear. A person can go through several of these cycles before it occurs to him that the process is unending. There are cycles within cycles; the person has now come to fear fear itself. But this is only another, though more basic, cycle, and it too subsides. It may return several times, but more important, during this time the person is becoming dimly aware that something more is being demanded of him. He is quite willing to feel fear now, if that is required. In a sense, he is like a child who is willing to cry if that is the effect his parent's punishment is intended to produce. Soon the child cries at the mere threat of punishment. The situation has become quite false, but the child is satisfied to have warded off real punishment by his symbolic gesture. He even takes a certain comfort in his cries.

Dread Sets In

But in the psychedelic experience the purely symbolic quickly crumbles. The person senses he will not get off with symbolic fear and a certain dread sets in. More layers of fear are peeled away in an attempt to assuage the dread. Finally, only a figment of the person remains, and beyond this, he begins to suspect, lies nothing. It is this last figment of a person that is being asked for. The last remaining fear must be lost if the cycle is to be ended. The last fear and the last stronghold of the person are identical. And when this is removed, an opening is revealed that leads into a great emptiness. The person falls through the hole into an abyss with no sides and no bottom.

The sense of falling great distances can produce fear again. Perhaps a trace of the person or the habit of fear still remains. In any case, the person is quite helpless and soon gives up to the inevitable. At this point two things happen. The person realizes there is no bottom to the abyss and that he will fall indefinitely without ever coming closer to the bottom than he is at that moment. He then realizes that nothing has really changed. In relation to infinity he is always finite; his falling is relative to nothing but his own sense of falling. He has by then stopped falling, or he may continue, enjoying the sensation. Falling has become fun. He has now begun his real trip.

Same Conclusion

Since the psychedelic experience up to this point is determined by the particular psychological make-up of the person, it differs from individual to individual. For some this part may constitute nearly the whole experience, for others it may be very brief, and others may pass it by completely. But for everybody the experience points to the same conclusion: the ground is no more solid than the water; underneath both is the abyss. The person under psychedelics must somehow come to terms with this nothingness. In it anything is possible, and the choice is whether to fear it—thus retiring to the only tangible thing available, the inner bedrock of fear itself—or to delight in the possibilities suddenly opened up. To delight, to allure, to entice, in other words, to play with the world, to sense it in all its aspects. This in effect is what the psychedelic experience opens up on. To play is also to be surprised, to invite surprise. Alice goes down the rabbit hole or through the mirror and arrives in Wonderland. It is a polymorphous world in which the ugly becomes beautiful, the fragile strong, the colorful drab; fear blends into delight, delight into something else again, perhaps laughter, which may merge into weeping. The perverse suddenly seems normal and right. Even fear is seen as a phantom that has its dark place, a visitation that will also pass.

If the nada of Hemingway is all there is, then the choice is one of either creating life out of this nothing, or the opposite, becoming frozen with fear which turns to destructive energy and a sort of hell on earth. Exactly how this choice is made, or comes about, is a mystery, possibly tied to the origin of the emotions which seem to constitute the self. The help of other persons is possible. The "guide" in the psychedelic experience, a person outside the experience but familiar with the terrain from previous trips, is of considerable importance. He helps the person to tune in by suggestion and encouragement, but finally the person is on his own. He must sense if he is to enter a relationship with his environment. This process of action and reaction, of going backward and forward, seems to be necessary to generate the heat of the emotions, to generate the self. A case could probably be made for the world operating on friction. Both the exhilaration and the ecstasy reported in psychedelic experiences are products of unions with the environment. These go beyond feelings of pleasure or joy or delight. People who have taken LSD often refer to several distinct levels of perception. At the top of an ascending scale is the perception of the molecular structure of the world, a vision of pure energy or pure light. This perception is accompanied by the sensation of a pure, even heat generated throughout the body. The ordinary world of daily life seems ages away.

'Extra Day'

"Trip" describes the psychedelic experience very well. It is gratuitous, "an extra day in the week," one saying goes, and the sense of this experience being unearned is perhaps the common feature of all the attitudes that have grown up around it. It shapes the disbelief of those who have not experienced it, and, paradoxically, it confirms the belief that something quite so rich in life experience must somehow always be a gift and unmerited. The view of ordinary life is nearly always altered after a trip, but this does not mean the style of post-psychedelic life is set, or naturally follows. Egos are still distinct, twins in their variety, and the egoless, the genuine LSD-head can't really be said to have returned from his trip. You can't bring the universe home with you. Perhaps all you can do is choose your home.

The nuttiness is spreading in our land.

I get on this plane recently. An emergency trip—out to Chicago and back again. No time to make reservations, and it seems that when you're really in a hurry the only seat you can ever get is on the Champagne—Red Carpet Flight. The others are all booked up weeks ahead of time.

I Hear America Singing; or
"Leaves of Grass" revisited, like

And so I find myself going through this great big chute. You don't walk into airplanes any more; they inject you into them. The airplane is mainlining people. You walk through this tube —the same air-conditioning and Muzak that is in the terminal— you never know you're on a plane. It's like a big tunnel that runs from the Time-Life Building straight to Chicago.

This really is the Jet Age. In order to Keep Your Finger on the Pulse of Life you've got to do it at 700 miles per hour, or slightly below the sonic barrier. Because, Dad, that's where it's happening. That is where the story is being spelled out.

But one thing—at subsonic speeds you've got to really look at it hard in order to see it, because sometimes it's moving so fast it's just a blur. Trailing smoke.

You've got the picture. I am injected into this enormous silver monster, floating gently on a sea of barely audible Muzak, the sweet Karo Syrup of Existence. I am strapped into my seat. My safety belt is a delicate baby-blue shade, matching the cloud-blue and spun-silver interior décor of this about-to-hurtle projectile.

Muzak rises to a crescendo and we take off. Instantly we are high over this big chunk of land, and the world has become a blurred Kodachrome slide.

A man today never feels so alive as when he is hurtling from one point to another on the azimuth. My nerves are tingling. I'm

Adapted from *Mademoiselle*, 59 (August, 1964), 243 ff. Reprinted with permission of Conde Nast, Inc., and the author.

ready to devour Life in great chunks. In the Champagne—Red Carpet—First Class—VIP—Very Expensive Section.

Silently the red velour is rolled out and baby-blue and silver *houris* are plying me with stuff to eat—which if my mother knew I was eating she would really know I have gone to hell. By God, caviar and Moët *brut* and diced lamb's-liver pâté at 8:17 A.M., over Altoona.

Suddenly, with no warning, from behind me I hear the sound. I have never heard anything like this ever in a jet plane. Or in a biplane for that matter. Or even a Fokker trimotor. I'm sitting there knocking down the caviar, slurping up the champagne, when from behind me I hear the sound, the unmistakable twang, the soul-searing biting buzz of a *guitar!*

A plaintive G-minor chord mingled with the sounds of ice cubes and plastic swizzle sticks . . .

Boing . . . boing . . . twaaannng . . .

And then, a heartbroken voice. It's the voice of America Singing:

500 Miles! ! ! !

It echoes through the pressurized cabin, bouncing from one curved baby-blue bulkhead to the next, and finally fading out somewhere near the "Occupied" sign at the far end of our sealed capsule:

500 Miles! ! ! !

For crying out loud! A Lonesome Traveler! On a jet flight for Chicago, Meat Packer to the World, City of the Broad Shoulders, where the fog creeps in on little cat's feet. A Lonesome Traveler in the Champagne—Red Carpet—First Class—VIP—Very Expensive Section!

I turn around. And here's this angry, beat-looking kid sprawled out there in his foam rubber seat, his safety belt unhooked, a battered guitar case beside him. This angry kid, all tanned from Fire Island where the Crusade for Truth is swelling like a mighty organ chord that cannot be ignored. He's tanned, and wearing a pair of Levis carefully torn in all the right places. It cost his old man a lot of bucks for that pair of Levis—torn, faded, and worn as if they've been worn building the Union Pacific by hand, fighting the Terrible Depression of the Thirties, scrabbling out of the stony soil a hard crust of bread for a poor, honest man, just a-livin' in This Land, just a-tryin' to Love and a-tryin' to Understand and Live as a simple, pure Heart with his Fellows, his Brothers and Sisters all over This Land. A pure White Dove, a-sailin', a-sailin', a-sailin' . . .

The Times They Are a-Changin'

This guy's singing there and the tears are just a-streamin' down between the champagne glasses and the olive picks. . . . There was hardly a dry eye in the house. I am surrounded by a horde of college students, all empathizing like mad with the plight of the Common Man Fighting Against the Forces of Evil, the forces of a rotten, decadent Society.

This kid is on his way to his junior year at the University of Iowa, all the way Champagne Flight, all the way it's been all of his life.

If I Had a Hammer

There he sat, honest tears a-coursin' down those hardened, tan cheeks of his, hardened by so many hard, terrible, awful, wrenchin' scrabblin' weeks at Bar Harbor.

WE SHALL OVERCOME

He's getting *real* bugged now.

WE SHALL NOT BE MOVED

The stewardess bends over to say, "More champagne, sir?" "Yeah, fill it up . . ."

If I Had My Way

I'm sitting there and all of a sudden I realize that today's Lonesome Traveler travels *only* First Class. And more and more I realized that the plight of the Common Man is now in the hands of the Uncommon Man. With plenty of jack.

One of the wildest things about this whole new Suffering Traveler bit that is spreading throughout the campuses today is that the higher a guy is in *actual* social status, the more he em-

pathizes with the real strugglers. More and more you'll find that
the "folk" groups are the most clean-scrubbed, most obviously
well-heeled people you'll ever see in your life. You just can't
imagine Peter, Paul and Mary *ever* hungry. Or Joan Baez, either,
for that matter.

There I sit with champagne glass in hand, trying to figure out
just exactly why all this vaguely bugged me. It reminded me of
something else that I couldn't quite remember. Sort of like trying to remember just how *Swan Lake* goes, or something.

The guitar hit a lovely A-minor chord as the feckless youth
behind me plumbed even deeper into his social consciousness.
The stewardess's baby-blue bottom undulated up the aisle,
toward Chicago. And suddenly I knew. Marie Antoinette! And
then I recalled something out of my almost completely forgotten
European history courses.

Marie Antoinette—now it came back. Just before the French
Revolution . . . I could even remember a few pedantic phrases
from my European History II textbook:

"Just before the French Revolution there was a tremendous
upsurge of interest in and empathy for the peasant on the part of
the idle nobility. It reached the point where Marie Antoinette and
her ladies-in-waiting, with selected noblemen and their pages,
would spend weekends in the country, dressed as milkmaids and
simple peasants of the field."

Aha!

"In the forests around Versailles the decadent French court
built simple peasant cottages in which to live the 'rough' life and
to sing the praises of the rough singular man living his hard,
stony life, tilling from the soil of France the barest essentials of
existence. They actually *did* empathize with him. There was a
movement led by Rousseau, the Rousseau Naturalism Movement . . ."

I toyed moodily with a morsel of Belgian mint jelly as behind
me the Simple Peasant of the Field once again raised his sorrow-
ful voice:

This Land Is Your Land

My left hand made the chord changes instinctively as he sang
out.

Another section of European history came floating back to me on the scent of delicate candied baby yams:

"It is difficult to imagine what the *real* peasants and laborers and milkmaids of France thought when they observed Marie Antoinette and the noblemen at play. Some French writers believe that the sight so enraged them that the course of Revolution was then truly set."

Nervously, I signaled for more wine. I thought, high over Ohio, of the folk music audiences and singers I had seen. There hadn't been many Downtrodden and Defeated people in those crowds. Could it be that the lower down a man really is on the social scale, the less he identifies with the Folk Freedom Fighters, until finally, in the actual slums themselves, you'll find *no* guys singing:

This Land Is Your Land

I looked down through 37,500 feet of cumulus mist. I wondered how many guys were looking up out of tenements at this whistlin' lonesome jet carrying all these guys in the Champagne Section, winging on their way toward Northwestern, Indiana University, U.C.L.A., the University of Michigan. First Class.

A big blonde across the aisle, with an O.S.U. sticker on her Pan-Am flight bag, had joined in. Another white dove a-sailin' and a-sailin'. I wondered if that chick knew what a tumbrel was. Hard to say. American people are not historically minded. She probably thinks that a tumbrel is a seven-letter word (46 Across) meaning "a small cart."

A tall, skinny, crewcut kid, tweed jacket, Daks slacks, with a "Ban the Bomb" button in his lapel, bumped past me, trailing the scent of Brandy and Benedictine. He was heading for the john.

Ban the bomb. I guess that kid figures that history started in 1945. Everything before that was some kind of bad TV show starring Rip Torn as the company commander who chickened out.

I started in on the mousse. Not bad. Ladyfingers soaked in Virgin Islands rum. The big blonde grinned at me over her copy of *The Realist*. Yes, by God, I was surrounded by Realists.

Another phrase from Eur. His. II jiggled into form:

"One school of thought holds that what happened in France

can happen in any society at a certain point in that society's existence, when life becomes so unreal, abstract, to so many people that they begin to long hungrily for the life that they *imagine* is 'Real,' usually the life of men who are tilling the soil or suffering social injustices at the hands of the imaginers themselves."

Hmmmm. Seven or eight pilgrims had joined in the singing, led by a thin, sharp-faced, dark-haired, high-cheekboned girl in a burlap skirt from Jax. A nice bottom. I wondered if she knew what a tumbrel was.

This crowd was as much at home in a jet plane as they were in a taxicab. Belting it out:

> *I'm a lonesome, lonesome traveler*
> *along the hard, rocky road of life* . . .

sitting in the back seat of a Yellow Cab, the meter ticking away.

> *I'm a lonesome, lonesome Yellow Cab*
> *Rider a-travelin' on the old man's*
> *Diners' Club card.*

One thing I've noticed about jet flying is that once you're at cross-country altitude, you rarely feel the slightest bump of a transient air pocket or rough crosswind. At 600 miles per hour plus, you just hang there, suspended. And it is easy to lose all sense of time, space, and reality. The old DC-3's and 4's and even the 6's bumped and banged along, and you knew damn well that something was out there battering at that fuselage, trying to get in. I guess the place to have a fantasy, if you don't want Reality to come creeping in on gnarled vulture claws, is in a jet, just hanging there.

I felt vaguely drunk. Every junky and pothead I've ever known, as well as drinkers of all variety, somehow always use the word "high." By God, we really *were* high! Half a snootful at 37,500 feet is *high*, Dad! Just look out of the misty, ovoid window and there it is, big, fat, and luscious—that fat old earth. I knew one guy who said every time he smoked a joint or two he felt as though he were slowly volplaning around, doing an easy Immelmann, looking down at everybody. He could see it *all*. Of course, the truth is he was five feet six and a very nervous cat.

In real life he didn't look down at much, except maybe a gopher or two, and it all scared him. Maybe that's part of the key, too. I don't know.

The hostess began serving brandies and liqueurs. Our little First Class section was now a tightly knit, jet-propelled hootenanny. Bagged to the gills and feeling the rich, heady hot blood of Social Protest coursing through our veins. Solidarity! Love! Ah, it was good to be alive. And not only alive, but a vibrant, sensitive, Aware person who knew where injustice and human misery were. And we knew what to do about it. *Sing* about it.

I could no longer fight back the urge to join in with my fellow men. Yes, we had been through hell together. Together we had seen it.

A thin, pale young man stood in the aisle. His crystal-clear boy soprano quivering with exultation, he led us on to further glories. True, he reminded me of Audrey Hepburn, who never was exactly my type. His little-boy bangs carelessly brushed down over his forehead, his clearly symbolic denim-blue workshirt open, nay, *ripped* open, à la fist-fightin' Millhand, he was the very image of a Master Sufferer Singer of our time. In the overheated air of our First Class cabin you could almost see his head starkly outlined in a grainy black and white photograph— towering above the rubble of an American street—a perfect Album Cover head. One of the New Breed—the New Breed of fiction artists edging out the old crowd who had used writing as a medium to create fictional characters in novels and plays and short stories, characters that were clearly recognized as make-believe.

The New Breed has gone one important step farther. They use their own lives as a medium for fiction and their own persons as fictional characters. The New Breed can imagine himself to be anything, and believe it—Cowhand, Lumberjack, Negro, Itinerant Fruit-Picker, Bullfighter—any romantic figure that fits his fancy. So, at 19 or 20, a man can have lived a full, rich, dangerous life and feel that he is a worn-out, misery-scarred pilgrim. And what's more, his followers believe him, because they work in the same medium.

Denim Shirt's China-blue eyes burned with the feverish light of the Creative Artist, believing himself to be a rough-hewn hunk who had traveled many roads, "rode freight trains for kicks and got beat up for laughs, cut grass for quarters and sang for dimes," and now he was singing out all the pain of all those old wounds, a spent, scarred Singer for Truth who had been there and known it all. At 22.

If I Had a Hammer

sang the pale, wispy lad.

Up near the forward bulkhead two shaggy-browed 45-year-old tractor salesmen with the obvious tribal markings of retired paratroopers raised their snouts from the champagne trough. The port-side ex-sergeant glared backward down the aisle.

"For God's sake, sonny, will you keep it down?" With which the old battler went back to his jug.

For a brief moment the plane became very aggressive. A classical—if you will excuse the expression—pregnant moment.

And then, bravely, as he had always done, Young Audrey sang on. . . .

I looked at the bulging back of Old Sarge, and I wondered how many roads *that* old son of a gun had walked down. From Bizerte to Remagen, up the Po Valley and back; 7,000 miles, from Kiska to Iwo. And still on the Goddamn road.

Beat up for laughs! The grizzled specimen next to Old Sarge had the chewed ears of a guy who had fist-fought his way through every Off Limits bar from Camp Kilmer to the Kit Kat Klub on the Potzdamer Platz, and all for laughs.

The dark chick glowered up the cabin at the back of Old Sarge's head. He and his buddy were boffing it up. She glanced meltingly, at young Denim Shirt, her blue and white "Fight for Freedom" button gleaming like an angry shield above her tiny black-T-shirted bosom.

Her glance spoke volumes: "Those clods! What do they know of Suffering, of fighting for Good, for Ideals? What do they know of the hard, flinty back alleys of Life, of Injustice? Only Youth *understands* and knows. Do not be afraid. I, an angry Girl-Type Lonesome Traveler, will protect you."

The lissome lad, taking heart, began again with renewed spirit and passion.

She was right. What *did* Old Sarge know about true Suffering?

His swarthy, grizzled neck bent defiantly forward, back to the trough, that neck which still bore a permanent mahogany stain of 10,000 suns, the Libyan Desert, Tinian, the Solomons, Burma Road, Corregidor . . .

Chewed Ear glanced over his hunched shoulder for a brief instant at the button-wearer, the leer that had impaled broad-beamed, ripe-bosomed females from Dakar to Adelaide, a glance primeval and unmistakable. She flushed. She obviously was not used to heavy artillery.

Blowin' in the Wind

The black-T-shirted White Dove fluttered, confused, in the sand for a few wing beats and then scurried out of range.

The undergrad hootenanny swung into the chorus. Someone had produced a Kentucky mandolin, jangling high above the passionate Ovaltine voices. . . . The cabin was filled with the joyous sound. Old Sarge, after the last note died echoing in the soft light-blue carpeting, turned suddenly. "Hey kid, do any of you guys know 'Dirty Gertie from Bizerte'?"

He laughed obscenely, not realizing he was disrupting a Religious service. The congregation plunked, embarrassed.

"How 'bout 'Lili Marlene'?" Without any warning, Chewed Ear tuned up—*a cappella*.

> *I've been workin' on the railroad,*
> *all the Goddamned day . . .*

He sang in the cracked voice that had sung itself out over 9,000 miles of Canadian-Pacific track, laying every spike in the frozen tundra personally.

> *I've been workin' on the railroad,*
> *just to pass the time away . . .*

he bellowed.

Blue Jeans in the seat behind me, in a put-down stage whisper to O.S.U. Bag:

"For God sake, 'I've Been Working on the Railroad'! This old guy wouldn't know a Work Song if he heard it."

The apple-cheeked youth, his fingers calloused by countless

hours of guitar-pick-clutching, slumped knowingly against the cushions of his seat.

Can't you hear those whistles blowin' . . .

The whiskey-cracked calliope, honed and sharpened against the cold winds blowing over countless flatbed coal cars and short-coupled reefers, ground to a stop.

FASTEN YOUR SEAT BELTS. NO SMOKING PLEASE. The soft yellow warning broke up the action.

"This is the Captain speaking. We are making our final approach to O'Hare Airport. We should be on the ground in three minutes. The ground temperature in Chicago—fifty-seven degrees. There is a slight crosswind. I hope you've enjoyed your trip. We hope to see you soon. Please fasten your seat belts."

Our great silver arrow knifed down through the thick underlayer of cloud and smoke. Red-roofed houses and lines of crawling blue Fords rose up toward us. The great flaps creaked and clanked into position. The bird paused for a brief instant, and we touched the runway.

"This is your stewardess. It has been a pleasure to have you aboard. Please keep your seat belts fastened until we come to a full stop. We hope you have had a pleasant trip, and hope to see you again soon."

The jet stopped rolling, and outside my porthole I could see the Chicago end of the Great Tube being inserted into our bird. Behind me, the angry snap of a guitar case clasp. We moved up the aisle. From somewhere ahead, a piping adolescent voice:

"Hey Freddie, I'll see ya next weekend at the big hoot in Ann Arbor. Dylan's gonna make the scene. Maybe Baez!"

Old Sarge, hat jammed down over his ears, made one last verbal swipe at the stewardess who stood by the exit as we filed out. She smiled blandly.

"I hope you enjoyed your trip, sir."

Our little band of Lonesome Travelers toiled up the chute toward the City of the Broad Shoulders, Meat Packer to the World. The party was over.

No aspect of human life seethes with so many unexorcised demons as does sex. No human activity is so hexed by super-stition, so haunted by residual tribal lore, and so harassed by socially induced fear. Within the breast of urban-secular man, a toe-to-toe struggle still rages between his savage and his bourgeois forebears. Like everything else, the images of sex

Sex and Secularization

which informed tribal and town society are expiring along with the eras in which they arose. The erosion of traditional values and the disappearance of accepted modes of behavior have left contemporary man free, but somewhat rudderless. Abhorring a vacuum, the mass media have rushed in to supply a new code and a new set of behavioral prototypes. They appeal to the un-exorcised demons. Nowhere is the persistence of mythical and metalogical denizens more obvious than in sex, and the shamans of sales do their best to nourish them. Nowhere is the humaniza-tion of life more frustrated. Nowhere is a clear word of exorcism more needed.

How is the humanization of sex impeded? First it is thwarted by the parading of cultural-identity images for the sexually dispossessed, to make money. These images become the tyrant gods of the secular society, undercutting its liberation from religion and transforming it into a kind of neotribal culture. Second, the authentic secularization of sex is checkmated by an anxious clinging to the sexual standards of the town, an era so recent and yet so different from ours that simply to transplant its sexual ethos into our situation is to invite hypocrisy of the worst degree.

Let us look first at the spurious sexual models conjured up for our anxious society by the sorcerers of the mass media and the advertising guild. Like all pagan deities, these come in pairs— the god and his consort. For our purposes they are best sym-bolized by The Playboy and Miss America, the Adonis and

Reprinted with permission of The Macmillan Company from *The Secular City* by Harvey Cox. Copyright © Harvey Cox 1965.

Aphrodite of a leisure-consumer society which still seems unready to venture into full postreligious maturity and freedom. The Playboy and Miss America represent The Boy and The Girl. They incorporate a vision of life. They function as religious phenomena and should be exorcised and exposed.

The Residue of Tribalism

Let us begin with Miss America. In the first century B.C., Lucretius wrote this description of the pageant of Cybele:

> Adorned with emblem and crown . . . she is carried in awe-inspiring state. Tight-stretched tambourines and hollow cymbals thunder all round to the stroke of open hands, hollow pipes stir with Phrygian strain. . . . She rides in procession through great cities and mutely enriches mortals with a blessing not expressed in words. They straw all her path with brass and silver, presenting her with bounteous alms, and scatter over her a snow-shower of roses.

Now compare this with the annual twentieth-century Miss America pageant in Atlantic City, New Jersey. Spotlights probe the dimness like votive tapers, banks of flowers exude their varied aromas, the orchestra blends feminine strings and regal trumpets. There is a hushed moment of tortured suspense, a drumroll, then the climax—a young woman with carefully prescribed anatomical proportions and exemplary "personality" parades serenely with scepter and crown to her throne. At TV sets across the nation throats tighten and eyes moisten. "There she goes, Miss America—" sings the crooner. "There she goes, your ideal." A new queen in America's emerging cult of The Girl has been crowned.

Is it merely illusory or anachronistic to discern in the multiplying pageants of the Miss America, Miss Universe, Miss College Queen type a residuum of the cults of the pre-Christian fertility goddesses? Perhaps, but students of the history of religions have become less prone in recent years to dismiss the possibility that the cultural behavior of modern man may be significantly illuminated by studying it in the perspective of the mythologies of bygone ages. After all, did not Freud initiate a revolution in social science by utilizing the venerable myth of Oedipus to help make sense out of the strange behavior of his

Viennese contemporaries? Contemporary man carries with him, like his appendix and his fingernails, vestiges of his tribal and pagan past.

In light of this fertile combination of insights from modern social science and the history of religions, it is no longer possible to see in the Miss America pageant merely an overpublicized prank foisted on us by the advertising industry. It certainly is this, but it is also much more. It represents the mass cultic celebration, complete with a rich variety of ancient ritual embellishments, of the growing place of The Girl in the collective soul of America.

This young woman—though she is no doubt totally ignorant of the fact—symbolizes something beyond herself. She symbolizes The Girl, the primal image, the One behind the many. Just as the Virgin appears in many guises—as our Lady of Lourdes or of Fatima or of Guadalupe—but is always recognizably the Virgin, so with The Girl.

The Girl is also the omnipresent icon of consumer society. Selling beer, she is folksy and jolly. Selling gems, she is chic and distant. But behind her various theophanies she remains recognizably The Girl. In Miss America's glowingly healthy smile, her openly sexual but officially virginal figure, and in the name-brand gadgets around her, she personifies the stunted aspirations and ambivalent fears of her culture. "There she goes, your ideal."

Miss America stands in a long line of queens going back to Isis, Ceres, and Aphrodite. Everything from the elaborate sexual taboos surrounding her person to the symbolic gifts at her coronation hints at her ancient ancestry. But the real proof comes when we find that the function served by The Girl in our culture is just as much a "religious" one as that served by Cybele in hers. The functions are identical—to provide a secure personal "identity" for initiates and to sanctify a particular value structure.

Let us look first at the way in which The Girl confers a kind of identity on her initiates. Simone de Beauvoir says in *The Second Sex* that "no one is *born* a woman." One is merely born a female, and "*becomes* a woman" according to the models and meanings provided by the civilization. During the classical Christian centuries, it might be argued, the Virgin Mary served in part as this model. With the Reformation and especially with the Puritans, the place of Mary within the symbol system of the Protestant countries was reduced or eliminated. There are those who claim that this excision constituted an excess of zeal that greatly impoverished Western culture, an impoverishment from which it has never recovered. Some would even claim that the alleged failure of American novelists to produce a single great heroine (we have no Phaedra, no Anna Karenina) stems from this self-imposed lack of a central feminine ideal.

Without entering into this fascinating discussion, we can certainly be sure that, even within modern American Roman Catholicism, the Virgin Mary provides an identity image for few American girls. Where then do they look for the "model" Simone de Beauvoir convincingly contends they need? For most, the prototype of femininity seen in their mothers, their friends, and in the multitudinous images to which they are exposed on the mass media is what we have called The Girl.

In his significant monograph *Identity and the Life Cycle,* Erik Erikson reminds us that the child's identity is not modeled simply on the parent but on the parent's "super-ego." Thus in seeking to forge her own identity the young girl is led beyond her mother to her mother's ideal image, and it is here that what Freud called "the ideologies of the superego . . . the traditions of the race and the people" become formative. It is here also that The Girl functions, conferring identity on those for whom she is— perhaps never completely consciously—the tangible incarnation of womanhood.

To describe the mechanics of this complex psychological process by which the fledgling American girl participates in the life of The Girl and thus attains a woman's identity would require a thorough description of American adolescence. There is little doubt, however, that such an analysis would reveal certain striking parallels to the "savage" practices by which initiates in the mystery cults shared in the magical life of their god.

For those inured to the process, the tortuous nightly fetish by which the young American female pulls her hair into tight bunches secured by metal clips may bear little resemblance to the incisions made on their arms by certain African tribesmen to make them resemble their totem, the tiger. But to an anthropologist comparing two ways of attempting to resemble the holy one, the only difference might appear to be that with the Africans the torture is over after initiation, while with the American it has to be repeated every night, a luxury only a culture with abundant leisure can afford.

In turning now to an examination of the second function of The Girl—supporting and portraying a value system—a comparison with the role of the Virgin in the twelfth and thirteenth centuries may be helpful. Just as the Virgin exhibited and sustained the ideals of the age that fashioned Chartres Cathedral, as Henry Adams saw, so The Girl symbolizes the values and aspirations of a consumer society. (She is crowned not in the political capital, remember, but in Atlantic City or Miami Beach, centers associated with leisure and consumption.) And she is not entirely incapable of exploitation. If men sometimes sought to buy with gold the Virgin's blessings on their questionable causes, so The Girl now dispenses her charismatic favor on watches, refrigerators, and razor blades—for a price. Though The Girl has built no cathedrals, without her the colossal edifice of mass persuasion would crumble. Her sharply stylized face and figure beckon us from every magazine and TV channel, luring us toward the beatific vision of a consumer's paradise.

The Girl is *not* the Virgin. In fact she is a kind of anti-Madonna. She reverses most of the values traditionally associated with the Virgin—poverty, humility, sacrifice. In startling contrast, particularly, to the biblical portrait of Mary in Luke 1:46–55, The Girl has nothing to do with filling the hungry with "good things," hawking instead an endless proliferation of trivia on TV spot commercials. The Girl exalts the mighty, extols the rich, and brings nothing to the hungry but added despair. So The Girl does buttress and bring into personal focus a value system, such as it is. In both social and psychological terms, The Girl, whether or not she is really a goddess, certainly acts that way.

Perhaps the most ironic element in the rise of the cult of The Girl is that Protestantism has almost completely failed to notice it, while Roman Catholics have at least given some evidence of sensing its significance. In some places, for instance, Catholics are forbidden to participate in beauty pageants, a ruling not entirely inspired by prudery. It is ironic that Protestants have traditionally been most opposed to lady cults while Catholics have managed to assimilate more than one at various points in history.

If we are correct in assuming that The Girl *functions* in many ways as a goddess, then the cult of The Girl demands careful Protestant theological criticism. Anything that functions, even in part, as a god when it is in fact not God, is an idol. When the Reformers and their Puritan offspring criticized the cult of Mary it was not because they were antifeminist. They opposed anything—man, woman, or beast (or dogma or institution)—that usurped in the slightest the prerogatives that belonged alone to God Almighty. As Max Weber has insisted, when the prophets of Israel railed against fertility cults, they had nothing against fertility. It is not against sexuality but against a cult that protest is needed. Not, as it were, against the beauty but against the pageant.

Thus the Protestant objection to the present cult of The Girl must be based on the realization that The Girl is an *idol*. She functions as the source of value, the giver of personal identity. But the values she mediates and the identity she confers are both spurious. Like every idol she is ultimately a creation of our own hands and cannot save us. The values she represents as ultimate satisfactions—mechanical comfort, sexual success, unencumbered leisure—have no ultimacy. They lead only to endless upward mobility, competitive consumption, and anxious cynicism. The devilish social insecurities from which she promises to deliver us are, alas, still there, even after we have purified our breaths, our skins, and our armpits by applying her sacred oils. She is a merciless goddess who draws us farther and farther into the net of accelerated ordeals of obeisance. As the queen of commodities in an expanding economy, the fulfillment she promises must always remain just beyond the tips of our fingers.

Why has Protestantism kept its attention obsessively fastened on the development of Mariolatry in Catholicism and not noticed the sinister rise of this vampirelike cult of The Girl in our society? Unfortunately, it is due to the continuing incapacity of theological critics to recognize the religious significance of cultural phenomena outside the formal religious system itself. But the rise of this new cult reminds us that the work of the reformer is never done. Man's mind is indeed—as Luther said—a factory busy making idols. The Girl is a far more pervasive and destructive influence than the Virgin, and it is to her and her omnipresent altars that we should be directing our criticism.

Besides sanctifying a set of phony values, The Girl compounds her noxiousness by maiming her victims in a Procrustean bed of uniformity. This is the empty "identity" she panders. Take the Miss America pageant, for example. Are these virtually indistinguishable specimens of white, middle-class postadolescence really the best we can do? Do they not mirror the ethos of a mass-production society, in which genuine individualism somehow mars the clean, precision-tooled effect? Like their sisters, the finely calibrated Rockettes, these meticulously measured and pretested "beauties" lined up on the Boardwalk bear an ominous similarity to the faceless retinues of goose-steppers and the interchangeable mass exercisers of explicitly totalitarian societies. In short, *who* says this is beauty?

The caricature becomes complete in the Miss Universe contest, when Miss Rhodesia is a blonde, Miss South Africa is white, and Oriental girls with a totally different tradition of feminine beauty are forced to display their thighs and appear in spike heels and Catalina swim suits. Miss Universe is as universal as an American adman's stereotype of what beauty should be.

The truth is that The Girl can*not* bestow the identity she promises. She forces her initiates to torture themselves with starvation diets and beauty-parlor ordeals, but still cannot deliver the satisfactions she holds out. She is young, but what happens when her followers, despite added hours in the boudoir, can no longer appear young? She is happy and smiling and loved. What happens when, despite all the potions and incantations, her disciples still feel the human pangs of rejection and loneliness? Or what about all the girls whose statistics, or "personality" (or color) do not match the authoritative "ideal"?

After all, it is God—not The Girl—who is God. He is the center and source of value. He liberates men and women from the bland uniformity of cultural deities so that they may feast on the luxurious diversity of life He has provided. The identity He confers frees men from all pseudo-identities to be themselves, to fulfill their human destinies regardless whether their faces or figures match some predetermined abstract "ideal." As His gift, sex is freed from both fertility cults and commercial exploitation to become the thoroughly human thing He intended. And since it is one of the last items we have left that is neither prepackaged nor standardized, let us not sacrifice it too hastily on the omnivorous altar of Cybele.

The Playboy, illustrated by the monthly magazine of that name, does for the boys what Miss America does for the girls. Despite accusations to the contrary, the immense popularity of this magazine is not solely attributable to pin-up girls. For sheer nudity its pictorial art cannot compete with such would-be competitors as *Dude* and *Escapade. Playboy* appeals to a highly mobile, increasingly affluent group of young readers, mostly between eighteen and thirty, who want much more from their drugstore reading than bosoms and thighs. They need a total image of what it means to be a man. And Mr. Hefner's *Playboy* has no hesitation in telling them.

Why should such a need arise? David Riesman has argued that the responsibility for character formation in our society has shifted from the family to the peer group and to the mass-media peer-group surrogates. Things are changing so rapidly that one who is equipped by his family with inflexible, highly internalized values becomes unable to deal with the accelerated pace of change and with the varying contests in which he is called upon to function. This is especially true in the area of consumer values toward which the "other-directed person" is increasingly oriented.

Within the confusing plethora of mass-media signals and peer-group values, *Playboy* fills a special need. For the insecure young man with newly acquired free time and money who still feels uncertain about his consumer skills, *Playboy* supplies a comprehensive and authoritative guidebook to this forbidding new world to which he now has access. It tells him not only who to be; it tells him *how* to be it, and even provides consolation outlets for those who secretly feel that they have not quite made it.

In supplying for the other-directed consumer of leisure both the normative identity image and the means for achieving it, *Playboy* relies on a careful integration of copy and advertising material. The comic book that appeals to a younger generation with an analogous problem skillfully intersperses illustrations of incredibly muscled men and excessively mammalian women with advertisements for body-building gimmicks and foam-rubber brassière supplements. Thus the thin-chested comic-book readers of both sexes are thoughtfully supplied with both the ends and the means for attaining a spurious brand of maturity. *Playboy* merely continues the comic-book tactic for the next age group. Since within every identity crisis, whether in teens or twenties, there is usually a sexual-identity problem, *Playboy* speaks to those who desperately want to know what it means to be a man, and more specifically a *male*, in today's world.

Both the image of man and the means for its attainment exhibit a remarkable consistency in *Playboy*. The skilled consumer is cool and unruffled. He savors sports cars, liquor, high fidelity, and book-club selections with a casual, unhurried aplomb. Though he must certainly *have* and *use* the latest consumption item, he must not permit himself to get too attached to it. The style will change and he must always be ready to adjust. His persistent anxiety that he may mix a drink incorrectly, enjoy a jazz group that is passé, or wear last year's necktie style is comforted by an authoritative tone in *Playboy* beside which papal encyclicals sound irresolute.

"Don't hesitate," he is told, "this assertive, self-assured weskit is what every man of taste wants for the fall season." Lingering doubts about his masculinity are extirpated by the firm assurance that "real men demand this ruggedly masculine smoke" (cigar ad). Though "the ladies will swoon for you, no matter what they promise, don't give them a puff. This cigar is for men only." A fur-lined canvas field jacket is described as "the most masculine thing since the cave man." What to be and how to be it are both made unambiguously clear.

Since being a male necessitates some kind of relationship to females, *Playboy* fearlessly confronts this problem too, and solves it by the consistent application of the same formula. Sex becomes one of the items of leisure activity that the knowledgeable consumer of leisure handles with his characteristic skill and detachment. The girl becomes a desirable—indeed an indispensable—"Playboy accessory."

In a question-answering column entitled "The Playboy Adviser," queries about smoking equipment (how to break in a meerschaum pipe), cocktail preparation (how to mix a Yellow Fever), and whether or not to wear suspenders with a vest alternate with questions about what to do with girls who complicate the cardinal principle of casualness either by suggesting marriage or by some other impulsive gesture toward a permanent relationship. The infallible answer from the oracle never varies: sex must be contained, at all costs, within the entertainment-recreation area. Don't let her get "serious."

After all, the most famous feature of the magazine is its monthly fold-out photo of a *play*mate. She is the symbol par excellence of recreational sex. When playtime is over, the playmate's function ceases, so she must be made to understand the rules of the game. As the crew-cut young man in a *Playboy* cartoon says to the rumpled and disarrayed girl he is passionately embracing, "Why speak of love at a time like this?"

The magazine's fiction purveys the same kind of severely departmentalized sex. Although the editors have recently dressed up the *Playboy* contents with contributions by Hemingway, Bemelmans, and even a Chekhov translation, the regular run of stories relies on a repetitious and predictable formula. A successful young man, either single or somewhat less than ideally married—a figure with whom readers have no difficulty identifying—encounters a gorgeous and seductive woman who makes no demands on him except sex. She is the prose duplication of the cool-eyed but hot-blooded playmate of the fold-out.

Drawing heavily on the fantasy life of all young Americans, the writers utilize for their stereotyped heroines the hero's schoolteacher, his secretary, an old girl friend, or the girl who brings her car into the garage where he works. The happy issue is always a casual but satisfying sexual experience with no entangling alliances whatever. Unlike the women he knows in real life, the *Playboy* reader's fictional girl friends know their place and ask for nothing more. They present no danger of permanent involvement. Like any good accessory, they are detachable and disposable.

Many of the advertisements reinforce the sex-accessory identification in another way—by attributing female characteristics
to the items they sell. Thus a full-page ad for the MG assures us
that this car is not only "the smoothest pleasure machine" on
the road and that having one is a "love-affair," but most important, "you drive it—it doesn't drive you." The ad ends with the
equivocal question "Is it a date?"

Playboy insists that its message is one of liberation. Its gospel
frees us from captivity to the puritanical "hatpin brigade." It
solemnly crusades for "frankness" and publishes scores of letters
congratulating it for its unblushing "candor." Yet the whole
phenomenon of which *Playboy* is only a part vividly illustrates
the awful fact of a new kind of tyranny.

Those liberated by technology and increased prosperity to new
worlds of leisure now become the anxious slaves of dictatorial
tastemakers. Obsequiously waiting for the latest signal on what
is cool and what is awkward, they are paralyzed by the fear that
they may hear pronounced on them that dread sentence occasionally intoned by "The Playboy Adviser": "You goofed!"
Leisure is thus swallowed up in apprehensive competitiveness,
its liberating potential transformed into a self-destructive compulsion to consume only what is *à la mode*. *Playboy* mediates the
Word of the most high into one section of the consumer world,
but it is a word of bondage, not of freedom.

Nor will *Playboy's* synthetic doctrine of man stand the test of
scrutiny. Psychoanalysts constantly remind us how deep-seated
sexuality is in the human being. But if they didn't remind us,
we would soon discover it ourselves anyway. Much as the human
male might like to terminate his relationship with a woman as
he would snap off the stereo, or store her for special purposes
like a camel's-hair jacket, it really can't be done. And anyone
with a modicum of experience with women knows it can't be
done. Perhaps this is the reason *Playboy's* readership drops off
so sharply after the age of thirty.

Playboy really feeds on the existence of a repressed fear of
involvement with women, which for various reasons is still
present in many otherwise adult Americans. So *Playboy's* version
of sexuality grows increasingly irrelevant as authentic sexual
maturity is achieved.

The male identity crisis to which *Playboy* speaks has at its roots a deep-set fear of sex, a fear that is uncomfortably combined with fascination. *Playboy* strives to resolve this antinomy by reducing the proportions of sexuality, its power and its passion, to a packageable consumption item. Thus in *Playboy's* iconography the nude woman symbolizes total sexual accessibility but demands nothing from the observer. "You drive it—it doesn't drive you." The terror of sex, which cannot be separated from its ecstasy, is dissolved. But this futile attempt to reduce the *mysterium tremendum* of the sexual fails to solve the problem of being a man. For sexuality is the basic form of all human relationship, and therein lies its terror and its power.

Karl Barth has called this basic relational form of man's life *Mitmensch,* co-humanity. This means that becoming fully human, in this case a human male, requires not having the other totally exposed to me and my purposes—while I remain uncommitted—but exposing myself to the risk of encounter with the other by reciprocal self-exposure. The story of man's refusal so to be exposed goes back to the story of Eden and is expressed by man's desire to control the other rather than to *be with* the other. It is basically the fear to be one's self, a lack of the "courage to be."

Thus any theological critique of *Playboy* that focuses on its "lewdness" will misfire completely. *Playboy* and its less successful imitators are not "sex magazines" at all. They are basically antisexual. They dilute and dissipate authentic sexuality by reducing it to an accessory, by keeping it at a safe distance.

4

The People

An age is finally remembered most for the people who walked through it. Older books would talk of the heroes of a generation; new books might list our antiheroes; but we have chosen rather to speak of people. Each one of the people in this section is in his own way very much a part of the Sixties.

If no age has any contemporary heroes but only a surfeit of popular figures, so, too, no age has a contemporary who is seen as totally representative. The six people in this chapter do, however, represent some part of the Sixties. It would be presumptuous to try to describe their representativeness (their names alone do that). What they have in common is style. Not a common style—certainly Lenny Bruce is different from Pope John XXIII, but they each have a recognizable individuality that can reach others.

Bogey, for example, is a rediscovery made by the Sixties in search of a style. Heidegger represents another kind of influence, perhaps more profound, certainly less visible. *Zein und Zeit* was translated in the Sixties and will become more and more a part of our consciousness of ourselves and our world.

Jimmy Breslin, the Sixties' version of a Front Page newspaperman, describes his reactions to the now well-established species, *Homo suburbis*.

Robert Kennedy and Pope John are truly people of the Sixties. Let's say that each in his own way was able to communicate to millions something that those millions wanted to know.

GERALD WEALES

Anyone entangled, emotionally and aesthetically, in the movies of the 1930's and 1940's, as I am, is likely to view with suspicion the phenomenon of the revival, the festival dedicated to a single performer, director or genre. No one wants the sontag-cum-serendipity crowd camping where he lives, giggling its way through his childhood, adolescence and early manhood. A

The Bogart Vogue: Character and Cult

theater in Philadelphia recently offered four hours of Batman serials, stitched together to form an evening's entertainment, winking from its marquee, "Is it pop art or is it camp?" I stayed away because I know how bad the Batman serials are, I have no emotional investment in them (I was too old when they began to appear) and I am slightly nauseated by the kind of laughter they invoke, the superior snottiness that thinks it is funny to put comic captions on stills from old movies and photographs of babies and animals.

On the other hand, I went to the Gallery of Modern Art to see Busby Berkeley and Ruby Keeler when they came out of retirement to appear on a program, along with more than two hours of Berkeley musical numbers laid end to end, honoring the work of the most important musical director of the 1930's. Even so, there was an unhealthy ambiguity about the occasion. Along with a genuine nostalgia for Miss Keeler and a real admiration for Berkeley's inventiveness, even when it became ridiculous, there was an air of chi-chi, for in some circles it has become fashionable laughingly to admire Ruby Keeler simply because she was so bad as an actress, a singer and a dancer.

Humphrey Bogart is no Batman and he never played opposite Ruby Keeler (it was Cagney who danced with her in "Footlight Parade"), but I feel some of the same sense of distrust about the Bogart vogue. Praise for him on the lips of anyone under 35 makes me suspicious, particularly when he is called "Bogey," the man's nickname transferred to the actor. I always called him

From *Commonweal*, 83 (March 11, 1966), 664–666. Reprinted by permission of Commonweal Publishing Co., Inc.

"Humphrey Bogart," or, at my most familiar, "Bogart." This "Bogey" thing sounds culty to me, as though it might have been imported with the French *nouvelle vague,* a transplant from "Breathless" ("Son of Bogie" proclaims the January *Esquire* in an article on Belmondo), an exotic flower growing in home soil where simple Bogart fans once flourished.

Although there is something about the Bogart boom that is as deceptively genuine as Sydney Greenstreet's smile in "The Maltese Falcon," there is something solid too. There is more to it than a momentary Batman or Flash Gordon resurgence. It has lasted too long, for one thing. Not long after Bogart's death in 1957, fanning out from Harvard, where film festivals are born, the Bogart revivals began in cities all across the country. This was not a case of rediscovery, for he was a top box-office star right to the end of his life. In his last 10 years, however, beginning with "Treasure of Sierra Madre," he made conscious and often successful attempts to create characters only distantly related to the personality that is now called "Bogey." One of the purposes of the festivals was to reestablish that personality, to see that the films of the early forties were played alongside his later successes. While we went to "Sierra Madre" or "The African Queen" at first-run theaters, we watched the all-night houses for a chance to see again "High Sierra," "The Maltese Falcon," "The Big Sleep."

The even earlier Bogart films, the parade of ordinary 1930's feature pictures, were not available at all until Warner Bros. dumped its movies on the television market. Then we could see Bogart playing second fiddle to Pat O'Brien in "The Great O'Malley" or Edward G. Robinson in "Kid Galahad"; we could reaffirm our half-remembered conviction that once, as a wrestling impresario, Bogart set up a match between Nat Pendleton and Louise Fazenda—in "Swing Your Lady." It is on television that the most persistent if casual Bogart festivals play, because hardly a week goes by without at least one Bogart film available at some time of day or night in every viewing area. The testimony to Bogart made at the box-offices of art houses or in the early morning hours in front of television sets can now be echoed in bookstores. In the fall of 1965, four books on Humphrey Bogart were published, three of them entitled *Bogey.*

(*Bogey, The Films of Humphrey Bogart,* by Clifford McCarty, Citadel, $6.95; *Humphrey Bogart, The Man and His Films,* by Paul Michael, Bobbs-Merrill, $7.95; *Bogey, The Man, The Actor, The Legend,* by Jonah Ruddy and Jonathan Hill, Tower, 75¢; *Bogey: Good-Bad Guy,* by Ezra Goodman, Lyle Stuart, $4.95.) I have not seen the Goodman book.

The Bogart that the books celebrate, the figure who looms a little larger than any one of his films is chiefly a product of a handful of Warner movies made between 1941 and 1946, from "High Sierra" to "The Big Sleep." He was a long time getting there. Bogart played a number of minor roles on Broadway during the 1920's. It is usually said that he spent those years dressed in flannels, carrying a tennis racket, but the Bogart role that sticks in my mind from a later reading of the play is the prim and earnest young man in Larry E. Johnson's "It's a Wise Child" (1929), who, always willing to sacrifice romance to his career, loses the girl to Minor Watson. Bogart made several unsuccessful bids for a Hollywood career (nine movies for four companies from 1930 to 1932), but it was not until his success as Duke Mantee in "The Petrified Forest" (1936), a repetition of his Broadway role, that his movie career began in earnest. He was no star even then. Featured, he appeared in five films in 1936, seven in 1937, six in 1938, seven in 1939, a functioning cog in the Warner machine, a busy bush-league gangster on the turf ruled by Cagney and Robinson. He had played a gangster as far back as 1932, in "Three on a Match," in which he drove poor Ann Dvorak to suicide, but it was his Duke Mantee that convinced the Warner typecasters that they had a good thing. Given that many movies in that short a time, he played a variety of parts, but the tough-guy roles predominated and became his identification tag.

Walking Through His Roles

He was never an actor with a great range and in those days he did little but walk through stereotypical parts. The Ruddy-Hill book, which is admiring in tone, admits, "A close-up would often fail to reveal whether he was shooting it out with the FBI or making passionate love to his leading lady." As the Irish horse trainer in "Dark Victory," he conveyed nothing at all; he was saved in the movie because his face carried over a certain amount of amiable menace (which had nothing to do with "Dark Victory") from his customary roles and also because the film's leading man, George Brent, was so obviously a block of wood that Bogart seemed alive by comparison. In more conventional parts, dead-pan quality was a virtue. Cagney, Robinson, Muni, Raft, all the leading film gangsters worked within a comfortable stereotype and the small-part gangsters, Joe Sawyer, George E. Stone, Allen Jenkins, wore their familiar faces as obviously as the stock figures in Restoration comedy. Bogart became an adept performer, as so many of the Hollywood stars and contract players did, by learning to operate with skill and with apparent ease within the confines of a self- and studio-defined personality.

As this endless string of unimportant feature pictures rolled off the Warner lot, two things were in operation helping to prepare the transition to the next Bogart—one had to do with Bogart himself, one with the genre. Although the directors of the gangster movies occasionally attempted to get a kind of tawdry realism on film, as background to the action, the genre itself was highly stylized. Even in serious films, it was difficult to take the villainy at more than face value; much more difficult, when the same Bogart went through his menacing paces in comedies in which the wisecrack shared screen space with mayhem—"Kid Galahad" or "Brother Orchid." While the genre insisted that we pay attention to a stereotyped figure, the actor playing that figure was impressing himself on audiences.

Much is made of Bogart's rugged handsomeness or attractive ugliness—depending on what fan magazine you read—but that kind of generalization explains very little. I suspect that two details of Bogart's face prepared audiences to accept his presumed toughness as a mask. One was the heavy eyebrows, dark even when they were plucked thinner than usual, which gave a deep-set quality to his eyes; the second was a kind of vulnerability about the lower lip and chin. All he needed was the roles to convince us that he was a tough guy with a soft streak just under the surface ("High Sierra") or a soft-hearted, idealistic guy who wore toughness as a disguise and a defense ("The Maltese Falcon"). There had been embryo Bogeys earlier—his Red Kennedy in "San Quentin" (1937)—but it was "Sierra" and "Falcon," coming together in 1941, that established the Bogart we know. Even after he attempted to go beyond that character, he returned to it in almost pure form in "Beat the Devil" (1954) and in certain details of some of his more famous later roles— Charlie Allnut in "The African Queen" and Harry Dawes in "The Barefoot Contessa." Its most famous embodiment, of course, was Rick in "Casablanca."

A Bogus Nonchalance

This Bogart came at just the right time for my generation. The idealism of the 1930's was coming to a confused end; after years of political optimism, the country was becoming aware that it had vaulted out of the depression, only to come down in a major war. Those of us who were going to have to go directly from high school to war had no intention of being sucked into overt patriotism. If we were going to have to be heroic, we knew how to do the job obliquely, out of the corner of our mouths. I do not want to blow up Bogart into a major symbol, but it was from him, and other Hollywood stars, that we found the manner that let us carry off a dirty and necessary war with a certain bogus nonchalance.

John Clellan Holmes summed him up well in a recent article on the movies of the 1930's (*Harper's*, December, 1965), although the Bogart he described really belongs to the 1940's: "He is always pre-eminently the Existential Knight, suspicious of sentiment, verbosity, and cheap idealism." The existential label (André Bazin used it earlier) is out of time, although accurate enough. It is in the Bogart character's assumption that real feeling, displayed, becomes rhetoric that his appeal for us lay. It is the same quality that must have appealed to a whole new generation in the 1950's. In the last few years, idealism has begun to come out from underground, but until a generation comes along which can proclaim itself without ambivalence, Bogart will keep his hold on new audiences; his world-weary Galahad will continue to speak to young men who want to do the right thing in the wrong tone of voice.

To know the character, however, better keep an eye out for a chance to see a movie like "All Through the Night" (1942). There, more than in "Casablanca" or any of the films that asks to be taken seriously, Bogart can be seen most clearly. He walks his soft-hearted, hard-fisted, wise-cracking way through that movie, flanked by Frank McHugh and William Demarest, and in the end he saves the heroine and the country from the Nazi menace of Conrad Veidt, Peter Lorre and Judith Anderson.

There is a risk for the critic to speak of a turning point in Heidegger's thought. For nearly every position taken by the later Heidegger one can find a passage in the earlier work that prepares the way. Thus one could speak just as well of the remarkable continuity of this thought rather than of any abrupt turning point or points that it takes. Continuity and discontinuity in

Martin Heidegger: The Turning Point

the case of any organic development go together and are complementary: from acorn to oak is one continuous process, yet what emerges at different stages of growth will be remarkably unlike what went before. The change in Heidegger is not at all a repudiation of earlier positions but an enlargement upon them. It is primarily a change in emphasis, in temper and tone. The later Heidegger is far more the historical prophet, his tone is more sweeping and apocalyptic, and the themes of his thought are the total historical perspectives of Western civilization.

Here are the central points in this change:

1. Metaphysics, and indeed philosophy itself, is finished. The earlier Heidegger had spoken of his efforts as a destruction of traditional ontology. But this destruction would itself be a form of ontology, which Heidegger called "fundamental ontology." Moreover, in the essay *What is Metaphysics?*, Heidegger thought of himself as still doing metaphysics, as the title itself of the essay shows. Twenty years later, in a foreword to this essay, he corrects this idea: his thought has gone beyond metaphysics altogether.

It should be remarked here, by the way, that when he speaks of metaphysics, and indeed of philosophy itself, as finished, he does not mean that thinking is finished; on the contrary, thought is merely in transition to a new historical epoch.

2. In *Being and Time* there had been two propositions that sounded paradoxical enough to provoke puzzlement and misunderstanding among many readers:

a. There is no Being (*Sein*) without man (*Dasein*); and
b. There is no "World" without man (*Dasein*).

At first glance these statements sound like the most extreme subjectivism, even solipsism. But of course Heidegger did not mean to assert that there would be no beings—no stars, planets, rocks, and trees—without man. Such a position would be a piece of colossal and arrogant philosophical egotism. Nor did he intend that the world, in the sense of physical universe, was the creation of man. His meaning, rather, was that Being as sheer presence—the Is of what-is—in its full temporal and historical concreteness is present only with man, or any other creature in the universe, if there be such, who is constituted by the possibilities of *Dasein*. Similarly, there can be no world, in Heidegger's sense of world—namely as the total field of possibilities that man inhabits—without man, or some creature like him. In short, Being and World reveal themselves phenomenologically as structural components of the human *Dasein*.

But with all subjectivistic misinterpretations aside, these two propositions still carry a very marked emphasis upon man as the center of the whole field of Being. He is the creator and destroyer of worlds, as has been repeatedly shown in history through the emergence and destruction of very different world-perspectives at different epochs. The picture of man, or one part of the picture, that emerges from *Being and Time* is that of a creature who actively creates himself through his own projects: man is a self-projecting project. This is the aspect of his thought which Sartre fastens on almost exclusively and develops to the point where the human project seems to detach itself altogether from the background of Being. Given some (though not all) the emphases in his earlier work, Heidegger himself might have trod this path. It is most significant that he did not, and that the later Heidegger diverges even more sharply from the Sartrian brand of existentialism.

The emphasis of the later Heidegger is not upon man as the active center of Being, but upon Being itself as that which perpetually claims man. Man is not only *ek-sistenz*—the creature who actively transcends himself—but also an *in-sistenz*—a being who, however he may stand beyond himself, must always stand within Being itself. Man is not the Lord of Being, a creature who transforms and bulldozes the world of nature; rather, he is the shepherd of Being: the creature who carefully tends and guards Being in all its revelations. The first is the technician, the second the poet.

3. Consequent upon this last change there is a de-emphasis upon all assertions of will. Activity and human self-assertion have been the distinguishing features of Western civilization since the time of the Renaissance. By contrast, the Oriental civilizations, and even the earlier civilizations in the West, have been characterized more by a passive acceptance rather than the active will to transform nature. This overwhelming emphasis upon activity has found expression in the various philosophies of the will that have emerged within the modern period and reached their culmination in Hegel and Nietzsche.

To all of this Heidegger is opposed. This opposition does not mean that he wishes flaccidity and torpor to replace the will to action. In any case, the wheels of a civilization cannot be turned back by simple fiat. Activity and the will to action have resulted in the colossal achievements of modern times that we could not easily dispense with even if we really wanted to. The point is that the tremendous fever of activity of modern man can cut him off from his roots and launch him into the void. Activity, activity at all costs—that almost becomes the watchword in some sectors of modern society. Heidegger refers to this tendency within modern thought as *"the will to will"*—implying by this phrase that it ceases to be a concern what end is willed so long as the will itself is operative. What the late Heidegger persistently opposes to this frenzied "will to will" is the notion of "letting-be": at some point in the midst of his feverish drive to action man must learn to let-be if he is not to twist truth into the total distortions of some ideological fanaticism. To let-be is to let oneself be claimed by Being in its sheer presence. This is why the voice of the poet is so necessary in this time of need, and also why, Heidegger says in echo of Hölderlin, the poet is deemed useless in a spiritually impoverished time. This emphasis of the late Heidegger is conveyed through the title of a little book published in 1959: *Gelassenheit*—surrender or abandonment. That is to say, Being discloses itself to man only when, having given up the fearful claims of the will to action, he surrenders himself to the presence and the mystery of things.

These changes in Heidegger's views developed over a rather considerable period—from the late nineteen-twenties through the forties. In a sense, then, there is no dramatic turning point; if we have applied such a label in connection with the two essays —*What is Metaphysics?* and *On the Nature of Cause*—our point is that in these two works he had pushed certain views too far to continue to maintain them within the philosophical framework that he had already built up, so that in time he had to change the framework.

For example, in *What is Metaphysics?* he ends by describing metaphysics as "the fundamental happening within human existence." This, of course, is not at all the traditional sense of metaphysics as a discipline that aims to study being as being, what-is just insofar as it is. Heidegger was led into this characterization of metaphysics because he set out to describe man's encounter with Being as a living and dramatic event in human existence rather than a mere conceptual cerebration about the most general and empty of concepts. But once he had gone so far as to depict metaphysics in this way, he was bound to recognize that his thinking was not metaphysical at all and had in fact gone beyond metaphysics.

It is a rather ironical little coincidence that the positivist Rudolf Carnap published a severe criticism of Heidegger's essay, demolishing it for errors in logic and grammar, under the title: "The Surpassing of Metaphysics" (*Die Überwindung der Metaphysik*). Much later Heidegger himself was to publish an essay with the same title. Needless to say, the two destructions of metaphysics—the positivistic and the Heideggerian—have very little in common beyond their title. For Heidegger, positivism is still all too metaphysical—and without knowing it.

What is Metaphysics?, delivered as his public inaugural lecture at Freiburg, is concerned mainly with discussing the nature of the Nothing (*das Nichts*). On the face of it this must strike common sense as a perfectly absurd thing for a savant to be discussing publicly before a company of savants. It must have been a strange and rather uncanny experience at that time for Heidegger's hearers, the faculty and scholars of Freiburg University, to hear a discourse on this unlikely subject—a discourse, moreover, into which the lecturer flung himself with such passion and abandonment. But philosophers and "common sense," despite the present insistence of British philosophers, are not at all points essential bedmates, or the "common sense" of the ancient Athenians would not have judged Socrates to be such a monster and condemned him to drink the hemlock just for being odd and different. Philosophers are a queer breed, in the eyes of common sense, and they must be allowed to treat whatever strange subjects their roving and restless spirit leads them to. The question of Non-Being, moreover, has had an ancient, if somewhat hidden, place in the tradition of philosophy, beginning with Plato's elaborate discussion in his dialogue "The Sophist." Plato is led into that discussion not out of some antic spirit of novelty or oddity, but because the themes of his thought essentially lead him there: it is necessary to understand Non-Being if one is to understand the finitude of the particular beings within the sensible world.

Heidegger's discussion of the Nothing follows just as essentially from the themes of his own thought. His examination of Nothingness is not a frivolous play on words, but a serious attempt to confront directly certain modes of experience that are inescapable in human life: the negative is always present in the positive, and indeed, to put it somewhat paradoxically, the positive posits the negative as its very ground. Moreover, in the way it differs from the traditional account of Non-Being, Heidegger's derives from his own radically different understanding of Being, and helps us to understand this latter.

The traditional position, founded by Aristotle and solidified through centuries of Scholasticism, had regarded all negative being as purely mental or conceptual. According to this tradition, being (ens, that-which-is) is divided into two kinds:

1. *Ens reale,* a real entity, which has positive existence within the world of things (*in rerum natura*), like this table on which I am writing, or the tree there outside the window; and

2. *Ens rationis,* an entity of reason, a merely conceptual entity, like a centaur or a round square.

Thus all real existence is positive existence; the negative has its place only in the human mind which can conceive and speak of things other than they actually are. The color non-green, for example, is not a real entity but a concept for all the colors that exist positively as yellow, blue, red, etc.—all colors other than green. And this holds true for all negative or privative modes of being: blindness, for example, as the absence of vision, is not itself a solid object in the world of things, and therefore is an *ens rationis*. It is, of course, a fact that a given individual may be blind, but the positive reality is a material growth over the eyes, a lesion in the optic nerve, or whatever other real entity, existing positively *in rerum natura*, makes impossible that form of *consciousness* that we call vision. There would not be such a thing as blindness if there were not consciousness; and this is the sense in which it would be listed as an *ens rationis*, an entity of reason.

So too, for example, with the *absence* of a dead person from a house where she has always lived with her family. That absence is not a real entity, like a physical body really present now within the house, however much that absence may haunt the survivors of the deceased. This absence is real only insofar as there are human minds that feel it. Hence it has reality only within consciousness; it is an *ens rationis*.

This distinction between the two modes of being is quite unexceptionable within the terms of its own analysis. For certain purposes of logical discourse it secures clarity and order; and it does get rid of certain intangible and somewhat ghostly entities that do not belong in the solid world of reality. It is, moreover, an analysis that is perfectly in line with one form of common sense.

Yet this disjunction between real and conceptual being harbors within itself the seed that blossoms as the dichotomy between object (*ens reale*) and subject (*ens cogitans*). Those who would make Descartes the villain for creating the Western dualism between subject and object ought to reconsider this judgment in the light of the traditional distinction between the two modes of being: the Cartesian dualism was already implicit within the traditional way in which Western philosophy conceived of Being. Real Being is what actually and positively exists, ultimately substances and their attributes; everything negative in experience—the so-called "negative facts" about whose status philosophers have so much debated—derives from human consciousness. But how then can the mind bring into reality something that is not found there without it? The mind becomes something intrinsically different and therefore alien from the substantial and positive things that exist outside it *in rerum natura*.

To understand the negative in experience we have then to go over to a radically different concept of Being. If we do not locate Being primarily in physical substances outside the mind, nor in the mind that apprehends data of which these physical objects may be the cause, but rather in the enveloping presence—the Is of what-is—that encompasses both thing and mind, then the disjunction between positive and negative being turns out to be provisional and useful but not absolute. This present situation in which I find myself surrounded by things is always penetrated through and through by the negative. This is particularly evident if we do not forget the temporal sense of the Is. This present moment, in which a world containing things and other people surrounds and grips me, is penetrated by the future, which is *not* yet, and torn from the past, which is *no* more. Thus the present, which traditionally has been taken as the real and actual point of time, is essentially constituted by two negatives. Therefore, the positive reality of the present is what it is through the negative of future and past that penetrate it. Moreover, the world as it presents itself is always indefinite and finite; and however far we may extend our horizon, beyond it there is always —Nothing. Readers of James Joyce's *Portrait of the Artist as a Young Man* may remember the passage where Stephen Dedalus as a young boy encounters Nothingness in trying to locate his own individual presence in the world:

> He turned to the flyleaf of the geography and read what he had written there: himself, his name and where he was.
>
>> Stephen Dedalus
>> Class of Elements
>> Clongowes Wood College
>> Sallins
>> County Kildare
>> Ireland
>> Europe
>> The World
>> The Universe

. . . Then he read the flyleaf from the bottom to the top till
he came to his own name. That was he: and he read down
the page again. What was after the universe? Nothing.

If this be deprecated as the mere naiveté of the child trying to
draw imaginary boundaries to the world, it is on the other hand
a naiveté that does not disfigure experience as it is given to us:
no matter how we try to locate ourselves within the world, we do
not escape the Nothing. We must always project the world
against the background of Nothingness, and we ourselves are a
human project within Nothingness. Heidegger, however, does
not follow the path of Joyce's young hero in trying to locate
Nothing as something that lies beyond the barriers of the world.
On the contrary, since however far we go in trying to fix our
place within the world the Nothing must be invoked, or if not
invoked then left unspoken at the end of our address, this Nothing is therefore essentially involved with and internal to our
human project of defining our world. The Nothing is not empty
space outside the universe, but a possibility within human
existence itself, insofar as this existence always projects its
world.

   This essential link between Nothing and World is also the link
between the two essays, *What is Metaphysics?* and *On the
Nature of Cause.* As the first is concerned with the Nothing, the
latter deals with man insofar as he seeks a support or ground for
his world. We have spoken of both essays as marking a turning
point in Heidegger's thought, but it is the second that more
clearly goes to an extreme toward which the early thought of
Heidegger had been leading. For what he does in the essay, *On
the Nature of Cause,* is to transform the traditional search by
philosophers for a First Cause or Ultimate Ground of the universe into a search by man for some ultimate support to his own
existence. Man is placed here more sharply and extremely at the
center of the world than in any other of Heidegger's writings.
For a thinker who has proclaimed that his thought eschews
every form of subjectivism, Heidegger's point of view here seems
strangely anthropocentric. It is, in fact, a form of Nietzschean
humanism: Man, freed from the search for God, appears as the
creator and destroyer of worlds. Man has taken the place of God.
The later Heidegger was to go on and repudiate every form of

humanism as incomplete and rootless, since it leaves unasked and unanswered the question in what man's humanity is to be rooted. For the later Heidegger, the figure of Nietzsche marks the end of Western philosophy, beyond which thought must slowly and patiently seek for new beginnings, because Nietzsche has gone to the very end and posed the question of humanism in its extreme and recisive form. But in this earlier essay, though the name of Nietzsche is not involved, the perspective seems thoroughly Nietzschean throughout.

To be sure, a good deal of this is *sotto voce*. The quiet and academic tone of the essay masks the audacity of Heidegger's proposals. He begins, as if he were only another plodding professor, by citing passages from Aristotle, Leibnitz, and other philosophers that have to do with the notion of principle, cause, or ground. Then, without the fanfare of any announcement, he has transformed the whole theme into his own key. The metaphysical quest for a First Cause of the cosmos is transformed into a question of the "fundamental ontology" of human existence: of the *Dasein* that has within itself the possibility of grounding its own existence—though it must always be a ground that is incomplete and therefore involves the negative. (It is from this essay that Sartre derives his own dictum that man seeks to be God—i.e., seeks to establish an absolute ground for his own existence, but must perpetually fail.) Man takes the place of God, as he must in every form of humanism when pushed to its limit. But man, as this Nietzschean creator of his world, must always move within the Void. This is something that Heidegger, however much he may have moved toward Nietzsche in the year 1929, did not forget. The figure of Hölderlin, his complementary guardian angel, was to remind him that this Void, before which Nietzsche attempts such exuberance and bravado, is also the dark night of the world from which the gods have fled.

At any rate, after this essay Heidegger's thought ceases to have any kinship with anything we might call humanism, whether this humanism call itself "existentialist" (Sartre) or not.

The wife of a new neighbor from up on the corner came down and walked up to my wife and started acting nice, which must have exhausted her.

This woman is one of the people I have to live with. Four years ago, in the true style of an amateur, I "moved out a bit." I moved onto a block with a lot of other people who live side by

The Sign in Jimmy Breslin's Front Yard

side in houses. Now, people are all right. Get them alone and they're pretty good. But put five of them together and they start conforming and after that all they are is trouble. Put sixteen families on the same block, the way it is on mine, and they become unbelievable. They are not people any more. They are enemies. On my block they sweep the lawn and have the waxer polish the front walk and all of them ring doorbells about kid fights and if everything isn't the same, and everybody doesn't worry about things that show, they bother you as an occupation. Anybody who has his own mind and moves out of a beautiful, anonymous Manhattan apartment and goes to a house on a block is crazy.

For four years now, so many of the neighbors have come to the door, or had their kids run up like stool pigeons to report some crime my kids committed, that now I sit at the front window and watch one of them come down the block and as he walks I dream of a big black car pulling up and three guys in big hats jumping out and breaking both my neighbor's legs.

It is this bad to live with these people, and this woman could get first on the whole block.

"I haven't gotten a chance to see you since the baby," the new one said. "How nice. This is, uh, your . . . ?"

She knew the number, she knows everything. She knew my take-home pay by the end of the first week she was on the block.

"Fifth," my wife said.

From *The World of Jimmy Breslin* by Jimmy Breslin. Copyright © 1963, 1964, 1965, 1966, 1967 by Jimmy Breslin. All rights reserved. Reprinted by permission of The Viking Press, Inc.

"How wonderful," she said. "And did you plan this one?"

"Oh, yes," my wife said sweetly. "Why, everybody I know plans their fifth baby."

The woman got mad and walked away. Which was great. And I was going to say something to her that she could tell her husband for me, but I didn't have the time. I had to stay on Walter, from the Dazzle Sign Painting Company, who was on my lawn and acting like a coward.

"Put it up, Walter," I told him.

"Not in the daylight," Walter said.

Walter had two big wooden posts and a lot of tools in his arms.

"An argument is an argument, but if you do this it lets everybody know that you're crazy," my wife says.

"Put it up, Walter," I said. "I want these people to read my sign right now."

Walter shook his head. Then he dropped everything and began jamming one of the posts into the lawn. My wife ran inside the house. She is the former Rosemary Dattolico and she is very Italian. She likes knives on black nights, not big posters in broad daylight.

"Let's go, Walter," I said, and Walter, from the Dazzle Sign Painting Company, put in both the stakes and tacked the sign on, and when he was finished, right there on the lawn was the most beautiful sign you ever saw.

It was about three feet high and five feet wide and it was in three bright colors and it read real good. On the top, in two lines of big red upper-case letters, the sign said:

SORRY TO MAKE YOU LOOK AT THIS BECAUSE I KNOW HOW TIRED YOU PEOPLE GET MOVING YOUR LIPS WHEN YOU READ

Underneath this, in smaller, but still real big blue letters, was a line which said: PEOPLE I'M NOT TALKING TO THIS YEAR.

The line was centered. Right under it, in neat columns, like a service honor roll, was the name of everybody who lives on my block. Everybody. All the couples, all the mothers-in-law, and all the kids. Every single person alive on my block had his name printed on that sign by Walter, from the Dazzle Sign Painting

Company. And at the end of the list of names, I had Walter put "Dugan" for the bread man and "Stylon" for the dry-cleaning guy and "Borden's" for the fat milkman I don't like.

The best was at the bottom. In clear orange italics, the little passage said: "*I also am announcing a special service for people who ring my bell to tell me what my children did. This service includes a man who answers the doorbell. Why don't you come and ring my bell and see what happens to you?*"

Walter and I stepped back to look at the sign. The white pasteboard looked nice in the sunlight. It was the greatest sign I ever saw.

"Nobody ever had a sign like this," Walter said. "Nobody. I paint 'Fire Sale' and 'Prices Slashed' and for gin mills I do 'Under New Management' or 'Sunday Cocktail Hour,' but I never in my life done a sign like this."

"Beautiful," I said. I stood back and admired it. This was my message, my own personal message to everybody on the block. How could you find a better way to put it across? For a year now, my wife has been hissing at the neighbors, "He's writing a novel about the block and you're in it because he hid a tape recorder under your kitchen table." But this sign of mine beat any book. And even those Burma Shave signs—"She went wild/When he went woolly"—they never read as good as my personal sign.

"The sign costs $27.50," Walter said.

"Walter, it's worth $100," I said. "Look at that." I grabbed his arm. "Look at that woman up the block, Walter. She just saw the sign. She's dying to come up here and see it, I bet. Look at her, Walter. She's dying. Wait'll she comes up here and sees what it says. Can you imagine the face on her when she does that, Walter? Boy, this takes care of them. Why don't you stay around so we can both look out the window and watch?"

"I think you're sick," Walter said.

"No, I'm not, I just hate those people."

I hate them all. In the whole area where we live, I hate them all. Once I thought we got a break. A big gangster from Brooklyn moved out and tried to live quietly with his two Cadillacs parked in front of the house and his pearl-gray hat stuck on his head even when he came out for the milk. But the guy was in the neighborhood only three months and then he got arrested and he was all over the papers. People began detouring two blocks so they wouldn't go near his house, and the fellow stayed holed up so much that you never could meet him. He finally moved, and left me with all the garbage. One thing you can bet, I wouldn't have had Walter, from the Dazzle, put the gangster's name on my sign.

After I had watched my sign for a while, and Walter left with his truck from the Dazzle, I went into the kitchen and had coffee and waited until this friend of mine called Bad Eddie showed up. Bad Eddie is called this because he doesn't do anything nice, and I had things I wanted him to do to my neighbors that aren't nice.

"There's a lot of people out on the block," Bad Eddie said.

"That's good, we're going to get rid of them all," I said.

"Oh, dear Lord, look at this," my wife said. "They're coming from the other block, too."

"They could get hurt, too, and I wouldn't complain," I said.

Then I got down to business with Bad Eddie. "Now look," I said, "we're going to do this big-time. We'll get white mice and put them in someone's house. That'll fix them. Now, look out the window. See that guy up there in his back yard? Walking around the bushes? We don't even mess with him. He goes."

"What do you mean, he goes?" Bad Eddie said.

"Any way you want to do it," I said. "But he goes. We're going to do this right, just like Capone. We'll use mice, threats, beatings, anything we want."

Bad Eddie did not look up from his coffee.

"Don't that joint of his give him any vacation?" he asked my wife. "He needs a rest." Nobody answered.

"It's going to be crowded out there," my wife said. "Almost like the day Jason Robards and Lauren Bacall were across the street."

That was the biggest day in the history of the block and the people did just what you'd expect them to do. They acted like jerks. They walked back and forth, then back and forth again, or they stood on the sidewalk and gaped at Mr. Robards and his wife. They were visiting their accountant, who lives across the street and doesn't talk to me, but they should have charged admission for coming out in the front of the house.

When they left, the block went back to normal. Which means all that ever happens is some grown man, pushed out by his wife with an adolescent's mind, comes up to the door and tells you, "Your Jimmy tried to strangle my son the other day." And you tell him, "I'm awfully sorry. I'm awfully sorry Jimmy messed up the job and didn't kill your kid."

Now, for the rest of this day, I sat over coffee with Eddie and plotted doing things to people, and, outside, the people stopped to look at the sign and they stumbled through the reading and then went on. And in one day everybody got my personal message.

They never did get Bad Eddie's message because he spent the whole day sitting at the kitchen table and shaking his head and when he left he only said one thing. "Get yourself a good rest," Bad Eddie said.

Since then the sign has come down, but it's in the garage and it can go up any time, just like a flag. That is, if there is a garage left. As a precaution against a slow real-estate market when we find something in town and put the house up for sale, I had Marvin the Torch over one day. He is a man who burns down things for a living.

He went out in the front and dug a fingernail into the wood and looked around.

"Not too good," he said. "The wood is green. Too green. To do this sure, I might have to load it up, and that would mean taking out half the block."

"Don't let that stand in your way," I told him. The new one was right up the block looking at us.

ANDREW KOPKIND

Robert Kennedy is on to something. He hovers over it like a pig in the *Perigord* sniffing a truffle. It is just below the surface; he can't quite see it; he doesn't know its size or shape or worth or even what it's called. He only knows it's there, and he is going to get it.

Where does he look? Among the grape-pickers on strike in

He's a Happening: Robert Kennedy's Road to Somewhere

central California, in Cloth Market Square in Cracow, on the Ole Miss campus, in a Senate hearing room. And always with the same single-minded, almost frightening intensity. Perhaps the young know what it is; Kennedy spends an inordinate amount of time at schools and colleges talking with them. Maybe the poor know; he studies the condition of the urban ghettoes. Is it in Latin America? He'll go and see. Is it in South Africa? Get him a visa.

Whatever the object of his quest, Kennedy is unlikely to find it. He is looking not for a thing, but for a happening—what is happening to politics, to people. "In the 1930's, just going to college was a struggle," he said last week, feet up on his cluttered desk, drinking hot tea late in the afternoon of a hot day. "Then the war in the 'forties, then the Korean war. So now there's time, and people have more of a realization of things. When you obtain knowledge it creates internal problems."

Everything Kennedy says about other people has an auto-biographical ring. That may be the characteristic of a good novelist, but not frequently the mark of the customary politician. But then no one argues that he is an ordinary politician. He is an elusive phenomenon, even more than the other Kennedys. He is not a liberal or a conservative or a hawk or a dove or a machine politician or an independent. The favorite journalistic game these days is to examine his motives. Is he making a cal-

From *The New Republic* (April 2, 1966), 18–22. Reprinted with the permission of *The New Republic*, copyright 1966, Harrison-Blaine of New Jersey, Inc.

culated, almost diabolical drive for the Presidency? Is he on
some joy ride in politics, doing and saying the first thing that
pops into his head?

Neither question elicits the answers that make sense in
politics. Certainly he wants to be President, and he hardly can
help weighing his actions on the scale of long-range goals. But
the choices are wide open, and Kennedy is opting more and
more for the high-risk, high-gain issue. Nothing in the book of
common political practice demands that he approve of blood
donations for the Viet Cong, that he champion the grape-strikers'
cause, that he criticize the Justice Department's refusal to allow
burial of a Communist in Arlington cemetery. He does not have
to make diplomatic trouble by going to South Africa. He can
talk about the "urban crisis" without suggesting that whole
blocs of ghetto Negroes migrate to the suburbs. He could have
addressed the rally in Mississippi without belittling Ross Barnett.
He can involve himself in automobile safety without bludgeoning
the president of General Motors at Senate hearings. Yet he has
done all those things. He thinks some of them have done him
political harm. He finds the pain delicious.

He can afford the luxury of the free rein because he has a
precious commodity—time. Nothing much is likely to happen
to him for five years, maybe more. He neither needs nor wants
to harden the lines around his constituency. His speech recognizing the stake of the Viet Cong in any Vietnam settlement won
him exaggerated enthusiasm from student radicals and "peace-
niks," but he will not be their champion. He commands the
hearts of the Irish Catholics from the 1960 campaign, but he is
not their property; he may even offend some of them with talk
of birth control and divorce law reform. A current theory has
Kennedy grabbing the "liberals" in the Democratic Party from
under the nose of Vice President Hubert Humphrey, like so many
apples. But what will he do with them? No Kennedy carries the
mantle of "liberalism" comfortably.

Kennedy is not yet capturing a bloc, or putting together a
coalition, or hewing out a program. What is happening is less
dramatic: around him are gathering people in government and
outside who in the very loosest sense constitute a Kennedy
Party. It does not caucus, and very few in it would be able to

identify themselves as members. There are a few senators, several old New Frontiersmen scattered about Washington, and many more "exiles," in one sense or another in law offices, universities or businesses around the country. There is no "party line," or at least nothing in manifesto form. But the Kennedy Party is, as one Democratic senator said, "the only alternative power source to that famous Consensus. If you're against Johnson, you've got to be for it"—or be a Republican.

As the informal party leader—as the only reason for its existence—Kennedy has peculiar credits and liabilities. His name makes slavish zombies out of otherwise rational humans. The movie-star aura that gave the White House something of the flavor of the MGM back lot during the early 'sixties has settled on him. More than that, he radiates power: for three years he was at the very heart of it (closer by far than any mere Vice President) and he is changed for the experience.

Robert Kennedy's past, and to a certain extent his manner, will always haunt him. In the early 'fifties he was a committed McCarthyite. Then he became so engrossed in the prosecution of Jimmy Hoffa that he lost sight of some refinements discernible to other Americans who care deeply about individual rights. Neither the politics nor the personality that Robert Kennedy expressed in those years fits the expectations of those who are now his fondest followers. So they get rid of what doubts linger by postulating a theory of "flux." Kennedy's life, an old associate suggests, is discontinuous. Other men may develop in an orderly, serial way; Kennedy's career is seen in episodes side by side. There was the Senate investigating episode, the Justice Department episode, and now the senatorial episode. Like Picasso's various periods, they do follow logically one from the other.

In his current incarnation, Kennedy is cast in the role of a "presidential" Democrat from New York State—the first since Franklin Roosevelt. He comes to Washington with a lot of political linen laid out for him. It is taken for granted that he will be an aggressively "liberal" senator; New York does that to its elected officials. Besides, his colleague in the Senate is a Republican, Jacob Javits, who is constantly pushing Kennedy to more aggressive positions. Kennedy has to be strong on civil rights, dedicated to urban development, for Israel and against Arabs, for reapportionment, welfare, education, housing—and so on down the line.

But as a very junior senator, Kennedy can be experimental. He can test out ideas without the sense of responsibility that he had as part of a national administration, or that older senators sometimes feel as middling-to-elder statesmen. He can be a "good Democrat" and support the Great Society programs to the hilt. That would be enough to ensure his reelection, and with everything else working for him, enough to keep him alive as a presidential candidate.

But the wilder tacks he takes—the sudden, spontaneous, half-understood acts of calculated risk—define the Kennedy Party. It puts Robert Kennedy apart from the politics of his own youth, and even some distance from the New Frontier. Someone calls it "post-Stevenson politics," which does not provide much of a definition. It is what comes after rationalized public welfare, full employment, desegregation and the sensible conduct of a Cold War. It deals with an age of systems-analysis, ghetto warfare, labor and corporate centralization, and post-postwar diplomacy.

Kennedy is not a conceptualizer; at least, he does not talk much about broad concepts. But he seems to have an intuitive sense of the changes going on in the country, and he responds to them. Just before he flew to the grape-pickers' strike he asked an assistant, "Why am I going there?" There were places where farm workers got lower wages, or had worse living conditions, or more oppression. But that strike is perhaps the definitive labor war of the decade—and Kennedy felt it before he understood it. The point was that the workers in the grape fields do not want just better wages or conditions, but *recognition*, as a source of power, as a community, as people capable of making their own decisions. To get it, they have to fight some elements of big labor as well as the big growers. It did not, as it turned out, take Kennedy long to grasp it all. He tore into the growers in two days of hearings, and won the confidence of the strikers.

He knows that "conscience" is becoming a major element in political behavior. He likes to quote an inscription which he says was found on an Egyptian pyramid: "No one was angry enough to speak out." Last week he said, "There's a sharp difference between this generation and the last. Young people today have that motivation—idealism and dissatisfaction." He has an affinity for protest, if not a taste for protesters. He likes people who are making "that effort"—"whatever their particular politics happen to be." Kennedy denounces "easy solutions" in many speeches, but more than that he seems to dislike solutions in general. Still, there are distant goals. "I'd be discouraged if I thought it was all just an exercise," he says. But certainty? He quotes Learned Hand approvingly in praise of "the spirit which is not too sure it is right.'"

The Outsider

Kennedy's position in the Senate reflects these intuitions. Many of his colleagues get the idea that he doesn't think much of Congress at all. "He's a visitor, a boarder," a senatorial aide said. Unlike his brother, Teddy, who is working his way into the Senate "establishment," Robert Kennedy remains almost totally outside. He does not defer to older senators; he sometimes insults them. During one session of the car-safety hearings in February, Kennedy exploded at Republican Sen. Carl Curtis for not letting Ralph Nader, a leading critic of the automobile industry, give his full testimony.

"What I don't understand is why you don't let Mr. Nader read his statement to find out if in fact—" Kennedy growled at Curtis.

"I have no objection to his reading his statement," Curtis replied.

"Then maybe we would understand his position," Kennedy went on. "I don't know how you can reach a conclusion about his position, First you admit you haven't read his book; and, secondly, you haven't heard his testimony. Why don't you listen to his testimony and then criticize?"

"I have no objection to hearing his testimony," Curtis reiterated meekly, "but when he loses me with—"

"With big words?" Kennedy smiled.

That's not very nice for a junior senator. But Kennedy asks few favors from senators; it was he who finally had his brother, Teddy, withdraw the nomination of Francis X. Morrissey from the confirmation fight over a judgeship last fall in the Senate.

Congress is too slow, too ineffectual, too deliberative for Robert Kennedy. It is not where the action is. Like John Kennedy, he feels it is somewhat of an anachronism, that the affairs of a vast and complex society cannot be dealt with by such a windy, old-fashioned collection of egotists.

To delve into the effect of the assassination on Robert Kennedy is to indulge too much in pocketbook Freud. Many of those close to him think it did not drastically change his way of life, but reinforced certain tendencies—his fatalism about politics, his alienation from establishments, his sense of the importance of individual acts of conscience. It was obvious to everyone who saw him that it intensified the brooding, the pained introspection that for a while became a public manner. Slowly, that is changing. His friends say that he can now make almost casual remarks about President Kennedy—even little jokes, with a touch of the macabre.

The political effects of the assassination on Robert Kennedy's life are as difficult to sort out as the psychological effects. It quickly made him a leading contender for the Presidency, but at the same time put new obstacles in his way. He certainly wants the office, but he is not going to go about it in the same way John Kennedy did. "One of the questions we ask," an aide says, "is what the political consequences of a speech will be. But it is very rarely the first question." "You have to remember," another adviser warns, "that no presidential campaign can be planned more than two years in advance. There are too many variables before that."

In the normal course of things, Kennedy can do nothing about the Presidency until 1972, and it may turn out to be later than that. The "scenarios" which some people have constructed involving a move in 1968 seem to have little foundation in foreseeable realities. In the meantime, the Kennedy Party at best can become a focus for disaffection in varying degrees with the Johnson Administration.

Kennedy himself is less than enthralled with the Johnson Administration; it is clearly not his style. But neither is he about to begin guerrilla warfare against it. Relations with his successor at the Justice Department, Attorney General Katzenbach, are under some strain. Kennedy is justly proud of his own record at Justice; he sometimes feels that Katzenbach responds too quickly to White House pressure, and has little taste for innovation. Kennedy disliked Katzenbach's stand against the burial of Robert Thompson, a Communist, at Arlington. He disagreed with Katzenbach's arguments against providing legal aid to poor defendants at the very beginning of criminal cases—in the police station. The Administration repays such opposition with small unkindnesses: Kennedy was conspicuously excluded from a recent White House meeting with senators interested in judicial matters.

It is doubtful whether Kennedy will ever express publicly anything less than support for Johnson. It is not merely good politics and good taste; Kennedy knows Johnson's problems and the difficulties of the Presidency. But others are becoming more alienated. The war has cut deeply into the natural affection the New Frontier had for the Great Society. And the Kennedy Party could be an anti-war government-in-exile.

It already is a home for many of the New Frontier officials who were ripped untimely from their jobs. There is a kind of "shadow cabinet" which Kennedy uses both for ideas and to a lesser extent for political activity. Burke Marshall, the former head of the Justice Department's Civil Rights Division and now general counsel at IBM, has the civil rights portfolio. Roswell Gilpatric, former Undersecretary of Defense, is a key source on strategy. Richard Goodwin, a former White House speechwriter, does work on foreign policy (he helped write the speech on Vietnam and the Viet Cong), and so does Arthur Schlesinger Jr. Kennedy has close ties with Robert McNamara and Orville Freeman, and he gets help from Theodore Sorensen on speeches (both Sorensen and Schlesinger are useful as gagwriters, among other things, but Schlesinger is considered the better of the two). Schlesinger actually writes few speeches that are delivered as written.

At a different level, Kennedy is developing a cadre of "idea men" as distinct from personal advisers. Some of them are New Frontier holdovers, former members of "Kennedy's guerrillas," a middle-echelon network of government officials with a special loyalty to the attorney general in those days. Some of them are still in federal agencies: Leonard Duhl, a psychiatrist and social planner now at Housing and Urban Development. Richard Boone, formerly head of Community Action at the Poverty Program, is another ex-guerrilla. Now he is director of the Citizens Crusade Against Poverty, a Walter Reuther-sponsored private antipoverty action group. A few journalists are close to Kennedy; most prominent is Joseph Kraft, the columnist. Since his rather abrupt entry into New York, Kennedy has developed another level of advisers around his state: he talks with Dr. Eugene McCarthy of Columbia University on health problems, and through him Kennedy has made contact with the "pro-Medicare" doctors (many of them teachers) in New York. He admires James Allen, the state Commissioner of Education, and solicits his ideas on school problems. Through Alan Campbell, of the Maxwell School of Public Administration at Syracuse, he has plugged into a vigorous group of upstate intellectuals.

Kennedy is playing New York politics cool. He manages to stay detached from the identifiable factions, and yet encourages and often supports them all as the need arises and conditions allow. He is more than courteous to the Reform Democrats in New York; they almost feel wanted by him. Last month, he spent a day at a conference on problems of underdeveloped nations, sponsored by Rep. William Fitts Ryan, the reform Democrat *par excellence*. He calls on reform leaders; recently he invited one to his hotel room and greeted the astounded visitor in his undershorts. The truth is that everyone needs him more than he needs them.

Kennedy has a small organization of his own in New York, presided over by Stephen Smith, in the tradition of Kennedy brothers-in-law. John Burns, the state party chairman, was a Kennedy choice. But there is not yet anything like a Kennedy machine in the state. "He could hand-pick the candidates for any office," a New Yorker said, "but he's staying aloof."

Who Are the New Boys?

The point is that Kennedy does not have to rule New York with a heavy hand. It is his own turf, and no one is in sight to challenge him. Elsewhere around the country, he has not begun to make new contacts. He is naturally close to old friends from 1960; after all, he cultivated them, and they will maintain a certain allegiance to him. In one way, that could prove to be something of a liability. Kennedy may personally be attuned to new political forces—the challengers of the big-city machines, for instance—but if he has only the old boys, his activities will be tightly circumscribed. His advisers say, however, that there is time enough to form new alliances, and it is in fact the part of wisdom to wait out the inevitable conflicts before moving in.

In the meantime, the Kennedy Party will concentrate on ideas rather than men, on creating a political mood rather than building a political organization. Already the mood is beginning to take shape. It began with the speeches Kennedy made last year on nuclear proliferation. He suggested that the US join with the Soviet Union, and China, if possible, to oppose the spread of atomic weapons. There were cries of "appeasement," but Kennedy's point was made: if ideology prohibits diplomacy, change the ideology. He continually pressed the Johnson Administration on a Vietnam settlement. He criticized the President for regarding the war as "purely a military problem." It was one of the factors which forced the Administration to devote at least some energies to "social reform." Then he spoke out against bombing North Vietnam. Finally, in his famous statement on the Viet Cong, he asked the President to recognize that a settlement in Vietnam could not come without participation, at some level, of the rebel forces.

The storm which the speech—and the subsequent "clarifications" which followed it—caused, has not yet subsided. Kennedy is said to think that he made many mistakes during those first days—not for what he said, but because he was unprepared to deal with the reaction. The problem was in his analysis of the nature of political tempers all around. One of his advisers likens the affair to the meeting Kennedy had, after the Birmingham civil rights conflict in 1963, with James Baldwin and a collection of well-known Negro public figures in New York. Kennedy's instincts in arranging the meeting were good, and again ahead of the game (it is hard to imagine anyone in the White House or the Cabinet today even thinking of such a notion). But he did not comprehend what was going on in the Negro world (very few whites did in those days) and when Baldwin said later, "he doesn't understand us," he was right.

"I made the speech because I thought there was something that was worth saying," Kennedy said last week. "We hadn't really discussed with any completeness or thoroughness the heart of what our policy should be. I made some mistakes in handling it. I think it was unpopular politically. But I would do it all over again if I had to."

What Kennedy only sensed about the Vietnam speech was that he was establishing a position of opposition, not presenting a program for enactment. When the inevitable political counter-attack came from the Administration, Kennedy saw how vulnerable he was. All the big guns were against him. He retreated to avoid destruction. The principal effect of the act—to legitimize criticism and make alternative policies in Vietnam thinkable—was somewhat diluted.

Breaking Up the Ghetto

Kennedy has worked hard on education and civil rights legislation, but his principal domestic enthusiasms so far were contained in three speeches delivered in New York in late January. He called them "A Program for the Urban Crisis"; they included major proposals for housing, education and employment for the poor, in particular, Negroes. But the most intriguing part of the speeches was the analysis of the problem of the poor. Kennedy went further than any major political figure has done so far in seeing what underlies the "breakup of the Negro family" (as the President referred to it in his Howard University speech last June) and the "lack of motivation" (as the poverty program officials call it) of Negroes.

"The deeper part," Kennedy said, ". . . is in the gulf which separates the Negro from the white power structure that governs him, and in the failure of the Establishment to afford him full participation in shaping the governmental services he receives. For 300 years the Negro has been a nation apart, a people governed by a repression that has been softened to the point where it is now only a massive indifference. The Watts riots were as much a revolt against official indifference, an explosion of frustration at the inability to communicate and participate, as they were an uprising about inferior jobs and education and housing."

No one in the Administration yet is talking out loud about eliminating the ghetto, but Kennedy said, "Wiping out the ghetto is essential to the future of the Negro and of the city itself. It is essential because the ghetto is not a neighborhood. Rather it is a vast undifferentiated mass. . . . If we can break down the massive housing segregation of the ghetto, we can break down the other forms of segregation which it has caused. The ghetto, for example, makes it practically impossible to achieve meaningful racial balance in the schools. . . . The existence of smaller Negro and integrated neighborhoods throughout the metropolitan area would, on the other hand, permit the achievement of improved racial balance."

If Kennedy understands the powerlessness of ghetto-dwellers, he knows more about America than any of his Senate colleagues. It is still problematic whether he can translate such feelings into political action. He probably will not be a major framer of legislation. As John Kennedy did, he will use the Senate as a sounding board, dropping in and out as the occasions arise (he has spent more time outside than in Washington this year). Kennedy has his friends inside the Senate (his brother, Senators Tydings, Jackson, McGovern, Bayh and a few others, such as Church and Clark, with whom he often works), but it is the loosest of all factions. Kennedy is too much of a loner to start a Senate club. He has admirers on the House side, but no cohesive following there, either (Humphrey, on the other hand, had his own House club).

In the next few years, Kennedy's biggest problem will be to convince people of the significance of his new "episode." "Long ago," one Washington politician mused recently, "Robert Kennedy discovered that no one was going to like him, in the sense that people liked Roosevelt, or Stevenson, or Jack Kennedy. So he decided to make people follow him because of the power of his ideas, or the rightness of his positions." Even so, Kennedy still has to project his own intuitions over long distances to the voting public. Communication—which most politicians find so easy—is his biggest "hang-up."

At times it seems he can talk winningly only to young people. "Given a choice, he'll pick up an appearance at a school rather than at a civic club," an aide says. He begins to glow with a young audience, but he rarely gets past cool charm with adults. More cynical politicians suppose that he is carefully cultivating the new generation in hopes that he will win their votes in a half-dozen years. There may be some of that; at a Washington high school he told a student who asked when he would run for President, "when you're old enough to vote for me."

Pope John died yesterday.

A holy and good man: and he was both because he was first of all a *man*—that is to say, a fully human being. This is the great meaning of his papacy, of the Council, of *Pacem in Terris*. Being a man, he was concerned with other men. (One felt that Pope Pius XII, for example, was more concerned with *principles*.)

Pope John XXIII

Pope John was not just a humanist. He was deeply concerned with the humanity which he shared with his fellow man. *Pacem in Terris* is not theology. It simply says that war is a sin because it is *inhuman*.

Certainly everybody recognized this and responded to the Encyclical sincerely. Even the Russians. In fact one feels that some of those who responded least to this deep humaneness of the Pope were men close to him in Rome. It is a shameful but nevertheless understandable fact.

May he rest in peace, this great good Father, whom I certainly loved, who had been personally very kind to me. I do not think he has stopped being a father to us and to me. If we last long enough, we will canonize him. I do not hesitate to ask his intercession now.

Curious effect of newspaper stories of Pope John's death read over and over in the refectory. They are all really one story, but from different papers, different sources, different angles. The total effect of hearing the same material over and over, the same details, repeated each time in a slightly new arrangement, is like a story by Robbe-Grillet. One is left with a strange, neutral sense of dreamlike objectivity. The cast-iron bed, the thick red carpet, the four relatives from Sotto il Monte, the bed table with the black telephone and bottles of medicine. The thick red carpet to muffle the sound of feet. The cast-iron bed. Relatives from Sotto il Monte, Xaverio, Giuseppe, (one whose name I forget), and Assunta, who had been a nurse. The Pope was dying in a cast-iron bed. His sister who had been a nurse was by his (cast-iron) deathbed. Since she had been a nurse she knew what to do. Xaverio and Giuseppe and the other one were not nurses, but they also knew what to do. They sat there. The Pope called his relatives to his bedside. It was a cast-iron bed. There was a rosary on the bed table. The Pope called his relatives. They sat there. Assunta was formerly a nurse. There was a thick red carpet so that when the relatives came closer the sound of their footsteps was not heard. They sat there. The Pope said: "Think of Papa and Mama." He said it in Bergamesque dialect. His relatives were from Sotto il Monte, near Bergamo. Assunta dipped a cloth in a silver bowl of water and mopped the Pope's brow, and the newspapermen knew by this that she had truly been a nurse. They all told about her dipping a cloth in the silver bowl and mopping the Pope's brow. "Think of Papa and Mama," said the Pope. They sat there and thought. The four relatives were there. They sat in four red-damask chairs. The black telephone did not ring. A rosary on the table. The silver bowl . . . The Pope died in a cast-iron bed.

Poor Pope John: none of this idiot mishmash can change his greatness, he suffers nothing from it: even this bug-eyed surrealistic view of his death chamber is somehow great and dignified (much more so than the macabre details—the photographer, etc.—at the death of Pope Pius. One of the first things Pope John had done as Pope had been to protest against the vulgarity and indecency of those who permitted these indiscretions at the death of his predecessor.)

Nothing can change the fact that this was a holy death, a deeply Christian death, a death that was not a pseudo-death and a pontifical cliché. The world knows it, and understands.

ALBERT GOLDMAN

Several months ago in Chicago, the comedian Lenny Bruce was convicted of obscenity and sentenced to one year in jail and a $1000 fine. Shortly afterward, he was also convicted by a Los Angeles court of narcotics possession. These convictions, currently being appealed, are by no means the only run-ins Bruce has had with the authorities. Since returning from his world

The Comedy of Lenny Bruce

tour last year, Bruce has been arrested seven times in all: twice in Los Angeles on suspicion of narcotics possession; four times for obscenity (he was acquitted in San Francisco and Philadelphia); and once for assault in Van Nuys, California. Earlier, he had been twice barred from entering England; on the first occasion, he was turned back within an hour at the airport, when authorities simply denied him a work permit. The second time, entering England via Ireland, and bearing with him affidavits attesting to his probity, sobriety, and general moral earnestness, Bruce was allowed to stay the night, only to become on the following day the subject of emergency intervention by the Home Secretary, who declared his presence not to be "in the public interest." On these occasions, as in previous encounters with the agencies of law-enforcement, Bruce showed himself courteous, even disarmingly so, to his antagonists and a trifle bewildered, it seemed, at the havoc he could create merely by turning up. He boarded a plane and went back home.

Bruce has been called "blasphemous," "obscene," and "sick" —and not only in the expected quarters (Walter Winchell, Robert Ruark, assorted *Variety* pundits, etc.) but by critics like Benjamin DeMott and Kenneth Alcott. On the other hand, of course, there are equally sophisticated critics like Robert Brustein and Kenneth Tynan who have arrived at opposite conclusions, finding Bruce not only essentially "healthy," but the physician, as it were, for the illness from which all of us are suffering.

From *Commentary*, 36 (October, 1963), 312–317. Reprinted from *Commentary*, by permission; copyright © 1963 by the American Jewish Committee and the author.

While certain spokesmen for an American "underground" have claimed him for their own, Bruce has also earned a vast popular following, far exceeding the limits of any coterie. Long before his present notoriety, indeed, he was one of the most successful nightclub performers in the country, earning on the average of $5,000 a week and with his record-album sales totaling well over $100,000. Fellow comics are among Bruce's keenest admirers, and, if not always admitting their debt to him publicly, frequently reveal it by imitation. Among his most articulate disciples are the British social satirists of groups like "The Establishment" and "Beyond the Fringe," who have been even more unstinting than the Americans in acknowledging both his fascination and his influence.

What, then, explains Bruce's unique effect? Certainly, his impact cannot be attributed to his material alone. By now, so completely have the so-called "sick" comics caught on—and so quickly has the authentic radical satire of a few years ago been rendered innocuous by sheer acceptance and then imitation— that it no longer requires daring, originality, or courage to attack sacred cows like integration, Mother's Day, the Flag. Such things are done, albeit in diluted form, virtually on every network. Yet Bruce seems immune from that permissiveness that is in the end perhaps more subversive of true protest than censorship. Uniquely among members of his profession (and matched in others perhaps only among jazz musicians), Bruce continues to shock, to infuriate, to be the subject on the one hand of a passionate and almost unprecedented advocacy, and on the other of a constant surveillance amounting to persecution, so that today, at the height of his drawing power, it is doubtful whether a club in New York would dare to book him.

Bruce slouches onstage in a crumpled black raincoat ("dressed for the bust," as he confidingly informs the audience, in anticipation of arrest); pale, unshaven, with long black sideburns— beat, raffish, satanic. Ordering the lights up, he surveys the house: "Yeah. You're good-looking. You got lotsa bread." He pauses. "Good looking chicks always got lotsa bread. That's a hooker syllogism." Having opened on this amiable note, he abruptly switches his tone and manner to lull the audience into temporary security, then launches into an apparently off-the-cuff discourse on themes of the moment:

> You know? Liberals will buy anything a bigot writes. They really support it. George Lincoln Rockwell's probably just a very knowledgeable businessman with no political convictions whatsoever. He gets three bucks a head working mass rallies of nothing but angry Jews, shaking their fists and wondering why there are so many Jews there.

Even in this relatively minor bit, the distinctive qualities of Bruce's satire are in evidence—it is authenticaly shocking and nihilistic to a degree that is not altogether apparent at first. To make fun of liberals these days is an act of conventional daring; to make fun of George Lincoln Rockwell these days is an act of slightly less conventional daring; but to make fun of a "proper" moral response to George Lincoln Rockwell constitutes the violation of a taboo. What Bruce is doing by finding in George Lincoln Rockwell an ordinary businessman out for the main chance, goes far beyond the modish cliché of "the guilt we all share"—it amounts to an implication of normality itself in the monstrous. Perhaps this accounts for the slightly hysterical quality of the laughter that his performances usually elicit. It is helplessness in the face of a truly nihilistic fury that makes the parody currently fashionable in the nightclubs and the off-Broadway theaters seem safe and cautious.

Bruce's vision forbids the smallest hint of self-congratulation, allows no comfortable perch from which the audience can look complacently down on the thing satirized. Even his "conventional" routines take a bizarre and violent course which transforms them into something quite different from mere parody. There is one, for instance, in which an "ordinary white American" tries to put a Negro he has met at a party at ease. The predictable blunders with their underlying viciousness ("That Joe Louis was a hell of a fighter . . . Did you eat yet? I'll see if there's any watermelon left . . .") are within the range of any gifted satirist with his heart in the right place; but Bruce gives the screw an added turn by making the protagonist, besotted with temporary virtue, a forthright and entirely ingenuous Jew-hater as well—sincerely making common cause with the Negro.

This is closer to surrealism than to simple farce, a fantasy on the subject of bigotry far more startling than a merely perfect sociological rendition of the accents of race hatred would have been. And as the routine proceeds, the fantasy gets wilder and wilder, with the white man becoming more and more insinuatingly confidential in his friendliness ("What is it with you guys? Why do you always want to ——— everybody's sister? . . . You really got a big ——— on you, huh? Hey, could I see it?") and the Negro becoming progressively stiffer and more bewildered.

Similarly, Bruce has a fairly conventional routine that might have been dreamed up in its general outline fifteen years ago by a stand-up comedian from the Lower East Side, but that he pushes to what would have been unthinkable lengths fifteen years ago. The performer, in the guise of himself, encounters a "typical" Jewish couple while on a Midwestern tour; they are at first shy and admiring, until the inevitable question is asked and the discovery is made—Bruce is Jewish; then their respect and timidity give way first to a slightly insulting familiarity and finally to overt, violent aggression. The routine which, again, would once have been played for folksiness, becomes bizarre and disturbing when Bruce uses it to expose within the couple depths of prurient malevolence far in excess of their apparent "human" failings. The climax is an orgy of vituperation in the familial mode that becomes a glaring and devastating comment on Jewish life in America.

Until a few years ago, this kind of humor had never been seen in a night club or theater. It appeared to be completely original, yet obviously it mined a rich, seemingly inexhaustible vein and was, moreover, enforced by a highly finished technique. Critics responded to Bruce at first as though he were *sui generis*, a self-created eccentric of genius without discernible origins. Yet nothing could be further from the truth. What Lenny is saying today in public had been done for years in private, not only by him, but by dozens of amateurs all over New York City—at private parties, on street corners, in candy stores. His originality consists in his having been the first to use this private urban language in public, and his genius lies in his ability to express the ethos out of which he comes in unadulterated form.

He is, in other words, a genuine folk artist who stands in a relation to the lower-middle-class adolescent Jewish life of New York not unlike that of Charlie Parker to the Negroes of Harlem. And like Parker, he derives his strength from having totally available to himself—and then being able to articulate—attitudes, ideas, images, fragments of experience so endemic to a culture that they scarcely ever come to conscious awareness. Thus for many people the shock of watching Bruce perform is primarily the shock of recognition.

Bruce—who grew up in Brooklyn, the son of an "exotic dancer" who now runs a school for strippers and coaches comics —grew up as part of the adolescent "underground" that exists beneath the lower-middle-class gentility of such Brooklyn neighborhoods as Bensonhurst, Borough Park, and Brighton Beach. Adolescent defiance is scarcely unique, but the group of which Bruce was a part acted out its anger not only by rubbing shoulders with the socially outlawed (pushers, prostitutes, loafers, show-business types, Negro jazzmen) but also through staging sessions of ritualistic parody in which they vented their contempt for the life around them. On Saturday nights, for instance, they would get together and everyone would have his turn "onstage" to review the events of the week—each performer egging himself on to greater heights of exaggeration, outrage, and sheer fantasy in describing things that had happened in the family, in the neighborhood, and in the dark sexual corners of their world. It was in this "home-cooking" school that Bruce learned how to free-associate on his feet, and it was here also that he trained himself in the technique of the "spritz"—the spontaneous satire that gathers momentum and energy as it goes along, spiraling finally into the exhilarating anarchy of total freedom from inhibition.

The psychological mechanism of this kind of comedy is well enough known by now: it is a means of expressing hatred and contempt and still escaping punishment. But the matter is complicated by the fact that the comic's sensitivity to imperfection and ugliness is heightened by a conviction of his own inadequacy, vulgarity, and hypocrisy, leading him to become doubly intolerant of these faults in others. They haunt him, they are demons which he seeks to exorcise by comic confrontation. The psychological source of such satire is, thus, a persistent, ineradicable hatred of the self, and this is particularly striking in the case of Bruce, whose sense of moral outrage is intimately connected with an awareness of his own corruption. ("I can't get worked up about politics. I grew up in New York, and I was hip as a kid that I was corrupt and that the mayor was corrupt. I have no illusions.") If the practitioner of this kind of comedy is in any way morally superior to his audience, it is only because he is *honest,* and willing to face himself, while they, the audience, are blind enough to think *they* are pure.

From Brooklyn, Bruce went into the Navy, was discharged at the end of the War, and after serving a hitch in the Merchant Marine, returned to New York where he submerged himself in the show-business jungle of Times Square. For several years he moved around digging other comics, haunting their hangouts, trying to work out an act of his own. Finally, in 1951, he appeared on the Arthur Godfrey Talent Show and won. Soon he was doing a conventional "single" at the Strand and other burlesque houses, but he loathed "the business" as much as he despised the Brooklyn of his youth, and for many of the same reasons.

The decisive moment for his career came in 1958 while Bruce was working on the West Coast as a screen writer and nightclub emcee. At about this time Mort Sahl, also on the Coast, was becoming famous. ("I was just a product of my time," Sahl has said. "This license was lying around waiting for someone to pick it up.") Nevertheless, the novelty of Sahl's act undoubtedly stimulated Bruce's own breakthrough and there was an audience ready to respond to Bruce's first original creation—a series of satirical bits based on a potent symbol evolved in the early "homecooking" days—the shingle man.

A type of "con" man prevalent in the Forties, the shingle man spent much of his time on the road, usually traveling in groups, doing comic routines, smoking marijuana, taking time off now and then to talk gullible slum residents into buying new roofing. Though strictly a small-time operator, the ruthlessly manipulating shingle man came, in Bruce's universe, to represent any and all wielders of power and authority—up to and including the most grandiose. The great world, in short—all political, social, or religious activity—is nothing but a gigantic racket run by shingle men. In a Bruce routine called "Religion, Inc.," for example, organized religion was reduced to a threeway phone conversation between the Pope, Billy Graham, and Oral Roberts making plans in hipster jargon ("Hey, John! What's shaking, Baby?") for a world-wide religious revival complete with give-away items (a cigarette lighter in the form of a cross and cocktail napkins bearing the imprint, "Another martini for Mother Cabrini").

Similarly, in another routine of this period, Bruce portrays Hitler as the brainstorm of a couple of shrewd theatrical agents, who discover the new "star" while he is painting their office and set him up with costumes (an armband with the four "7's"), music, routines—in short, an act. Lavishly applying the metaphor of the shingle man to every social institution in the book, Bruce embarked upon a career whose underlying intention has remained constant, though his style has gone through many changes; to set up a remorselessly unqualified identification of power and respectability with corruption.

It is a mistake to regard Bruce simply as a social satirist, for he has long since transcended the limitations of that role, just as he has long since gone beyond mere irreverence in his routines. Indeed, for the most apposite metaphor describing what Bruce does, one must turn from show business to the seemingly remote domain of cultural anthropology. Gèzà Roheim's description of the *shaman*, exorciser of public demons, sharply reveals the true character of Lenny Bruce's present "act."

> In every primitive tribe we find the *shaman* in the center of society and it is easy to show that he is either a neurotic or a psychotic, or at least that his art is based on the same mechanisms as a neurosis or psychosis. The *shaman* makes both visible and public the systems of symbolic fantasy that are present in the psyche of every adult member of society. They are the leaders in an infantile game and the lightning conductors of common anxiety. They fight the demons so that others can hunt the prey and in general fight reality.

Although "sick" humor appears to be a remarkably unfeeling reaction to misery, particularly to physical deformity, it actually is an oblique protest against the enforced repression of those in-

stinctive emotions of revulsion, anxiety, and guilt evoked by
deformity. It represents a distorted rebellion against the piety
that demands automatic sympathy for literally every form of
human limitation. Though neither Mort Sahl nor Bruce can be
wholly identified with "sick" comedy, the shock techniques used
by both gave them something in common with the outrageous
jokes that were spreading through the country during the mid-
and late fifties. (With Sahl, also, Bruce shares other things—
the technique of the encyclopedic monologue, the courage to
deal in forbidden subjects, the use of hipster language, and an
obvious identification with the jazz world.) For a time Bruce's
act was sprinkled with "sick" jokes, but they never constituted
more than a small portion of his verbal arsenal.

Unlike Sahl, however, whose specialty is political satire, Bruce
has never had much to say about politics; the abuse is too
obvious. There is a further difference: Sahl is primarily a wit
and a social commentator; while Bruce's imagination is a more
creative one, which has enabled him to produce a remarkable
variety of characters, situations, and lines of comic action. The
next stage in Bruce's development saw the shingle man super-
seded by a richer, more personal metaphor—show business itself. Balancing his own profound self-contempt against his
loathing for the "business," Bruce created his most complex
parable, a routine called "The Palladium." A cocksure little
nightclub comic, crude, untalented, but "on the make" for success, is disgusted with working the "toilets" (second-rate clubs)
and determines to take a crack at the big-time. Booked into the
London Palladium, he is slated to follow "Georgia Gibbs," a performer who knows exactly what the public wants and "puts them
away" every time. His vulgar, corny gags fail to get a laugh and
he "dies." Desperate to succeed, he begs for another chance, but
is swamped in the wake of the singer, who caps her cunningly
contrived performance with a lachrymose tribute to "the boys
who died over there."

The little comic lacks the wit to change even a single line of
his mechanical act, and again he is about to "die" when, con-
fronting disaster, he blindly ad libs a line: "Hey folks, How
'bout this one—screw the Irish!" This puerile bid for attention

instantly transforms the somnolent audience into a raging mob who sweep the comic off the stage and wreck the theater.

Clearly, show business for Bruce stands for American society itself—and, indeed, in no other country have entertainers come to be more profoundly symbolic of national values than here. The anxiety to please which takes the form of tearjerking sentimentality and fake humanitarianism in "Georgia Gibbs" is no less ruthlessly dramatized in the portrait of the brash little comedian, whom we can take as a comic degradation of Bruce himself, and whose story is a reflection of Bruce's own development. Not only does he expose the agonies that assault the performer whose very life depends on his success with the audience; he also satirizes one of the most remarkable features of his own present role as *shaman*—the direct, brutal onslaught on the passions and prejudices of his audience that stems from desperation in the face of failure and that sets off an appalling explosion of primitive hatred.

While he lacks the dramatic gifts of Elaine May, Sid Caesar, or Jonathan Winters—with their actors' techniques of mimicry, foreign accents, and sound effects—Bruce is nevertheless at his best in personal narratives put across with just a suggestion of the dramatic. His work, in fact, is intensely personal and provides an obvious outlet for his private rage; nevertheless, there is a part of Bruce that is utterly disinterested. Like any satirist, he knows that the only effective way to attack corruption is to expose and destroy it symbolically; that the more elaborately and vividly this destruction is imagined, the greater will be his own satisfaction, and the more profound the cathartic effect on the audience. Thus, gradually moving from a wholly conventional act through a series of increasingly wild and outspoken routines, Bruce has indeed become the *shaman*: he has taken on himself the role of exorcising the private fears and submerged fantasies of the public by articulating in comic form the rage and nihilistic savagery hidden beneath the lid of social inhibition. . . .

This routine vividly illustrates Bruce's attitude toward his audience; he regards it as an object of sadistic lust, he hates and loves it; it is the enticing enemy, and he attacks it repeatedly.

In the past his aggression was masked, but now it is naked. He may pick up a chair and menace a patron; if the audience laughs, he will observe soberly that he might have killed the man and that if he had, everyone would have accepted the murder as part of the act. Here he demonstrates, almost in the manner of a classroom exercise, the repressed violence of modern society. By making the audience *laugh* at incipient murder he has tricked them into exposing their own savage instincts. The implication is that given the slightest excuse for condoning a killing, even the absurd rationale of its being part of a nightclub act, society would join eagerly in the violence it so conscientiously deplores.

This public display of the ugly, the twisted, the perverse—offensive though it is at times—nevertheless serves a vital function, for it gives the audience a profound sense, not only of release, but of self-acceptance. Again and again, Bruce violates social taboos—and he does not die! Like the witch doctor or the analyst, he brings the unconscious to light, and thereby lightens the burden of shame and guilt. By its very nature his material cannot come out clear, decorous, and beautifully detached; it must be, and is, charged with self-pity, self-hatred, fear, horror, crudity, grotesquerie.

What is unsatisfactory in Bruce's work is his frequent failure to transmute his rage into real comedy. Sometimes he has nothing more to offer than an attitude ("Everything is rotten. Mother is rotten. The flag is rotten. God is rotten.") At other times, what starts with a promise of rounded development will flatten out into a direct and insulting statement. A sophisticated listener forgives the comic these lapses, understanding that the ad lib approach and the often intractable material are apt to betray the performer into mere obscenity; but people with no natural sympathy for this approach are shocked and offended—there has never been a lack of people in the audience to walk out during Bruce's act.

The reason for these occasional lapses into crudity is the almost total lack of "art" in Bruce's present act; he deliberately destroys the aesthetic distance which is a convention of the theater established by tacit agreement between audience and performer that what is happening on the stage is an illusion of life, rather than life itself. Like other performers who deal in direct communication, Bruce has always tried to *reduce* the barrier between the stage and reality. He has never wanted to appear as an entertainer doing an act, but rather as himself, no different onstage from off, not really a performer, but a man who performs in order to share with others his most secret thoughts and imaginings. The desire, however, to eradicate the distinction between art and reality has at this stage almost completely destroyed the artistry with which Bruce formerly presented his material. Gone, now, are the metaphors of the shingle man and the show business manipulator; done, too, are the story-telling devices of the personal narrative and the dramatic impersonations. All that remains are sketchy, often underdeveloped, sometimes incoherent, scraps of former routines.

The new material consists of deep, psychologically primitive fantasies, hurled at a defenseless audience without the mitigating intervention of art. Frequently, Bruce assaults his listeners with scatological outbursts consisting of the crudest and most obvious anal and oral sadistic fantasies, undisguised. There is currently a comic picture book in circulation (*Stamp Help Out*) with a photograph of Bruce on the cover, stripped to the waist like a heroic frontiersman, engaged in shattering a toilet bowl with an axe—Bruce's comment on the surgically white "powder room" of our culture.

Much of his current material is in fact unquotable—not so much because of the language but because its comic effect depends on nonverbal associations and is thereby scarcely intelligible in the reading. In one bit, for instance, he tells how, when the Avon representative called at his house, he drugged her, stripped her, decked her out with galoshes and moustache, raped her, and then wrote on her belly, "You were balled."

In another long and complicated routine, which changes from one performance to another, he explains that the Lone Ranger's bullets are really pellets of Ehrlich's 606. . . . This deliberate perpetration of outrage on the persons of the most innocuous figures of American folklore—the Lone Ranger, the Avon representative—is, of course, one of the leitmotifs of the recent "sick" humor. The same thing was once done in a grimier way in those pornographic comic books that showed the heroes of the comic strip—familiar to every American child—in complicated sexual situations.

As his material has become more direct, Bruce has tended more and more to *be* the act. Because the imaginative impulse is naked, unsublimated, Bruce's intention is less and less communicated by what he says, and depends now, to a great extent, on affective devices—his manner, his tone, especially his physical appearance. Whereas in the past Bruce would walk briskly out on the floor, good-looking, impeccably groomed, wearing a chic Italian suit, now he comes on stiff-legged and stooped, wearing shabby clothes, his face a pale mask of dissipation. Having discarded the civilized mask that people wear in public to protect themselves, Bruce comes before his audience as a mythic figure—beat, accused junkie, "underground" man—who has suffered in acting-out their own forbidden desires. Where they are cautious, he is self-destructive, alternately terrifying the audience (the very fact that *he doesn't care* is awesome) and arousing their sympathy and concern. (He now regularly opens his act by enacting and commenting on his recent arrests.) Merely looking at Bruce these days is a disturbing experience.

Finally, Bruce is dramatizing his role as *shaman* by embellishing his act for the first time with consciously contrived bits of hocus-pocus. He turns the lights on and off, strikes drums and cymbals, swings into crude chants. He prowls about the stage, sometimes exposing himself to the audience, at other times crouching in the darkness and hiding from it. He opens and closes doors and climbs onto furniture to symbolize his power over the bewildered spectators.

In the darkened, cave-like club, charged with tension, the audience sits hunched over, tense, breathless, their eyes fastened on the weird figure in the center of the magic circle. While the tribe looks on with fearful absorption, the medicine man puts himself into a trance in preparation for the terrible struggle with the tribal demons (anxieties). And then—when the performance is over and the "unspeakable" has been shouted forth —there is mingled with the thunderous applause a sigh of release. Purged of their demons by the *shaman*, the tribe has been freed, for the moment, to "hunt the prey and in general fight reality."

5

The Negro

The Sixties and the Negro had to come together. There is a nice irony, for those who care to note such things, in the fact that the Sixties marked the centennial of the Civil War. As books about Grant and Lee, Lincoln and Davis, and Gettysburg, Shiloh, Antietam, and Vicksburg poured off the presses, we lived through the battles that opened the second hundred years. Selma, Birmingham, Watts, Cambridge in Maryland, and Cicero in Illinois—these were the scenes of the struggle that began in Harper's Ferry and has not yet seen its end.

The Negro is the social problem of the Sixties largely because most Americans still think of "The Negro" and not of individual men. This section presents the views of some of the men engaged in the civil rights movement of the Sixties. Stokely Carmichael, Martin Luther King, and Claude Brown speak for the Negro. Murray Kempton, Robert Penn Warren, and Norman Podhoretz talk about what it means for white men to try to see those "other men."

The Negro is not an isolated phenomenon of the Sixties. No social revolution begins at some arbitrary date. The Negro has left the farm and inherited the city. The secular city that defines midcentury America has redefined the Negro. The violence that disturbs Philip Roth (see "Writing American Fiction" in Section 9, *Literature*) is a fact of Negro life.

The Negro Revolution offers evidence in support of Teilhard de Chardin's eloquently argued view of the continuing evolution of consciousness. No people is ready for a revolution until it is aware of itself and its situation. Stokely Carmichael can tell us what Negroes want because he is a child of this time with a clear consciousness of what white men are, should be, and have been.

In the mutual relations between Negro and whites during the hundred years since the 1860's both parties have grown in nothing so much as their painful consciousness of each other. These selections record some parts of that awareness.

MARTIN LUTHER KING, JR.

Five score years ago, a great American, in whose symbolic shadow we stand, signed the Emancipation Proclamation. This momentous decree came as a great beacon light of hope to millions of Negro slaves who had been seared in the flames of withering injustice. It came as a joyous daybreak to end the long night of captivity.

"I Have a Dream . . ."

But one hundred years later, we must face the tragic fact that the Negro is still not free. One hundred years later, the life of the Negro is still sadly crippled by the manacles of segregation and the chains of discrimination. One hundred years later, the Negro lives on a lonely island of poverty in the midst of a vast ocean of material prosperity. One hundred years later, the Negro is still languished in the corners of American society and finds himself an exile in his own land. So we have come here today to dramatize an appalling condition.

In a sense we have come to our nation's Capital to cash a check. When the architects of our republic wrote the magnificent words of the Constitution and the Declaration of Independence, they were signing a promissory note to which every American was to fall heir. This note was a promise that all men would be guaranteed the unalienable rights of life, liberty, and the pursuit of happiness.

It is obvious today that America has defaulted on this promissory note insofar as her citizens of color are concerned. Instead of honoring this sacred obligation, America has given the Negro people a bad check; a check which has come back marked "insufficient funds." But we refuse to believe that the bank of justice is bankrupt. We refuse to believe that there are insufficient funds in the great vaults of opportunity of this nation. So we have come to cash this check—a check that will give us upon demand the riches of freedom and the security of justice. We have also come to this hallowed spot to remind America of the fierce

Authorized text reprinted by permission of Martin Luther King, Jr.

urgency of *now*. This is no time to engage in the luxury of cooling off or to take the tranquilizing drug of gradualism. *Now* is the time to make real the promises of Democracy. *Now* is the time to rise from the dark and desolate valley of segregation to the sunlit path of racial justice. *Now* is the time to open the doors of opportunity to all of God's children. *Now* is the time to lift our nation from the quicksands of racial injustice to the solid rock of brotherhood.

It would be fatal for the nation to overlook the urgency of the moment and to underestimate the determination of the Negro. This sweltering summer of the Negro's legitimate discontent will not pass until there is an invigorating autumn of freedom and equality. 1963 is not an end, but a beginning. Those who hope that the Negro needed to blow off steam and will now be content will have a rude awakening if the nation returns to business as usual. There will be neither rest nor tranquillity in America until the Negro is granted his citizenship rights. The whirlwinds of revolt will continue to shake the foundations of our nation until the bright day of justice emerges.

But there is something that I must say to my people who stand on the warm threshold which leads into the palace of justice. In the process of gaining our rightful place we must not be guilty of wrongful deeds. Let us not seek to satisfy our thirst for freedom by drinking from the cup of bitterness and hatred. We must forever conduct our struggle on the high plane of dignity and discipline. We must not allow our creative protest to degenerate into physical violence. Again and again we must rise to the majestic heights of meeting physical force with soul force. The marvelous new militancy which has engulfed the Negro community must not lead us to a distrust of all white people, for many of our white brothers, as evidenced by their presence here today, have come to realize that their destiny is tied up with our destiny and their freedom is inextricably bound to our freedom. We cannot walk alone.

And as we walk, we must make the pledge that we shall march ahead. We cannot turn back. There are those who are asking the devotees of civil rights, "When will you be satisfied?" We can never be satisfied as long as the Negro is the victim of the unspeakable horrors of police brutality. We can never be satisfied as long as our bodies, heavy with the fatigue of travel, cannot gain lodging in the motels of the highways and the hotels of the cities. We cannot be satisfied as long as the Negro's basic mobility is from a smaller ghetto to a larger one. We can never be satisfied as long as a Negro in Mississippi cannot vote and a Negro in New York believes he has nothing for which to vote. No, no, we are not satisfied, and we will not be satisfied until justice rolls down like waters and righteousness like a mighty stream.

I am not unmindful that some of you have come here out of great trials and tribulations. Some of you have come fresh from narrow jail cells. Some of you have come from areas where your quest for freedom left you battered by the storms of persecution and staggered by the winds of police brutality. You have been the veterans of creative suffering. Continue to work with the faith that unearned suffering is redemptive.

Go back to Mississippi, go back to Alabama, go back to South Carolina, go back to Georgia, go back to Louisiana, go back to the slums and ghettos of our northern cities, knowing that somehow this situation can and will be changed. Let us not wallow in the valley of despair.

I say to you today, my friends, that in spite of the difficulties and frustrations of the moment I still have a dream. It is a dream deeply rooted in the American dream.

I have a dream that one day this nation will rise up and live out the true meaning of its creed: "We hold these truths to be self-evident; that all men are created equal."

I have a dream that one day on the red hills of Georgia the sons of former slaves and the sons of former slaveowners will be able to sit down together at the table of brotherhood.

I have a dream that one day even the state of Mississippi, a desert state sweltering with the heat of injustice and oppression, will be transformed into an oasis of freedom and justice.

I have a dream that my four little children will one day live in a nation where they will not be judged by the color of their skin but by the content of their character.

I have a dream today.

I have a dream that one day the state of Alabama, whose governor's lips are presently dripping with the words of interposition and nullification, will be transformed into a situation where little black boys and black girls will be able to join hands with little white boys and white girls and walk together as sisters and brothers.

I have a dream today.

I have a dream that one day every valley shall be exalted, every hill and mountain shall be made low, the rough places will be made plain, and the crooked places will be made straight, and the glory of the Lord shall be revealed, and all flesh shall see it together.

This is our hope. This is the faith with which I return to the South. With this faith we will be able to hew out of the mountain of despair a stone of hope. With this faith we will be able to transform the jangling discords of our nation into a beautiful symphony of brotherhood. With this faith we will be able to work together, to pray together, to struggle together, to go to jail together, to stand up for freedom together, knowing that we will be free one day.

This will be the day when all of God's children will be able to sing with new meaning

> My country, 'tis of thee,
> Sweet land of liberty,
> Of thee I sing:
> Land where my fathers died,
> Land of the pilgrims' pride,
> From every mountain-side
> Let freedom ring.

And if America is to be a great nation this must become true. So let freedom ring from the prodigious hilltops of New Hampshire. Let freedom ring from the mighty mountains of New York. Let freedom ring from the heightening Alleghenies of Pennsylvania!

Let freedom ring from the snowcapped Rockies of Colorado!

Let freedom ring from the curvacious peaks of California!

But not only that; let freedom ring from Stone Mountain of Georgia!

Let freedom ring from Lookout Mountain of Tennessee!

Let freedom ring from every hill and molehill of Mississippi. From every mountainside, let freedom ring.

When we let freedom ring, when we let it ring from every village and every hamlet, from every state and every city, we will be able to speed up that day when all of God's children, black men and white men, Jews and Gentiles, Protestants and Catholics, will be able to join hands and sing in the words of the old Negro spiritual, "Free at last! free at last! thank God almighty, we are free at last!"

The most consistent quality of white America's experience with the Negro is that almost nothing happens that we—or perhaps even he—expects to have happen. Faithful to that tradition, Washington waited most of the summer for the avenging Negro army to march on Washington for Jobs and Freedom; what came was the largest religious pilgrimage of Americans that any of us is ever likely to see.

The March on Washington

When it was over, Malcolm X, the Muslim, was observed in the lobby of the Statler. It had, he conceded, been something of a show. "Kennedy," said Malcolm X, "should win the Academy Award—for direction." Yet while the President may have triumphed as director-manipulator, he was also deftly manipulated by those whom he strove to direct.

"When the Negro leaders announced the march, the President asked them to call it off," Bayard Rustin, its manager, remembered the next day. "When they thumbed—when they told him they wouldn't—he almost smothered us. We had to keep raising our demands . . . to keep him from getting ahead of us."

Rustin and A. Philip Randolph are men who had to learn long ago that in order to handle they must first permit themselves to be handled. The moment in that afternoon which almost strained belief was near its end, when Rustin led the assemblage in a mass pledge never to cease until they had won their demands. A radical pacifist, every sentence punctuated by his upraised hand, was calling for a $2 an hour minimum wage. Every television camera at the disposal of the networks was upon him. No expression one-tenth so radical has ever been seen or heard by so many Americans.

To produce this scene had taken some delicate maneuvering.

From *The New Republic*, 149 (September 14, 1963), 19–20. Reprinted by permission of *The New Republic*, copyright © 1963, Harrison-Blaine of New Jersey, Inc.

Randolph called the march last spring at a moment when the civil rights groups had fallen into a particularly painful season of personal rancor. Randolph is unique because he accepts everyone in a movement whose members do not always accept one another. His first support came from the non-violent actionists; they hoped for passionate protest. That prospect was Randolph's weapon; the moderates had to come in or be defenseless against embarrassing disorder. Randolph welcomed them not just with benevolence but with genuine gratitude. When President Kennedy expressed his doubts, Randolph answered that some demonstration was unavoidable and that what had to be done was to make it orderly.

It was the best appeal that feeling could make to calculation. The White House knew that the ordinary Negro cherishes the Kennedy brothers and that the larger the assemblage the better disposed it would be not to embarrass them. When the President finally mentioned the march in public, he issued something as close as possible to a social invitation.

No labor leader since John L. Lewis in 1933 has succeeded in employing the President of the United States as an organizer. Even Lewis only sent his organizers about the pits telling the miners that the President wanted them to join the union, and was careful never to tell Mr. Roosevelt about it. Randolph got his President live, whole and direct.

If the march was important, it was because it represented an acceptance of the Negro revolt as part of the American myth, and so an acceptance of the revolutionaries into the American establishment. That acceptance, of course, carries the hope that the Negro revolt will stop where it is. Yet that acceptance is also the most powerful incentive and assurance that the revolt will continue. The children from Wilmington, North Carolina, climbed back on their buses with the shining memory of a moment when they marched with all America—a memory to sustain them when they return to march alone. So it was, too, for all the others who came from Birmingham, Montgomery, Danville, Gadsden and Jackson—places whose very names evoke not only the cause but the way it is being won.

Gray from Jail, Haggard from Tension

The result of such support—the limits it placed on the spectacle
—was illustrated by the experience of John Lewis, chairman of
the Student Non-Violent Coordinating Committee. Lewis is only
25; his only credential for being there was combat experience;
he has been arrested 22 times and beaten half as often. The
Student Non-Violent Coordinating Committee is a tiny battalion,
its members gray from jail and exhausted from tension. They
have the gallant cynicism of troops of the line; they revere
Martin Luther King (some of them) as a captain who has faced
the dogs with them and they call him with affectionate irreverence, "De Lawd." We could hardly have had this afternoon without them.

Lewis, in their spirit, had prepared a speech full of temerities
about how useless the civil rights bill is and what frauds the
Democrats and Republicans are. Three of the white speakers
told Randolph that they could not appear at a platform where
such sedition was pronounced, and John Lewis had to soften his
words in deference to elders. Equal rights for the young to say
their say may, perhaps, come later.

Yet Lewis' speech, even as laundered, remained discomfiting
enough to produce a significant tableau at its end. "My friends,"
he said, "let us not forget that we are engaged in a significant
social revolution. By and large American politics is dominated
by politicians who build their careers on immoral compromising
and ally themselves with open forums of political, economic and
social exploitation." When he had finished, every Negro on the
speakers' row pumped his hand and patted his back; and every
white one looked out into the distance.

So even in the middle of this ceremony of reconciliation, the
void between the Negro American and a white one remained.
Or rather, it did and it didn't. At one point, Martin King mentioned with gratitude the great number of white people (about
40,000 to 50,000 out of an estimated 200,000) who had joined
the march. There was little response from the platform—where
it must have seemed formal courtesy—but as the sound of those
words moved across the great spaces between King and the vis-
itors from the Southern towns, there was the sudden sight and
sound of Negroes cheering far away. Nothing all afternoon was

quite so moving as the sight of these people, whose trust has been violated so often in the particular, proclaiming it so touchingly intact in the general.

We do not move the Negro often, it would seem, and we do it only when we are silent and just standing there. On the speakers' stand there was the inevitable Protestant, Catholic and Jew without which no national ceremony can be certified. Is it hopeless to long for a day when the white brother will just once accept the duty to march, and forego the privilege to preach? Dr. Eugene Carson Blake of the National Council of Churches told the audience that the Protestants were coming and "late we come." It was the rarest blessing—an apology. We have begun to stoop a little; and yet it is so hard for us to leave off condescending.

We cannot move the Negro by speaking, because the public white America seems to know no words except the ones worn out from having been so long unmeant. Even if they are meant now, they have been empty too long not to *sound* empty still; whatever our desires, our language calls up only the memory of the long years when just the same language served only to convey indifference.

Yet the Negro moves us most when he touches our memory, even as we chill him most when we touch his. August 28 was to many whites only a demonstration of power and importance until Mahalia Jackson arose to sing the old song about having been rebuked and scorned and going home. Then King near the end began working as country preachers do, the words for the first time not as to listeners but as to participants, the intimate private conversation of invocation and response. For just those few minutes, we were back where this movement began and has endured, older than the language of the society which was taking these pilgrims in, but still fresh where the newer language was threadbare.

The Negro comes from a time the rest of us have forgotten; he seems new and complicated only because he represents something so old and simple. He reminds us that the new, after which we have run so long, was back there all the time. Something new will some day be said, and it will be something permanent, if it starts from such a memory.

"Run!"
Where?
Oh, hell! Let's get out of here!
"Turk! Turk! I'm shot!"
I could hear Turk's voice calling from a far distance, telling me not to go into the fish-and-chips joint. I heard, but I didn't

Manchild in the Promised Land

understand. The only thing I knew was that I was going to die.

I ran. There was a bullet in me trying to take my life, all thirteen years of it.

I climbed up on the bar yelling, "Walsh, I'm shot. I'm shot." I could feel the blood running down my leg. Walsh, the fellow who operated the fish-and-chips joint, pushed me off the bar and onto the floor. I couldn't move now, but I was still completely conscious.

Walsh was saying, "Git outta here, kid. I ain't got no time to play."

A woman was screaming, mumbling something about the Lord, and saying, "Somebody done shot that poor child."

Mama ran in. She jumped up and down, screaming like a crazy woman. I began to think about dying. The worst part of dying was thinking about the things and the people that I'd never see again. As I lay there trying to imagine what being dead was like, the policeman who had been trying to control Mama gave up and bent over me. He asked who had shot me. Before I could answer, he was asking me if I could hear him. I told him that I didn't know who had shot me and would he please tell Mama to stop jumping up and down. Every time Mama came down on that shabby floor, the bullet lodged in my stomach felt like a hot poker.

Another policeman had come in and was struggling to keep the crowd outside. I could see Turk in the front of the crowd.

Reprinted by permission of The Macmillan Company from *Manchild in the Promised Land* by Claude Brown. Copyright © 1965 by the Author.

Before the cops came, he asked me if I was going to tell them that he was with me. I never answered. I looked at him and wondered if he saw who shot me. Then his question began to ring in my head: "Sonny, you gonna tell 'em I was with you?" I was bleeding on a dirty floor in a fish-and-chips joint, and Turk was standing there in the doorway hoping that I would die before I could tell the cops that he was with me. Not once did Turk ask me how I felt.

Hell, yeah, I thought, I'm gonna tell 'em.

It seemed like hours had passed before the ambulance finally arrived. Mama wanted to go to the hospital with me, but the ambulance attendant said she was too excited. On the way to Harlem Hospital, the cop who was riding with us asked Dad what he had to say. His answer was typical: "I told him about hanging out with those bad-ass boys." The cop was a little surprised. This must be a rookie, I thought.

The next day, Mama was at my bedside telling me that she had prayed and the Lord had told her that I was going to live. Mama said that many of my friends wanted to donate some blood for me, but the hospital would not accept it from narcotics users.

This was one of the worst situations I had ever been in. There was a tube in my nose that went all the way to the pit of my stomach. I was being fed intravenously, and there was a drain in my side. Everybody came to visit me, mainly out of curiosity. The girls were all anxious to know where I had gotten shot. They had heard all kinds of tales about where the bullet struck. The bolder ones wouldn't even bother to ask: they just snatched the cover off me and looked for themselves. In a few days, the word got around that I was in one piece.

On my fourth day in the hospital, I was awakened by a male nurse at about 3 A.M. When he said hello in a very ladyish voice, I thought that he had come to the wrong bed by mistake. After identifying himself, he told me that he had helped Dr. Freeman save my life. The next thing he said, which I didn't understand, had something to do with the hours he had put in working that day. He went on mumbling something about how tired he was and ended up asking me to rub his back. I had already told him that I was grateful to him for helping the doctor save my life.

While I rubbed his back above the beltline, he kept pushing my hand down and saying, "Lower, like you are really grateful to me." I told him that I was sleepy from the needle a nurse had given me. He asked me to pat his behind. After I had done this, he left.

The next day when the fellows came to visit me, I told them about my early-morning visitor. Dunny said he would like to meet him. Tito joked about being able to get a dose of clap in the hospital. The guy with the tired back never showed up again, so the fellows never got a chance to meet him. Some of them were disappointed.

After I had been in the hospital for about a week, I was visited by another character. I had noticed a woman visiting one of the patients on the far side of the ward. She was around fifty-five years old, short and fat, and she was wearing old-lady shoes. While I wondered who this woman was, she started across the room in my direction. After she had introduced herself, she told me that she was visiting her son. Her son had been stabbed in the chest with an ice pick by his wife. She said that his left lung had been punctured, but he was doing fine now, and that Jesus was so-o-o good.

Her name was Mrs. Ganey, and she lived on 145th Street. She said my getting shot when I did "was the work of the Lord." My gang had been stealing sheets and bedspreads off clotheslines for months before I had gotten shot. I asked this godly woman why she thought it was the work of the Lord or Jesus or whoever. She began in a sermonlike tone, saying, "Son, people was gitting tired-a y'all stealing all dey sheets and spreads." She said that on the night that I had gotten shot, she baited her clothesline with two brand-new bedspreads, turned out all the lights in the apartment, and sat at the kitchen window waiting for us to show.

She waited with a double-barreled shotgun.

The godly woman said that most of our victims thought that we were winos or dope fiends and that most of them had vowed to kill us. At the end of the sermon, the godly woman said, "Thank the Lord I didn't shoot nobody's child." When the godly woman had finally departed, I thought, Thank the Lord for taking her away from my bed.

Later on that night, I was feeling a lot of pain and couldn't get to sleep. A nurse who had heard me moaning and groaning came over and gave me a shot of morphine. Less than twenty minutes later, I was deep into a nightmare.

I was back in the fish-and-chips joint, lying on the floor dying. Only, now I was in more pain than before, and there were dozens of Mamas around me jumping up and screaming. I could feel myself dying in a rising pool of blood. The higher the blood rose the more I died.

I dreamt about the boy who Rock and big Stoop had thrown off that roof on 149th Street. None of us had stayed around to see him hit the ground, but I just knew that he died in a pool of blood too. I wished that he would stop screaming, and I wished that Mama would stop screaming. I wished they would let me die quietly.

*   *   *

I dreamt about waking up in the middle of the night seven years before and thinking that the Germans or the Japs had come and that the loud noises I heard were bombs falling. Running into Mama's room, I squeezed in between her and Dad at the front window. Thinking that we were watching an air raid, I asked Dad where the sirens were and why the street lights were on. He said, "This ain't no air raid—just a whole lotta niggers gone fool. And git the hell back in that bed!" I went back to bed, but I couldn't go to sleep. The loud screams in the street and the crashing sound of falling plate-glass windows kept me awake for hours. While I listened to the noise, I imagined bombs falling and people running through the streets screaming. I could see mothers running with babies in their arms, grown men running over women and children to save their own lives, and the Japs stabbing babies with bayonets, just like in the movies. I thought, Boy, I sure wish I was out there. I bet the Stinky brothers are out there. Danny and Butch are probably out there having all the fun in the world.

The next day, as I was running out of the house without underwear or socks on, I could hear Mama yelling, "Boy, come back here and put a hat or something on your head!" When I reached the stoop, I was knocked back into the hall by a big man carrying a ham under his coat. While I looked up at him, wondering what was going on, he reached down with one hand and snatched me up, still holding the ham under his coat with his other hand. He stood me up against a wall and ran into the hall with his ham. Before I had a chance to move, other men came running through the hall carrying cases of whiskey, sacks of flour, and cartons of cigarettes. Just as I unglued myself from the wall and started out the door for the second time, I was bowled over again. This time by a cop with a gun in his hand. He never stopped, but after he had gone a couple of yards into the hall, I heard him say, "Look out, kid." On the third try, I got out of the building. But I wasn't sure that this was my street. None of the stores had any windows left, and glass was everywhere. It seemed that all the cops in the world were on 145th Street and Eighth Avenue that day. The cops were telling everybody to move on, and everybody was talking about the riot. I went over to a cop and asked him what a riot was. He told me to go on home. The next cop I asked told me that a riot was what had happened the night before. Putting two and two together I decided that a riot was "a whole lotta niggers gone fool."

I went around the corner to Butch's house. After I convinced him that I was alone, he opened the door. He said that Kid and Danny were in the kitchen. I saw Kid sitting on the floor with his hand stuck way down in a gallon jar of pickled pigs' ears. Danny was cooking some bacon at the stove, and Butch was busy hiding stuff. It looked as though these guys had stolen a whole grocery store. While I joined the feast, they took turns telling me about the riot. Danny and Kid hadn't gone home the night before; they were out following the crowds and looting.

My only regret was that I had missed the excitement. I said, "Why don't we have another riot tonight? Then Butch and me can get in it."

Danny said that there were too many cops around to have a riot now. Butch said that they had eaten up all the bread and that he was going to steal some more. I asked if I could come along with him, and he said that I could if I promised to do nothing but watch. I promised, but we both knew that I was lying.

When we got to the street, Butch said he wanted to go across

the street and look at the pawnshop. I tagged along. Like many
of the stores where the rioters had been, the pawnshop had been
set afire. The firemen had torn down a sidewall getting at the
fire. So Butch and I just walked in where the wall used to be.
Everything I picked up was broken or burned or both. My feet
kept sinking into the wet furs that had been burned and
drenched. The whole place smelled of smoke and was as dirty as
a Harlem gutter on a rainy day. The cop out front yelled to us to
get out of there. He only had to say it once.

After stopping by the seafood joint and stealing some shrimp
and oysters, we went to what was left of Mr. Gordon's grocery
store. Butch just walked in, picked up a loaf of bread, and
walked out. He told me to come on, but I ignored him and went
into the grocery store instead. I picked up two loaves of bread
and walked out. When I got outside, a cop looked at me, and
I ran into a building and through the backyard to Butch's house.
Running through the backyard, I lost all the oysters that I had;
when I reached Butch's house, I had only two loaves of bread
and two shrimp in my pocket.

Danny, who was doing most of the cooking, went into the
street to steal something to drink. Danny, Butch, and Kid were
ten years old, four years older than I. Butch was busy making
sandwiches on the floor, and Kid was trying to slice up a loaf of
bologna. I had never eaten shrimp, but nobody seemed to care,
because they refused to cook it for me. I told Butch that I was
going to cook it myself. He said that there was no more lard in
the house and that I would need some grease.

I looked around the house until I came up with some Vaseline
hair pomade. I put the shrimp in the frying pan with the hair
grease, waited until they had gotten black and were smoking,
then took them out and made a sandwich. A few years later, I
found out that shrimp were supposed to be shelled before cooking. I ate half of the sandwich and hated shrimp for years
afterward.

The soft hand tapping on my face to wake me up was Jackie's.
She and Della had been to a New Year's Eve party. Jackie wanted
to come by the hospital and kiss me at midnight. This was the
only time in my life that I ever admitted being glad to see Jackie.

I asked them about the party, hoping that they would stay and talk to me for a while. I was afraid that if I went back to sleep, I would have another bad dream.

The next thing I knew, a nurse was waking me up for breakfast. I didn't recall saying good night to Jackie and Della, so I must have fallen asleep while they were talking to me. I thought about Sugar, how nice she was, and how she was a real friend. I knew she wanted to be my girl friend, and I liked her a lot. But what would everybody say if I had a buck-toothed girl friend. I remembered Knoxie asking me how I kissed her. That question led to the first fight I'd had with Knoxie in years. No, I couldn't let Sugar be my girl. It was hard enough having her as a friend.

The next day, I asked the nurse why she hadn't changed my bed linen, and she said because they were evicting me. I had been in the hospital for eleven days, but I wasn't ready to go home. I left the hospital on January 2 and went to a convalescent home in Valhalla, New York. After I had been there for three weeks, the activity director took me aside and told me that I was going to New York City to see a judge and that I might be coming back. The following morning, I left to see that judge, but I never got back to Valhalla.

I stood there before Judge Pankin looking solemn and lying like a professional. I thought that he looked too nice to be a judge. A half hour after I had walked into the courtroom, Judge Pankin was telling me that he was sending me to the New York State Training School for Boys. The judge said that he thought I was a chronic liar and that he hoped I would be a better boy when I came out. I asked him if he wanted me to thank him. Mama stopped crying just long enough to say, "Hush your mouth, boy."

Mama tried to change the judge's mind by telling him that I had already been to Wiltwyck School for Boys for two and a half years. And before that, I had been ordered out of the state for at least one year. She said that I had been away from my family too much; that was why I was always getting into trouble.

The judge told Mama that he knew what he was doing and that one day she would be grateful to him for doing it.

I had been sent away before, but this was the first time I was ever afraid to go. When Mama came up to the detention room in Children's Court, I tried to act as though I wasn't afraid. After I told her that Warwick and where I was going were one and the same, Mama began to cry, and so did I.

Most of the guys I knew had been to Warwick and were too old to go back. I knew that there were many guys up there I had mistreated. The Stinky brothers were up there. They thought that I was one of the guys who had pulled a train on their sister in the park the summer before. Bumpy from 144th Street was up there. I had shot him in the leg with a zip gun in a rumble only a few months earlier. There were many guys up there I used to bully on the streets and at Wiltwyck, guys I had sold tea leaves to as pot. There were rival gang members up there who just hated my name. All of these guys were waiting for me to show. The word was out that I couldn't fight any more—that I had slowed down since I was shot and that a good punch to the stomach would put my name in the undertaker's book.

When I got to the Youth House, I tried to find out who was up at Warwick that I might know. Nobody knew any of the names I asked about. I knew that if I went up to Warwick in my condition, I'd never live to get out. I had a reputation for being a rugged little guy. This meant that I would have at least a half-dozen fights in the first week of my stay up there.

It seemed the best thing for me to do was to cop out on the nut. For the next two nights, I woke up screaming and banging on the walls. On the third day, I was sent to Bellevue for observation. This meant that I wouldn't be going to Warwick for at least twenty-eight days.

While I was in Bellevue, the fellows would come down and pass notes to me through the doors. Tito and Turk said they would get bagged and sent to Warwick by the time I got there. They were both bagged a week later for smoking pot in front of the police station. They were both sent to Bellevue. Two weeks after they showed, I went home. The judge still wanted to send me to Warwick, but Warwick had a full house, so he sent me home for two weeks.

The day before I went back to court, I ran into Turk, who had just gotten out of Bellevue. Tito had been sent to Warwick, but Turk had gotten a walk because his sheet wasn't too bad. I told him I would probably be sent to Warwick the next day. Turk said

he had run into Bucky in Bellevue. He told me that he and Tito
had voted Bucky out of the clique. I told him that I wasn't going
for it because Bucky was my man from short-pants days. Turk
said he liked him too, but what else could he do after Bucky had
let a white boy beat him in the nutbox? When I heard this, there
was nothing I could do but agree with Turk. Bucky had to go.
That kind of news spread fast, and who wanted to be in a clique
with a stud who let a paddy boy beat him?

The next day, I went to the Youth House to wait for Friday
and the trip to Warwick. As I lay in bed that night trying to
think of a way out, I began to feel sorry for myself. I began to
blame Danny, Butch, and Kid for my present fate. I told myself
that I wouldn't be going to Warwick if they hadn't taught me
how to steal, play hookey, make homemades, and stuff like that.
But then I thought, aw, hell, it wasn't their fault—as a matter
of fact, it was a whole lotta fun.

I remembered sitting on the stoop with Danny, years before,
when a girl came up and started yelling at him. She said that
her mother didn't want her brother to hang out with Danny any
more, because Danny had taught her brother how to play
hookey. When the girl had gone down the street, I asked Danny
what hookey was. He said it was a game he would teach me as
soon as I started going to school.

Danny was a man of his word. He was my next-door neighbor,
and he rang my doorbell about 7:30 A.M. on the second day of
school. Mama thanked him for volunteering to take me to school.
Danny said he would have taught me to play hookey the day
before, but he knew that Mama would have to take me to school
on the first day. As we headed toward the backyard to hide our
books, Danny began to explain the great game of hookey. It
sounded like lots of fun to me. Instead of going to school, we
would go all over the city stealing, sneak into a movie, or go up
on a roof and throw bottles down into the street. Danny suggested that we start the day off by waiting for Mr. Gordon to put
out his vegetables; we could steal some sweet potatoes and cook
them in the backyard. I was sorry I hadn't started school sooner,
because hookey sure was a lot of fun.

Before I began going to school, I was always in the streets

with Danny, Kid, and Butch. Sometimes, without saying a word, they would all start to run like hell, and a white man was always chasing them. One morning as I entered the backyard where all the hookey players went to draw up an activity schedule for the day, Butch told me that Danny and Kid had been caught by Mr. Sands the day before. He went on to warn me about Mr. Sands, saying Mr. Sands was that white man who was always chasing somebody and that I should try to remember what he looked like and always be on the lookout for him. He also warned me not to try to outrun Mr. Sands, "because that cat is fast." Butch said, "When you see him, head for a backyard or a roof. He won't follow you there."

During the next three months, I stayed out of school twenty-one days. Dad was beating the hell out of me for playing hookey, and it was no fun being in the street in the winter, so I started going to school regularly. But when spring rolled around, hookey became my favorite game again. Mr. Sands was known to many parents in the neighborhood as the truant officer. He never caught me in the street, but he came by my house many mornings to escort me to class. This was one way of getting me to school, but he never found a way to keep me there. The moment my teacher took her eyes off me, I was back on the street. Every time Dad got a card from Mr. Sands, I got bruises and welts from Dad. The beatings had only a temporary effect on me. Each time, the beatings got worse; and each time, I promised never to play hookey again. One time I kept that promise for three whole weeks.

The older guys had been doing something called "catting" for years. That catting was staying away from home all night was all I knew about the term. Every time I asked one of the fellows to teach me how to cat, I was told I wasn't old enough. As time went on, I learned that guys catted when they were afraid to go home and that they slept everywhere but in comfortable places. The usual places for catting were subway trains, cellars, unlocked cars, under a friend's bed, and in vacant newsstands.

One afternoon when I was eight years old, I came home after a busy day of running from the police, truant officer, and storekeepers. The first thing I did was to look in the mailbox. This had become a habit with me even though I couldn't read. I was looking for a card, a yellow card. That yellow card meant that I would walk into the house and Dad would be waiting for me with his razor strop. He would usually be eating and would pause just long enough to say to me, "Nigger, you got a ass whippin' comin'." My sisters, Carole and Margie, would cry almost as much as I would while Dad was beating me, but this never stopped him. After each beating I got, Carole, who was two years older than I, would beg me to stop playing hookey. There were a few times when I thought I would stop just to keep her and Margie, my younger sister, from crying so much. I decided to threaten Carole and Margie instead, but this didn't help. I continued to play hookey, and they continued to cry on the days that the yellow card got home before I did.

Generally, I would break open the mailbox, take out the card, and throw it away. Whenever I did this, I'd have to break open two or three other mailboxes and throw away the contents, just to make it look good.

This particular afternoon, I saw a yellow card, but I couldn't find anything to break into the box with. Having some matches in my pockets, I decided to burn the card in the box and not bother to break the box open. After I had used all the matches, the card was not completely burned. I stood there getting more frightened by the moment. In a little while, Dad would be coming home; and when he looked in the mailbox, anywhere would be safer than home for me.

This was going to be my first try at catting out. I went looking for somebody to cat with me. My crime partner, Buddy, whom I had played hookey with that day, was busily engaged in a friendly rock fight when I found him in Colonial Park. When I suggested that we go up on the hill and steal some newspapers, Buddy lost interest in the rock fight.

We stole papers from newsstands and sold them on the subway trains until nearly 1 A.M. That was when the third cop woke us and put us off the train with the usual threat. They would always promise to beat us over the head with a billy and lock us up. Looking back, I think the cops took their own threats more seriously than we did. The third cop put us off the Independent Subway at Fifty-ninth Street and Columbus Circle. I wasn't afraid of the cops, but I didn't go back into the subway—the next cop might have taken me home.

In 1945, there was an Automat where we came out of the subway. About five slices of pie later, Buddy and I left the Automat in search of a place to stay the night. In the center of the Circle, there were some old lifeboats that the Navy had put on display.

Buddy and I slept in the boat for two nights. On the third day, Buddy was caught ringing a cash register in a five-and-dime store. He was sent to Children's Center, and I spent the third night in the boat alone. On the fourth night, I met a duty-conscious cop, who took me home. That ended my first catting adventure.

Dad beat me for three consecutive days for telling what he called "that dumb damn lie about sleeping in a boat on Fifty-ninth Street." On the fourth day, I think he went to check my story out for himself. Anyhow, the beatings stopped for a while, and he never mentioned the boat again.

Before long, I was catting regularly, staying away from home for weeks at a time. Sometimes the cops would pick me up and take me to a Children's Center. The Centers were located all over the city. At some time in my childhood, I must have spent at least one night in all of them except the one on Staten Island.

The procedure was that a policeman would take me to the Center in the borough where he had picked me up. The Center would assign someone to see that I got a bath and was put to bed. The following day, my parents would be notified as to where I was and asked to come and claim me. Dad was always in favor of leaving me where I was and saying good riddance. But Mama always made the trip. Although Mama never failed to come for me, she seldom found me there when she arrived. I had no trouble getting out of Children's Centers, so I seldom stayed for more than a couple of days.

When I was finally brought home—sometimes after weeks of catting—Mama would hide my clothes or my shoes. This would mean that I couldn't get out of the house if I should take a notion to do so. Anyway, that's how Mama had it figured. The truth of the matter is that these measures only made getting out of the house more difficult for me. I would have to wait until one of the fellows came around to see me. After hearing my plight, he would go out and round up some of the gang, and they would steal some clothes and shoes for me. When they had the clothes and shoes, one of them would come to the house and let me know. About ten minutes later, I would put on my sister's dress, climb down the back fire escape, and meet the gang with the clothes.

If something was too small or too large, I would go and steal the right size. This could only be done if the item that didn't fit was not the shoes. If the shoes were too small or large, I would have trouble running in them and probably get caught. So I would wait around in the backyard while someone stole me a pair.

Mama soon realized that hiding my clothes would not keep me in the house. The next thing she tried was threatening to send me away until I was twenty-one. This was only frightening to me at the moment of hearing it. Ever so often, either Dad or Mama would sit down and have a heart-to-heart talk with me. These talks were very moving. I always promised to mend my bad ways. I was always sincere and usually kept the promise for about a week. During these weeks, I went to school every day and kept my stealing at a minimum. By the beginning of the second week, I had reverted back to my wicked ways, and Mama would have to start praying all over again.

The neighborhood prophets began making prophecies about my life-span. They all had me dead, buried, and forgotten before my twenty-first birthday. These predictions were based on false tales of policemen shooting at me, on truthful tales of my falling off a trolley car into the midst of oncoming automobile traffic while hitching a ride, and also on my uncontrollable urge to steal. There was much justification for these prophecies. By the time I was nine years old, I had been hit by a bus, thrown into the Harlem River (intentionally), hit by a car, severely beaten with a chain. And I had set the house afire.

While Dad was still trying to beat me into a permanent conversion, Mama was certain that somebody had worked roots on me. She was writing to all her relatives in the South for solutions, but they were only able to say, "that boy musta been born with the devil in him." Some of them advised Mama to send me down there, because New York was no place to raise a child. Dad thought this was a good idea, and he tried to sell it to Mama. But Mama wasn't about to split up her family. She said I would stay in New York, devil or no devil. So I stayed in New York, enjoying every crazy minute.

Mama's favorite question was, "Boy, why you so bad?" I tried many times to explain to Mama that I wasn't "so bad." I tried to make her understand that it was trying to be good that generally got me into trouble. I remember telling her that I played hookey to avoid getting into trouble in school. It seemed that whenever I went to school, I got into a fight with the teacher. The teacher would take me to the principal's office. After I had fought with the principal, I would be sent home and not allowed back in school without one of my parents. So to avoid all that trouble, I just didn't go to school. When I stole things, it was only to save the family money and avoid arguments or scoldings whenever I asked for money.

Mama seemed silly to me. She was bothered because most of the parents in the neighborhood didn't allow their children to play with me. What she didn't know was that I never wanted to play with them. My friends were all daring like me, tough like me, dirty like me, ragged like me, cursed like me, and had a great love for trouble like me. We took pride in being able to hitch rides on trolleys, buses, taxicabs and in knowing how to steal and fight. We knew that we were the only kids in the neighborhood who usually had more than ten dollars in their pockets. There were other people who knew this too, and that was often a problem for us. Somebody was always trying to shake us down or rob us. This was usually done by the older hustlers in the neighborhood or by storekeepers or cops. At other times, older fellows would shake us down, con us, or Murphy us out of our loot. We accepted this as the ways of life. Everybody was stealing from everybody else. And sometimes we would shake down newsboys and shoeshine boys. So we really had no complaints coming. Although none of my sidekicks was over twelve years of age, we didn't think of ourselves as kids. The other kids my age were thought of as kids by me. I felt that since I knew more about life than they did, I had the right to regard them as kids.

In the fall of 1945, I was expelled from school for the first time. By the time February rolled around, I had been expelled from three other schools in Harlem. In February, Mama sent me downtown to live with Grandpapa on Eldridge Street. Papa enrolled me in a public school on Forsythe and Stanton Streets. It was cold that winter, and I usually went to school to be warm.

For weeks, everybody thought things were going along fine. The first day I didn't come home from school, Papa ignored it, thinking that I had gone uptown. But the next day, Mama received a card from Bellevue Hospital's psychiatric division informing her that I was undergoing psychiatric observation and that she was allowed to visit me on Wednesdays and Sundays. My grandfather knew nothing about any of this, so when Mama (his oldest daughter) came to him wanting to know what her son was doing in Bellevue, Papa asked, "How did he get there?" They both came over to Bellevue believing I had gone crazy. Dad didn't bother to come, because, as he put it, "That's where he shoulda been years ago." I was glad Dad didn't come, because he might not have believed that I was falsely accused of trying to push a boy in school out of a five-story window. Mama had already heard my teacher's version of the window incident, and now I was trying to explain my side of the story. My teacher had told her that I persuaded a boy to look out of the window to see an accident that hadn't taken place. Because of the window's wide ledge, I was holding his legs while he leaned out of the window. The boy started screaming and calling for help. When he got down out of the window, the boy said that I had been trying to push him out of the window. Just because we had fought the day before and I was the only one who saw the accidents, I ended up in the nutbox.

I don't think my story completely convinced Mama or Papa, but they gave me the benefit of the doubt. Mama told me that I would have to stay in the hospital for a few weeks. Her eyes were filled with tears when she said good-bye, and I tried to look sad too, but I was actually happy. I thought about how nice it was going to be away from Dad. Also, there were a few of my friends there, and we were sure to find something to get into. I had already had a couple of fights and won, so this was going to be a real ball.

I had lots of fun in the nutbox and learned a lot of new tricks, just as I thought. I didn't know it at the time, but many of the boys I met in Bellevue would also be with me at Wiltwyck and Warwick years later. Some of those I had bullied in the nutbox would try to turn the tables later on in life. Some would succeed.

There were a few things around to steal. There were plenty of guys to fight with and lots of adults to annoy. The one drawback that the nutbox had was school and teachers. But I found the nutbox to be such a nice place that I was sad when Mama came to take me home.

When I returned home, I was told that my former school had refused to readmit me. This was the best news I had heard since I started going to school. I thought that I had finally gotten out of going to school. But two weeks later, I was enrolled in another school in Harlem.

Within two months from the time I had left Bellevue, I found myself in Manhattan's Children Court for the first time. The reason was that I had been thrown out of two more schools, and there weren't any more in Manhattan that would accept me. The judge told Mama that if I was still in New York State when the fall semester began, he would send me someplace where I would be made to go to school. After Mama had promised the judge that I would not be in New York when September rolled around, we went home.

This was the first time that Mama had been in court, and she was pretty angry about the whole thing. All the way uptown on the bus, Mama kept telling me that I should be ashamed of myself for making her come down to that court and face those white people. Every ten or twelve blocks, Mama would stop preaching just long enough to look at me and say, "Child, maybe that head doctor was right about you," or, "Boy, why you so damn bad?" She didn't understand what the psychiatrist was talking about when he was telling her about my emotional problems. Since she couldn't understand the terms he was using, Mama thought he was trying to tell her in a nice way that I was crazy. Of course, she didn't believe him. "That ole big-nose, thick-eyeglasses white man, he looked kinda crazy his own self," she said. No, she didn't believe him, whatever it was that he had said—but sometimes she wondered if that man might have been right.

When we got back uptown, Mrs. Rogers, who lived next door to us, came over to find out how things had gone in court. Mrs. Rogers, Danny's mother, had made many trips to Manhattan's Children Court. Now she had come to sympathize with Mama. Mrs. Rogers—who was also a jackleg preacher (she did not have a church)—called everybody "child," "brother," or "sister." What a person was called by Mrs. Rogers depended on whether or not he was "saved." To be saved meant to live for the Lord. Mrs. Rogers was saved, and so was her husband; she couldn't understand why all her children had not yet been "hit by spirit."

Mrs. Rogers, a big, burly woman about fifteen years older than Mama, always called Mama "child." I can remember her saying to Mama when we came home from court that day, "Child, ain't that Lexington Avenue bus the slowest thing in this whole city?" I always found Mrs. Rogers' visits hard to take. She was a very nice meddlesome old woman, but too godly to have around constantly. Poor Danny, he had to live with it. Mrs. Rogers had told Mama that Danny was so bad because his behavior was the Lord's way of testing her faith. Dad called Mrs. Rogers the "preacher woman." He believed that Mrs. Rogers was going against the Lord's Word and that this was the reason for her son's behavior. He had often said that "the Lord never told no woman to go out and preach the Gospel to nobody." Dad said that if the Lord had wanted a woman to preach, he would have chosen a woman to be one of his apostles.

On this day, Mrs. Rogers' advice was no different from the other times. After Mama had told Mrs. Rogers about what had happened in court, Mrs. Rogers began her usual sermon, saying, "Child, you just gotta pray, you just gotta pray and trust in the Lord." I always left the house at this point, because our house would be used as a practice pulpit for the next two or three hours.

As I ran down the stairs, I tried to imagine what was going on in the house. In a little while, Mrs. Rogers would be patting her foot real fast, and she would start talking real loud, clapping her hands, shaking her head, and every other word would be "Jesus" or "Lord." I wondered why Mrs. Rogers never got tired of talking about the Lord. Before Mrs. Rogers finished her private sermon, she would have Mama talking about the Lord and patting her feet. By the time Mrs. Rogers was ready to leave, she would have Mama promising to come to a church where she was preaching next Sunday. Mama would promise, and Mrs. Rogers would start telling her how good it is to be saved, to walk with Jesus, and to let God into your soul. Even though Mama knew Dad wasn't going to let her go to a sanctified church with that "jackleg preacher woman," she still promised to go. Dad always said, "All those sanctified people is just a bunch of old hypocrites, and none of 'em ain't a bit more saved than nobody else."

Mrs. Rogers never talked about saving Dad. She said, "That man got the devil in him," and I believed it. As a matter of fact, I had suspected something like that long before Mrs. Rogers did.

We had all been to Mrs. Rogers' Sunday sermon once. All of us except Dad. She was preaching that time in what looked like a church-apartment to me and a church-store to Carole. I think most of the people there were relatives of Mrs. Rogers. All of her family was there except for Danny; he had escaped on the way to church. June, one of Mrs. Rogers' daughters, was playing an old, out-of-tune upright piano. Another one of Danny's sisters was banging two cymbals together and mumbling something about Jesus. She seemed to be in a trance. Mr. Rogers was shaking a tambourine and singing about Jesus with a faraway look in his eyes. Mrs. Rogers, who was dressed in a white robe, got up and started preaching. After Mrs. Rogers had been preaching for about fifteen minutes, an old lady got up and started screaming and shouting, "Help me, Lord Jesus!" She was still throwing her arms up and shouting for Jesus to help her when a younger woman jumped up and hollered, "Precious Lord Jesus, save me!" Mrs. Rogers' voice was getting louder all the time.

For two hours, she preached—and for two hours, people were getting up, shouting, jumping up and down, calling to Jesus for help and salvation, and falling out exhausted. Some of these "Holy Rollers," as Dad called them, would fall to the floor and start trembling rapidly; some of them even began to slobber on themselves. When I asked Mama what was wrong with those people and what they were doing on the floor, she told me that the "spirit" had hit them. When Carole heard this, she began to cry and wanted to get out of there before the spirit hit us. Mrs. Rogers had gone over to a man who was rolling on the floor, slobbering on himself, and babbling as if he were talking to the Lord. She held the man's hand very tight and told him repeatedly to walk with the Lord and not to fear Jesus. She was saying to the man, "Brother, say, 'Yes, Jesus; yes, Jesus.'" After a while, the man calmed down, and Mrs. Rogers said he had been saved.

Carole and Margie were frightened by these strange goings-on. I had been fascinated until now. But now this spirit thing had Mama jumping up and shouting. I joined Carole and Margie in a crying chorus, and the three of us started pulling on Mama. After Mama had jumped, clapped her hands, and had her say about Jesus, she fell back in her chair, tired and sweating. One of Mrs. Rogers' blood sisters had started fanning Mama. Carole, Margie, and I had stopped crying, but we were still scared, because we didn't know if Mama was all right or not.

In the makeshift pulpit, Mrs. Rogers was looking real pleased with herself, probably thinking that she had saved a lot of people. I think Mrs. Rogers judged her sermon by the number of people who were hit by the spirit and fell down during her sermon. She cautioned the people who were saved about "back-slidin'" and told them about how happy they were going to be with Jesus in their lives. She also asked some of the old saved souls to "testify." After three or four saved souls had told about what a good friend Jesus had been to them, Mrs. Rogers began her third request for money. The ushers, who were also relatives of Mrs. Rogers, passed a china bowl down each row. Carole and Margie dropped the nickel that Mama had given to each of them in the bowl, then they turned and looked at me. Although that was the first time we had ever been to church together, they would have been surprised if I had put my nickel in the bowl. I didn't surprise them that day.

While Carole and Margie were busy telling Mama about me not putting my nickel in the bowl, I was pulling a chair from the aisle behind us. All the chairs in the place were kitchen chairs, and they weren't all the same size. Before I could get the chair into our aisle, a big fat shiny dark-skinned woman with a man's voice said, "Boy, leave dat chair 'lone." I was frightened by the heavy, commanding voice, but not as much as I was after I looked up and saw that great big old woman giving me the evil eye. My first thought was that she was a witch or a hag, what-

ever that was. I knew she couldn't be the boogeyman; not in
church. But the longer I looked, the more I doubted her being
anything other than the boogeyman. About thirty seconds later,
when I had gotten my voice back, I meekly said, "Dat ain't your
chair." The next thing I heard was the sound of Mama's hand
falling heavily across my mouth. As I started crying, I heard
Mama say, "What I tole you about sassin' ole people?" While I
went on crying, Mama was telling me about the dangers of talking back to old people. I remember her saying, "If one of these
ole people put the bad mouth on you, maybe you'll be satisfied."

For years afterward, the mention of church always reminded
me of the day that we went to hear Mrs. Rogers preach. To me,
a church was a church-apartment where somebody lined up a lot
of kitchen chairs in a few rows, a preacher did a lot of shouting
about the Lord, people jumped up and down until they got
knocked down by the spirit, and Mrs. Rogers put bowls of money
on a kitchen table and kept pointing to it and asking for more.
It was a place where I had to stand up until I couldn't stand any
more and then had to sit down on hard wooden chairs. The one
good thing I got out of going to hear Mrs. Rogers preach was a
new threat to use on Carole and Margie. Whenever Carole and
Margie would threaten to tell on me, I told them that if they did,
the spirit would hit them the way it hit those people in Mrs.
Rogers' church-apartment.

Maybe Dad was right when he said Mrs. Rogers was just rob-
bing people in the name of the Lord. Anyway, I felt pretty good
about her not getting my nickel.

Even though Dad didn't care for preachers and churches, he
had a lot of religion in his own way. Most of the time, his religion didn't show. But on Saturday night, those who didn't see
it heard it. Sometimes Dad would get religious on Friday nights
too. But Saturday night was a must. Because it always took
liquor to start Dad to singing spirituals and talking about the
Lord, I thought for years that this lordly feeling was something
in a bottle of whiskey. To me, it was like castor oil or black
draught. You drink it and the next thing you know, you're doing
things.

I was introduced to religion on Saturday night. I don't recall just when, but as far back as I can remember, Saturday night was the Lord's night in our house. Whenever Dad was able to make it home on his own two feet, he would bring a recording of a spiritual, a plate of pigs' feet and potato salad from the corner delicatessen or a plate of fish-and-chips from the wine joint around the corner, and whatever was left of his last bottle of religion. He usually got home about three o'clock in the morning, and the moment he hit the block I could hear him singing (or yelling) the record he had. By the time he got upstairs, everybody in the building knew the song and hated it. Before Dad was in the house, I could hear him calling me.

By the time he finished unlocking and relocking the door at least six times, kicking on it, cursing out the lock and the neighbors who had tried to quiet him down, I was up and had already turned on the phonograph. On her way to the door, Mama would say, "Boy, turn that thing off and git back in that bed." While Mama told Dad how disgusting he was, I would be busily picking out the pigs' feet or fish-and-chips with the least amount of hot sauce on them. When Mama had gotten tired of competing with Dad's singing, she went back to bed. As Dad gave me the record —usually by Sister Rosetta Tharpe, the Dixie Hummingbirds, or the Four Blind Boys—he would tell me how somebody I had never heard of sang it in the cotton fields or at somebody's wedding or funeral "down home." After listening to the record at least a dozen times, Dad would turn the phonograph off, and we would sing the song a few times. Before dawn started sneaking through the windows, Dad and I had gone through his entire repertoire of spirituals. By daybreak, we were both drunk and had fallen on the floor, and we stayed there until we awoke later in the day.

If we—and . . . I mean the relatively conscious whites
and the relatively conscious blacks, who must, like lovers,
insist on, or create, the consciousness of the others—do not
falter in our duty now, we may be able, handful that we
are, to end the racial nightmare, and achieve our country,
and change the history of the world.

JAMES BALDWIN

My Negro Problem—and Ours

Two ideas puzzled me deeply as a child growing up in Brooklyn
during the 1930's in what today would be called an integrated
neighborhood. One of them was that all Jews were rich; the
other was that all Negroes were persecuted. These ideas had
appeared in print; therefore they must be true. My own experience and the evidence of my senses told me they were not true,
but that only confirmed what a day-dreaming boy in the provinces—for the lower-class neighborhoods of New York belong as
surely to the provinces as any rural town in North Dakota—
discovers very early: *his* experience is unreal and the evidence
of his senses is not to be trusted. Yet even a boy with a head full
of fantasies incongruously synthesized out of Hollywood movies
and English novels cannot altogether deny the reality of his own
experience—especially when there is so much deprivation in
that experience. Nor can he altogether gainsay the evidence of
his own senses—especially such evidence of the senses as comes
from being repeatedly beaten up, robbed, and in general hated,
terrorized, and humiliated.

And so for a long time I was puzzled to think that Jews were
supposed to be rich when the only Jews I knew were poor, and
that Negroes were supposed to be persecuted when it was the
Negroes who were doing the only persecuting I knew about—
and doing it, moreover, to *me*. During the early years of the war,
when my older sister joined a left-wing youth organization, I
remember my astonishment at hearing her passionately denounce my father for thinking that Jews were worse off than

Negroes. To me, at the age of twelve, it seemed very clear that Negroes were better off than Jews—indeed, than *all* whites. A city boy's world is contained within three or four square blocks, and in my world it was the whites, the Italians and Jews, who feared the Negroes, not the other way around. The Negroes were tougher than we were, more ruthless, and on the whole they were better athletes. What could it mean, then, to say that they were badly off and that we were more fortunate? Yet my sister's opinions, like print, were sacred, and when she told me about exploitation and economic forces I believed her. I believed her, but I was still afraid of Negroes. And I still hated them with all my heart.

It had not always been so—that much I can recall from early childhood. When did it start, this fear and this hatred? There was a kindergarten in the local public school, and given the character of the neighborhood, at least half of the children in my class must have been Negroes. Yet I have no memory of being aware of color differences at that age, and I know from observing my own children that they attribute no significance to such differences even when they begin noticing them. I think there was a day—first grade? second grade?—when my best friend Carl hit me on the way home from school and announced that he wouldn't play with me any more because I had killed Jesus. When I ran home to my mother crying for an explanation, she told me not to pay any attention to such foolishness, and then in Yiddish she cursed the *goyim* and the *schwartze,* the *schwartzes* and the *goyim.* Carl, it turned out, was a *schwartze,* and so was added a third to the categories into which people mysteriously divided.

Sometimes I wonder whether this is a true memory at all. It is blazingly vivid, but perhaps it never happened: can anyone really remember back to the age of six? There is no uncertainty in my mind, however, about the years that followed. Carl and I hardly ever spoke, though we met in school every day up through the eighth or ninth grade. There would be embarrassed moments of catching his eye or of his catching mine—for whatever it was that had attracted us to one another as very small children remained alive in spite of the fantastic barrier of hostility that had grown up between us, suddenly and out of nowhere. Nevertheless, friendship would have been impossible, and even if it had been possible, it would have been unthinkable. About that, there was nothing anyone could do by the time we were eight years old.

Item: The orphanage across the street is torn down, a city housing project begins to rise in its place, and on the marvelous vacant lot next to the old orphanage they are building a playground. Much excitement and anticipation as Opening Day draws near. Mayor LaGuardia himself comes to dedicate this great gesture of public benevolence. He speaks of neighborliness and borrowing cups of sugar, and of the playground he says that children of all races, colors, and creeds will learn to live together in harmony. A week later, some of us are swatting flies on the playground's inadequate little ball field. A gang of Negro kids, pretty much our own age, enter from the other side and order us out of the park. We refuse, proudly and indignantly, with superb masculine fervor. There is a fight, they win, and we retreat, half whimpering, half with bravado. My first nauseating experience of cowardice. And my first appalled realization that there are people in the world who do not seem to be afraid of anything, who act as though they have nothing to lose. Thereafter the playground becomes a battleground, sometimes quiet, sometimes the scene of athletic competition between Them and Us. But rocks are thrown as often as baseballs. Gradually we abandon the place and use the streets instead. The streets are safer, though we do not admit this to ourselves. We are not, after all, sissies—that most dreaded epithet of an American boyhood.

Item: I am standing alone in front of the building in which I live. It is late afternoon and getting dark. That day in school the teacher had asked a surly Negro boy named Quentin a question he was unable to answer. As usual I had waved my arm eagerly ("Be a good boy, get good marks, be smart, go to college, become a doctor") and, the right answer bursting from my lips, I was held up lovingly by the teacher as an example to the class. I had seen Quentin's face—a very dark, very cruel, very Oriental-looking face—harden, and there had been enough threat in his eyes to make me run all the way home for fear that he might catch me outside.

Now, standing idly in front of my own house, I see him approaching from the project accompanied by his little brother who is carrying a baseball bat and wearing a grin of malicious anticipation. As in a nightmare, I am trapped. The surroundings are secure and familiar, but terror is suddenly present and there is no one around to help. I am locked to the spot. I will not cry out or run away like a sissy, and I stand there, my heart wild, my throat clogged. He walks up, hurls the familiar epithet ("Hey, m——r"), and to my surprise only pushes me. It is a violent push, but not a punch. A push is not as serious as a punch. Maybe I can still back out without entirely losing my dignity. Maybe I can still say, "Hey, c'mon Quentin, whaddya wanna do *that* for. I dint do nothin' to *you*," and walk away, not too rapidly. Instead, before I can stop myself, I push him back—a token gesture—and I say, "Cut that out, I don't wanna fight, I ain't got nothin' to fight about." As I turn to walk back into the building, the corner of my eye catches the motion of the bat his little brother has handed him. I try to duck, but the bat crashes colored lights into my head.

The next thing I know, my mother and sister are standing over me, both of them hysterical. My sister—she who was later to join the "progressive" youth organization—is shouting for the police and screaming imprecations at those dirty little black bastards. They take me upstairs, the doctor comes, the police come. I tell them that the boy who did it was a stranger, that he had been trying to get money from me. They do not believe me, but I am too scared to give them Quentin's name. When I return to school a few days later, Quentin avoids my eyes. He knows that I have not squealed, and he is ashamed. I try to feel proud, but in my heart I know that it was fear of what his friends might do to me that had kept me silent, and not the code of the street.

Item: There is an athletic meet in which the whole of our junior high school is participating. I am in one of the seventh-grade rapid-advance classes, and "segregation" has now set in with a vengeance. In the last three or four years of the elementary school from which we have just graduated, each grade had been divided into three classes, according to "intelligence." (In the earlier grades the divisions had either been arbitrary or else unrecognized by us as having anything to do with brains.)

These divisions by IQ, or however it was arranged, had resulted in a preponderance of Jews in the "1" classes and a corresponding preponderance of Negroes in the "3's," with the Italians split unevenly along the spectrum. At least a few Negroes had always made the "1's," just as there had always been a few Jewish kids among the "3's" and more among the "2's" (where Italians dominated). But the junior high's rapid-advance class of which I am now a member is overwhelmingly Jewish and entirely white —except for a shy lonely Negro girl with light skin and reddish hair.

The athletic meet takes place in a city-owned stadium far from the school. It is an important event to which a whole day is given over. The winners are to get those precious little medallions stamped with the New York City emblem that can be screwed into a belt and that prove the wearer to be a distinguished personage. I am a fast runner, and so I am assigned the position of anchor man on my class's team in the relay race. There are three other seventh-grade teams in the race, two of them all Negro, as ours is all white. One of the all-Negro teams is very tall—their anchor man waiting silently next to me on the line looks years older than I am, and I do not recognize him. He is the first to get the baton and crosses the finishing line in a walk. Our team comes in second, but a few minutes later we are declared the winners, for it has been discovered that the anchor man on the first-place team is not a member of the class. We are awarded the medallions, and the following day our home-room teacher makes a speech about how proud she is of us for being superior athletes as well as superior students. We want to believe we deserve the praise, but we know we could not have won even if the other class had not cheated.

That afternoon, walking home, I am waylaid and surrounded by five Negroes, among whom is the anchor man of the disqualified team. "Gimme my medal, . . ." he grunts. I do not have it with me and I tell him so. "Anyway, it ain't yours," I say foolishly. He calls me a liar on both counts and pushes me up against the wall on which we sometimes play handball. "Gimme my . . . medal," he says again. I repeat that I have left it home. "Let's search the li'l . . . ," one of them suggests, "he prolly got it *hid* in his . . . *pants*." My panic is now unmanageable. (How

many times had I been surrounded like this and asked in soft
tones, "Len' me a nickel, boy." How many times had I been called
a liar for pleading poverty and pushed around, or searched, or
beaten up, unless there happened to be someone in the maraud-
ing gang like Carl who liked me across that enormous divide
of hatred and who would therefore say, "Aaah, c'mon, le's git
someone else, *this* boy ain't got no money on 'im.") I scream at
them through tears of rage and self-contempt, "Keep your . . .
filthy lousy black hands offa me! I swear I'll get the cops." This
is all they need to hear, and the five of them set upon me. They
bang me around, mostly in the stomach and on the arms and
shoulders, and when several adults loitering near the candy
store down the block notice what is going on and begin to shout,
they run off and away.

I do not tell my parents about the incident. My team-mates,
who have also been waylaid, each by a gang led by his opposite
number from the disqualified team, have had their medallions
taken from them, and they never squeal either. For days, I walk
home in terror, expecting to be caught again, but nothing happens. The medallion is put away into a drawer, never to be worn
by anyone.

Obviously experiences like these have always been a common
feature of childhood life in working-class and immigrant neighborhoods, and Negroes do not necessarily figure in them. Wherever, and in whatever combination, they have lived together
in the cities, kids of different groups have been at war, beating
up and being beaten up: micks against kikes against wops
against spicks against polacks. And even relatively homogeneous
areas have not been spared the warring of the young: one block
against another, one gang (called in my day, in a pathetic effort
at gentility, an "S.A.C.," or social-athletic club) against another.
But the Negro-white conflict had—and no doubt still has—a
special intensity and was conducted with a ferocity unmatched
by intramural white battling.

In my own neighborhood, a good deal of animosity existed between the Italian kids (most of whose parents were immigrants
from Sicily) and the Jewish kids (who came largely from East
European immigrant families). Yet everyone had friends, some-

times close friends, in the other "camp," and we often visited one another's strange-smelling houses, if not for meals, then for glasses of milk, and occasionally for some special event like a wedding or a wake. If it happened that we divided into warring factions and did battle, it would invariably be half-hearted and soon patched up. Our parents, to be sure, had nothing to do with one another and were mutually suspicious and hostile. But we, the kids, who all spoke Yiddish or Italian at home, were Americans, or New Yorkers, or Brooklyn boys; we shared a culture, the culture of the street, and at least for a while this culture proved to be more powerful than the opposing cultures of the home.

Why, *why* should it have been so different as between the Negroes and us? How was it borne in upon us so early, white and black alike, that we were enemies beyond any possibility of reconciliation? Why did we hate one another so?

I suppose if I tried, I could answer those questions more or less adequately from the perspective of what I have since learned. I could draw upon James Baldwin—what better witness is there? —to describe the sense of entrapment that poisons the soul of the Negro with hatred for the white man whom he knows to be his jailer. On the other side, if I wanted to understand how the white man comes to hate the Negro, I could call upon the psychologists who have spoken of the guilt that white Americans feel toward Negroes and that turns into hatred for lack of acknowledging itself as guilt. These are plausible answers and certainly there is truth in them. Yet when I think back upon my own experience of the Negro and his of me, I find myself troubled and puzzled, much as I was as a child when I heard that all Jews were rich and all Negroes persecuted. How could the Negroes in my neighborhood have regarded the whites across the street and around the corner as jailers? On the whole, the whites were not so poor as the Negroes, but they were quite poor enough, and the years were years of Depression. As for the white hatred of the Negro, how could guilt have had anything to do with it? What share had these Italian and Jewish immigrants in the enslavement of the Negro? What share had they—down-trodden people themselves breaking their own necks to eke out a living— in the exploitation of the Negro?

No, I cannot believe that we hated each other back there in Brooklyn because they thought of us as jailers and we felt guilty toward them. But does it matter, given the fact that we all went through an unrepresentative confrontation? I think it matters profoundly, for if we managed the job of hating each other so well without benefit of the aids to hatred that are supposedly at the root of this madness everywhere else, it must mean that the madness is not yet properly understood. I am far from pretending that I understand it, but I would insist that no view of the problem will begin to approach the truth unless it can account for a case like the one I have been trying to describe. Are the elements of any such view available to us?

At least two, I would say, are. One of them is a point we frequently come upon in the work of James Baldwin, and the other is a related point always stressed by psychologists who have studied the mechanisms of prejudice. Baldwin tells us that one of the reasons Negroes hate the white man is that the white man refuses to *look* at him: the Negro knows that in white eyes all Negroes are alike; they are faceless and therefore not altogether human. The psychologists, in their turn, tell us that the white man hates the Negro because he tends to project those wild impulses that he fears in himself onto an alien group which he then punishes with his contempt. What Baldwin does *not* tell us, however, is that the principle of facelessness is a two-way street and can operate in both directions with no difficulty at all. Thus, in my neighborhood in Brooklyn, *I* was as faceless to the Negroes as they were to me, and if they hated me because I never looked at them, I must also have hated them for never looking at *me*. To the Negroes, my white skin was enough to define me as the enemy, and in a war it is only the uniform that counts and not the person.

So with the mechanism of projection that the psychologists talk about: it too works in both directions at once. There is no question that the psychologists are right about what the Negro represents symbolically to the white man. For me as a child the life lived on the other side of the playground and down the block on Ralph Avenue seemed the very embodiment of the values of the street—free, independent, reckless, brave, masculine, erotic. I put the word "erotic" last, though it is usually stressed above all others, because in fact it came last, in consciousness as in importance. What mainly counted for me about Negro kids of my own age was that they were "bad boys." There were plenty of bad boys among the whites—this was, after all, a neighborhood with a long tradition of crime as a career open to aspiring talents—but the Negroes were *really* bad, bad in a way that beckoned to one, and made one feel inadequate. *We* all went home every day for a lunch of spinach-and-potatoes; *they* roamed around during lunch hour, munching on candy bars. In winter *we* had to wear itchy woolen hats and mittens and cumbersome galoshes; *they* were bare-headed and loose as they pleased. *We* rarely played hookey, or got into serious trouble in school, for all our street-corner bravado; *they* were defiant, forever staying out (to do what delicious things?), forever making disturbances in class and in the halls, forever being sent to the principal and returning uncowed. But most important of all, they were *tough*; beautifully, enviably tough, not giving a damn for anyone or anything. To hell with the teacher, the truant officer, the cop; to hell with the whole of the adult world that held *us* in its grip and that we never had the courage to rebel against except sporadically and in petty ways.

This is what I saw and envied and feared in the Negro: this is what finally made him faceless to me, though some of it, of course, was actually there. (The psychologists also tell us that the alien group which becomes the object of a projection will tend to respond by trying to live up to what is expected of them.) But what, on his side, did the Negro see in me that made me faceless to *him*? Did he envy me my lunches of spinach-and-potatoes and my itchy woolen caps and my prudent behavior in the face of authority, as I envied him his noon-time candy bars and his bare head in winter and his magnificent rebelliousness? Did those lunches and caps spell for him the prospect of power and riches in the future? Did they mean that there were possibilities open to me that were denied to him? Very likely they did. But if so, one also supposes that he feared the impulses within himself toward submission to authority no less powerfully than I feared the impulses in myself toward defiance. If I represented the jailer to him, it was not because I was oppressing him or keeping him down: it was because I symbolized for him the dangerous and probably pointless temptation toward greater repression, just as he symbolized for me the equally perilous tug toward greater freedom. I personally was to be rewarded for this repression with a new and better life in the future, but how many of my friends paid an even higher price and were given only gall in return.

We have it on the authority of James Baldwin that all Negroes hate whites. I am trying to suggest that on their side all whites— all American whites, that is—are sick in their feelings about Negroes. There are Negroes, no doubt, who would say that Baldwin is wrong, but I suspect them of being less honest than he is, just as I suspect whites of self-deception who tell me they have no special feeling toward Negroes. Special feelings about color are a contagion to which white Americans seem susceptible even when there is nothing in their background to account for the susceptibility. Thus everywhere we look today in the North, we find the curious phenomenon of white middle-class liberals with no previous personal experience of Negroes—people to whom Negroes have always been faceless in virtue rather than faceless in vice—discovering that their abstract commitment to the cause of Negro rights will not stand the test of a direct confrontation. We find such people fleeing in droves to the suburbs as the Negro population in the inner city grows; and when they stay in the city we find them sending their children to private school rather than to the "integrated" public school in the neighborhood. We find them resisting the demand that gerrymandered school districts be re-zoned for the purpose of overcoming *de facto* segregation; we find them judiciously considering whether the Negroes (for their own good, of course) are not perhaps pushing too hard; we find them clucking their tongues over Negro militancy; we find them speculating on the question of whether there may not, after all, be something in the theory that the races are biologically different; we find them saying that it will take a very long time for Negroes to achieve full equality, no matter what anyone does; we find them deploring the rise of black nationalism and expressing the solemn hope that the leaders of the Negro community will discover ways of containing the impatience and incipient violence within the Negro ghettos.

But that is by no means the whole story; there is also the phenomenon of what Kenneth Rexroth once called "crow-jimism." There are the broken-down white boys like Vivaldo Moore in Baldwin's *Another Country* who go to Harlem in search of sex or simply to brush up against something that looks like primitive vitality, and who are so often punished by the Negroes they meet for crimes that they would have been the last ever to commit and of which they themselves have been as sorry victims as any of the Negroes who take it out on them. There are the writers and intellectuals and artists who romanticize Negroes and pander to them, assuming a guilt that is not properly theirs. And there are all the white liberals who permit Negroes to blackmail them into adopting a double standard of moral judgment, and who lend themselves—again assuming the responsibility for crimes they never committed—to cunning and contemptuous exploitation by Negroes they employ or try to befriend.

And what about me? What kind of feelings do I have about Negroes today? What happened to me, from Brooklyn, who grew up fearing and envying and hating Negroes? Now that Brooklyn is behind me, do I fear them and envy them and hate them still? The answer is yes, but not in the same proportions and certainly not in the same way. I now live on the upper west side of Manhattan, where there are many Negroes and many Puerto Ricans, and there are nights when I experience the old apprehensiveness again, and there are streets that I avoid when I am walking in the dark, as there were streets that I avoided when I was a child. I find that I am not afraid of Puerto Ricans, but I cannot restrain my nervousness whenever I pass a group of Negroes standing in front of a bar or sauntering down the street. I know now, as I did not know when I was a child, that power is on my side, that the police are working for me and not for them. And knowing this I feel ashamed and guilty, like the good liberal I have grown up to be. Yet the twinges of fear and the resentment they bring and the self-contempt they arouse are not to be gainsaid.

But envy? Why envy? And hatred? Why hatred? Here again the intensities have lessened and everything has been complicated and qualified by the guilts and the resulting over-compensations that are the heritage of the enlightened middle-class world of which I am now a member. Yet just as in childhood I envied Negroes for what seemed to me their superior masculinity, so I envy them today for what seems to me their superior physical grace and beauty. I have come to value physical grace very highly, and I am now capable of aching with all my being when I watch a Negro couple on the dance floor, or a Negro playing baseball or basketball. They are on the kind of terms with their own bodies that I should like to be on with mine, and for that precious quality they seem blessed to me.

The hatred I still feel for Negroes is the hardest of all the old feelings to face or admit, and it is the most hidden and the most overlarded by the conscious attitudes into which I have succeeded in willing myself. It no longer has, as for me it once did, any cause or justification (except, perhaps, that I am constantly being denied my right to an honest expression of the things I earned the right as a child to feel), How, then, do I know that this hatred has never entirely disappeared? I know it from the insane rage that can stir in me at the thought of Negro anti-Semitism; I know it from the disgusting prurience that can stir in me at the sight of a mixed couple; and I know it from the violence that can stir in me whenever I encounter that special brand of paranoid touchiness to which many Negroes are prone.

This, then, is where I am; it is not exactly where I think all other white liberals are, but it cannot be so very far away either. And it is because I am convinced that we white Americans are— for whatever reason, it no longer matters—so twisted and sick in our feelings about Negroes that I despair of the present push toward integration. If the pace of progress were not a factor here, there would perhaps be no cause for despair: time and the law and even the international political situation are on the side of the Negroes, and ultimately, therefore, victory—of a sort, anyway—must come. But from everything we have learned from observers who ought to know, pace has become as important to the Negroes as substance. They want equality and they want it *now,* and the white world is yielding to their demand only as much and as fast as it is absolutely being compelled to do. The Negroes know this in the most concrete terms imaginable, and it is thus becoming increasingly difficult to buy them off with rhetoric and promises and pious assurances of support. And so within the Negro community we find more and more people declaring—as Harold R. Isaacs recently put it—that they want *out:* people who say that integration will never come, or that it will take a hundred or a thousand years to come, or that it will come at too high a price in suffering and struggle for the pallid and sodden life of the American middle class that at the very best it may bring.

The most numerous, influential, and dangerous movement that has grown out of Negro despair with the goal of integration is, of course, the Black Muslims. This movement, whatever else we may say about it, must be credited with one enduring achievement: it inspired James Baldwin to write an essay * which deserves to be placed among the classics of our language. Everything Baldwin has ever been trying to tell us is distilled here into a statement of overwhelming persuasiveness and prophetic magnificence. Baldwin's message is and always has been simple. It is this: "Color is not a human or personal reality; it is a political reality." And Baldwin's demand is correspondingly simple: color must be forgotten, lest we all be smited with a vengeance "that does not really depend on, and cannot really be executed by, any person or organization, and that cannot be prevented by any police force or army: historical vengeance, a cosmic vengeance based on the law that we recognize when we say, 'Whatever goes up must come down.'" The Black Muslims Baldwin portrays as a sign and a warning to the intransigent white world. They come to proclaim how deep is the Negro's disaffection with the white world and all its works, and Baldwin implies that no American Negro can fail to respond somewhere in his being to their message: that the white man is the devil, that Allah has doomed him to destruction, and that the black man is about to inherit the earth. Baldwin of course knows that this nightmare inversion of the racism from which the black man has suffered can neither win nor even point to the neighborhood in which victory might be located. For in his view the neighborhood of victory lies in exactly the opposite direction: the transcendence of color through love.

* Originally published in *The New Yorker* under the title "Letter from a Region in My Mind," subsequently published in book form (along with a new introduction) under the title *The Fire Next Time*.

Yet the tragic fact is that love is not the answer to hate—not in the world of politics, at any rate. Color is indeed a political rather than a human or a personal reality and if politics (which is to say power) has made it into a human and a personal reality, then only politics (which is to say power) can unmake it once again. But the way of politics is slow and bitter, and as impatience on the one side is matched by a setting of the jaw on the other, we move closer and closer to an explosion and blood may yet run in the streets.

Will this madness in which we are all caught never find a resting-place? Is there never to be an end to it? In thinking about the Jews I have often wondered whether their survival as a distinct group was worth one hair on the head of a single infant. Did the Jews have to survive so that six million innocent people should one day be burned in the ovens of Auschwitz? It is a terrible question and no one, not God himself, could ever answer it to my satisfaction. And when I think about the Negroes in America and about the image of integration as a state in which the Negroes would take their rightful place as another of the protected minorities in a pluralistic society, I wonder whether they really believe in their hearts that such a state can actually be attained, and if so *why* they should wish to survive as a distinct group. I think I know why the Jews once wished to survive (though I am less certain as to why we still do): they not only believed that God had given them no choice, but they were tied to a memory of past glory and a dream of imminent redemption. What does the American Negro have that might correspond to this? His past is a stigma, his color is a stigma, and his vision of the future is the hope of erasing the stigma by making color irrelevant, by making it disappear as a fact of consciousness.

I share this hope, but I cannot see how it will ever be realized unless color does in *fact* disappear: and that means not integration, it means assimilation, it means—let the brutal word come out—miscegenation. The Black Muslims, like their racist counterparts in the white world, accuse the "so-called Negro leaders" of secretly pursuing miscegenation as a goal. The racists are wrong, but I wish they were right, for I believe that the wholesale merging of the two races is the most desirable alternative for everyone concerned. I am not claiming that this alternative can be pursued programmatically or that it is immediately feasible as a solution; obviously there are even greater barriers to its achievement than to the achievement of integration. What I am saying, however, is that in my opinion the Negro problem can be solved in this country in no other way.

I have told the story of my own twisted feelings about Negroes here, and of how they conflict with the moral convictions I have since developed, in order to assert that such feelings must be acknowledged as honestly as possible so that they can be controlled and ultimately disregarded in favor of the convictions. It is *wrong* for a man to suffer because of the color of his skin. Beside that clichéd proposition of liberal thought, what argument can stand and be respected? If the arguments are the arguments of feeling, they must be made to yield; and one's own soul is not the worst place to begin working a huge social transformation. Not so long ago, it used to be asked of white liberals, "Would you like your sister to marry one?" When I was a boy and my sister was still unmarried, I would certainly have said no to that question. But now I am a man, my sister is already married, and I have daughters. If I were to be asked whether I would like a daughter of mine "to marry one," I would have to answer: "No, I wouldn't *like* it at all. I would rail and rave and rant and tear my hair. And then I hope I would have the courage to curse myself for raving and ranting, and to give her my blessing. How dare I withhold it at the behest of the child I once was and against the man I now have a duty to be?"

In recognizing the justice of the Negro's demands there are many temptations to sentimentality. One such temptation is to assume that it is all a matter of feeling—that we must consult our feelings in order to do justice. When Martin Luther King, standing on a platform, addressing an off-stage white society, says, "You don't have to love me to quit lynching me," he is dis-

Who Speaks for the Negro?

infecting his doctrine of *agapē* from sentimentality—from the notion of easy solutions by easy love. He is also making a grim and paradoxical joke, which Negroes greatly appreciate—to judge by the titter and applause. The joke frees them; it frees them from the need to be "lovable"—lovable by some set of white standards, i.e., servile—in order not to be lynched.

But the joke is one for the white man to ponder. For it frees him, too: from the need to "love" in order not to lynch. Translated, the joke frees him from the need to love in order to refrain from doing a whole lot of things—such as segregating buses, bombing churches, and conniving in racial covenants in housing developments.

In an ideal world, of course, our feelings would all be good— we would "love" all men—and the good feelings would express themselves immediately and effortlessly in good acts. There would be no moral problem—in fact, it might be said that there would be no moral consciousness, therefore no moral life. But in this world, the issue is not, so Dr. King is saying, one of achieving perfection; it is one of achieving a proper awareness of, and attitude toward, our imperfection. In this world, we may aspire to be pure in heart, but we can't wait for that far-off divine event before trying to be reasonably decent citizens who, with all their failings, may believe in justice. Since the odds are that, in this imperfect world, the old human heart remains rather impure, we can scarcely consult it to find out what to do. Rather than depend on our spontaneous and uncriticized feelings we had

---

better consult our intelligence, fallible as it is, to see what is reasonable, decent, socially desirable—and even just—and then, as best we can, act on that.

When, in the South, a white woman says to me, as not a few have said, "I pray to God to change my feelings," she is recognizing the old human split—between her intellectual recognition that makes her pray for a change, and her feelings which she prays that God will change. But if the split exists—and the recognition of such splits is the ground fact of our moral life— there is no ultimately compelling reason why she should wait on the mystic change of feeling before she can take a practical step. To wait for the regeneration of feeling is sentimentality, a self-flattering indulgence and an alibi.

If we want to change feelings we can remember that the performing of an act does a good deal to change the feelings of the performer of the act. In fact, one of the surest ways for an intellectual recognition to change feelings is to put the recognition, in however minimal a way, into action. But it is sentimental, again, to expect immediate, easy, and absolute regeneration of feelings just because you have joined the NAACP or sent a contribution to CORE or marched in a demonstration. It is absurd to expect such cataclysmic, glorious, and easy purgation on the particular point of racial brotherhood, when you know that you have to live in a shifting complex of feelings about mother, father, sister, brother, wife, child, friend, the U.S.A., and God Almighty. Why should you think that feelings on the question of racial brotherhood are to be exempted from the ordinary complexities of life?

* * *

Another form of sentimentality appears in the notion that the Negro—*qua* Negro—is intrinsically "better." This betterness is described in many forms, but, strangely enough, you never hear *the* Negro admired as a better philosopher, mathematician, nuclear physicist, banker, soldier, lawyer, or administrator. It would seem that the betterness is always something that can be attributed to the Noble Savage—if we give a rather generous interpretation to that term. This modern American Noble Savage is admired for athletic prowess, musicality, grace in the dance, heroic virtue, natural humor, tenderness with children, patience, sensitivity to nature, generosity of spirit, capacity to forgive, life

awareness, and innocent sexuality. A white man may choose the
particular version of the Noble Savage to suit his tastes. Here is
Jack Kerouac, in a now well-advertised passage, making his
choice:

> At lilac evening I walked with every muscle aching among
> the lights of 27th and Welton in the Denver colored section,
> wishing I were a Negro, feeling that the best the white world
> had afforded was not enough ecstasy for me, not enough
> life, joy, kicks, darkness, music, not enough night.*

It would, I imagine, be a very dull Negro who did not catch
here the note of condescension. James Baldwin, who is definitely
not dull, caught the tone, and remarked: "I would hate to be in
Jack Kerouac's shoes if he should ever be mad enough to read
this aloud from the stage of the Apollo Theater [in Harlem]."

Over and over again, directly or as irony, we may encounter
the Negro's resentment at such white man's praise. For instance,
we may remember how Stokely Carmichael resented the praise
and even the popularity he found at Bronx High. He read the
condescension in it—and worse, the special condescension in the
fact that he was being addressed as *the* Negro and not as himself. We may remember the classic example of unconscious condescension in the notion in the old sociology textbook by Park
and Burgess, of the Negro as "the lady of the races."

The risk of condescension is always present in any romantic
attachment to the simple—or to what, sometimes erroneously,
may sometimes be taken as simple: Wordsworth's peasant, child,
and idiot; Leatherstocking; the "worker" of the 1930's; folk song.
Now that *the* Negro, from Ray Charles to Martin Luther King,
is in for special attention, we find special versions of condescension. Even in the admiration, sometimes abject, for a man like
King—who is far from peasant, child, idiot, "worker," Indian
scout, or box-beater—the paradox of inferiority-superiority, the
sense of the complex person (white) recognizing simple worth
(black), the psychology of the appeal of the pastoral poem,
lurks in the very abjectness of the admiration granted.

*   *   *

There is one more kind of sentimentality that the white man
cannot afford: a sentimentality about himself. He cannot afford

* *The Subterraneans.*

to feel that he is going to redeem the Negro. For the age of philanthropy is over, and it would be vicious illusion for the white man to think that he, by acting alone, can reach a solution and pass it down to gratefully lifted black hands.

It would be an even more vicious illusion to think that in trying to solve the problem he would be giving something away, would be "liberal," or would be performing an act of charity, Christian or any other kind. The safest, soberest, most humble, and perhaps not the most ignoble way for him to think of grounding action is not on generosity, but on a proper awareness of self-interest.

It is self-interest to want to live in a society operating by the love of justice and the concept of law. We have not been living in such a society. It is self-interest to want all members of society to contribute as fully as possible to the enrichment of that society. The structure of our society has prevented that. It is self-interest to seek out friends and companions who are congenial in temperament and whose experience and capacities extend our own. Our society has restricted us in this natural quest. It is self-interest to want to escape from the pressure to conform to values which we feel immoral or antiquated. Our society has maintained such pressures. It is self-interest to want to escape from the burden of vanity into the hard and happy realization that in the diminishment of others there is a deep diminishment of the self. Our society has been organized for the diminishment of others.

More than a half-century ago, in *The Souls of Black Folk,* W.E.B. Du Bois called us "this happy-go-lucky nation which goes blundering along with its Reconstruction tragedies, its Spanish War interludes and Philippine matinees, just as though God were really dead." A lot has happened since he said that, but perhaps God is not dead yet.

It would be sentimentality to think that our society can be changed easily and without pain. It would be worse sentimentality to think that it can be changed without some pain to our particular selves—black and white. It would be realism to think that that pain would be a reasonable price to pay for what we all, selfishly, might get out of it.

One of the tragedies of the struggle against racism is that up to now there has been no national organization which could speak to the growing militancy of young black people in the urban ghetto. There has been only a civil rights movement, whose tone of voice was adapted to an audience of liberal whites. It served as a sort of buffer zone between them and angry young blacks.

Power and Racism

None of its so-called leaders could go into a rioting community and be listened to. In a sense, I blame ourselves—together with the mass media—for what has happened in Watts, Harlem, Chicago, Cleveland, Omaha. Each time the people in those cities saw Martin Luther King get slapped, they became angry; when they saw four little black girls bombed to death, they were angrier; and when nothing happened, they were steaming. We had nothing to offer that they could see, except to go out and be beaten again. We helped to build their frustration.

For too many years, black Americans marched and had their heads broken and got shot. They were saying to the country, "Look, you guys are supposed to be nice guys and we are only going to do what we are supposed to do—why do you beat us up, why don't you give us what we ask, why don't you straighten yourselves out?" After years of this, we are at almost the same point—because we demonstrated from a position of weakness. We cannot be expected any longer to march and have our heads broken in order to say to whites: come on, you're nice guys. For you are not nice guys. We have found you out.

An organization which claims to speak for the needs of a community—as does the Student Nonviolent Coordinating Committee—must speak in the tone of that community, not as somebody else's buffer zone. This is the significance of black power as a slogan. For once, black people are going to use the words they

From *The New York Review of Books*, September 22, 1966. Originally titled "What We Want." Reprinted with permission of the Student Nonviolent Coordinating Committee; Copyright © 1966, *The New York Review of Books*.

want to use—not just the words whites want to hear. And they
will do this no matter how often the press tries to stop the use
of the slogan by equating it with racism or separatism.

An organization which claims to be working for the needs of
a community—as SNCC does—must work to provide that community with a position of strength from which to make its voice
heard. This is the significance of black power beyond the slogan.

Black power can be clearly defined for those who do not attach
the fears of white America to their questions about it. We should
begin with the basic fact that black Americans have two problems: they are poor and they are black. All other problems arise
from this two-sided reality: lack of education, the so-called
apathy of black men. Any program to end racism must address
itself to that double reality.

Almost from its beginning, SNCC sought to address itself to
both conditions with a program aimed at winning political
power for impoverished Southern blacks. We had to begin with
politics because black Americans are a propertyless people in a
country where property is valued above all. We had to work for
power, because this country does not function by morality, love,
and nonviolence, but by power. Thus we determined to win
political power, with the idea of moving on from there into
activity that would have economic effects. With power, the
masses could *make or participate in making* the decisions which
govern their destinies, and thus create basic change in their
day-to-day lives.

But if political power seemed to be the key to self-determination, it was also obvious that the key had been thrown down a
deep well many years earlier. Disenfranchisement, maintained
by racist terror, made it impossible to talk about organizing for
political power in 1960. The right to vote had to be won, and
SNCC workers devoted their energies to this from 1961 to 1965.
They set up voter registration drives in the Deep South. They
created pressure for the vote by holding mock elections in Mississippi in 1963 and by helping to establish the Mississippi Freedom
Democratic Party (MFDP) in 1964. That struggle was eased,
though not won, with the passage of the 1965 Voting Rights Act.
SNCC workers could then address themselves to the question:

"Who can we vote for, to have our needs met—how do we make our vote meaningful?"

SNCC had already gone to Atlantic City for recognition of the Mississippi Freedom Democratic Party by the Democratic convention and been rejected; it had gone with the MFDP to Washington for recognition by Congress and been rejected. In Arkansas, SNCC helped thirty Negroes to run for School Board elections; all but one were defeated, and there was evidence of fraud and intimidation sufficient to cause their defeat. In Atlanta, Julian Bond ran for the state legislature and was elected—twice—and unseated—twice. In several states, black farmers ran in elections for agricultural committees which make crucial decisions concerning land use, loans, etc. Although they won places on a number of committees, they never gained the majorities needed to control them.

All of the efforts were attempts to win black power. Then, in Alabama, the opportunity came to see how blacks could be organized on an independent party basis. An unusual Alabama law provides that any group of citizens can nominate candidates for county office and, if they win 20 per cent of the vote, may be recognized as a county political party. The same then applies on a state level. SNCC went to organize in several counties such as Lowndes, where black people—who form 80 per cent of the population and have an average annual income of $943—felt they could accomplish nothing within the framework of the Alabama Democratic Party because of its racism and because the qualifying fee for this year's elections was raised from $50 to $500 in order to prevent most Negroes from becoming candidates. On May 3, five new county "freedom organizations" convened and nominated candidates for the offices of sheriff, tax assessor, members of the school boards. These men and women are up for election in November—if they live until then. Their ballot symbol is the black panther: a bold, beautiful animal, representing the strength and dignity of black demands today. A man needs a black panther on his side when he and his family must endure—as hundreds of Alabamians have endured—loss of job, eviction, starvation, and sometimes death, for political activity. He may also need a gun and SNCC reaffirms the right of black men everywhere to defend themselves when threatened or attacked. As for initiating the use of violence, we hope that such programs as ours will make that unnecessary; but it is not for us to tell black communities whether they can or cannot use any particular form of action to resolve their problems. Responsibility for the use of violence by black men, whether in self-defense or initiated by them, lies with the white community.

This is the specific historical experience from which SNCC's call for "black power" emerged on the Mississippi march last July. But the concept of "black power" is not a recent or isolated phenomenon: It has grown out of the ferment of agitation and activity by different people and organizations in many black communities over the years. Our last year of work in Alabama added a new concrete possibility. In Lowndes county, for example, black power will mean that if a Negro is elected sheriff, he can end police brutality. If a black man is elected tax assessor, he can collect and channel funds for the building of better roads and schools serving black people—thus advancing the move from political power into the economic arena. In such areas as Lowndes, where black men have a majority, they will attempt to use it to exercise control. This is what they seek: control. Where Negroes lack a majority, black power means proper representation and sharing of control. It means the creation of power bases from which black people can work to change statewide or nationwide patterns of oppression through pressure from strength—instead of weakness. Politically, black power means what it has always meant to SNCC: the coming-together of black people to elect representatives and *to force those representatives to speak to their needs.* It does not mean merely putting black faces into office. A man or woman who is black and from the slums cannot be automatically expected to speak to the needs of black people. Most of the black politicians we see around the country today are not what SNCC means by black power. The power must be that of a community, and emanate from there.

SNCC today is working in both North and South on programs of voter registration and independent political organizing. In some places, such as Alabama, Los Angeles, New York, Philadelphia, and New Jersey, independent organizing under the black panther symbol is in progress. The creation of a national "black panther party" must come about; it will take time to build, and it is much too early to predict its success. We have no infallible master plan and we make no claim to exclusive knowledge of how to end racism; different groups will work in their own different ways. SNCC cannot spell out the full logistics of self-determination but it can address itself to the problem by helping black communities define their needs, realize their strength, and go into action along a variety of lines which they must choose for themselves. Without knowing all the answers, It can address itself to the basic problem of poverty; to the fact that in Lowndes County, 86 white families own 90 per cent of the land. What are black people in that county going to do for jobs, where are they going to get money? There must be reallocation of land, of money.

Ultimately, the economic foundations of this country must be shaken if black people are to control their lives. The colonies of the United States—and this includes the black ghettoes within its borders, north and south—must be liberated. For a century, this nation has been like an octopus of exploitation, its tentacles stretching from Mississippi and Harlem to South America, the Middle East, southern Africa, and Vietnam; the form of exploitation varies from area to area but the essential result has been the same—a powerful few have been maintained and enriched at the expense of the poor and voiceless colored masses. This pattern must be broken. As its grip loosens here and there around the world, the hopes of black Americans become more realistic. For racism to die, a totally different America must be born.

This is what the white society does not wish to face; this is why that society prefers to talk about integration. But integration speaks not at all to the problem of poverty, only to the problem of blackness. Integration today means the man who "makes it," leaving his black brothers behind in the ghetto as fast as his new sports car will take him. It has no relevance to the Harlem wino or to the cottonpicker making three dollars a day. As a lady I know in Alabama once said, "the food that Ralph Bunche eats doesn't fill my stomach."

Integration, moreover, speaks to the problem of blackness in a despicable way. As a goal, it has been based on complete acceptance of the fact that *in order to have* a decent house or education, blacks must move into a white neighborhood or send their children to a white school. This reinforces, among both black and white, the idea that "white" is automatically better and "black" is by definition inferior. This is why integration is a subterfuge for the maintenance of white supremacy. It allows the nation to focus on a handful of Southern children who get into white schools, at great price, and to ignore the 94 per cent who are left behind in unimproved all-black schools. Such situations will not change until black people have power—to control their own school boards, in this case. Then Negroes become equal in a way that means something, and integration ceases to be a one-way street. Then integration doesn't mean draining skills and energies from the ghetto into white neighborhoods; then it can mean white people moving from Beverly Hills into Watts, white people joining the Lowndes County Freedom Organization. Then integration becomes relevant.

Last April, before the furor over black power, Christopher Jencks wrote in a *New Republic* article on white Mississippi's manipulation of the anti-poverty program:

> The war on poverty has been predicated on the notion that there is such a thing as *a community* which can be defined geographically and mobilized for a collective effort to help the poor. This theory has no relationship to reality in the Deep South. In every Mississippi county there are *two* communities. Despite all the pious platitudes of the moderates on both sides, these two communities habitually see their interests in terms of conflict rather than cooperation. Only when the Negro community can muster enough political, economic and professional strength to compete on somewhat equal terms, will Negroes believe in the possibility of true cooperation and whites accept its necessity. En route to integration, the Negro community needs to develop greater independence—a chance to run its own affairs and not cave in whenever "the man" barks . . . Or so it seems to me, and to most of the knowledgeable people with whom I talked in Mississippi. To OEO, this judgment may sound like black nationalism . . .

Mr. Jencks, a white reporter, perceived the reason why America's anti-poverty program has been a sick farce in both North and South. In the South, it is clearly racism which prevents the poor from running their own programs; in the North, it more often seems to be politicking and bureaucracy. But the results are not so different: In the North, non-whites make up 42 per cent of all families in metropolitan "poverty areas" and only 6 per cent of families in areas classified as not poor. SNCC has been working with local residents in Arkansas, Alabama, and Mississippi to achieve control by the poor of the program and its funds; it has also been working with groups in the North, and the struggle is no less difficult. Behind it all is a federal government which cares far more about winning the war on the Vietnamese than the war on poverty; which has put the poverty program in the hands of self-serving politicians and bureaucrats rather than the poor themselves; which is unwilling to curb the misuse of white power but quick to condemn black power.

To most whites, black power seems to mean that the Mau Mau are coming to the suburbs at night. The Mau Mau are coming, and whites must stop them. Articles appear about plots to "get Whitey," creating an atmosphere in which "law and order must be maintained." Once again, responsibility is shifted from the oppressor to the oppressed. Other whites chide, "Don't forget— you're only 10 per cent of the population; if you get too smart, we'll wipe you out." If they are liberals, they complain, "what about me?—don't you want my help any more?" These are people supposedly concerned about black Americans, but today they think first of themselves, of their feelings of rejection. Or they admonish, "you can't get anywhere without coalitions," without considering the problems of coalition with whom?; on what terms? (coalescing from weakness can mean absorption, betrayal); when? Or they accuse us of "polarizing the races" by our calls for black unity, when the true responsibility for polarization lies with whites who will not accept their responsibility as the majority power for making the democratic process work.

White America will not face the problem of color, the reality of it. The well-intended say: "We're all human, everybody is really decent, we must forget color." But color cannot be "forgotten" until its weight is recognized and dealt with. White America will not acknowledge that the ways in which this country sees itself are contradicted by being black—and always have been. Whereas most of the people who settled this country came here for freedom or for economic opportunity, blacks were brought here to be slaves. When the Lowndes County Freedom Organization chose the black panther as its symbol, it was christened by the press "the Black Panther Party"—but the Alabama Democratic Party, whose symbol is a rooster, has never been called the White Cock Party. No one ever talked about "white power" because power in this country *is* white. All this adds up to more than merely identifying a group phenomenon by some catchy name or adjective. The furor over that black panther reveals the problems that white America has with color and sex; the furor over "black power" reveals how deep racism runs and the great fear which is attached to it.

Whites will not see that I, for example, as a person oppressed because of my blackness, have common cause with other blacks who are oppressed because of blackness. This is not to say that there are no white people who see things as I do, but that it is black people I must speak to first. It must be the oppressed to whom SNCC addresses itself primarily, not to friends from the oppressing group.

From birth, black people are told a set of lies about themselves. We are told that we are lazy—yet I drive through the Delta area of Mississippi and watch black people picking cotton in the hot sun for fourteen hours. We are told, "If you work hard, you'll succeed"—but if that were true, black people would own this country. We are oppressed because we are black—not because we are ignorant, not because we are lazy, not because we're stupid (and got good rhythm), but because we're black.

I remember that when I was a boy, I used to go to see Tarzan movies on Saturday. White Tarzan used to beat up the black natives. I would sit there yelling, "Kill the beasts, kill the savages, kill 'em!" I was saying: Kill *me*. It was as if a Jewish boy watched Nazis taking Jews off to concentration camps and cheered them on. Today, I want the chief to beat hell out of Tarzan and send him back to Europe. But it takes time to become free of the lies and their shaming effect on black minds. It takes time to reject the most important lie: that black people inherently can't do the same things white people can do, unless white people help them.

The need for psychological equality is the reason why SNCC today believes that blacks must organize in the black community. Only black people can convey the revolutionary idea that black people are able to do things themselves. Only they can help create in the community an aroused and continuing black consciousness that will provide the basis for political strength. In the past, white allies have furthered white supremacy without the whites involved realizing it—or wanting it, I think. Black people must do things for themselves; they must get poverty money they will control and spend themselves, they must conduct tutorial programs themselves so that black children can identify with black people. This is one reason Africa has such importance: The reality of black men ruling their own nations gives blacks elsewhere a sense of possibility, of power, which they do not now have.

This does not mean we don't welcome help, or friends. But we want the right to decide whether anyone is, in fact, our friend. In the past, black Americans have been almost the only people whom everybody and his momma could jump up and call their friends. We have been tokens, symbols, objects—as I was in high school to many young whites, who liked having "a Negro friend." We want to decide who is our friend, and we will not accept someone who comes to us and says: "If you do X, Y, and Z, then I'll help you." We will not be told whom we should choose as allies. We will not be isolated from any group or nation except by our own choice. We cannot have the oppressors telling the oppressed how to rid themselves of the oppressor.

I have said that most liberal whites react to "black power" with the question, What about me?, rather than saying: Tell me what you want me to do and I'll see if I can do it. There are answers to the right question. One of the most disturbing things about almost all white supporters of the movement has been that they are afraid to go into their own communities—which is where the racism exists—and work to get rid of it. They want to run from Berkeley to tell us what to do in Mississippi; let them look instead at Berkeley. They admonish blacks to be nonviolent; let them preach nonviolence in the white community. They come to teach me Negro history; let them go to the suburbs and open up freedom schools for whites. Let them work to stop America's racist foreign policy; let them press this government to cease supporting the economy of South Africa.

There is a vital job to be done among poor whites. We hope to see, eventually, a coalition between poor blacks and poor whites. That is the only coalition which seems acceptable to us, and we see such a coalition as the major internal instrument of change in American society. SNCC has tried several times to organize poor whites; we are trying again now, with an initial training program in Tennessee. It is purely academic today to talk about bringing poor blacks and whites together, but the job of creating a poor-white power bloc must be attempted. The main responsibility for it falls upon whites. Black and white can work together in the white community where possible; it is not possible, however, to go into a poor Southern town and talk about integration. Poor whites everywhere are becoming more hostile—not less— partly because they see the nation's attention focused on black poverty and nobody coming to them. Too many young middle-class Americans, like some sort of Pepsi generation, have wanted to come alive through the black community; they've wanted to be where the action is—and the action has been in the black community.

Black people do not want to "take over" this country. They don't want to "get whitey"; they just want to get him off their backs, as the saying goes. It was for example the exploitation by Jewish landlords and merchants which first created black resentment toward Jews—not Judaism. The white man is irrelevant to blacks, except as an oppressive force. Blacks want to be in his place, yes, but not in order to terrorize and lynch and starve him. They want to be in his place because that is where a decent life can be had.

But our vision is not merely of a society in which all black men have enough to buy the good things of life. When we urge that black money go into black pockets, we mean the communal pocket. We want to see money go back into the community and used to benefit it. We want to see the cooperative concept applied in business and banking. We want to see black ghetto residents demand that an exploiting landlord or storekeeper sell them, at minimal cost, a building or a shop that they will own and improve cooperatively; they can back their demand with a rent strike, or a boycott, and a community so unified behind them that no one else will move into the building or buy at the store. The society we seek to build among black people, then, is not a capitalist one. It is a society in which the spirit of community and humanistic love prevail. The word love is suspect; black expectations of what it might produce have been betrayed too often. But those were expectations of a response from the white community, which failed us. The love we seek to encourage is within the black community, the only American community where men call each other "brother" when they meet. We can build a community of love only where we have the ability and power to do so: among blacks.

As for white America, perhaps it can stop crying out against "black supremacy," "black nationalism," "racism in reverse," and begin facing reality. The reality is that this nation, from top to bottom, is racist; that racism is not primarily a problem of "human relations" but of an exploitation maintained—either actively or through silence—by the society as a whole. Camus and Sartre have asked, can a man condemn himself? Can whites, particularly liberal whites, condemn themselves? Can they stop blaming us, and blame their own system? Are they capable of the shame which might become a revolutionary emotion?

We have found that they usually cannot condemn themselves, and so we have done it. But the rebuilding of this society, if at all possible, is basically the responsibility of whites—not blacks. We won't fight to save the present society, in Vietnam or anywhere else. We are just going to work, in the way *we* see fit, and on goals *we* define, not for civil rights but for all our human rights.

6

God

"It is incomprehensible that God should exist and incomprehensible that he should not." Thus Pascal brought into sharp focus a question that has become one of the major dilemmas of religious thinkers in our time. Faced with the steady diminution of the supernatural by the advance of science and human knowledge, religious men have been forced to redefine the fundamental principles of their belief. In the Sixties this redefinition took a number of forms, but the best known was the adoption by a group of young theologians of Nietzsche's phrase "God is dead."

Because of its dramatic shock appeal, the phrase proved to be an effective rallying cry for those who wished to confront head-on the question of the relevance of religion to contemporary life. It had become painfully obvious that the traditional religions no longer wielded the ethical, social or spiritual influence they once had. The young theologians called for a new theological reformation. The old formulas had to be re-examined and reinterpreted according to the moral realities of twentieth-century life. At the foundation of this reformation was to be a re-examination of that most fundamental question—what is the nature of God?

The essays printed here by John A. T. Robinson, the Anglican Bishop of Woolwich, England, and Leslie Dewart, a Catholic theologian, represent two attempts at redefinition. They are notable for their unflinching honesty and their insistence on new modes of thought.

Less obviously revolutionary but possibly even more profoundly probing of traditional theological thinking are the two other positions represented here. Abraham Heschel redirects our attention to the prophets of the Old Testament and their intense experience of the reality of God's presence. In the final essay, the novelist John Updike attempts to summarize the nature and sources of the thought of Karl Barth. Barth readily grants God's incomprehensibility and the absurdity of the attempt to "prove" His existence, but asserts that this fact merely testifies to His absolute, unintelligible otherness and the radically curtailed limits of human experience.

JOHN A. T. ROBINSON

Must Christianity Be 'Supranaturalist'?

Traditional Christian theology has been based upon the proofs for the existence of God. The presupposition of these proofs, psychologically if not logically, is that God might or might not exist. They argue from something which everyone admits exists

The End of Theism?

(the world) to a Being beyond it who could or could not be there. The purpose of the argument is to show that he must be there, that his being is 'necessary'; but the presupposition behind it is that there is an entity or being 'out there' whose existence is problematic and has to be demonstrated. Now such an entity, even if it could be proved beyond dispute, would not be God: it would merely be a further piece of existence, that might conceivably not have been there—or a demonstration would not have been required.

Rather, we must start the other way round. God is, by definition, ultimate reality. And one cannot argue whether ultimate reality *exists*. One can only ask what ultimate reality is like— whether, for instance, in the last analysis what lies at the heart of things and governs their working is to be described in personal or impersonal categories. Thus, the fundamental theological question consists not in establishing the 'existence' of God as a separate entity but in pressing through in ultimate concern to what [Paul] Tillich calls 'the ground of our being.'

What he has to say at this point is most readily summarized in the opening pages of the second volume of his *Systematic Theology*, where he restates the position he has argued in the first volume and defends it against his critics.

The traditional formulation of Christianity, he says, has been in terms of what he calls 'supranaturalism.' According to this way of thinking, which is what we have all been brought up to,

From *Honest to God* by John A. T. Robinson. Published in the U.S.A., by The Westminster Press; © SCM Press Ltd., 1963. Used by permission.

God is posited as 'the highest Being'—out there, above and beyond this world, existing in his own right alongside and over against his creation. As Tillich puts it elsewhere, he is

> a being beside others and as such part of the whole of reality. He certainly is considered its most important part, but as a part and therefore as subjected to the structure of the whole . . . He is seen as a self which has a world, as an ego which is related to a thou, as a cause which is separated from its effect, as having a definite space and an endless time. He is a being, not being-itself.[1]

The caricature of this way of thinking is the Deist conception of God's relation to the world. Here God is the supreme Being, the grand Architect, who exists somewhere out beyond the world —like a rich aunt in Australia—who started it all going, periodically intervenes in its running, and generally gives evidence of his benevolent interest in it.

It is a simple matter to shoot down this caricature and to say that what *we* believe in is not Deism but Theism, and that God's relationship to the world is fully and intimately personal, not this remote watchmaker relationship described by the Deists. But it is easy to modify the *quality* of the relationship and to leave the basic structure of it unchanged, so that we continue to picture God as a Person, who looks down at this world which he has made and loves from 'out there.' We know, of course, that he does not exist in space. But we think of him nevertheless as defined and marked off from other beings *as if* he did. And this is what is decisive. He is thought of as *a* Being whose separate existence over and above the sum of things has to be demonstrated and established.

It is difficult to criticize this way of thinking without appearing to threaten the entire fabric of Christianity—so interwoven is it in the warp and woof of our thinking. And, of course, it *is* criticized by those who reject this supranaturalist position as a rejection of Christianity. Those who, in the famous words of Laplace to Napoleon, 'find no need of this hypothesis' attack it in the name of what they call the 'naturalist' position. The most influential exponent of this position in England today, Professor Julian Huxley, expressly contrasts 'dualistic supernaturalism'

[1] *The Courage to Be* (1952), p. 175.

with 'unitary naturalism.' The existence of God as a separate
entity can, he says, be dismissed as superfluous; for the world
may be explained just as adequately without positing such a
Being.

The 'naturalist' view of the world identifies God, not indeed
with the totality of things, the universe, *per se*, but with what
gives meaning and direction to nature. In Tillich's words,

> The phrase *deus sive natura*, used by people like Scotus
> Erigena and Spinoza, does not say that God is identical
> with nature but that he is identical with the *natura natu-*
> *rans*, the creative nature, the creative ground of all natural
> objects. In modern naturalism the religious quality of these
> affirmations has almost disappeared, especially among
> philosophizing scientists who understand nature in terms
> of materialism and mechanism.[2]

Huxley himself has indeed argued movingly for religion as a
necessity of the human spirit. But any notion that God really
exists 'out there' must be dismissed: 'gods are peripheral phenomena produced by evolution.' True religion (if that is not a
contradiction in terms, as it would be for the Marxist) consists
in harmonizing oneself with the evolutionary process as it develops ever higher forms of self-consciousness.

'Naturalism' as a philosophy of life is clearly and consciously
an attack on Christianity. For it 'the term "God" becomes interchangeable with the term "universe" and therefore is semanti-
cally superfluous.' But the God it is bowing out is the God of the
'supranaturalist' way of thinking. The real question is how far
Christianity is identical with, or ultimately committed to, this
way of thinking.

Must Christianity Be 'Mythological'?

Undoubtedly it has been identified with it, and somewhere deep
down in ourselves it still is. The whole world-view of the Bible,
to be sure, is unashamedly supranaturalistic. It thinks in terms
of a three-storey universe with God up there, 'above' nature. But

---

[2] *Systematic Theology*, vol. II, p. 7.

even when we have refined away what we should regard as the crudities and literalism of this construction, we are still left with what is essentially a mythological picture of God and his relation to the world. Behind such phrases as 'God created the heavens and the earth,' or 'God came down from heaven,' or 'God sent his only-begotten Son,' lies a view of the world which portrays God as a person living in heaven, *a* God who is distinguished from the gods of the heathen by the fact that 'there is no god beside me.'

In the last century a painful but decisive step forward was taken in the recognition that the Bible does contain 'myth,' and that this is an important form of religious truth. It was gradually acknowledged, by all except extreme fundamentalists, that the Genesis stories of the Creation and Fall were representations of the deepest truths about man and the universe in the form of myth rather than history, and were none the less valid for that. Indeed, it was essential to the defence of Christian truth to recognize and assert that these stories were *not* history, and not therefore in competition with the alternative accounts of anthropology or cosmology. Those who did not make this distinction were, we can now see, playing straight into the hands of Thomas Huxley and his friends.

In this century the ground of the debate has shifted—though in particular areas of Christian doctrine (especially in that of the last things) the dispute that raged a hundred years ago in relation to the first things has still to be fought through to its conclusion, and the proper distinction established between what statements are intended as history and what as myth. But the centre of today's debate is concerned not with the relation of particular myths to history, but with how far Christianity is committed to a mythological, or supranaturalist, picture of the universe at all. Is it necessary for the Biblical faith to be expressed in terms of this world-view, which in its way is as primitive philosophically as the Genesis stories are primitive scientifically? May it not be that the truth of Christianity can be detached from the one as much as from the other—and may it not be equally important to do so if it is to be defended properly today? In other words, is the reaction to naturalism the rehabilitation of supranaturalism, or can one say that Julian Huxley is performing as valuable a service in detaching Christianity from the latter as

we now see his grandfather was in shaking the Church out of its
obscurantism in matters scientific?

This is the problem to which Bultmann has addressed himself. And he answers boldly, 'There is nothing specifically Christian in the mythical view of the world as such. It is simply the
cosmology of a pre-scientific age.' The New Testament, he says,
presents redemption in Christ as a supranatural event—as the
incarnation from 'the other side' of a celestial Being who enters
this earthly scene through a miraculous birth, performs signs
and wonders as an indication of his heavenly origin, and after
an equally miraculous resurrection returns by ascent to the
celestial sphere whence he came. In truth, Bultmann maintains,
all this language is not, properly speaking, describing a supranatural transaction of any kind but is an attempt to express the
real depth, dimension and significance of the *historical* event of
Jesus Christ. In this person and event there was something of
ultimate, unconditional significance for human life—and that,
translated into the mythological view of the world, comes out as
'God' (a Being up there) 'sending' (to 'this' world) his only-
begotten 'Son.' The transcendental significance of the historical
event is 'objectivized' as a supranatural transaction.

I do not wish here to be drawn into the controversy which
Bultmann's programme of demythologizing has provoked. Much
of it has, I believe, been due to elements in his presentation
which are to some extent personal and fortuitous. Thus,

(*a*) Bultmann is inclined to make statements about what 'no
modern man' could accept (such as 'It is impossible to use electric light and the wireless and believe . . .') which reflect the
scientific dogmatism of a previous generation. This gives to
some of his exposition an air of old-fashioned modernism.

(*b*) The fact that he regards *so much* of the Gospel history as
expendable (e.g., the empty tomb *in toto*) is due to the fact
that purely in his capacity as a New Testament critic he is
extremely, and I believe unwarrantably, distrustful of the tradition. His historical scepticism is not necessarily implied in his
critique of mythology.

(*c*) His heavy reliance on the particular philosophy of
(Heidegger's) Existentialism as a replacement for the mythological world-view is historically, and indeed geographically,
conditioned. He finds it valuable as a substitute for the contem-

porary generation in Germany; but we are not bound to embrace it as the only alternative.

One of the earliest and most penetrating criticisms of Bultmann's original essay was made by Bonhoeffer, and to quote it will serve as a transition to his own contribution. 'My view of it today,' he writes from prison in 1944,

> would be not that he went too far, as most people seem to think, but that he did not go far enough. It is not only the mythological conceptions such as the miracles, the ascension and the like (which are not in principle separable from the conceptions of God, faith and so on) that are problematic, but the 'religious' conceptions themselves. You cannot, as Bultmann imagines, separate God and miracles, but you do have to be able to interpret and proclaim *both* of them in a 'non-religious' sense.[3]

Must Christianity Be 'Religious'?

What does Bonhoeffer mean by this startling paradox of a non-religious understanding of God?

> I will try to define my position from the historical angle. The movement beginning about the thirteenth century (I am not going to get involved in any arguments about the exact date) towards the autonomy of man (under which head I place the discovery of the laws by which the world lives and manages in science, social and political affairs, art, ethics and religion) has in our time reached a certain completion. Man has learned to cope with all questions of importance without recourse to God as a working hypothesis. In questions concerning science, art, and even ethics, this has become an understood thing which one scarcely dares to tilt at any more. But for the last hundred years or so it has been increasingly true of religious questions also: it is becoming evident that everything gets along without 'God,' and just as well as before. As in the scientific field, so in human affairs generally, what we call 'God' is being more and more edged out of life, losing more and more ground.

[3] Dietrich Bonhoeffer, *Letters and Papers from Prison* (1953), p. 125; reprinted by permission of The Macmillan Company and SCM Press Ltd. Copyright 1953 by The Macmillan Company.

Catholic and Protestant historians are agreed that it is in this development that the great defection from God, from Christ, is to be discerned, and the more they bring in and make use of God and Christ in opposition to this trend, the more the trend itself considers itself to be anti-Christian. The world which has attained to a realization of itself and of the laws which govern its existence is so sure of itself that we become frightened. False starts and failures do not make the world deviate from the path and development it is following; they are accepted with fortitude and detachment as part of the bargain, and even an event like the present war is no exception. Christian apologetic has taken the most varying forms of opposition to this self-assurance. Efforts are made to prove to a world thus come of age that it cannot live without the tutelage of 'God.' Even though there has been surrender on all secular problems, there still remain the so-called ultimate questions—death, guilt—on which only 'God' can furnish an answer, and which are the reason why God and the Church and the pastor are needed. Thus we live, to some extent by these ultimate questions of humanity. But what if one day they no longer exist as such, if they too can be answered without 'God'? . . .

The attack by Christian apologetic upon the adulthood of the world I consider to be in the first place pointless, in the second ignoble, and in the third un-Christian. Pointless, because it looks to me like an attempt to put a grown-up man back into adolescence, i.e., to make him dependent on things on which he is not in fact dependent any more, thrusting him back into the midst of problems which are in fact not problems for him any more. Ignoble, because this amounts to an effort to exploit the weakness of man for purposes alien to him and not freely subscribed to by him. Un-Christian, because for Christ himself is being substituted one particular stage in the religiousness of man.[4]

Bonhoeffer speaks of the God of 'religion' as a *deus ex machina*. He must be 'there' to provide the answers and explanations beyond the point at which our understanding or our capacities fail. But such a God is constantly pushed further and further back as the tide of secular studies advances. In science, in politics, in ethics the need is no longer felt for such a stop-gap or long-stop; he is not required in order to guarantee anything, to solve anything, or in any way to come to the rescue. In the same vein Julian Huxley writes:

[4] *Op. cit.*, pp. 145–7.

The god hypothesis is no longer of any pragmatic value for the interpretation or comprehension of nature, and indeed often stands in the way of better and truer interpretation. Operationally, God is beginning to resemble not a ruler but the last fading smile of a cosmic Cheshire Cat.[5]

It will soon be as impossible for an intelligent, educated man or woman to believe in a god as it is now to believe that the earth is flat, that flies can be spontaneously generated, that disease is a divine punishment, or that death is always due to witchcraft. Gods will doubtless survive, sometimes under the protection of vested interests, or in the shelter of lazy minds, or as puppets used by politicians, or as refuges for unhappy and ignorant souls.[6]

And it is in this final haunt, says Bonhoeffer, that the God who has been elbowed out of every other sphere has a 'last secret place,' in the private world of the individual's need. This is the sphere of 'religion' and it is here that the Churches now operate, doing their work among those who feel, or can be induced to feel, this need.

The only people left for us to light on in the way of 'religion' are a few 'last survivals of the age of chivalry,' or else one or two who are intellectually dishonest. Would they be the chosen few? Is it on this dubious group and none other that we are to pounce, in fervour, pique, or indignation, in order to sell them the goods we have to offer? Are we to fall upon one or two unhappy people in their weakest moment and force upon them a sort of religious coercion? [7]

Bonhoeffer's answer is that we should boldly discard 'the religious premise,' as St. Paul had the courage to jettison circumcision as a precondition of the Gospel, and accept 'the world's coming of age' as a God-given fact. 'The only way to be honest is to recognize that we have to live in the world *etsi deus non daretur*—even if God is not 'there.' Like children outgrowing the secure religious, moral and intellectual framework of the home, in which 'Daddy' is always there in the background, 'God is teaching us that we must live as men who can get along very well without him.'

[5] *Religion without Revelation*, 2nd ed., p. 58.

[6] *Ibid.*, p. 62. Cf. S. Freud, *The Future of an Illusion* (1928), pp. 76 f.

[7] *Op. cit.*, p. 122.

The God who makes us live in this world without using him as a working hypothesis is the God before whom we are ever standing. Before God and with him we live without God. God allows himself to be edged out of the world, and that is exactly the way, the only way, in which he can be with us and help us. . . . This is the decisive difference between Christianity and all religions. Man's religiosity makes him look in his distress to the power of God in the world; he uses God as a *Deus ex machina*. The Bible however directs him to the powerlessness and suffering of God; only a suffering God can help. To this extent we may say that the process we have described by which the world came of age was an abandonment of a false conception of God, and a clearing of the decks for the God of the Bible, who conquers power and space in the world by his weakness. This must be the starting point for our 'worldly' interpretation.[8]

Transcendence for Modern Man

Bonhoeffer here touches on what he would put in the place of what he has demolished, and to this we shall return in the chapters that follow. This chapter has been concerned with 'clearing the decks' and it has inevitably therefore been destructive. I have called it 'The End of Theism?', following Tillich's lead. For, as he says, theism as ordinarily understood 'has made God a heavenly, completely perfect person who resides above the world and mankind.' Classical Christian theology has not in fact spoken of God as a 'person' (partly because the term was already pre-empted for the three 'persons' of the Trinity), and the Church's best theologians have not laid themselves open to such attack. They would have been content with the essential orthodoxy of Professor Norman Pittenger's description of God as 'the Reality undergirding and penetrating through the whole derived creation.' Yet popular Christianity has always posited such a supreme personality. And Julian Huxley cannot be blamed for seeing 'humanity in general, and religious humanity in particular,' as 'habituated to thinking' of God 'mainly in terms of an external, personal, supernatural, spiritual being.' Indeed, if

[8] *Op. cit.*, p. 164.

I understand them aright, it is still about the existence or non-existence of such a Being that our contemporary linguistic philosophers, for all their sophistication, continue to do battle. 'The theist,' says I. M. Crombie, 'believes in God as a transcendent *being*,' and G. F. Woods regards R. W. Hepburn as stating the issue 'concisely and accurately' when he writes, 'The language of "transcendence," the thought of God as a personal being, wholly other to man, dwelling in majesty—this talk may well collapse into meaninglessness, in the last analysis. And yet to sacrifice it seems at once to take one quite outside Christianity.'

It is precisely the identification of Christianity—and transcendence—with this conception of theism that I believe we must be prepared to question. Does the Gospel stand or fall with it? On the contrary, I am convinced that Tillich is right in saying that 'the protest of atheism against such a highest person is correct.' And this protest, which today is made in the name of the 'meaninglessness' of any such metaphysical statement, has seemed to others a matter of much greater existential concern. And to understand them we should be prepared to see how it looks to them. Huxley contents himself with saying, 'For my own part, the sense of spiritual relief which comes from rejecting the idea of God as a supernatural being is enormous.' But, earlier, men like Feuerbach and Nietzsche, whom Proudhon correctly described as 'antitheists' rather than atheists, saw such a supreme Person in heaven as the great enemy of man's coming of age. This was the God they must 'kill' if man was not to continue dispossessed and kept in strings. Few Christians have been able to understand the vehemence of their revolt because for them he has not been the tyrant they portrayed, who impoverishes, enslaves and annihilates man. Indeed, for most non-Christians also he has been more of a Grandfather in heaven, a kindly Old Man who could be pushed into one corner while they got on with the business of life. But the nature of his *character* is here secondary. What is important is whether such a Being represents even a distorted image of the Christian God. Can he be rehabilitated, or is the whole conception of that sort of a God, 'up there,' 'out there,' or however one likes to put it, a projection, an idol, that can and should be torn down?

For an answer to that question I should like to end not with a theological analysis but with a personal testimony—from John Wren-Lewis, who believes that it was just such a superstition from which he was delivered in order to become a Christian:

> I cannot emphasize too strongly that acceptance of the Christian faith became possible for me *only* because I found I did not have to go back on my wholesale rejection of the superstitious beliefs that had hitherto surrounded me. The faith I came to accept was not merely different from what I had hitherto believed Christianity to be—it was utterly opposed to it, and I still regard that sort of 'religion' as an unmitigated evil, far, far more anti-Christian than atheism. This is a truth to which I do not think religious apologists pay nearly enough attention. There is a misplaced sense of loyalty which makes many Christians feel reluctant to come out in open opposition to anything that calls itself by the same name, or uses words like 'God' and 'Christ'; even Christians who in practice dislike superstition as much as I do still often treat it as a minor aberration to be hushed up rather than a radical perversion to be denounced. For example, Christian writers whose positive views are, as far as I can judge, very similar to my own, even though they may use different language to express them, still feel constrained to produce 'refutations' of the Freudian case against religion, although in fact a very large proportion of what passes for religion in our society is exactly the sort of neurotic illness that Freud describes, and the first essential step in convincing people that Christianity can be true in spite of Freud is to assert outright that belief based on the projection mechanisms he describes is false, however much it may say 'Lord, Lord.' It is not enough to describe such beliefs as childish or primitive, for this implies that the truth is *something* like them, even though much more 're-fined' or 'enlightened,' whereas in reality *nothing like* the 'God' and 'Christ' I was brought up to believe in can be true. It is not merely that the Old Man in the Sky is only a mythological symbol for the Infinite Mind behind the scenes, nor yet that this Being is benevolent rather than fearful: the truth is that this whole way of thinking is wrong, and if such a Being did exist, he would be the very devil. [9]

That, I believe, is an exaggeration. To speak thus one is in danger, like the Psalmist, of condemning a whole generation—

[9] *They Became Anglicans*, ed. Dewi Morgan, pp. 168 f. Quoted by kind permission of A. R. Mowbray and Co., Ltd. and Morehouse-Barlow Co., Inc.

indeed many, many generations—of God's children. It is still the language of most of his children—and particularly his older children. There is nothing intrinsically wrong with it, any more than there was with the symbolism of a localized heaven. There will be many—and indeed most of us most of the time—for whom it presents no serious difficulties and no insuperable barriers to belief. In fact, its demolition will be the greater shock to faith and will appear to leave many people bereft and 'without God in the world.' Nevertheless, I am firmly convinced that this whole way of thinking can be the greatest obstacle to an intelligent faith—and indeed will progressively be so to all except the 'religious' few. We shall eventually be no more able to convince men of the existence of a God 'out there' whom they must call in to order their lives than persuade them to take seriously the gods of Olympus. If Christianity is to survive, let alone to recapture 'secular' man, there is no time to lose in detaching it from this scheme of thought, from this particular theology or *logos* about *theos*, and thinking hard about what we should put in its place. We may not have a name yet with which to replace 'theism': indeed, it may not prove necessary or possible to dispense with the term (hence the query in the title of this chapter). But it is urgent that we should work away at framing a conception of God and the Christian Gospel which does not depend upon that projection. And to this, very tentatively, I now turn.

But before turning to it it will be well to say at once that our concern will not be simply to substitute an immanent for a transcendent Deity, any more than we are implying that those who worked with the previous projection thought of him as being *only* 'out there' and denied his immanence. On the contrary, the task is to validate the idea of transcendence for modern man. But this means restating its reality in other than what Bultmann has called the 'objectivized,' mythological terms which merely succeed in making nonsense of it to him. For, as Professor R. Gregor Smith has said, 'The old doctrine of transcendence is nothing more than an assertion of an outmoded view of the world.' Our concern is in no way to change the Christian doctrine of God but precisely to see that it does not disappear with this outmoded view.

LESLIE DEWART

The Relation of Scholastic Philosophy to Modern Atheism

So far we have considered certain inadequacies of Christian theism resulting from the hellenization of the Christian faith. The hellenization of the Christian faith's speculation has produced certain parallel inadequacies in Catholic philosophical

The Future of Belief

thought. The most obvious of these is not directly relevant to the question of theism and, therefore, will be but mentioned here. The Catholic's loyalty to his community should not blind him to the distressing fact that since the end of the middle ages Catholic philosophical thought has not produced very many contributions to man's understanding of himself or of reality. Its conception of knowledge of truth, of enquiry, of man, of change, of time, of reality, and even its conception of philosophy itself— all these conspire to deny Scholasticism the possibility of becoming so dissatisfied with its own real and valuable truth that it must consciously and intentionally seek to surpass itself. This is surely not unrelated to the yet more surprising fact that among the many theological developments that in recent times have facilitated and justified the renewal of the Church, and which continue to serve it, few if any have been inspired by Scholasticism. Insofar as Catholic theology today needs philosophy, it needs a philosophy that would not preclude *creative* development. It cannot be well served by a philosophy that permits no more than the eduction of act from potency. Creative Catholic theology has therefore increasingly turned to non-Scholastic (which means almost exclusively non-Catholic, indeed, non-Christian) philosophical thought. One can only hope that this unfortunate state of affairs will not continue indefinitely.

There is, however, another inadequacy of the traditional Catholic philosophy which is pertinent to our theme. I now refer to the hellenization of Christian philosophical speculation as constituting, in point of historical fact, the condition of the pos-

sibility of modern atheism. In this summary account I will restrict myself to bare fundamentals. It will make, nevertheless,
a somewhat complex recital.

It is not by chance that the problem of the existence of God
has been historically paralleled by the problem of the existence
of objects of knowledge. To understand the connection between
the two let us note that Greek philosophy and Scholasticism
share a fundamental principle which makes them both "metaphysical." This is Parmenides' postulate of the equivalence of
being and intelligibility.[1] The Greek metaphysical tradition which
began with Plato and Aristotle never doubted the existence of
intelligible reality or the reliability of knowledge, because in
addition to the postulate of Parmenides it assumed that being
existed necessarily—the Greek cultural experience would hardly
have permitted Greek philosophers to think otherwise. Scholasticism, however, adopted the Parmenidean principle, but consciously rejected (on account of its evident inconsistency with
the Christian faith) the only condition that made it epistemo-
logically viable, namely, the existential necessity of the actual as
such.

For the Greeks the necessity of being meant the necessity of
being *as such*. Evidently, they were not unaware that in a certain sense the beings of this material world are not necessary.
But this only meant that the individual being was contingent
insofar as it was material and potential. But every being *as such*,
and not only the Supreme Being, was necessary. It was necessarily actual (that is, necessarily existing and necessarily intelligible), insofar as it participated in being, that is, precisely
insofar as it was in act. For example, this individual *man* may be
contingent precisely as individual, as concretized in matter. But
Man, the species, is necessary, indeed eternal. For being as such,
since it is necessary, is also eternal. Thus, although every individual being in the material world is subject to change and is in
a sense contingent, for it has a beginning and an end, the world
as a whole is necessary, eternal, unmoving and without beginning or end.

Now, like the Greeks, the Christian philosophers thought that
the Supreme Being was necessary. But unlike the Greeks they

[1] "That which can be thought is identical with that which can be,"
Fr. 3, (Freeman trans.).

could not countenance even the foregoing relative necessity of
creatures: it is precisely as created *beings* that God's creatures
must be totally contingent if the gratuitous self-communication
of an utterly transcendent God is to be upheld. Pressed thus by
Greek philosophy on the one side, and by the Christian faith on
the other, Scholasticism sought to escape its dilemma with an
ingeniously simple solution, namely, by restricting the necessity
of creatures exclusively to their intelligibility, that is, to their
essence. After Parmenides, Greek metaphysics had identified the
necessity of being and the necessity of intelligibility through the
identity of being and intelligibility. The Scholastics simply
distinguished the necessity of intelligibility from that of being,
so that a creature could have (as in Greek philosophy) a necessary intelligibility and nevertheless (as in the Christian faith)
remain totally contingent precisely as being and as actual—the
difficulty was that the Scholastics also retained the Parmenidean
identification of being and intelligibility.

The story has been often and ably told of the metaphysical
revolution that this simple solution entailed, and particularly
the transformation of metaphysics itself from the science of
being as *substance* (*ousia*) to that of being as *being,* properly so
called. For our purposes, however, we need only note that the
retrenchment of necessity to the bastion of essence implied the
doctrine of the real distinction in creatures between *essence* and
existence. For this was, indeed, the effect actually intended by
the restriction of necessity to essence, namely, to make the *whole*
actuality of the being of creatures totally contingent while
nevertheless retaining the Parmenidean identity of being (and,
therefore, of necessity) with intelligibility. But in God, of course,
the opposite was required, since in him actuality and necessity
should go together with each other and with intelligibility. In
brief, the Scholastic modificaion of Greek metaphysics in order
to bring it into line with the Christian faith, consisted in the twofold doctrine that (a) there is in creatures a real distinction
between essence and existence, but (b) in God essence and
existence are identically the same.

*   *   *

Nevertheless, what is radically unforeseeable may well be
empirically predictable: though we may not say what final goal

we are bound to arrive at, we can determine in which direction we are already going. We can forecast what points we are likely to traverse, on the basis of the decisions we have already taken and on the assumption that we will follow them through.

I will not deal here with Protestant Christianity, a subject apart. But the Catholic Church in recent years has freely taken certain basic decisions which, to be sure, are in principle reversible, but which for the present remain a defining point of its orientation. The principal one was manifested most clearly, perhaps, in the general acceptance by the Church of the directive contained in Pope John's opening address to Vatican II. It was the decision to adopt a historical perspective: to "look to the present, to new conditions and new forms of life . . . to dedicate ourselves with an earnest will and without fear to that work which our era demands of us." In the single moment of unhesitating acclamation with which this proposal was greeted —even if not a few among those who subscribed it were possibly not fully conscious of its ultimate import—the reversal took place of a policy which Christianity unconsciously began to develop at some time between the days of patristic hellenism and the age of medieval Scholasticism, and which had been implicitly espoused since the beginning of the sixteenth century and consciously abided by since the end of the eighteenth. This policy was, for the sake of protecting the truth and purity of the Christian faith, to resist the factual reality, and to deny the moral validity, of the historical development of man's self-consciousness, especially as revealed in cultural evolution. In the person of John XXIII the Catholic Church made an act of faith in the precisely opposite idea: that the truth of Christianity needs for its health, protection and development the reality of man's individual and cultural growth in self-consciousness. Despite hesitations and misgivings that have abounded as the implications of this act of faith have come to light, this remains for the present the Church's most fundamental principle of self-guidance— and, as we all sense, one which could not now be forsworn without the certainty of disaster.

In relation to the Christian faith in God it is not difficult to ascertain in principle what will be the consequence of this historic decision: it will be the remedying of the Christian faith's unwarranted and inexpedient inadequacy. This remedy should in turn mean, in negative terms, the conscious rejection of every form of absolute theism. It should mean, in positive terms, at first the restoration, and ultimately the deepening and perfecting of, the relative theism which inspires the Christian faith.

But how will this be manifested? How are we likely to conceive God—rather, in what way is our conception of God likely to shift—as these changes take effect? This is much more difficult to discern. In order to avoid in what follows the constant qualification that would be required as one attempted to answer these questions, I will stress at this point once for all the highly tentative and exploratory nature which speculation on the matter must necessarily have. We now stand on a very uncertain terrain. We are justified in exploring it solely for the attempt's possible heuristic value.

The Being and Existence of God

The Christian theism of the future might not conceive God as *a being*. I place the stress not merely on the indeterminate article *a* but also on the substantive *being*. In Scholastic philosophy God is not conceived as *a* being, but he is nevertheless conceived as *being (ens)*. We might eventually go beyond this as well, if the methodological principle which may be operative in our future concept of God should transcend that which in Greek and, later, in Christian thought has always been at work. I refer again to the *metaphysical* method which rests on Parmenides' postulate of the convertibility of being and intelligibility. If reality is not assumed to be constituted by intelligibility—or by any (possible or actual) relation to mind [2]—reality can no longer be identified with that-which-is (which is the usual meaning of *being, ens*).

_____

[2] I stipulate the latter because in the philosophy of Sartre and certain other existentialists there is a confusion between the *neutrality* of being, as it were, with relation to mind (I mean, the mere *non-mental* character of reality as such), and its supposed *absurdity*. In this confusion we find the last refuge of the Parmenidean principle of mind-being equivalence. Sartre's transcendence of realism-idealism is less radical than he imagines. To understand reality as absurd is to understand it as intrinsically related to mind (albeit by a relation of mutual exclusion).

To be sure, reality will still be as a matter of fact intelligible.
But its intelligibility will now be a matter of *fact*, not of *necessity*.
Being is intelligible, but not *as such*. Things can be understood,
and can be conceived as being, because if they in fact exist they
will also have a history—and this history makes them relatable to
mind. Essences, therefore, what things are, are always created,
whether created by another or self-created (in the case of consciousness).

Thus, man is most truly a being, because he is present to himself as an object. Transcending the subjectivity of mere objects
and the objectivity of mere subjects, he understands himself
as being. His transcendence, his spirituality, consists in being
conscious and thus being able to be whatever he makes himself
to be.[3] On the other hand, the open background against which he
becomes conscious of transcendence and which is grasped in
that empirical attitude which permits faith to emerge, is precisely
that which is beyond man, beyond transcendence, and therefore
beyond being. In Christian language this is called the uncreated-
ness of God. Well, then, the Christian must believe that God is
uncreated. God cannot be created, whether by another or by himself. He should therefore not be conceived as being.

It should be made clear that this proposition is to be taken
literally. Since the method which produces it is not that of
Scholasticism, it does *not* mean this: that since God must in
some real sense be a being because otherwise he would be nothing, yet he cannot be univocally said to be a being, we must *both*
affirm and deny being of him, so that the proposition "God is not
a being" really means "God is a super-being." What it means is
literally what it says, that God is not a being at all. What the
religious experience of God discloses is a reality *beyond* being.
Nor do I suggest that if God is beyond being he is empirically
unknowable, or that he is (unless we use the term hyper-
bolically) ineffable. Nor does saying that God is a reality beyond
being mean that he can be experienced only mystically or through
affective knowledge or connaturality. For unless we retain the
Greek metaphysical outlook, the ordinary facts of Christian experience are sufficient to establish that we do *experience* God,
but that we do not experience him as *being*. This proposition
should be obvious and commonplace to the philosophically un-

[3] Marcel, *Homo Viator*, pp. 13–28.

prejudiced Christian believer. In fact, since it is a matter of simple observation it should be one of the starting points of a Christian philosophical enquiry that would rise to the empirical level of methodology to which philosophy has been developed in our time. We should determine what consequences for our understanding of God follow from this observation, rather than the consequences for our understanding of faith, within the general presuppositions of the Greek theories of knowledge, that follow from the presupposition that the God in whom we believe is the Supreme Being. God is, among other ways in which we can conceptualize the matter, that which we experience as the open background of consciousness and being. There is no need, if we discard Parmenides, to make God fit the mould of being (and afterwards say that the mould is really a Procrustean bed of analogical being). On the contrary, what we must do is to open ourselves to that which transcendence reveals.

By the same token, God cannot be said to exist. But there are two things which are *not* meant by this proposition. The first thing it does not mean is this: that although actually "God exists," this proposition must be complemented by its opposite, "God does not exist," in order to signify that the existence of God is only analogous to that of creatures, and that therefore "God, who does not exist, super-exists." The second thing it does not mean is this: that there is no reality transcending our experience of totality or of being, or that reality is exhausted by being, or that the openness of human transcendence is only a logical void, filled not by any reality but by nothing.

The reason why the latter construction should be rejected will appear as the positive aspect of this concept of God, namely, his *presence,* is developed below. But we can anticipate part of it. The affirmation that "God does not exist at all" takes nothing away from God's reality and presence. For *to exist* and to be *present* are quite different things. As Marcel has remarked, "we could say that the man sitting beside us was in the same room as ourselves, but that he was not really *present* there, that his *presence* did not make itself felt." [4] Conversely, God's real presence to us (and, therefore, his reality "in himself") does not depend upon his being a being or an object. In fact, our belief in the Christian God is post-primitive to the degree that we appre-

[4] *The Mystery of Being,* I, p. 205.

hend that although there is no super-being behind beings, no supreme being who stands at the summit of the hierarchy of being, nevertheless a reality beyond the totality of being reveals itself by its *presence*. There can be, beyond the totality of all actually existing being, something *present* to us in our experience, in the sense that "when somebody's presence does really make itself felt . . . it reveals me to myself, it makes me more fully myself than I should be if I were not exposed to its impact." [5] The reality of human transcendence discloses the presence of a reality beyond all actual and possible empirical intuition, *if* in the presence of myself to myself I find that over and above my own agency (and indeed as the ultimate condition of the possibility of that agency) there is a presence which "reveals me to myself" in a supererogatory and gratuitous way, that is, by making me "more fully myself than I should be if I were not exposed to its impact." [6]

[5] *Ibid.*

[6] This, which is the only valid "proof" for the "existence" of God that I know of, I take to incorporate all that which seems valid in Maritain's "sixth way," *Approaches to God*, (London, 1955), pp. 62–65. I estimate, however, that Maritain's insight (that "the operations of the human intellect . . . [which] emanate from a subject or from a person" reveal by their self-insufficiency the existence of their source, God), is fundamentally voided by his confusion of God's *presence* with God's *sufficient causality*. It is therefore also marred by his consequent conceptualization of God as that in which the thinking self "pre-existed" or "existed before itself in a first existence distinct from every temporal existence." In point of fact, the question of *priority* and *posteriority*, metaphysical or otherwise, does not enter into it any more than does *causality*. On the contrary, the presence of God does not exhibit him as a prior, anterior, supra-temporal or eternal reality: it manifests him as a *present* one. The point can hardly be missed once we rid ourselves of any hellenic compulsion to think of God as the First (or the Last) Cause, or as the *arche* and *aitia* of existence, or as the Supreme Being.

I should underline that the "proof" I have suggested above not only has nothing to say about God's "existence" properly so called, but that it is hardly a proof in the classical sense of the term. It concerns a reality which is not the object of any actual or possible empirical intuition. Therefore, it is an essentially *unverifiable* argument. It is always possible to look at the same facts and find nothing but the *absence* of God. This is why I have formulated the argument in hypothetical form.

The other construction of the original assertion above is to be rejected because as a means of developing the Christian concept of God the method of analogical predication is no longer useful. Its true value has been limited and negative, namely, to have enabled Christian thought to preserve a *faith* in God's transcendence while *reasoning* about him as if he were not transcendent. The method has not and could not have enabled philosophy to *conceive* and *understand* God in an essentially more adequate way than was possible to Greek metaphysics. It has enabled Scholastic philosophy merely to *acknowledge* the inadequacy of its hellenic conception of God—or, rather, to admit it without consciously acknowledging it. When analogy has been used well, it has served to introduce a qualification to every positive statement about God, a qualification which, once made, philosophy could proceed to ignore. And even this limited value has been lost whenever it has been mistaken for an actual means whereby to make empirical concepts perform a role they cannot otherwise perform. Thus, the proposition that "God does not exist" (in the Scholastic sense) has sometimes served to *hide* the insufficiency of the proposition that "God exists"— which is the one that has been really operative. In other words, when philosophy follows this method it only *says* that it provides a *meta*-physical understanding of God: it only *says* that it describes God *per viam remotionis et eminentiae*. The method is rightly called analogical *predication*. It does not provide analogical *understanding*. It only provides a conception of God in strictly "physical," human terms which is modified by the (implicit) *statement* that these terms are inadequate.[7] It is true, of

[7] The doctrine of analogy is the logical outcome of attempting to explain how we can conceive God while holding simultaneously (a) that knowledge is an intentional intussusception through the means of concepts, (b) that all our concepts are derived from empirical intuition, and (c) that God is not, at least "here below," known to us by any empirical intuition. The solution consists in supposing that concepts derived from empirical intuition *can* adequately reach an object beyond empirical intuition if only we recognize, avow and state that such concepts *cannot* adequately reach an object beyond empirical intuition.

The key assumption is, of course, the first. In a theory of knowledge in which human cognition is not an intussusception but a relational

course, that the terms of the traditional Scholastic conception of God are inadequate; but Scholastics unduly attribute this inadequacy to their positive, empirical nature or to their human character. We can philosophically account for man's experience of God in terms which are not intrinsically inadequate, if we first account for human experience in more adequate terms than Scholasticism does.

The proposition that "God cannot be said to exist" can be properly and literally understood by the Christian believer in God, on the grounds that *to exist* (in the literal sense of the term, *to arise out of, to emerge*), is proper to a being, that is, to that which is created or creates itself and is, therefore, a thing (*res*), a that-which-has-essence. If God is not a *res* and if he has no essence, then he does not exist. To attribute existence to God is the most extreme form of anthropomorphism. This anthropomorphism Christian philosophy has had to indulge only because of the inability of hellenic metaphysical thinking to discern *reality* except in *ens*, that-which-is. To be sure, the Christian experience of God *can* be cast in the concept of being. It can also be cast, however, in the concept of reality, as the presence of that which (though not itself being) manifests itself in and

---

existing-with which results from the self-differentiation of consciousness, all our concepts are derived from empirical intuition. God can be adequately conceived by us in the concepts of empirical intuition because he is experienced by us as a reality given *in* empirical intuition. But since he is not an object of thought or a being, the experience of God is the experience of an inevident reality. Hence, the experience is, however "rational" and reasonable, an experience of the order of *belief*. Conversely, belief in God is, however inevident, contingent and gratuitous, neither supra-rational nor infra-empirical. It is an experience in essentially the same fundamental sense as any other: when we believe in God we *experience* him. This means that although God is not an *object* of empirical intuition, his self-communicating reality (that is, his-self as rendering itself *present* to us) is experienced by us *in* the empirical intuition of objects, principally and most immediately in the empirical intuition of consciousness, selfhood and existence as objects of thought. This is why the experience of God takes on the peculiar character of *faith;* it is also the reason why the reasonableness and correctness of any "demonstration" of the reality of God does not take away the need to believe in God if one is to *experience* and *know* him at all.

through being, that-which-is. That-which-exists is *as such* a manifestation of God. But it is not God himself.

The idea that God should not be conceived as existing incorporates, but goes beyond, the attempt of some contemporary Catholic thinkers, notably Gilson, to conceive God as "beyond essence," but nonetheless as "subsisting existence itself." The insight that "God has no essence," that "God is as a beyond-essence," [8] is valid. But it must be taken seriously and followed through. It means, among other things, that the reality of God does not have an *objective* meaning. God does not have meaning in-and-for-himself, though he can have, of course, meaning for-us.

*   *   *

This would take nothing away from the reality of God, or from either the reasonableness or the truth of the Christian faith. It would, however, take away the problem of the existence of God. Indeed, the immediate meaning of the proposition is that the existence of God is not philosophically problematical—not any more than is the existence of "extramental" being. This does not mean that the existence, or even the reality, of God is self-evident. The existence of *things* is self-evident. But unlike the reality of being, God's is a transcendent reality. He is not merely present to us; he is both present and absent. It is in this sense that the reality of God is mysterious. The problem for Christian philosophy is to explore that reality and, in the first place, to try to understand the meaning of God's simultaneous presence and absence. But this does not mean: we must determine whether an actually existing thing-in-itself corresponds to the object of thought, God. What needs to be "proven" is not that a God-being objectively exists.[9] What requires "a demonstration," for it is not immediately obvious, is God's *presence*: whether, in what sense, in what way, and with what consequences, God is *present*. Present, in the first place to himself (though this is largely a

[8] Gilson, *Elements*, p. 133.
[9] The existence (properly so called) of God would remain *morally* problematic. That is, the question would always remain open whether our self-creation will or will not proceed so as to make God to-exist-for-us.

theological problem). Present, in any event, to being, present to world, present to man, present to man's faith, present to the Church, present to history, and present to the future that we create. The preoccupation with God's existence which characterized post-patristic thought, and thence post-medieval philosophy, is a result of conceiving God as an actual object of thought that is a possible objective being or thing-in-itself. But we should not place any *a priori* limits on the level of religious consciousness to which man may easily rise. In the future we may well learn to conceive God in a nobler way.

ABRAHAM HESCHEL

Understanding God

How should the question about the nature of the prophets' understanding of God be asked? The form in which the question is usually put—What is the prophets' idea of God?—is hardly adequate.

The Theology of Pathos

Having an idea of friendship is not the same as having a friend or living with a friend, and the story of a friendship cannot be fully told by what one friend thinks of the being and attributes of the other friend. The process of forming an idea is one of generalization, or arriving at a general notion from individual instances, and one of abstraction, or separating a partial aspect or quality from a total situation. Yet such a process implies a split between situation and idea, a disregard for the fullness of what transpires, and the danger of regarding the part as the whole. An idea or a theory of God can easily become a substitute for God, impressive to the mind when God as a living reality is absent from the soul.

The prophets had no theory or "idea" of God. What they had was an *understanding*. Their God-understanding was not the result of a theoretical inquiry, of a groping in the midst of alternatives about the being and attributes of God. To the prophets, God was overwhelmingly real and shatteringly present. They never spoke of Him as from a distance. They lived as witnesses, struck by the words of God, rather than as explorers engaged in an effort to ascertain the nature of God; their utterances were the unloading of a burden rather than glimpses obtained in the fog of groping.

The autonomy of ideas may result in their isolation or even in regarding them as independent, eternal, self-subsisting essences. To the prophets, the attributes of God were drives, challenges, commandments, rather than timeless notions detached from His Being. They did not offer an exposition of the nature of God, but rather an exposition of God's insight into man and His concern for man. They disclosed attitudes *of* God rather than ideas *about* God.

The bricks we collect in order to construct the biblical image of God are, as a rule, conceptual notions, such as goodness, justice, wisdom, unity. In terms of frequency of usage in biblical language, they are surpassed by statements referring to God's pathos, which, however, for a variety of reasons, has never been accorded proper recognition in the history of biblical theology.

Having described in the preceding chapters the place of the divine pathos in the thought of individual prophets, we shall now dwell on its general significance as a central category in prophetic theology.

The prophets, as said above, did not simply absorb the content of inspiration, they also claimed to understand its meaning, and sought to bring such meaning into coherence with all other knowledge they possessed. Moreover, inspiration was not their only source of knowledge. Together with receptivity to the word of God they were endowed with a receptivity to the presence of God. The presence and anxiety of God spoke to them out of manifestations of history. They had an intuitive grasp of hidden meanings, of an unspoken message.

A person's perception depends upon his experience, upon his assumptions, categories of thinking, degree of sensitivity, environment, and cultural atmosphere. A person will notice what he is conditioned to see. The prophet's perception was conditioned by his experience of inspiration.

By contrast to speculative knowledge, the pensive-intuitive attitude of the prophet to God, in which God is apprehended through His sensible manifestations, is to be characterized as *understanding*. Our intention of replacing in prophetology the traditional idea of knowledge of God by introduction of this new term is justified not only by the unsuitability of the former designation, but also by the usefulness of the latter. The prophets received their knowledge of God either through the moment of revelation or through intuitive contemplation of the surrounding world. In the first case, they received an inspiration as an expression of the divine Person; in the second, they sensed the signs of God's presence in history. They experienced the word as a living manifestation of God, and events in the world as effects of His activity. The given factor, whether the word or the event, was for them an expression of the divine. In both cases their comprehension consisted of an understanding of God through His expression, an understanding which proceeds from expressions addressed to them as well as from unspoken signs of their divine source or motivation.

The point of departure of such understanding is any datum which is felt to be an "expression" of God, the course it takes is a meditation on the meaning of this expression, and the final result is an increased sensitivity to the presence of God—not an impersonal knowledge. The culmination of prophetic fellowship with God is insight and unanimity—not union.

Understanding of God is contingent upon the distinction between being and expression. Its quality depends upon one's relationship with the divine. Since the time of Descartes it has been asserted that the understanding of other selves takes place through analogy. While it is true that we do not experience a person independently of his bodily actions or expressions, yet through, and in connection with, these expressions, other selves are experienced with the same immediacy with which we experience our own selves. Our conviction as to their existence is based upon directly experienced fellowship, not upon inference. To the prophet, knowledge of God was fellowship with Him, not attained by syllogism, analysis or induction, but by living together.

For a neutral observer, the comprehension of the expressions of love that come from a person who is in love may at times be possible only by way of analogy. However, the person for whom these expressions are intended has an immediate understanding of what they mean. These expressions are not perceived apart from the beloved person; the beloved person is sensed in that person's expressions. And although their meaning is experienced through understanding, it is nevertheless no *circulus vitiosus* to say that the immediacy of the understanding is the result of the meaning. The intuitive knowledge which the beloved person possesses is a primary factor in the act of understanding. This important factor is, of course, not inferred from the act of understanding, but is a determinative element of the understanding itself. The directedness of the divine acts of expression to the prophet thus conditions the peculiar immediacy of his act of apprehension, which does not require analogy in order to be possible.

Even if the prophets had affirmed the essential unknowability of God, they would still have insisted on the possibility of understanding Him by reflective intuition.

The God of Pathos

Prophecy consists in the inspired communication of divine attitudes to the prophetic consciousness. As we have seen, the divine pathos is the ground-tone of all these attitudes. A central category of the prophetic understanding for God, it is echoed in almost every prophetic statement.

To the prophet, we have noted, God does not reveal himself in an abstract absoluteness, but in a personal and intimate relation to the world. He does not simply command and expect obedience: He is also moved and affected by what happens in the world, and reacts accordingly. Events and human actions arouse in Him joy or sorrow, pleasure or wrath. He is not conceived as judging the world in detachment. He reacts in an intimate and subjective manner, and thus determines the value of events. Quite obviously in the biblical view, man's deeds may move Him, affect Him, grieve Him or, on the other hand, gladden and please Him. This notion that God can be intimately affected, that He possesses not merely intelligence and will, but also pathos, basically defines the prophetic consciousness of God.

The God of the philosophers is like the Greek *ananke*, unknown and indifferent to man; He thinks, but does not speak; He is conscious of Himself, but oblivious of the world; while the God of Israel is a God Who loves, a God Who is known to, and concerned with, man. He not only rules the world in the majesty of His might and wisdom, but reacts intimately to the events of

history. He does not judge men's deeds impassively and with
aloofness; His judgment is imbued with the attitude of One to
Whom those actions are of the most intimate and profound concern. God does not stand outside the range of human suffering
and sorrow. He is personally involved in, even stirred by, the
conduct and fate of man.

Pathos denotes, not an idea of goodness, but a living care;
not an immutable example, but an outgoing challenge, a dynamic
relation between God and man; not mere feeling or passive affection, but an act or attitude composed of various spiritual elements; no mere contemplative survey of the world, but a passionate summons.

Pathos and Passion

Did the prophets conceive of divine pathos as a passion such as
may powerfully grip a human being? [2] By passion we mean
drunkenness of the mind, an agitation of the soul devoid of
reasoned purpose, operating blindly "either in the choice of its
purpose, or, if this be supplied by reason, in its accomplishment;
for it is an emotional convulsion which makes it impossible to
exercise a free consideration of principles and the determination
of conduct in accordance with them." [3] In contrast, pathos was
understood not as unreasoned emotion, but as an act formed
with intention, depending on free will, the result of decision and
determination. Even "in the moment of anger" (Jer. 18:7), what
God intends is not that His anger should be executed, but that it
should be annulled by the people's repentance.

The divine reaction to human conduct does not operate automatically. Man's deeds do not necessitate but only occasion divine pathos. Man is not the immediate but merely the incidental
cause of pathos in God, the *"occasio"* or *"causa occasionalis,"*

---

[2] "By passions I mean desire, anger, fear, confidence, envy, joy,
friendly feeling, hatred, longing, jealousy, pity; and generally those
states of consciousness which are accompanied by pleasure or pain."
(Aristotle, *Nicomachean Ethics*, 1105b, 20 ff.; cf. *Eudemian Ethics*,
1220b, 12 ff.).

[3] Kant, *Critique of Judgment*, par. 29.

which freely calls forth a pathetic state in God. There is no nexus of causality, but only one of contingence between human and divine attitudes, between human character and divine pathos. The decisive fact is that of divine freedom. Pathos is not an attribute but *a situation.*

On the other hand, the divine pathos is not an absolute force which exists regardless of man, something ultimate or eternal. It is rather a reaction to human history, an attitude called forth by man's conduct; a response, not a cause. Man is in a sense an agent, not only the recipient. It is within his power to evoke either the pathos of love or the pathos of anger.

Pathos and Ethos

God's pathos was not thought of as a sort of fever of the mind which, disregarding the standards of justice, culminates in irrational and irresponsible action. There is justice in all His ways, the Bible insists again and again.

There is no dichotomy of pathos and ethos, of motive and norm. They do not exist side by side, opposing each other; they involve and presuppose each other. It is because God is the source of justice that His pathos is ethical; and it is because God is absolutely personal—devoid of anything impersonal—that this ethos is full of pathos.

Pathos, then, is not an attitude taken arbitrarily. Its inner law is the moral law; ethos is inherent in pathos. God is concerned about the world, and shares in its fate. Indeed, this is the essence of God's moral nature: His willingness to be intimately involved in the history of man.

The Transitive Character of the Divine Pathos

The divine pathos is not merely intentional; it is also transitive. The gods of mythology are self-centered, egotistic. The cowardice of Ares, the incontinence of Aphrodite, the lusts of Zeus, the jealousy of the gods, are reflexive passions. Zeus is "hit by the dart of desire and is inflamed with passion" for Io, with whom he desires "to enjoy the pleasures of Cypris" so that his "eye may be eased of its desire." [4]

Pathos, on the other hand, is not a self-centered and self-contained state; it is always, in prophetic thinking, directed outward; it always expresses a relation to man. It is therefore not one of God's attributes as such. It has a transitive rather than a reflexive character, not separated from history.

Man's Relevance to God

The theology of pathos brings about a shift in the understanding of man's ultimate problems. The prophet does not see the human situation in and by itself. The predicament of man is a predicament of God Who has a stake in the human situation. Sin, guilt, suffering, cannot be separated from the divine situation. The life of sin is more than a failure of man; it is a frustration to God. Thus, man's alienation from God is not the ultimate fact by which to measure man's situation. The divine pathos, the fact of God's participation in the predicament of man, is the elemental fact.

The essential meaning of pathos is, therefore, not to be seen in its psychological denotation, as standing for a state of the soul, but in its theological connotation, signifying God as involved in history. He is engaged to Israel—and has a stake in its destiny. The profundity of this insight can be sensed only in the light of the prophets' awareness of the mystery and transcendence of God. For the biblical understanding of history, the idea of pathos is as central as the idea of man being an image of God is for the understanding of creation.

The biblical writers were aware of the paradox involved in God's relation to man. "Behold, to the Lord your God belong heaven and the heaven of heavens, the earth with all that is in

[4] Aeschylus, *Prometheus Bound*, 645 ff. Pindar speaks of the morbid sexual passion of Zeus and Poseidon, *The Olympian Odes*, 1, 40–45.

it; yet the Lord set His heart in love upon your fathers and chose their descendants after them, you above all peoples, as at this day" (Deut. 10:14-15).

Never in history has man been taken as seriously as in prophetic thinking. Man is not only an image of God; he is a per-perpetual concern of God. The idea of pathos adds a new dimension to human existence. Whatever man does affects not only his own life, but also the life of God insofar as it is directed to man. The import of man raises him beyond the level of mere creature. He is a consort, a partner, a factor in the life of God.

The God of Pathos and the Wholly Other

As a reaction to excessive rationalism and the complete disregard of the mystery and uniqueness of the divine, twentieth-century theologians have often tended to go to the other extreme. God is the Wholly Other; religion has to be demonic in order to be authentic, opposed to reason in order to be unique; and God must have nothing in common with his creation.[5]

The God of the prophets is not the Wholly Other, a strange, weird, uncanny Being, shrouded in unfathomable darkness, but the God of the covenant, Whose will they know and are called upon to convey. The God they proclaim is not the Remote One, but the One Who is involved, near, and concerned. The Silent One may be the antithesis of man, but prophecy is God meeting man.

The Wholly Other is the sharp antithesis to the consciousness of man. However, all being, anything that is given to the mind, stands over against the mind as otherness. What meets the biblical man is a transcendent relatedness, a divine claim and demand.

Absolute antithesis is alien to the Hebrew mind. That the Lord has made known his ways to Moses (Ps. 103:7) is a certainty basic to biblical consciousness.

[5] Otherness is not a unique category. Evil, Plato suggests, is somehow mere nonexistence, or better, is "otherness," *heteroios* (*Parmenides*, 160–162).

Silence encloses Him; darkness is all around Him. Yet there is meaning beyond the darkness. God is *meaning beyond the mystery*.

Clouds and thick darkness are round about Him,
Righteousness and justice are the foundation of His throne.

Psalm 97:2

The numinous is not the supreme category for the prophets, else they would not have attacked the sacred, that which the people revered and which was set apart as holy. The primary object of their religious consciousness was a pathos rather than a numen.

Pathos, far from being intrinsically irrational, is a state which the prophet is able to comprehend morally as well as emotionally.

What Abraham and the prophets encountered was not a numen, but the fullness of God's care. The moral law may be obscured, but never suspended. The very act of addressing Abraham was experienced as care. It was because of the experience of God's responding to him in his plea for Sodom (Gen. 18:23 ff.) that Abraham did not question the command to sacrifice his only son, and it was the certainty of God's love and mercy that enabled the prophets to accept His anger.

The holy in the Bible is not a synonym for the weird. "He blessed the seventh day and made it holy" (Gen. 2:3), not weird or terrible. The Wholly Other stands outside all relations to man, whereas the very genitive "the Holy One of Israel" suggests the relatedness of God. Terrifying in His grandeur and demand, the Holy One evokes a sense of unworthiness and contrition. The Holy is otherness as well as nonotherness. This is why it is possible to speak of God's holiness as a pattern for man.

The Prophetic Sense of Life

To the prophets, the gulf that separates man from God is transcended by His pathos. For all the impenetrability of His being, He is concerned with the world and relates Himself to it. The tragic antithesis between man and the gods is powerfully ex-

pressed in a well-known Babylonian prayer of a righteous sufferer:

> I myself was thinking only of prayer and supplication:
> supplication was my concern, sacrifice my rule; the day of
> worship of the gods was my delight, the day of my goddess'
> procession was my profit and my wealth. . . . I taught my
> hand to observe the divine ordinances. . . . Oh, that I only
> knew that these things are well pleasing to a god! *What
> appears beautiful to man is abominable to the god, and what
> is odious to man's heart is most pleasing to the god.* Who
> has learnt [to understand] the will of the gods in heaven, the
> gods' plan, full of wisdom, who can comprehend it? When
> have stupid mortals ever understood the ways of the gods? [6]

This is a powerful expression of despair. One knows the power
of the gods, but, ignorant of their will, the mind cannot fathom
what is good in their eyes. In fact, the gods and man contradict each other. There is no meeting, there is no knowledge of
what counts most. "The god's anger, sickness, impurity, sin: it
all amounts to the same thing. We offend God even when we
ourselves neither know nor desire this; we are enemies of God,
and indeed for no other reason than that He is our enemy." [7]

This prayer expresses the tragic sense of life. In sharp contrast, the prophetic sense of life knows of no such contradiction, of no such ultimate darkness.

Underlying this contrast are two different conceptions of the
nature of sin. There is an awareness in many religions of a
blindly working guilt, of sin as a situation in which man is begotten, of sin which is involved in man's very being and stands
far above the ability of the individual man. Sin is not conceived
as something that happens, but as something that is and obtains
regardless of man's relationship to the gods. "Since we are what
we ought not to be, we also necessarily do what we ought not to
do. Therefore we need a complete transformation of our mind
and nature. That is the new birth. Although the guilt lies in
action, *operari*, yet the root of the guilt lies in our *essentia* and

---

[6] S. Langdon, *Babylonian Wisdom* (Paris, 1923), pp. 168 f. (Italics
mine, A. J. H.) Cf. *ANET*, p. 435. At the end of the poem the gods
have mercy on the sufferer and turn to him full of goodness.

[7] G. van der Leeuw, *Religion in Essence and Manifestation* (London, 1938), p. 520.

existentia, for out of these the *operari* necessarily proceeds. Accordingly our own true sin is really original sin." [8]

The Mesopotamians, while they knew themselves to be subject to the decrees of the gods, had no reason to believe that these decrees were necessarily just. Hence their penitential prayers abound in self-accusations of faults and misdeeds, but lack the awareness of disobedience to the divine will; they are vibrant with despair but not with contrition, with regret but not with return.

To the prophets, sin is not an ultimate, irreducible or independent condition, but rather a disturbance in the relationship between God and man; it is an adverb not a noun, a condition that can be surmounted by man's return and God's forgiveness.

The divine pathos is like a bridge over the abyss that separates man from God. It implies that the relationship between God and man is not dialectic, characterized by opposition and tension. Man in his essence is not the antithesis of the divine, although in his actual existence he may be rebellious and defiant. The fact that the attitudes of man may affect the life of God, that God stands in an intimate relationship to the world, implies a certain analogy between Creator and creature. The prophets stress not only the discrepancy of God and man, but also the relationship of reciprocity, consisting of God's engagement to man, not only of man's commitment to God. The disparity between God and the world is overcome in God, not in man.

Confronted with an unconditional and absolute will of God, with eternity and perfection, man in his brittleness appears as a complete antithesis. But the prophets face a God of compassion, a God of concern and involvement, and it is in such concern that the divine and the human meet. Pathos is the focal point for eternity and history, the epitome of all relationships between God and man. Just because it is not a final reality, but a dynamic modality, does pathos make possible a living encounter between God and His people.

The uniqueness and wealth of meaning implied in the divine pathos, and its essential significance for the understanding of the religious situation, lead us to regard it as a theological category *sui generis.*

[8] Schopenhauer, *The World as Will and Idea,* Bk. II, ch. 48.

Pathos and Covenant

The decisive importance of the idea of divine pathos emerges clearly when we consider the possible forms in which God's relation to the world may present itself. A purely ethical monotheism in which God, the guardian of the moral order, keeps the world subject to the law, would restrict the scope of God's knowledge and concern to what is of ethical significance. God's relation to man would, in general, run along the lines of a universal principle. The divine pathos alone is able to break through this rigidity and create new dimensions for the unique, the specific, and the particular.

It is not law and order itself, but the living God Who created the universe and established its law and order, that stands supreme in biblical thought. This differs radically from the concept of law as supreme, a concept found, for example, in the Dharma of Mahayana Buddhism. Before the Torah, the covenant was.

In contrast to our civilization, the Hebrews lived in a world of the covenant rather than in a world of contracts. The idea of contract was unknown to them. The God of Israel "cares as little for contract and the cash nexus as He cares for mere slavish obedience and obsequiousness. His chosen sphere is that of covenant." [9] His relationship to His partner is one of benevolence and affection. The indispensable and living instrument holding the community of God and Israel together is the law.

Prophecy is a reminder that what obtains between God and man is not a contract but a covenant. Anterior to the covenant is love, the love of the fathers (Deut. 4:37; 10:15), and what obtains between God and Israel must be understood, not as a legal, but as a personal relationship, as participation, involvement, tension. God's life interacts with the life of the people. To live in the covenant is to partake of the fellowship of God and His people. Biblical religion is not what man does with his solitariness, but rather what man does with God's concern for all men.

The idea of divine pathos throws light on many types of rela-

[9] W. F. Lofthouse, "*Hen* and *Hesed* in the Old Testament," *ZAW* (1933), pp. 29 ff.

tion between God and man unknown in apathetic religion. The covenant between God and Israel is an example. The category of divine pathos adds a new dimension to it. The covenant is an extraordinary act, establishing a reciprocal relation between God and man; it is conceived as a juridical commitment. Pathos, on the other hand, implies a constant concern and involvement; it is conceived as an emotional engagement. From the point of view of the unequivocal covenant-idea, only two forms of relationship between God and people are possible: the maintenance or the dissolution of the covenant. This rigid either–or is replaced by a dynamic multiplicity of forms of relationship implied in pathos.

The Meaning of Pathos

The basic features emerging from the above analysis indicate that the divine pathos is not conceived of as an essential attribute of God, as something objective, as a finality with which man is confronted, but as an expression of God's will; it is a functional rather than a substantial reality; not an attribute, not an unchangeable quality, not an absolute content of divine Being, but rather a situation or the personal implication in His acts.

It is not a passion, an unreasoned emotion, but an act formed with intention, rooted in decision and determination; not an attitude taken arbitrarily, but one charged with ethos; not a reflexive, but a transitive act. To repeat, its essential meaning is not to be seen in its psychological denotation, as standing for a state of the soul, but in its theological connotation, signifying God as involved in history, as intimately affected by events in history, as living care.

Pathos means: God is never neutral, never beyond good and evil. He is always partial to justice. It is not a name for a human experience, but the name for an object of human experience. It is something the prophets meet with, something eventful, current, present in history as well as in nature.

The prophets never identify God's pathos with His essence, because for them the pathos is not something absolute, but a form of relation. Indeed, prophecy would be impossible were the divine pathos in its particular structure a necessary attribute of God. If the structure of the pathos were immutable and remained unchanged even after the people had "turned," prophecy would lose its function, which is precisely so to influence man as to bring about a change in the divine pathos of rejection and affliction.

In sum, the divine pathos is the unity of the eternal and the temporal, of meaning and mystery, of the metaphysical and the historical. It is the real basis of the relation between God and man, of the correlation of Creator and creation, of the dialogue between the Holy One of Israel and His people. The characteristic of the prophets is not foreknowledge of the future, but insight into the present pathos of God.

JOHN UPDIKE

"There is no way from us to God—not even a *via negativa*—not even a *via dialectica* nor *paradoxa*. The god who stood at the end of some human way . . . would not be God." [1] This assertion, which would seem to discourage all theology, is by Karl Barth, the most prominent, prolific, and (it seems to me) persuasive of twentieth-century theologians. His theology has two

Faith in Search of Understanding

faces—the No and the Yes. The No, which first resounded in 1919, when the original edition of Barth's impassioned commentary on Romans was published, is addressed to all that is naturalistic, humanistic, demythologized, and merely ethical in the Christianity that German Protestantism had inherited from the nineteenth century. The liberal churches, as Barth saw them, were dedicated to "the god to whom in our pride and despair we have erected the tower of Babel; to the great personal or impersonal, mystical, philosophical, or naive Background and Patron Saint of our human righteousness, morality, state, civilization, or religion. . . . This god is really an unrighteous god, and it is high time for us to declare ourselves thoroughgoing doubters, skeptics, scoffers, and atheists in regard to him." The real God, the God men do not invent, is *totaliter aliter*—Wholly Other. We cannot reach Him; only He can reach us. This He has done as the Christ of Biblical revelation, and the Yes of Barth's theology is the reaffirmation, sometimes in radically original terms (for instance, his virtually antinomian doctrine of all-inclusive Grace),[2] of the traditional Christian message. As a critical

---

From *Assorted Prose* by John Updike. © Copyright 1963 by John Updike. Reprinted from *Assorted Prose*, by John Updike, by permission of Alfred A. Knopf, Inc.

[1] Most of the quotations not specifically assigned are from the collection of addresses titled *The Word of God and the Word of Man*, available as a Harper Torchbook and quite the best introduction to Barth's work. A brief life and full bibliography is provided by Georges Casalis in *Portrait of Karl Barth* (tr. Robert McAfee Brown. Doubleday; 1963).

[2] See *Christ and Adam* (Harper; 1957).

theologian, Barth ranks with Kierkegaard; as a constructive one, with Aquinas and Calvin. His elaboration of the Yes may be dated from 1932, when he began to publish the huge series of *Church Dogmatics,* which, after twelve volumes totalling nearly seven thousand pages, still engages him.

Between, as it were, the No and the Yes, Barth published, in 1931, a small book, *Anselm: Fides Quaerens Intellectum,* devoted to a detailed explication of the so-called "ontological" proof of God's existence definitely formulated by St. Anselm (1033–1109) in his treatise the *Proslogion.* Not until 1958 was it reprinted in German, and not until recently was it published in this country. Barth, in introducing the second German edition, expresses "sorrow and surprise" that "this book, on which at the time I expended special care and devotion, has remained until now in its first edition and has long been out of print." No doubt the Nazi interregnum is partly to blame for this neglect, but this essay on Anselm is, even for a piece of theology, uncommonly tedious and difficult, replete with untranslated passages of Latin, English words like "ontic," "noetic," and "aseity," and non-stop sentences of granitic opacity. Yet it is, for the author, a pivotal work; in his preface Barth writes, "In this book on Anselm I am working with a vital key, if not the key, to an understanding of that whole process of thought that has impressed me more and more . . . as the only one proper to theology."

This is surprising, because Barth's theology is intrinsically scornful of proofs and the kind of metaphysics that admits them. "Metaphysical absolutes," he has written, "are an abomination unto the Lord and abolished in Christ." In Volume II, Book 1, of *Church Dogmatics* he goes to some lengths to unmask the Catholic doctrine of *analogia entis* (the analogy of being, which argues toward the existence of God from the reality of created beings) as disguised natural theology, and as such non-Biblical, unrevealed, and worse than worthless. Even less stringent varieties of Christian thought have learned to do without proofs. The Very Reverend Walter Robert Matthews, Dean of St. Paul's, concludes his discussion of the traditional proofs in the Encyclopaedia Britannica with the mild claim that "in spite of their failure as demonstrative arguments they have great value as indicating lines of thought, suggested by experience, which tend to substantiate the Theistic theory." Certainly the traditional proofs, in the light of modern science, are no more than suggestive. The cosmological argument, which survived the shift from the Ptolemaic to the Newtonian cosmos, is hopelessly strained between the unimaginable macrocosm of super-stellar astronomy and the inscrutable microcosm of particle physics. And the teleological argument (i.e., many things—e.g., the human eye —are intricately designed for purposive ends; *ergo,* a directing Intelligence exists) was administered a mortal blow when Darwin demonstrated how the organic world, for all its seemingly engineered complexity, might be a self-winnowing chaos. Anselm's proof, unlike these, makes no appeal to the natural world; with peculiar elegance it sidesteps external phenomena entirely. It gives God a name, and seeks to demonstrate that the name excludes the possibility of non-existence.

Anselm's proof, as customarily expressed, is: "Something beyond which it is impossible to conceive anything greater" must exist in reality as well as in the mind, for if it existed only in the mind, it would not be "something beyond which it is impossible to conceive anything greater." The customary criticism, expressed by the Benedictine monk Gaunilo in Anselm's lifetime and since then by many others, including Aquinas and Kant, is that existence is not a quality but the precondition of all qualities. Gaunilo applied to the proof the *reductio ad absurdum* of the "perfect island," which, though undiscovered in a far-off sea, must, by Anselm's principle, exist because of its supposed perfection. Anselm's rebuttal was that God is conceived of as greater absolutely rather than as the greatest of a class of objects; though in all other instances essence and existence are separable, and a being may be conceived of as not existing, this is not possible in the single case of God. This reasoning was to be echoed by Descartes, one of the several post-medieval thinkers —Leibniz and Hegel are others—who have found in the ontological argument something more than an absurd transposition of fact and fancy. Indeed, the ontological argument is a kind of logical prism that, depending on how it is tipped, looks shallow as a mirror or profound as a well.

Anselm: Fides Quaerens Intellectum begins with Barth's analysis of how Anselm conceived of theology and what, specifically,

he meant by "prove." The terms *"probare"* and *"probatio"* were
first used, in connection with Anselm's proof in *Proslogion,* by
Gaunilo in his counter-work *Liber pro Insipiente* ("Book on
Behalf of the Fool"). Though Anselm accepted these terms and
employed them in his refutation, *Contra Gaunilonem,* his initial
description of what he is doing is not *probare* but *intelligere.* To
Anselm, as Barth reads him, theology is the attempt to understand what has already been given by faith; proof, far from being
the aim of this attempt, is the rather incidental "polemical-
apologetic result of *intelligere.*" In establishing this precedence
—understanding subsumed under faith, and proof under understanding—Barth contradicts the common impression of theology
as the justification *a nihilo* of the articles of faith. This, he says
in a footnote, "would be like trying to support Mount Olympus
with pegs and ropes." His conception of theology's role may
strike the non-Christian as scandalously modest: "The aim of
theology cannot be to lead men to faith, nor to confirm them in
the faith, nor even to deliver their faith from doubt. Neither
does the man who asks theological questions ask them for the
sake of the existence of his faith; his theological answers, however complete they may be, can have no bearing on the existence
of his faith." While the words are Barth's, ample footnotes root
them to Anselm; Barth's exposition follows the Latin so closely
that even an apparently spontaneous metaphor, "bats and owls
squabbling with eagles about the reality of the beams of the
midday sun," turns out to be a translation of *"vespertiliones et
noctuae non nisi in nocte caelum videntes de meridianis solis
radiis disceptent contra aquilas."*

The unbeliever, the bat or owl blind to the sun, the "fool
[*insipiens*] who has said in his heart, 'There is no God,'" may
well question the relevance to him of this theology, this utterly
secure exploration—Barth observes a "characteristic absence of
crisis in Anselm's theologizing"—of the terrain enclosed between
the subjective *credo* of personal belief and the objective Credo
of the Church. In a sense, to the faithless theology can have no
relevance. Its announced purpose is "to give the faithful joy
in believing by a demonstration of the *ratio* of their faith."
Anselm writes, *"Credo ut intelligam"* ("I believe in order to understand"). And Barth insists that Anselm insists on the impos-

sibility of the *intelligere* shifting itself to the alien ground of *non credo*. Yet Anselm, as aware as any medieval Christian of heathens and heretics, not to mention contentious Benedictine monks, is distinguished by an exceptional polemical mildness. "Perhaps Anselm did not know any other way of speaking of the Christian *Credo* except by addressing the sinner as one who has not sinned, the non-Christian as a Christian, the unbeliever as believer, on the basis of the great 'as if' which is really not an 'as if' at all, but which at all times has been the final and decisive means whereby the believer could speak to the unbeliever."

What Barth here describes is, of course, his own evangelical stance. In recent years he has rarely preached to any congregation except those of the prison of Basel. His sermons (collected as *Deliverance to the Captives*) repeatedly assure the inmates that he, "a professor of theology and as such presumably a convinced Christian if not a half-saint," is in fact as great a sinner and as much of a captive as they. In 1946, when the University of Bonn was half in ruins, Barth returned from Switzerland to Germany to deliver the series of lectures eventually published as *Dogmatics in Outline*.[3] Midway through this uncompromisingly supernaturalist exposition of the Apostles' Creed, he interrupted himself: "At this point I should like, in passing, to answer a

[3] Barth was an early and vigorous enemy of Nazism—"pure unreason, the product of madness and crime." Teaching theology at Bonn in 1933, Barth (with Martin Niemöller and others) transformed the Evangelical Church in Germany into the "Confessing Church"—confessing, that is, the Barmen Confession, which Barth wrote and which begins with a condemnation of the Hitler-supported "German Christians." In 1935 the Gestapo expelled Barth from Germany; he returned to his native city of Basel, on the German border, where he could oversee and with volumes of exhortation encourage the spiritual struggle against Nazism. In his foreword to *Dogmatics in Outline,* Barth describes his 1946 audience: "The audience consisted partly of theologians, but the larger part was of students from the other faculties. Most people in the Germany of to-day have in their own way and in their own place endured and survived much, almost beyond all measure. I noted the same in my Bonn lads. With their grave faces, which had still to learn how to smile again, they no less impressed me than I them, I who was an alien, the center of all sorts of gossip from old times. For me the situation will remain unforgettable. By a mere coincidence it was my fiftieth semester. And when it was past, my impression was that for me it was the best ever."

question which has been put to me several times during these weeks: 'Are you not aware that many are sitting in this class who are not Christians?' I have always laughed and said, 'That makes no difference to me.' "

Having defined and restricted the meaning of *probatio*, Barth examines Anselm's proof step by step. *Aliquid quo maius cogitari nequit* ("something beyond which it is impossible to conceive anything greater") is given as a name of God. Barth admires the designation as one purely negative, "designed to exclude just this conceivability of the non-existence or imperfection of God which lurks in the background of every ontic conception of God." That, so designated, God can exist as an idea in the mind of even non-believers is at some length established. With Barth's copious commentary solicitously ushering Anselm's terse Latin every inch of the way, the two theologians proceed side by side, and a certain suspense builds up as the reader anticipates the gigantic leap that lies ahead, from existence as a concept to existence as a fact—from *esse in intellectu* to *esse in re*. Then a strange thing happens. Anselm takes the leap, and Barth does not, yet he goes on talking as if he had never left Anselm's side. The medieval philosopher, having satisfied himself that to exist *in solo intellectu* is a limitation incompatible with the total superiority of God as conceived, writes:

> *Existit ergo procul dubio aliquid quo maius cogitari non valet, et in intellectu et in re.*

Literally translated: "There exists, therefore, without doubt, 'something beyond which it is impossible to conceive anything greater,' both in knowledge and objectively (in thing)." The three tiny words *"et in re"* carry an immense freight; indeed, it would be difficult to conceive of any words carrying more. For on their backs God rides from the realm of ideas into the realm of objective existence.

Barth glosses this crucial sentence as "Thus as God he cannot exist in knowledge as the one who merely exists in knowledge." Now, this is a typical Barthian remark, of a piece with "one cannot speak of God simply by speaking of man in a loud voice." It is also a fairly unexceptionable assertion, except perhaps to

Unitarians, pragmatists, and lunatics. That is, we cannot pray
to or believe in a God whom we recognize as a figment of our
own imaginations. But can this be all Anselm meant? Barth
firmly says so: "All that is proved is just this negative. The positive statement about the genuine and extra mental existence of
God (in the general sense of the concept 'existence') does not
stem from the proof and is in no sense derived from it but is
proved by the proof only in so far as the opposite statement
about God's merely intramental existence is shown to be absurd.
Where then does this positive statement come from? . . . The
positive statement cannot be traced back as it originates in revelation." To Barth, then, faith and faith alone, faith in the Christian revelation, has supplied the *"et in re."* Anselm's proof is
merely the scouring of a cup that is then filled from above.

Barth devotes the remainder of the book to arguing that his
conception of Anselm's proof and Anselm's own conception are
identical. Gaunilo is taken to task because "quite obstinately and
in actual fact very shortsightedly all he demanded was proof
that God exists in the manner of created things." Such, we must
weakly confess, is the proof that we had hoped for. And such—
it is our obstinate impression—was the kind of proof that Anselm
thought he had supplied. Barth's enthusiastic recommendation
of Anselm's proof differs only in emphasis from the traditional
criticisms: "The fact that God is infinite does not prove that he
exists. Rather the fact that God is infinite proves that (if he
exists) he exists differently from beings who are not infinite."
But, granted that Anselm built from faith and granted that he
conceived of God's existence as extending into dimensions beyond those of creaturely existence, surely he also believed that
he had rendered forever unnecessary the parenthetic "if he
exists" so conspicuous in Barth's paraphrase. The section of the
Proslogion containing the *probatio* concludes with a prayer
thanking God that now *"si te esse nolim credere, non possim non
intelligere"* ("even if I did not wish to believe Thine existence, I
could not but know it").

Whereas Barth admits that "By the miracle of foolishness it is
possible to think of God as not existing. But only by this miracle.
Anselm had certainly not reckoned with this." There is, then, a
difference between the modern and the medieval theologian—

the theologian of crisis and the theologian without a sense of crisis. They are separated by nine centuries in which the miracle of disbelief has so often recurred that to call it a miracle seems an irony. The gap between *credere* and *intelligere* across which Anselm slung his syllogism has grown so broad that only Jahweh's unappealable imperatives can span it: "God," Barth says, "shatters every syllogism." Several times Barth speaks of Anselm's formula *quo maius cogitari nequit* as an "embargo," as a Divine prohibition in the style of the First Commandment: "God is the One who manifests himself in the command not to imagine a greater than he." This "embargo" is in fact on freedom of thought, "the most inward and most intimate area of freedom. *Bene intelligere* means: to know once and for all, as a real ox knows its master or a true ass its master's stall." Here Barth's vocabulary and theology seem more Biblical than the Bible itself. The Christian believer, awaking from the medieval dream wherein Church and State, faith and science, thoughts and things seemed to merge, has been restored with a vengeance to his primitive desperation.

The understanding that faith seeks is, for Barth, fundamentally an understanding of what man and religion are *not*. Anselm's proof—"a model piece of good, penetrating, and neat theology"—interests him in its rigorous negativity, its perfect independence of natural phenomena, and the "key" it holds for him is, possibly, that it proves nothing—probes, that is, the nothingness from which rises the cry for God. In "The Task of the Ministry," Barth preached:

> We cannot speak of God. The mystics, and we all in so far as we are mystics, have been wont to *assert* that what annihilates and enters into man, the Abyss into which he falls, the Darkness to which he surrenders himself, the No before which he stands is *God;* but this we are incapable of *proving.* The only part of our assertion of which we are *certain,* the only part we can *prove,* is that man is negatived, negated.

7

War and Peace

Every era has its own war, and every era is shaped and defined by its response to that fact. The Spanish Civil War brought to an agonizing climax the social and ideological currents swirling throughout the Thirties. World War II dominated the Forties to such an extent that the two are all but synonymous in our minds. The Korean Conflict—somehow we never seemed able to call it a war—symbolized the frustrating, directionless and seemingly inconclusive character of the Fifties.

One measure of the men of an age is the distinction they bring to the act of killing one another. However, the Vietnamese war, which belongs to the Sixties, seems to define itself as the antithesis of what that age represents. The sense of purpose and renewal that informs many of the pages of this book is tragically undercut by the history of our experience in Viet Nam, an experience that threatens to leave America as ravaged morally as Viet Nam is physically. For a sizable and vocal segment of American society, the brightness with which the decade began has fallen from the air. As in all tragedies we have moved from "the dream of innocence" to "the fact of guilt." However beyond the specific tragedy of Viet Nam—succinctly formulated in Robert Lowell's "Open Letter to President Johnson"—lies a more fundamental problem: man's apparently irresponsible instinct for war. That critical question is examined from a variety of perspectives in the articles by Herman Kahn, Konrad Lorenz, and Leonard Kriegel.

DWIGHT D. EISENHOWER

Three days from now, after half a century in the service of our country, I shall lay down the responsibilities of office as, in traditional and solemn ceremony, the authority of the Presidency is vested in my successor.

This evening I come to you with a message of leavetaking and farewell, and to share a few final thoughts with you, my countrymen.

The Dangers of a Military-Industrial Complex

Like every other citizen, I wish the new President, and all who will labor with him, Godspeed. I pray that the coming years will be blessed with peace and prosperity for all.

Our people expect their President and the Congress to find essential agreement on issues of great moment, the wise resolution of which will better shape the future of the nation.

My own relations with the Congress, which began on a remote and tenuous basis when, long ago, a member of the Senate appointed me to West Point, have since ranged to the intimate during the war and immediate post-war period, and finally to the mutually interdependent during these past eight years.

In this final relationship, the Congress and the Administration have, on most vital issues, cooperated well, to serve the nation's good rather than mere partisanship, and so have assured that the business of the nation should go forward. So my official relationship with the Congress ends in a feeling, on my part, of gratitude that we have been able to do so much together.

We now stand ten years past the midpoint of a century that has witnessed four major wars among great nations—three of these involved our own country.

Despite these holocausts America is today the strongest, the most influential and most productive nation in the world. Understandably proud of this pre-eminence, we yet realize that America's leadership and prestige depend, not merely upon our unmatched material progress, riches and military strength, but on how we use our power in the interests of world peace and human betterment.

Reprinted from the New York *Times*, January 22, 1961.

Throughout America's adventure in free government, our basic purposes have been to keep the peace; to foster progress in human achievement, and to enhance liberty, dignity and integrity among peoples and among nations.

To strive for less would be unworthy of a free and religious people.

Any failure traceable to arrogance or our lack of comprehension or readiness to sacrifice would inflict upon us grievous hurt, both at home and abroad.

Crises there will continue to be. In meeting them, whether foreign or domestic, great or small, there is a recurring temptation to feel that some spectacular and costly action could become the miraculous solution to all current difficulties. A huge increase in newer elements of our defenses; development of unrealistic programs to cure every ill in agriculture; a dramatic expansion in basic and applied research—these and many other possibilities, each possibly promising in itself, may be suggested as the only way to the road we wish to travel.

But each proposal must be weighed in the light of a broader consideration; the need to maintain balance in and among national programs—balance between the private and the public economy, balance between the cost and hoped for advantages —balance between the clearly necessary and the comfortably desirable; balance between our essential requirements as a nation and the duties imposed by the nation upon the individual; balance between actions of the moment and the national welfare of the future. Good judgment seeks balance and progress; lack of it eventually finds imbalance and frustration.

The record of many decades stands as proof that our people and their Government have, in the main, understood these truths and have responded to them well in the face of threat and stress.

But threats, new in kind or degree, constantly arise. Of these, I mention two only.

A vital element in keeping the peace is our military establishment. Our arms must be mighty, ready for instant action, so that no potential aggressor may be tempted to risk his own destruction.

Our military organization today bears little relation to that

known of any of my predecessors in peacetime—or, indeed, by
the fighting men of World War II or Korea.

Until the latest of our world conflicts, the United States had no
armaments industry. American makers of plowshares could,
with time and as required, make swords as well.

But we can no longer risk emergency improvisation of national
defense. We have been compelled to create a permanent armaments industry of vast proportions. Added to this, three and a
half million men and women are directly engaged in the defense
establishment. We annually spend on military security alone
more than the net income of all United States corporations.

Now this conjunction of an immense military establishment
and a large arms industry is new in the American experience.
The total influence—economic, political, even spiritual—is felt
in every city, every state house, every office of the Federal Government. We recognize the imperative need for this development. Yet we must not fail to comprehend its grave implications.
Our toil, resources and livelihood are all involved; so is the very
structure of our society.

In the councils of Government, we must guard against the
acquisition of unwarranted influence, whether sought or un-
sought, by the military-industrial complex. The potential for the
disastrous rise of misplaced power exists and will persist.

We must never let the weight of this combination endanger
our liberties or democratic processes. We should take nothing
for granted. Only an alert and knowledgeable citizenry can compel the proper meshing of the huge industrial and military machinery of defense with our peaceful methods and goals, so that
security and liberty may prosper together.

Akin to, and largely responsible for the sweeping changes in
our industrial-military posture has been the technological revolution during recent decades.

In this revolution research has become central. It also becomes
more formalized, complex and costly. A steadily increasing share
is conducted for, by, or at the direction of the Federal Government.

Today the solitary inventor, tinkering in his shop, has been
overshadowed by task forces of scientists, in laboratories and
testing fields. In the same fashion, the free university, historic-

ally the fountainhead of free ideas and scientific discovery, has experienced a revolution in the conduct of research. Partly because of the huge costs involved, a Government contract becomes virtually a substitute for intellectual curiosity.

For every old blackboard there are now hundreds of new electronic computers.

The prospect of domination of the nation's scholars by Federal employment, project allocations and the power of money is ever present, and is gravely to be regarded.

Yet, in holding scientific research and discovery in respect, as we should, we must also be alert to the equal and opposite danger that public policy could itself become the captive of a scientific-technological elite.

It is the task of statesmanship to mold, to balance, and to integrate these and other forces, new and old, within the principles of our democratic system—ever aiming toward the supreme goals of our free society.

Another factor in maintaining balance involves the element of time. As we peer into society's future, we—you and I, and our Government—must avoid the impulse to live only for today, plundering, for our own ease and convenience, the precious resources of tomorrow.

We cannot mortgage the material assets of our grandchildren without risking the loss also of their political and spiritual heritage. We want democracy to survive for all generations to come, not to become the insolvent phantom of tomorrow.

During the long lane of the history yet to be written America knows that this world of ours, ever growing smaller, must avoid becoming a community of dreadful fear and hate, and be, instead, a proud confederation of mutual trust and respect.

Such a confederation must be one of equals. The weakest must come to the conference table with the same confidence as do we, protected as we are by our moral, economic and military strength. That table, though scarred by many past frustrations, cannot be abandoned for the certain agony of the battlefield.

Disarmament, with mutual honor and confidence, is a continuing imperative. Together we must learn how to compose differences—not with arms, but with intellect and decent purpose. Because this need is so sharp and apparent, I confess that

I lay down my official responsibilities in this field with a definite sense of disappointment. As one who has witnessed the horror and the lingering sadness of war, as one who knows that another war could utterly destroy this civilization which has been so slowly and painfully built over thousands of years, I wish I could say tonight that a lasting peace is in sight.

Happily, I can say that war has been avoided. Steady progress toward our ultimate goal has been made. But so much remains to be done. As a private citizen, I shall never cease to do what little I can to help the world advance along that road.

So, in this, my last good night to you as your President, I thank you for the many opportunities you have given me for public service in war and in peace.

I trust that in you—that, in that service, you find some things worthy. As for the rest of it, I know you will find ways to improve performance in the future.

You and I—my fellow citizens—need to be strong in our faith that all nations, under God, will reach the goal of peace with justice. May we be ever unswerving in devotion to principle, confident but humble with power, diligent in pursuit of the nation's great goals.

To all the peoples of the world, I once more give expression to America's prayerful and continuing aspiration:

We pray that peoples of all faiths, all races, all nations, may have their great human needs satisfied; that those now denied opportunity shall come to enjoy it to the full; that all who yearn for freedom may experience its spiritual blessings, those who have freedom will understand, also, its heavy responsibility; that all who are insensitive to the needs of others, will learn charity, and that the sources—scourges of poverty, disease and ignorance —will be made to disappear from the earth; and that in the goodness of time, all peoples will come to live together in a peace guaranteed by the binding force of mutual respect and love.

Now, on Friday noon, I am to become a private citizen. I am proud to do so. I look forward to it.

Thank you, and, good night.

HERMAN KAHN

Seventy-five years ago white slavery was rampant in England. Each year thousands of young girls were forced into brothels and kept there against their will. While some of the victims had been sold by their families, a large proportion were seized and held by force or fraud. The victims were not from the lower classes only; no level of English society was immune to having its

In Defense of Thinking

daughters seized. Because this practice continued in England for years after it had been largely wiped out on the Continent, thousands of English girls were shipped across the Channel to supply the brothels of Europe. One reason why this lasted as long as it did was that it could not be talked about openly in Victorian England; moral standards as to subjects of discussion made it difficult to arouse the community to necessary action. Moreover, the extreme innocence considered appropriate for English girls made them easy victims, helpless to cope with the situations in which they were trapped. Victorian standards, besides perpetuating the white slave trade, intensified the damage to those involved.

Social inhibitions which reinforce natural tendencies to avoid thinking about unpleasant subjects are hardly uncommon. The psychological factors involved in ostrich-like behavior have parallels in communities and nations.

Nevertheless, during the sixty years of the twentieth century many problems have come increasingly into the realm of acceptable public discussion. Among various unmentionable diseases, tuberculosis has lost almost all taint of impropriety; and venereal disease statistics can now be reported by the press. Mental illness is more and more regarded as unfortunate instead of shameful. The word "cancer" has lost its stigma, although the horror of the disease has been only partially abated by medical progress.

Despite the progress in removing barriers in the way of dis-

---

cussing diseases formerly considered shameful, there are doubtless thousands going without vital medical treatment today
because of their inhibitions against learning, thinking, or talking
about certain diseases. Some will not get treatment because they
do not know enough to recognize the symptoms, some because
they are consciously ashamed to reveal illness, and some because
they refuse to think about their condition—it seems too horrible
to think about.

It may now be possible to condemn unequivocally the extremes of Victorian prudery, but less doctrinaire forms of os-
trichism must be considered with more care; they are, after all,
often based on healthy instincts. Everyone is going to die, but
surely it is a good thing that few of us spend much time dwelling
on that fact. Life would be nearly impossible if we did. If thinking about something bad will not improve it, it is often better
not to think about it. Perhaps some evils can be avoided or reduced if people do not think or talk about them. But when our
reluctance to consider danger brings danger nearer, repression
has gone too far.

In 1960 I published a book [1] that attempted to direct attention
to the possibility of a thermonuclear war, to ways of reducing the
likelihood of such a war, and to methods for coping with the
consequences should war occur despite our efforts to avoid it.
The book was greeted by a large range of responses—some of
them sharply critical. Some of this criticism was substantive,
touching on greater or smaller questions of strategy, policy, or
research techniques. But much of the criticism was not concerned with the correctness or incorrectness of the views I expressed. It was concerned with whether any book should have
been written on this subject at all. It is characteristic of our times
that many intelligent and sincere people are willing to argue that
it is immoral to think and even more immoral to write in detail
about having to fight a thermonuclear war.

By and large this criticism was not personal; it simply reflected the fact that we Americans and many people throughout
the world are not prepared to face reality, that we transfer our
horror of thermonuclear war to reports about the realities of

[1] *On Thermonuclear War* (Princeton, N.J.: Princeton University
Press), hereafter referred to as *OTW*.

thermonuclear war. In a sense we are acting like those ancient kings who punished messengers who brought them bad news. This did not change the news; it simply slowed up its delivery. On occasion it meant that the kings were ill informed and, lacking truth, made serious errors in judgment and strategy.

In our times, thermonuclear war may seem unthinkable, immoral, insane, hideous, or highly unlikely, but it is not impossible. To act intelligently we must learn as much as we can about the risks. We may thereby be able better to avoid nuclear war. We may even be able to avoid the crises that bring us to the brink of war. But despite our efforts we may some day come face to face with a blunt choice between surrender or war. We may even have war thrust upon us without being given any kind of a choice. We must appreciate these possibilities. We cannot wish them away. Nor should we overestimate and assume the worst is inevitable. This leads only to defeatism, inadequate preparations (because they seem useless), and pressures toward either preventive war or undue accommodation.

Many terrible questions are raised when one considers objectively and realistically the problems created by the cold war and the armaments race. For some years I have spent my time on exactly these questions—both in thinking about ways to prevent war, and in thinking about how to fight, survive, and terminate a war, should it occur. My colleagues and I have sought answers to such questions as these:

How likely is accidental war? How can one make it less likely?

How dangerous is the arms race today? What will it be like in the future?

What would conditions be if a nuclear attack leveled fifty of America's largest cities? Would the survivors envy the dead?

How many million American lives would an American President risk by standing firm in differing types of crises? By starting a nuclear war? By continuing a nuclear war with the hope of avoiding surrender?

How many European and Soviet and other lives would he risk?

These questions can be put in a more concrete and hence more upsetting form. Consider, for example, the debate about the defense of Europe. We have increased our non-nuclear forces to meet without initial use of nuclear weapons a possible Soviet conventional attack in Europe. But our present doctrine also seems to indicate that if the strengthened forces prove inadequate to repel the attack, we will initiate the use of nuclear weapons.

The questions now become more unpleasant since we must acknowledge the likelihood that this use of nuclear weapons might not be limited. Whether we intend it or not, we may have obligated ourselves to go to an all-out central war. Attempts at restraint may turn out to be unreliable; passion, irrationality, and technical difficulties of control and discrimination might cause escalation into all-out war. In this context we must ask ourselves several questions. First, would we in fact initiate an all-out war if the Soviets attacked Europe? Would we even risk one by initiating a lesser response which could easily escalate into all-out war? What would be the European attitude toward fighting a "limited" nuclear (or even a large conventional) war on their territory?

In seeking the answers to these questions, the President must estimate the cohesion of the Alliance, and weigh the possibility of tens of millions, possibly hundreds of millions, of American and European casualties—not to speak of Russians and others. He must ask himself whether he is willing to sacrifice, or so much as risk, New York in order to defend Paris or London or revenge their destruction. If he concludes that he is not—and there are many who think that he would not willingly make the trade— then he must ask himself whether he wishes to change either his commitments or his preparations.

He may conclude that even if he is not willing to initiate a war or a limited reprisal that could easily develop into war, he must maintain a pretense of being willing. Perhaps the facade will work. After all, even if he is not willing to go to an all-out war, the Soviets cannot rely on this. The uncertainty regarding his response may deter them from testing his resolve.

The President may be unwilling to go to all-out war, and also unwilling to rely on the deterrent effect of Russian uncertainty about our response acting as a deterrent. In that case he has to have realistic contingency plans for lesser responses than all-out war, to be used in the event the Soviets are not deterred. He must then ask himself: Should he disclose these contingency plans to the Soviets so as to make credible the action we will take to make their aggression unprofitable? Should he keep these plans secret so that the Soviets will not be encouraged to expect a less than all-out response? How will our allies react to either policy? Will their attitude change in an intense crisis? Would we prefer an ally to be involved in a disastrous local war rather than see its resources added to the Communist bloc?

Perhaps, in addition to having a "wider choice than humiliation or holocaust," the President may wish to prepare for the possibility of holocaust, and for the problems involved in lessening the damage. Even if we are not willing to fight an all-out thermonuclear war, it may still be forced on us, or occur inadvertently.

Consider as well the problem of deterring the Soviets from striking the United States either because they may be planning an aggression or because there is some crisis in which U.S. policy (perhaps the mere existence of the United States) may threaten their ability to surmount the crisis. In desperation they may feel that striking the United States would be less risky than not striking. How risky must we make such an action? What kind of punishment would deter the Soviets even if they were desperate? The threat of 100 million dead Russians? Ten million? The destruction of Moscow and Leningrad? With their citizens? Without their citizens, i.e., evacuated? How certain must this threat be? Just how stable, then, is our present "balance of terror"? How is it most likely to break down? If it does break down what will be the consequence?

Consider another unpleasant question. When the movie "On the Beach" depicted a war in the early sixties, the result of which was the total annihilation of all humanity by radioactivity, almost all the reviewers and many scientists indicated that it was a realistic estimate of the results of a nuclear war. Are we really risking an end to all human life with our current system? If true, are we willing to risk it? Do we then prefer some degree of unilateral disarmament? If we do, will we be relying on the Russians to protect us from the Chinese? Will the world be more or less stable? Should we attempt to disarm unilaterally? If the answers to these last questions depend on the degree of damage that is envisaged, are we willing to argue that it is all right to risk a half billion or a billion people but not three billion?

There seem to be three basic objections to asking these types of questions:

1. No one should attempt to think about these problems in a detailed and rational way.

2. What thinking there is on these problems, should be done in secret by the military exclusively, or at least by the government.

3. Even if some of this thinking must be done outside the government the results of any such thought should not be made available to the public.

The arguments against hard thinking by anyone at all about the realities of thermonuclear war break down into a number of categories: First, it is argued that thinking about the indescribable horror of nuclear war breeds callousness and indifference to the future of civilization in our planners and decision makers. It is true that detailed and dispassionate discussion of such questions is likely to look incredibly hard-hearted. It should also be clear, at least to thoughtful readers, that such questions must be considered. The reality may be so unpleasant that decision makers would prefer not to face it; but to a great extent this reality has been forced on them, or has come uninvited. Thanks to our ever increasing technology we are living in a terrible and dangerous world; but, unlike the lady in the cartoon we cannot say, "Stop the world, I want to get off." We cannot get off. Even the most utopian of today's visionaries will have to concede that the mere existence of modern technology involves a risk to civilization that would have been unthinkable twenty-five years ago. While we are going to make major attempts to change the nature of this reality, accepting great risks if necessary, most of us are unwilling to choose either a pronounced degree of unilateral disarmament or a preventive war designed to "settle" our problems one way or another. We therefore must face the facts that thermonuclear bombs now exist in the hands of at least four powers; that at least one of these powers has announced it is interested in the destruction of our society, albeit by peaceful means if possible; that the number of thermonuclear powers may grow; that the power most likely to obtain these weapons next, China, stands on the thesis that war with us is inevitable; and, finally, that the possibilities of an immediate solution by negotiation are indeed slim. Unless we are willing to abdicate our responsibilities we are pledged to the maintenance of terrifying weapon systems with known and unknown, calculable and incalculable risks, unless and until better arrangements can be made.

If we are to have an expensive and lethal defense establishment, we must weigh all the risks and benefits. We must at least ask ourselves what are the likely and unlikely results of an inadvertent war, the possibilities of accident, irresponsibility, or unauthorized behavior on the other side as well as on our own.

A variation of the objection to careful consideration of these problems focuses on the personality of the thinker. This argument goes: Better no thought than evil thought; and since only evil and callous people can think about this, better no thought. Alternatively, the thinker's motives are analyzed: This man studies war; he must like war—much like the suspicion that a surgeon is a repressed sadist. Even if the charge were true, which in general it is not, it is not relevant. Like the repressed sadist who can perform a socially useful function by sublimating his urges into surgery, the man who loves war or violence may be able to successfully sublimate his desires into a careful and valuable study of war. It does indeed take an iron will or an unpleasant degree of detachment to go about this task. Ideally it should be possible for the analyst to have a disciplined empathy. In fact, the mind recoils from simultaneously probing deeply and creatively into these problems and being conscious at all times of the human tragedy involved.

This is not new. We do not continually remind the surgeon while he is operating of the humanity of his patient. We do not flash pictures of his patient's wife or children in front of him. We want him to be careful, and we want him to be aware of the importance and frailty of the patient; we do not want him to be distracted or fearful. We do not expect illustrations in a book on surgery to be captioned: "A particularly deplorable tumor," or "Good health is preferable to this kind of cancer." Excessive comments such as, "And now there's a lot of blood," or "This particular cut really hurts," are out of place although these are important things for a surgeon to know. To mention such things may be important. To dwell on them is morbid, and gets in the

way of the information. The same tolerance needs be extended
to thought on national security.

Some feel that we should consider these problems but view
them with such awe and horror that we should not discuss them
in normal, neutral, professional everyday language. I tend to
disagree, at least so far as technical discussions and research are
concerned. One does not do research in a cathedral. Awe is fine
for those who come to worship or admire, but for those who come
to analyze, to tamper, to change, to criticize, a factual and dispassionate, and sometimes even colorful, approach is to be preferred. And if the use of everyday language jars, that is all the
more reason for using it. Why would one expect a realistic discussion of thermonuclear war not to be disturbing?

The very complexity of the questions raised is another reason
why many object to their consideration. There is no doubt that
if we reject hard thinking about alternatives in favor of uncriti-
cal acceptance of an extreme position we make the argument
simpler—and most of us prefer simple arguments. Consider,
for example,[2] the following statement by C. P. Snow.

> We are faced with an either-or, and we haven't much
> time. The *either* is acceptance of a restriction of nuclear
> armaments. This is going to begin, just as a token, with an
> agreement on the stopping of nuclear tests. The United
> States is not going to get the 99.9 per cent "security" that it
> has been asking for.
> This is unobtainable, though there are other bargains that
> the United States could probably secure. I am not going to
> conceal from you that this course involves certain risks.
> They are quite obvious, and no honest man is going to blink
> them. That is the *either*. The *or* is not a risk but a certainty.
> It is this. There is no agreement on tests. The nuclear arms
> race between the United States and the U. S. S. R. not only
> continues but accelerates. Other countries join in. Within,
> at the most, six years, China and several other states will
> have a stock of nuclear bombs. Within, at the most, ten
> years, some of those bombs are going off. I am saying this
> as responsibly as I can. *That* is the certainty. On the one
> side, therefore, we have a finite risk. On the other side we
> have a certainty of disaster. Between a risk and a certainty,
> a sane man does not hesitate.

[2] C. P. Snow, "The Moral Un-neutrality of Science," *Science*, January 27, 1961.

The speech from which the above excerpt was taken attracted much favorable comment. In spite of the wide acclaim, and the scientific and literary distinction of the author, the statement is neither accurate nor responsible. The United States is *not* asking for 99.9 per cent security via the arms control route. In fact, we seem to be willing to accept agreements of a much lower reliability than almost anybody—even passionate arms controllers—would have been willing to accept a few years ago when they did not know how difficult it is to get reliably enforceable agreements. Much more important, the "or" described by C. P. Snow is not a certainty. Unless he has information denied to the rest of us, he cannot know that within ten years some of these bombs are going off. Even more important, he cannot know that some of these bombs going off will result in a *certainty* of disaster.

The reader may feel, possibly correctly, that I may have been unfair to C. P. Snow by taking his remarks too literally. Let me concede the possibility. What is startling is not so much that Sir Charles made the remarks, but that there was so little criticism of them. Imagine the uproar that would have occurred if an equally distinguished man had said that, "There is no probability at all of war in the next ten years." If the actual probability had been one-half, each remark might be equally off, at least in the arithmetical sense, but only the first would be regarded as an acceptable position by most people. It should be noted that either remark can be dangerous: The first by increasing the pressure for undue accommodation or preventive war; the second by decreasing the pressure for a reasonable compromise, and safety precautions.

I believe that the reason for the widespread acceptance of the attitude expressed by Sir Charles lies in his last sentence. It would be very simple indeed if all we had to do was to choose between a certainty and a risk of disaster. Responsible decision makers would not need to hesitate. Unfortunately for their peace of mind, however, it is by no means clear on which side the certainties and risks lie. It may even be true that there is a certainty of disaster no matter what we do. It is even conceivable that this certainty can be demonstrated; that some detached and infinitely wise observer can prove that it is impossible for us poor creatures on earth to get out of the difficulties we are in. He may even be able to show that, having weapons of mass destruction, we must sooner or later use them, and maybe more than once, until only the peace of utter destruction puts an end to the repetition.

On the other hand, there may be different paths to safety, each involving degrees of risk and varying outcomes. I believe there are. But I recognize that balancing the risks is difficult. It cannot be done rigorously, though analysis should help. In the end, the best of policies must involve judicious guesses, informed acts of faith, and careful steps in the dark. It is well to recognize these for what they are, to be conscious that some new and seemingly appealing path that avoids the familiar horrors may be riskier than the present perilous one.

The automatic balance of terror is not only a falsely simple view of the world, it is in some ways a comforting view. To see why this is so, consider Richard Nixon's remark to Khrushchev, "We must live together or die together." That is indeed a comforting remark because it indicates an easy choice between national sanity and insanity. Nixon could have said, "We must live together or one of us will die." This is not a comforting remark. It not only has a threatening sound, it indicates that carelessness can be dangerous and that survival is not necessarily dependent on one's own acts.

Both remarks are inaccurate, of course, but if I had to choose, I would say that the second is probably more accurate than the first for the time being. If one wishes to be accurate in these matters, he must be lengthy and complex. He can start by saying that we must live together or one of us will be hurt to a great degree and the other to a lesser degree, the exact amounts depending on such "technical details" as how the war starts, how it is fought, and how it is terminated.

The mutual annihilation view is also comforting to many idealistic individuals, particularly those who intrinsically abhor any use of force. The bizarreness of a war in which both sides expect to be annihilated confirms their intuition that this whole business of military preparations is silly: A stupid and dangerous game which we ought to discourage nations—our own country, at least—from playing. Those who believe this can afford to scoff at attempts to reduce casualties from, say, 100 million to 50 million Americans; the situation is hopeless anyway; the only respectable cause is the total elimination of war.

To summarize: Many people believe that the current system must inevitably end in total annihilation. They reject, sometimes very emotionally, any attempts to analyze this notion. Either they are afraid of where the thinking will lead them or they are afraid of thinking at all. They want to make the choice one between a risk and the certainty of disaster, between sanity and insanity, between good and evil; therefore, as moral and sane men they need no longer hesitate. I hold that an intelligent and responsible person cannot pose the problem so simply.

Interestingly enough, my view is somewhat comforting too. If C. P. Snow is right and if Bertrand Russell is also right in proclaiming that our irrational desire to maintain an obsolete system jeopardizes the future of the human race, one can make a very persuasive case for almost any kind of arms control, including unilateral disarmament and preventive war (to achieve forcible arms control), as being better than the current system. Disagreeing with both these gentlemen, I can counsel strongly against both. However one reason why many do not wish to consider these questions objectively is the fear that a case will be made for one of these extreme views.

Often the reluctance to think about these problems is not caused by the advocacy of any particular *Weltanschauung*. Rather it is based on nothing sounder than a supernatural fear of the magical power of words (to talk about cancer is to bring on cancer) or of actions (to build shelters is to create the need for their use). Many have this primitive belief that speaking of evil or preparing for evil creates evil. Some years ago there was a great outcry at the news that a study had been made of the possible conditions under which the United States might surrender during a war. Legislation was passed preventing appropriations for studies of this subject. One might ask whether failure to think about all the ways in which a war might end makes it more likely for us to win a war, or whether it merely prevents thinking about possible Soviet strategies designed to bring about our surrender. Or does it even prevent thinking about the possibility of achieving a peace treaty under relatively advantageous terms while sparing unnecessary slaughter?

An objection is frequently made on a more sophisticated level. An example is the so-called self-fulfilling prophecy: If you are hostile and suspicious toward someone, you will often act so. Even if he was innocent before, he will notice your attitude, which arouses hostility and suspicion in him. With your suspicions now confirmed you become more hostile, thus intensifying his suspicions. The mutual counteractions lead either to immediate violence or to a level of tension at which the possibility of violence is ever present.

The self-fulfilling prophecy sometimes occurs both between individuals and between nations, but realizing this does not settle the question. In 1959 and 1960, I gave a series of lectures. At almost every one of them, someone urged that mutual trust could act as self-fulfilling prophecy. Just before the first time it was brought up, I had been through a relevant experience. I described it then and have used it several times since to illustrate that prophecies can be self-defeating as well as self-fulfilling.

A person I know is an embezzler who has served time in jail twice. At the time I was first asked the question about self-fulfilling prophecies he was under indictment for the third time, and out on bail. After he had been indicted I asked him, "Why did you do it? You have already been caught twice. Why do you keep repeating this behavior? It's not only immoral, it obviously isn't successful. Why do you do it?" He looked me right in the eye and said, "I can't help it. People trust me."

He put the blame where he thought it belonged, on the excessive trust of others. He is an outgoing fellow; he does not have much character and he just cannot control himself when he is excessively tempted. His story is an example of a "self-defeating prophecy." His victims trusted him and did not guard against him; so they were victimized. If one worries about having funds embezzled one may take precautions that defeat an attempt at embezzlement. Self-defeating prophecies probably play a bigger role in human affairs than self-fulfilling prophecies. Similarly, if one prepares for war, one may possibly deter war. This can happen. Indeed it has often happened in the past.[3]

For this reason we simply cannot reject programs solely because they reflect some hostility and suspicion of the Soviet Union. Hostility and suspicion are justified. These occur even in ordinary private and commercial life; people have contracts, courts, and police. There are even better reasons to reject a totally trusting international policy toward the Soviet Union. Our suspicions were not created by our own imaginations working overtime. Indeed, some suspicion would exist even in an atmosphere of cordiality and entente. A policy that cannot co-exist with a degree of suspicion is not a viable policy in today's world, or indeed any world.

The last objection to detailed thought on thermonuclear war rests on the view that the subject is not only unpleasant but difficult.

Many people feel that it is useless to apply rationality and calculation in any area dominated by irrational decision makers. This is almost comparable to feeling that it would be impossible to design a safety system for an insane asylum by rational methods, since, after all, the inmates are irrational. Of course, no governor or superintendent would consider firing the trained engineer, and turning the design over to one of the lunatics. The engineer is expected to take the irrationality of the inmates into account by a rational approach. Rational discussions of war and peace can explicitly include the possibility of irrational behavior.

[3] For example, it is fair to say that from 1871 until its failure in 1914 through a series of coincidences, deterrence kept the peace. During this period the major nations of Europe remained at peace despite the fact that large segments of each nation desired war on numerous occasions, that there were bitter national antagonisms, and the consequences of war were not only nowhere near as serious as today, but were regarded as far less serious than they actually were. Both Soviet and U.S. behavior today over such controversies as Berlin indicate prudent behavior as a result of fear of war. Indeed the Soviet doctrine of coexistence sprang directly from an appreciation of the power of modern nuclear weapons. None of the above implies that deterrence is bound to work indefinitely (indeed the first example indicates how it might fail); only that it is possible to worsen our current situation by unwisely weakening deterrence.

Of course, analysts may be misled by oversimplified models or misleading assumptions, and their competence readily attacked. However, except for irrelevant references to game theory and computers, such attacks are rare, and are usually so half-hearted that it is clear that their main motivation is not to expose incompetency. Given the difficulty of the problems, one would expect the critics to work more effectively on the obvious methodological problems and other weaknesses of present-day analysts.

These weaknesses may make it impossible for the best-trained analyst to arrive at any better policy suggestions than relatively informed intuitions, no matter how objectively and carefully he works. In fact, the net effect of his research might be to make the analyst's recommendations persuasive rather than correct. Moreover, in his objective discussion of the case, he might weaken moral barriers, customs, and sanctions which might better be left strong. It is also conceivable that by raising these issues, he might automatically create a controversy which would impede the development of ideas or programs deriving from trial and error or originating in a spirit of compromise. Last, and possibly most important, by making recommendations which help make the current system acceptable, he may prevent the "patient" from going to the doctor and accepting the drastic surgery which is really necessary to cure his ills. There may be a great deal of wisdom in the ancient proverb that "the good is the enemy of the best."

For all of the above and other reasons it is possible that the most objective and careful discussions may still influence events in a wrong direction. Indeed, the final outcome of decisions that are well meaning, informed, and intelligent can be disastrous. However, few would argue that this is a good reason to be malevolent, uninformed, or stupid. Those of us who have not received any divine revelation as to the correct course must do the best we can with the knowledge and intellectual tools we have available. I for one do not believe that it makes sense to depend any more than can be helped on blind luck or faith—even though I concede we will need both if we are to negotiate safely the treacherous terrain before us.

The second class of objections seems to be that the study of warfare should be left to professional military officers. In fact, one reviewer of OTW said: [4]

> I can understand and respect career military officers who have chosen the "honorable profession of arms" as a way of life, often at a sacrifice in comfort and emoluments and who are subsequently assigned the duty of formulating war plans to meet all eventualities. But Mr. Kahn is a physicist, a scholar and a civilian. To be blunt, his book makes me ashamed that we are fellow countrymen.

Clemenceau once said, "War is too important to be left to the generals." A colleague of mine, Albert Wohlstetter, has paraphrased the remark to the even more appropriate, "Peace is too important to be left to the generals."

If we treat all questions of the deterrence and fighting of war as a subject to be entrusted solely to those in uniform we should not be surprised if we get narrow policies. The deterring or fighting of a thermonuclear war certainly needs specialists in and out of uniform; but it involves all of us and every aspect of our society.

Many liberals feel more confident knowing that civilians not directly in the governmental apparatus can influence military policy by the thought they give to its problems. But others do not; in fact, the research corporation working under contract with the United States Government has become a whipping-boy for certain sectors of the liberal press. There are many and good reasons, however, why these organizations exist, and will in all probability grow in the future.

The principal advantages of the private consultant are twofold: a lack of compulsion to deal with "first things first," and an independent point of view. As to the first of these, most people do not appreciate just how ill-equipped our government is to perform long-range planning. The most able officials are constantly involved in the meeting of day-to-day crises, Congressional investigations, budgetary problems, and administrative detail, with little time to devote to the long-range problems in which the civilian non-government research corporation specializes. Rarely, if ever, can a government agency allow one man to

[4] George Kirstein, in *The Nation*, January 14, 1961, pp. 34–35.

be free from what Professor Samuel Sharp calls the "tyranny of the in-and-out box" for more than just a few months. Moreover, it is especially unlikely that a man can be spared to work on a long-range problem that in all probability will never arise. However, we know that just this sort of problem can be vitally important.

The independence is equally important. Unless the researcher is allowed to make mistakes—indeed to be "irresponsible"—it is unlikely that he will consider carefully enough the full range of alternatives or make the kind of constructive advance in thinking that is, in effect, a devastating criticism of current thinking. We must even allow researchers to be wrongheaded and stubborn, since it is rare that new controversial ideas in the policy field are created fully documented, or that the documentation can be obtained without additional research or work that will only be done if the undocumented, unpopular idea is vigorously supported or pressed even in the absence of the necessary research. In effect, one of the main purposes of the independent research institution is to be a sort of loyal opposition which is privy to most of an agency's "secrets," and yet can be disowned by the agency.

There are other less important but still, by themselves, sufficient reasons for the existence of the independent research institute. They tend to be somewhat competitive and thus provide a freer market for ideas and skilled professional review and criticisms. It is difficult for "outsiders" to do this partly because of security reasons but mainly because technology is growing at an increasingly rapid rate. Paradoxical as it sounds, reality has left experience far behind, and central as "common sense" is, it is not enough. Even the simple study of weapons effects has grown so complicated that many scientists have spent almost a lifetime working on them alone. A detailed analysis of a military-political problem may occasionally involve computer studies or even fairly sophisticated problems in mathematics; it may involve economic analyses both of the input-output type and the more conventional kinds; it will unquestionably draw on engineering and physics, and, most important, it will require, in the words of William Lee Miller, "profound historical imagination, a playing on the possibilities in every direction, and an acute moral sense." [5] As in many other fields, life has become so complex that the individual must be supplemented and aided by the team. The question then arises as to why these groups cannot be employed solely and directly by the government. Some of them can be, and in fact are. However, on many problems independent research workers bring to their groups specialties and skills in short supply. Such institutions often provide a more efficient way to utilize scarce human resources.

Inevitably the fact that most people studying national defense are paid by some agency of the government gives rise to the allegation of subservience rather than independence, that their studies are bought. Alternatively, it is argued that the corruption is more subtle than purely monetary influence; the analyst is attracted by the excitement of knowing about or influencing national policy, or he is bought by being given access to information, to laboratories, etc. According to this view, the government gets the analyst, one way or another, to cooperate in producing distorted work.

There may be some germ of truth in such accusations, but by and large *ad hominem* charges are irrelevant. Any serious analy-

---

[5] From a review of *OTW* in *Worldview*, April, 1961. The review goes on to state, "Mr. Kahn, consequently, is surely right when he says that we need the thought of persons outside military strategy and mathematical calculation to deal with world politics in our strange era. And this, precisely, is what is lacking in *On Thermonuclear War*." I would not disagree too much with any part of this comment. Although it is important to keep strategists in their place, it is also important to realize that they have their place. Technical studies should not be allowed to dominate our thinking, but should be taken into account. Nor should these technical treatments of thermonuclear war be considered unacceptable unless they include extensive accounts of such related problems as foreign policy, limited war, arms control, or the moral and theological problems of war and peace. I certainly agree that every one of these related problems is of vital concern and the specialists on thermonuclear war must consider them either explicitly or implicitly. But the importance of related topics hardly diminishes the need for specialized studies of thermonuclear war—in itself a subject too vast to be completely grasped. It is certainly the case that technical and specialized studies on foreign policy, limited war, or arms control that do not include an extensive account of thermonuclear war seldom meet objection on this score.

sis should be studied, discussed, and answered on its own merits. The analyst's motivation may have some place in the discussion, but surely it is a minor one if the analysis is serious. I am reminded of a remark by Leo Szilard on the difference between politicians and scientists. He made the point that politicians always ask, "Why did he say it?" whereas scientists ask, "Is it true?" [6] Of course, a man's motives are important. But in a discussion of national security they are probably less important than, "Is he right?" Part of our national maturity must be the ability to discuss issues on their merits, whether they are brought up by generals, politicians, researchers, academicians, right-wingers, left-wingers, Russians, neutralists, or others.

It is undeniably true that research organizations vary in their independence and individuals in the most independent research organizations do sometimes seem to act more as advocates than as impartial scientists. Man is incurably partisan, but so long as the primary loyalty of the private research organization is clearly to intellectual integrity, the harm done by partisan individual researchers is small. Indeed their partisanship can have value. It increases the probability that a thorough study and a vigorous case will be made for the various partisan causes. Moreover, the demand for competent researchers is today so large that few of them could feel any economic pressure to slant their work. Finally, even if their freedom is not always complete, it is very large compared to that of a conscientious government official who is "locked in" by the commitments of his superiors. The government official is often torn by conflicting departmental and national loyalties as well as restricted by official channels. The private organization, where those who negotiate contracts are often divorced from those who perform the study, has many fewer such problems.

Critics frequently refer to the icy rationality of the Hudson Institute, the Rand Corporation, and other such organizations. I'm always tempted to ask in reply, "Would you prefer a warm, human error? Do you feel better with a nice emotional mistake?" We cannot expect good discussion of security problems if we are

---

[6] Szilard is probably being too respectful of his scientific colleagues who also seem to indulge in *ad hominem* arguments—especially when they are out of their technical specialty.

going to label every attempt at detachment as callous, every attempt at objectivity as immoral. Such attitudes not only block discussion of the immediate issues, they lead to a disunity and fragmentation of the intellectual community that can be disastrous to the democratic dialogue between specialist and layman. The former tends to withdraw to secret and private discussions; the latter becomes more and more innocent, or naive, and more likely to be outraged if he is ever exposed to a professional discussion.

Finally, there is the objection that thermonuclear war should not, at least in detail, be discussed publicly. Even some who admit the usefulness of asking unpleasant questions have advocated raising them only in secret. One objector pointed out to me that if a parent in a burning building is faced with the problem of having to save one of two children, but not both, he will make a decision on the spur of the moment; it wouldn't have made any difference if the parent had agonized over the problem ahead of time, and it would have been particularly bad to agonize in the presence of the children. This may be true, but other considerations dominate our nation's choices; our capabilities for action and the risks we are assuming for ourselves and thrusting on others will be strongly influenced by our preparations both intellectual and physical. Other reasons for this objection to public discussion range all the way from concern about telling the Soviets too much, and a fear of weakening the resolve of our own people, through a feeling that public discussion of death and destruction is distastefully comparable to a drugstore display of the tools, methods, and products of the mortician. Perhaps some or all of these objections to public discussion are well taken. I do not know for sure, but I think they are wrong.

They are wrong if we expect our people to participate rationally in the decision-making process in matters that are vital to their existence as individuals and as a nation. As one author has put it: "In a democracy, when experts disagree, laymen must resolve the disagreement." One issue is whether it is better that the lay public, which will directly or indirectly decide policy, be more or less informed. A second issue is whether the discussion itself may not be significantly improved by eliciting ideas from people outside of official policy-making channels.

There are in any case at least two significant obstacles to full public debate of national security matters. The first, of course, is the constantly increasing problem of communication between the technologist and the layman, because of the specialization (one might almost say fragmentation) of knowledge. The other lies in the serious and paramount need to maintain security. Technical details of weapons' capabilities and weaknesses must remain classified to some degree. Nonetheless, technical details may be of vital importance in resolving much broader problems.[7] Moreover, those who feel that in some areas "security" has been unnecessarily extended must concede that in certain areas it has its place. To that extent the functioning of the democratic processes must be compromised with the requirements of the cold war and modern technology. Certainly the wisdom of the Turkish Radar or the U-2 overflights were not amenable to the usual democratic processes of discussion. Fortunately, non-classified sources often give reasonable approximations to the classified data. I would say that many of the agonizing problems facing us today can be debated and understood just about as easily without classified material as with—provided one carefully considers the facts that are available.

It is quite clear that technical details are not the only important operative facts. Human and moral factors must always be considered. They must never be missing from policies and from public discussion. But emotionalism and sentimentality, as opposed to morality and concern, only confuse debates. Nor can experts be expected to repeat, "If, heaven forbid. . . . . ," before every sentence. Responsible decision makers and researchers cannot afford the luxury of denying the existence of agonizing questions. The public, whose lives and freedom are at stake, expects them to face such questions squarely and, where necessary, the expert should expect little less of the public.

[7] For instance, who can presume to say whether military advantages of atomic weapons testing outweigh the obvious political and physical disadvantages unless he knows what the military advantages are?

In reality, militant enthusiasm is a specialized form of communal aggression, clearly distinct from any yet functionally related to the more primitive forms of petty individual aggression. Every man of normally strong emotions knows, from his own experience, the subjective phenomena that go hand in hand with the response of militant enthusiasm. A shiver runs down

Ecce Homo!

the back and, as more exact observation shows, along the outside of both arms. One soars elated, above all the ties of everyday life, one is ready to abandon all for the call of what, in the moment of this specific emotion, seems to be a sacred duty. All obstacles in its path become unimportant; the instinctive inhibitions against hurting or killing one's fellows lose, unfortunately, much of their power. Rational considerations, criticism, and all reasonable arguments against the behavior dictated by militant enthusiasm are silenced by an amazing reversal of all values, making them appear not only untenable but base and dishonorable. Men may enjoy the feeling of absolute righteousness even while they commit atrocities. Conceptual thought and moral responsibility are at their lowest ebb. As a Ukrainian proverb says: "When the banner is unfurled, all reason is in the trumpet."

The subjective experiences just described are correlated with the following, objectively demonstrable phenomena. The tone of the entire striated musculature is raised, the carriage is stiffened, the arms are raised from the sides and slightly rotated inward so that the elbows point outward. The head is proudly raised, the chin stuck out, and the facial muscles mime the "hero face," familiar from the films. On the back and along the outer surface of the arms the hair stands on end. This is the objectively observed aspect of the shiver!

Anybody who has ever seen the corresponding behavior of the male chimpanzee defending his band or family with self-sacrificing courage will doubt the purely spiritual character of human enthusiasm. The chimp, too, sticks out his chin, stiffens his body, and raises his elbows; his hair stands on end, producing a terrifying magnification of his body contours as seen from the front. The inward rotation of his arms obviously has the purpose of turning the longest-haired side outward to enhance the effect. The whole combination of body attitude and hair-raising constitutes a bluff. This is also seen when a cat humps its back, and is calculated to make the animal appear bigger and more dangerous than it really is. Our shiver, which in German poetry is called a *"heiliger Schauer,"* a "holy" shiver, turns out to be the vestige of a prehuman vegetative response of making a fur bristle which we no longer have.

To the humble seeker of biological truth there cannot be the slightest doubt that human militant enthusiasm evolved out of a communal defense response of our prehuman ancestors. The unthinking single-mindedness of the response must have been of high survival value even in a tribe of fully evolved human beings. It was necessary for the individual male to forget all his other allegiances in order to be able to dedicate himself, body and soul, to the cause of the communal battle. *"Was schert mich Weib, was schert mich Kind"*—"What do I care for wife or child," says the Napoleonic soldier in a famous poem by Heinrich Heine, and it is highly characteristic of the reaction that this poet, otherwise a caustic critic of emotional romanticism, was so unreservedly enraptured by his enthusiasm for the "great" conqueror as to find this supremely apt expression.

The object which militant enthusiasm tends to defend has changed with cultural development. Originally it was certainly the community of concrete, individually known members of a group, held together by the bond of personal love and friendship. With the growth of the social unit, the social norms and rites held in common by all its members became the main factor holding it together as an entity, and therewith they became automatically the symbol of the unit. By a process of true Pavlovian conditioning plus a certain amount of irreversible imprinting these rather abstract values have in every human culture been substituted for the primal, concrete object of the communal defense reaction.

This traditionally conditioned substitution of object has important consequences for the function of militant enthusiasm. On the one hand, the abstract nature of its object can give it a definitely inhuman aspect and make it positively dangerous— what do I care for wife or child; on the other hand it makes it possible to recruit militant enthusiasm in the service of really ethical values. Without the concentrated dedication of militant enthusiasm neither art, nor science, nor indeed any of the great endeavors of humanity would ever have come into being. Whether enthusiasm is made to serve these endeavors, or whether man's most powerfully motivating instinct makes him go to war in some abjectly silly cause, depends almost entirely on the conditioning and/or imprinting he has undergone during certain susceptible periods of his life. There is reasonable hope that our moral responsibility may gain control over the primeval drive, but our only hope of its ever doing so rests on the humble recognition of the fact that militant enthusiasm is an instinctive response with a phylogenetically determined releasing mechanism and that the only point at which intelligent and responsible supervision can get control is in the conditioning of the response to an object which proves to be a genuine value under the scrutiny of the categorical question.

Like the triumph ceremony of the greylag goose, militant enthusiasm in man is a true autonomous instinct: it has its own appetitive behavior, its own releasing mechanisms, and, like the sexual urge or any other strong instinct, it engenders a specific feeling of intense satisfaction. The strength of its seductive lure explains why intelligent men may behave as irrationally and immorally in their political as in their sexual lives. Like the triumph ceremony, it has an essential influence on the social structure of the species. Humanity is not enthusiastically combative because it is split into political parties, but it is divided into opposing camps because this is the adequate stimulus situation to arouse militant enthusiasm in a satisfying manner. "If ever a doctrine of universal salvation should gain ascendancy over the whole earth to the exclusion of all others," writes Erich von Holst, "it would at once divide into two strongly opposing

factions (one's own true one and the other heretical one) and
hostility and war would thrive as before, mankind being—unfortunately—what it is!"

The first prerequisite for rational control of an instinctive behavior pattern is the knowledge of the stimulus situation which
releases it. Militant enthusiasm can be elicited with the pre-
dictability of a reflex when the following environmental situations arise. First of all, a social unit with which the subject identifies himself must appear to be threatened by some danger from
outside. That which is threatened may be a concrete group of
people, the family or a little community of close friends, or else
it may be a larger social unit held together and symbolized by its
own specific social norms and rites. As the latter assume the
character of autonomous values, in the way described in Chapter
Five, they can, quite by themselves, represent the object in whose
defense militant enthusiasm can be elicited. From all this it follows that this response can be brought into play in the service of
extremely different objects, ranging from the sports club to the
nation, or from the most obsolete mannerisms or ceremonials to
the ideal of scientific truth or of the incorruptibility of justice.

A second key stimulus which contributes enormously to the
releasing of intense militant enthusiasm is the presence of a
hated enemy from whom the threat to the above "values" ema-
nates. This enemy, too, can be of a concrete or of an abstract
nature. It can be "the" Jews, Huns, Boches, tyrants, etc., or
abstract concepts like world capitalism, Bolshevism, fascism,
and any other kind of ism; it can be heresy, dogmatism, scientific fallacy, or what not. Just as in the case of the object to be
defended, the enemy against whom to defend it is extremely
variable, and demagogues are well versed in the dangerous art
of producing supranormal dummies to release a very dangerous
form of militant enthusiasm.

A third factor contributing to the environmental situation
eliciting the response is an inspiring leader figure. Even the most
emphatically antifascistic ideologies apparently cannot do without it, as the giant pictures of leaders displayed by all kinds of
political parties prove clearly enough. Again the unselectivity of
the phylogenetically programmed response allows for a wide
variation in the conditioning to a leader figure. Napoleon, about

whom so critical a man as Heinrich Heine became so enthusiastic, does not inspire me in the least; Charles Darwin does.

A fourth, and perhaps the most important, prerequisite for the
full eliciting of militant enthusiasm is the presence of many
other individuals, all agitated by the same emotion. Their absolute number has a certain influence on the quality of the response. Smaller numbers at issue with a large majority tend to
obstinate defense with the emotional value of "making a last
stand," while very large numbers inspired by the same enthusiasm feel the urge to conquer the whole world in the name of
their sacred cause. Here the laws of mass enthusiasm are strictly
analogous to those of flock formation described in Chapter Eight;
here, too, the excitation grows in proportion, perhaps even in
geometrical progression, with the increasing number of individuals. This is exactly what makes militant mass enthusiasm
so dangerous.

I have tried to describe, with as little emotional bias as possible,
the human response of enthusiasm, its phylogenetic origin, its
instinctive as well as its traditionally handed-down components
and prerequisites. I hope I have made the reader realize, without
actually saying so, what a jumble our philosophy of values is.
What is a culture? A system of historically developed social
norms and rites which are passed on from generation to generation because emotionally they are felt to be values. What is a
value? Obviously, normal and healthy people are able to appreciate something as a high value for which to live and, if necessary, to die, for no other reason than that it was evolved in cultural ritualization and handed down to them by a revered elder.
Is, then, a value only defined as the object on which our instinctive urge to preserve and defend traditional social norms
has become fixated? Primarily and in the early stages of cultural
development this indubitably was the case. The obvious advantages of loyal adherence to tradition must have exerted a considerable selection pressure. However, the greatest loyalty and
obedience to culturally ritualized norms of behavior must not be
mistaken for responsible morality. Even at their best, they are
only functionally analogous to behavior controlled by rational
responsibility. In this respect, they are no whit different from the
instinctive patterns of social behavior. . . . Also they are just

as prone to miscarry under circumstances for which they have not been "programmed" by the great constructor, natural selection.

In other words, the need to control, by wise rational responsibility, all our emotional allegiances to cultural values is as great as, if not greater than, the necessity to keep in check our other instincts. None of them can ever have such devastating effects as unbridled militant enthusiasm when it infects great masses and overrides all other considerations by its single-mindedness and its specious nobility. It is not enthusiasm in itself that is in any way noble, but humanity's great goals which it can be called upon to defend. That indeed is the Janus head of man: The only being capable of dedicating himself to the very highest moral and ethical values requires for this purpose a phylogenetically adapted mechanism of behavior whose animal properties bring with them the danger that he will kill his brother, convinced that he is doing so in the interests of these very same high values. *Ecce homo!*

When I was telephoned last week and asked to read at the White House Festival of the Arts on June 14, I am afraid I accepted somewhat rapidly and greedily. I thought of such an occasion as a purely artistic flourish, even though every serious artist knows that he cannot enjoy public celebration without making subtle public commitments. After a week's wondering, I have decided

Open Letter to President Johnson

that I am conscience-bound to refuse your courteous invitation. I do so now in a public letter because my acceptance has been announced in the newspapers and because of the strangeness of the administration's recent actions.

Although I am very enthusiastic about most of your domestic legislation and intentions, I nevertheless can only follow our present foreign policy with the greatest dismay and distrust. What we will do and what we ought to do as a sovereign nation facing other sovereign nations seems to hang in the balance between the better and the worse possibilities. We are in danger of imperceptibly becoming an explosive and suddenly chauvinistic nation, and we may even be drifting on our way to the last nuclear ruin. I know it is hard for a responsible man to act; it is also painful for the private and irresolute man to dare criticism. At this anguished, delicate and perhaps determining moment, I feel I am serving you and our country best by not taking part in the White House Festival of the Arts.

Text of letter from the New York *World-Telegram and Sun.*

I have just returned from a visit to the Portuguese synagogue in Amsterdam. It is an old synagogue, almost three hundred years old, and it has, as do so many seventeenth century buildings here in Amsterdam, a light that is all its own. One recognizes that light from the painting by Emmanuel de Witte which hangs in the Rijksmuseum. But where de Witte depicts a synagogue

Jeremiah and the People Problem

filled with people as well as light, the synagogue I saw was empty. The concierge who accompanied me explained that it was much too cold in the winter; one had to wait until after *Pesach,* for the warm weather and the tourists, to see the synagogue as it was in the old days. Still, even empty, it was my home, and it spoke to me as few other buildings in this past we call Europe have spoken to me. It is mine, mine as a Jew, mine as a man whose father's family—my grandmother, grandfather, uncles, aunts, cousins—was destroyed by that very insanity which destroyed 90,000 of the 100,000 Jews living in Amsterdam before the German occupation, mine as a Westerner whose ancestral soul has been sucked dry by that very West which has so decisively rejected me as Jew. That concierge and I shared a heritage, and although she dropped an English word or two into her Dutch and I bravely wrestled with the unsayable in my own Dutch, each of us automatically shifted into Yiddish whenever we had something to say that the other simply had to understand. It was this past, this language, even that parchment of paper which, to our mutual shame, had sent Spinoza into the bravest of all exiles and which is still to be seen in the synagogue library, it was this that divided us from the world of non-Jews and this which we hugged in the secret recesses of whatever soul we shared (for we *knew,* even as we spoke, that we shared a soul) and this then enabled us, forced us even, to divide the world into *us* and *them.* We talked at some length as I walked through the synagogue. What she remembered best about the

From *American Judaism,* Fall, 1965. Reprinted by permission of *American Judaism* and the author.

war, she explained, was a single day in the spring of 1941, when
the Germans surrounded the Beth Hamidrash and seized six
hundred young boys. The boys, she insisted, were beautiful, "all
of them." Eight days later, the mothers of the boys—all except
one, whose son lived, because, as the concierge pointedly remarked, "Even God needs witnesses"—received letters informing
them that their sons had quite suddenly died of an unspecified
"illness." Whether the story is true or is merely a part of that old
woman's mythological baggage, the word itself is coldly accurate,
a testimonial to the spirit of that very meticulous German mind.
What other people could have created so narrow a vocabulary for
the imperative?

As she closed the door behind us, the impressive Portuguese
synagogue had become simply a *schul* and the old concierge
herself had become my dead Polish grandmother. And then that
old woman, who without knowing it had accepted the role Fitz-
gerald so willingly assigned to Edmund Wilson and who was
not only keeper of my conscience but, for the moment, keeper
of whatever conscience was left in the West, said, "Well, there's
a God in heaven. And He judges." How I loved her for that. But
she was a true daughter of Spinoza and I loved her even more
after she paused and added, "Maybe." It was the heritage we
shared that came out in that *maybe,* a triumph for the poetic
imagination.

I left her and walked to the corner to stand in the Water-
looplein, a lively square which contains an open-air market and
which also contains a statue I had heard a great deal about, the
famous *Dock Worker* of Amsterdam. It is a very thick figure,
arms thrusting outwards from the sides, partly in supplication,
partly in protest, a reminder of a time that was never its own.
It celebrates the general strike of February, 1941, which began
in the harbor and soon spread throughout all Amsterdam as a
protest against the German deportation of the Jews. "*Februari
Staking 1941. Daad van verzet der burgerij tegen de jodenver-
volging door de Duitse bezetters.*" "February Resistance 1941.
Act of protest of the citizens against the persecution of the Jews
by the German occupying forces." Surrounding the statue were
wreaths of flowers, what seemed to be hundreds of wreaths, all
of them faded, many of them with the inscription, "We shall

never forget." Almost all of the inscriptions were in Dutch, but I remember one in German and another in French. Some were printed on white streamers rather crudely designed to look like *talaytin* (prayer shawls). I stared at the wreaths and then I stared again at the statue and then I cried like the very frightened child I had suddenly become.

All of which is intended solely as a preface. For as I write this, I find myself reminded that the massive insanity of this most progressive of all centuries continues and there is, apparently, no end in sight, at least no end that I care to contemplate. Malcolm X was murdered and a good part of me aches for the flesh and blood that existed beneath all that rhetoric hailing his "black manhood"; Vietnam is the potential end I do not care to contemplate, and if we are all atomized on that account we shall, at least, have the solace of laughter when the men and the missiles merge; Ulbricht has returned from Egypt, a visit which, as a Dutch Marxist friend tearfully told me while our minds dueled against one another and against the effects of Dutch gin, is no more than "the celebration of the friendship of two great peoples" (it sounds even funnier in Dutch); and so on, apparently *ad infinitum, ad nauseam*. Not that any of this is particularly serious. Only the real can be serious, and we Americans have been so victimized by our own rhetoric that we can no longer accept the world as real; it is a world that has been turned inside out so many times that one simply ceases to care. We look for formulas, we collectivize guilt, and the result is a kind of moral absolutism that is as generalized as it is meaningless.

There are no people who are German—there are simply *the Germans*, to each of us a euphemism for that collective horror that stuffed our world into one or another gas chamber twenty years ago. Nor are we isolated in this by our Jewishness alone. A Dutch colleague and friend, a poet who is also an excellent historian, once quietly explained to me why it was not to be regretted that university students here in Holland did not read Thomas Mann. Mann, after all, remained *German,* a noun he did not so much say as spit. Another colleague expressed his avoidance of all things German as "a matter of hygiene." He had spent the entire war as a prisoner of the Japanese in Indonesia. But toward the Japanese he felt no animosity, or at least none that

I could discover, despite a great deal of personal suffering in the
P. W. camp. The Dutch, the Japanese, the Indonesians—they
were equally grasping but also equally human. His experience
was repeated, as well as his attitude, by a young girl who sometimes takes care of my two-year-old son. A university student of
French literature, she reads neither Mann nor Goethe; she dis-
likes the thought of traveling through or in Germany; she looks
upon all Germans as veritable lepers. One can still see the traces
of a broad scar on her forehead, the result, she quietly informed
me when I asked her about it, of an encounter with a Japanese
soldier who had been beating her mother and who answered her
five-year-old protests with a knife. When I wondered aloud how
she felt about the Japanese, she shrugged and said, "They really
weren't so bad. They had no business being in Indonesia. But,
then again, neither did we."

The world is divided into *us* and *them,* a division made by
psyches that have the geometric fragility of the designs children
make with Indian beads. Evil is as generalized as guilt and in the
mind of each of us, in my mind, in that old woman's mind, in
the minds of my Dutch colleagues, in the babysitter's mind, there
remains that terrible beast known as *they* or *them,* a question
of grammatical case alone. For all of us, *they* are *the Germans,*
whom we view as faceless messengers of death and destruction.
Now that the war has been over for twenty years, it feels rather
good—one is tempted to say spiritually cleansing—to be *us* and
to be so smugly conscious of *them.* Until, that is, we realize that
there are those in the world for whom *them* is *us.* From accuser
to accused, from victim to oppressor, from violated to violator.
The equation is there, all too uncomfortably there, and the gen-
eralities have turned and turned again.

For we are not the only prophets in the world shouting, "Vengeance is mine, saith the Lord." (And who is that Lord if not
our innermost voice? Vengeance belongs to us, not Him.) James
Baldwin, for instance, is another prophet, having recently described himself to cheering Cambridge students as a man who
had come among them as a Jeremiah. He has far more right to
that title than I have; he even has as much right to it as that old
woman who was among the one in ten who remained in Amsterdam. According to the international edition of the *New York
Times,* it was to these same Cambridge students that Mr. Baldwin

said, "Nothing you can do will save your son or daughter." I take it Mr. Baldwin means not only the son or daughter of his debating opponent, Mr. William F. Buckley, but also my son, as well as the sons and daughters of the vast majority of his Cambridge audience. Although I have great admiration for him as a writer, I am a bit suspect of Mr. Baldwin as Jeremiah—the prices are too high and the prophet business has lately become a bit too good. But Jeremiah only exists when *they* have called him into being, and, God knows, *they* have called him into being. Unfortunately, Mr. Baldwin's *they* includes a very substantial *me,* and not only the *me* of *me* but the *me* of my two-year-old-son. And that hurts. It hurts a great deal, since I do not care to think of my son's future in terms of Mr. Baldwin's prophecy. But what else are prophets for? The warning is clear, and the book brought into being by the pain of my ancestors has it all there, in black and white (the pun is intentional, for it clears the air). The sins of the fathers, etc.

But how tired I am of the judgment of prophets. How tired I am of Baldwin as Jeremiah, of myself as Jeremiah, of that old woman as Jeremiah, of my Dutch colleagues as Jeremiah. As distasteful as I find the prospect of linking my own name to that of William F. Buckley, I suspect that he is far more accurate than I would like to believe when he claims that Mr. Baldwin is treated with "unctuous servitude" by white Americans, especially by those white liberals who love to have their psyches rhetorically blistered, the kind of people for whom reality is measured by David Susskind's television program *Open End.* But this is no more than a pattern for our times; by itself, it may even have fairly positive results. What is so disturbing is that a writer as fine as Mr. Baldwin is now beginning to treat himself with "unctuous servitude"; one suspects that he can no longer see the self for the prophet. White is white, Jew and Gentile, the collective *they.* German is German, Catholic and Protestant, Mann and Hitler, the collective *they.* In the one case, my son is to pay the debt, perhaps with his life; in the other, the debt is obviously unpayable, except, in my own wildest fantasies, if the United States and the Soviet Union were to collaborate on ending the German problem by ending the Germans. The terrible beast rages in me, and as long as I can think of Germans as *they,* as long as I can avoid thinking of their children as possessing faces that are individual faces, as long as I can dehumanize myself as those SS guards doing their "duty" managed to dehumanize themselves, then I can relish the fantasy. But I can no longer believe that the children are faceless. I can no longer believe that all Germans are *they*, if for no other reason than that I now find the role of *they* so personally abhorrent. Collective guilt is not, in itself, sufficient retribution for collective cowardice. *They* is as much a fiction as *we*, and together they constitute a supreme fiction, one that threatens eventually to destroy the entire world. It is this process of abstraction that Mr. Baldwin himself has so brilliantly attacked in his essays, an abstraction as endemic to prophets as it is to madmen.

For if guilt and retribution are to be universal, then who is to decide where we are to begin in determining who pays what? Is it Mr. Baldwin? The old woman? My Dutch colleagues? Me? Are the Dutch at all responsible for the condition of the American Negro, since it was in a Dutch ship that the first African slaves were brought to America in 1619? To what extent are the English responsible since it was Englishmen who first made slavery so profitable a venture in Colonial America? And how much guilt do we apportion to the Arabs for their record as slave traders? And what bill do we present to the Africans, so many of whom sold their fellow Africans into slavery?

When will we stop the merry-go-round of guilt and retribution, of accusation and abstraction? Will the growing crescendo demanding vengeance and power lead us to any other solution than universal suicide? If that is what Mr. Baldwin means by coming among us as a Jeremiah, then at least let him say it. It seems, rather, that Baldwin has made a collective white man who is very similar to my collective German; he shares his *they* with his fellow American Negroes as well as most non-white people throughout the world, while I share mine with my fellow Jews and a great many Europeans. And having created a *they* for my own use, do I have the right to protest against being included in someone else's *they*? Quite obviously, the answer is no.

I am committed to the Negro's struggle in America today because it is the struggle of justice with injustice and because if that struggle is resolved as it should be resolved then my son may be able to know people who happen to be Negroes rather than *they*. For almost all whites I know, including those who are most militantly involved in the struggle for Negro rights—to the extent of turning themselves into virtual parodies of what *they* believe Negroes want to hear—cannot like or dislike Negroes as individuals. Negroes remain as invisible to them, to borrow Ralph Ellison's metaphor, as Jews were invisible to the majority of people living in Hitler's Germany, as Germans have become invisible to me and to my Dutch colleagues, and as I threaten to become invisible to Mr. Baldwin. We are groups, blocs, forces, cogs, masses, whites, Negroes, Jews, Germans, and God knows what else. We are in fact, everything but people.

I have simply had enough of guilt and retribution, especially when all I am promised is that my son shall have to go on paying until the tables are turned and black becomes white. Insofar, as Mr. Baldwin's war is a war for equality, for humanity, for brotherhood (and how embarrassed both reader and writer are even to see those words on a page, which is, by itself, sufficient reason for using them), it is my war, too. One works for justice not in the hope that the evil of the past can be undone but in the hope that there shall be a liveable future. Nothing can bring back my dead grandmother. There are simply too many people crying for retribution. Perhaps what we need today are fewer Jeremiahs and more Isaiahs. And perhaps the most flagrant example of disease on our planet is the fact that it has become so much easier to be a Jeremiah than to be an Isaiah.

Since reason for such defensiveness should be obvious, let me end on the following note: I am not arguing against Negro militancy. What the Negro has won in America, he has won largely because of his militancy; and what he shall win in the future, he shall probably win because of his militancy. But militancy stripped of prophecy, militancy which does not endow itself with *the* word straight from God, militancy motivated by the human rather than the divine—it is this kind of militancy which makes sense to me. And let us have an end to *they*, everybody's they, Mr. Baldwin's and mine and that of my Dutch colleagues. And let us, all of us, pack in the Jeremiah business. There are simply too many claimants to that prophet's mantle. And, God knows, it really is hard enough to be a *mensch*.

8

Man and Science

It was Robert Oppenheimer who gave the code name "Trinity" to the first atomic explosion. The year of "Trinity" is the year one of our world. In the beginning, in the moment when this new world was born, Ken Bainbridge turned from the fireball to Oppenheimer and said, "Now we are all sons-of-bitches." William Laurence was there and recreates that scene twenty years after the event in his essay "Alamogordo, Mon Amour," which captures something of the fear and fascination we have for the new power that helps to make us what we are.

Marshall McLuhan says, "It is one of the ironies of Western man that he has never felt any concern about invention as a threat to his way of life." Any McLuhanism is endlessly debatable, but this section on man and science concerns itself with science as a possible threat to all ways of life.

In an excerpt from an influential book, Don K. Price reflects on the new scientific establishment; the interlocking technocracy of science, government, industry, and education which shapes the world we know. Rachel Carson provides for the Sixties an updated version of the Frankenstein myth—the destruction of man by his mechanical creation. Lucy Eisenberg's article describes one of the newest frontiers of science, and an area of deep human concern—the possible transformation of the very stuff of humanity. And automation is, of course, science in the marketplace where all men finally define themselves. Ben Seligman (and Michael Harrington in Section 10, *The Sense of The Future*) offers a view of man the automated worker. The focus of this section, then, is on the ecology of science.

WILLIAM L. LAURENCE

History leaves us strange monuments. To the lives of illustrious dead men we have glittering memorials, often more dazzling than the mortals they enshrine. Graven tablets grace the scenes of long-past battles, births and deaths, that their fame might live on in perpetuity. But who knows where the first fire was lit? Or when? Where is the marker to indicate the birthplace of the

Alamogordo, Mon Amour

Stone Age or the place where the first wheel was made? No one knows, for History is less meticulous about such epochal matters. Perhaps it is not too surprising, therefore, that the birthplace of the Atomic Age is today marked only by a shabby wooden sign in the middle of a barren desert in New Mexico. Strange that it is marked at all. Its legend reads simply "Ground Zero"; nothing more. It is not engraved but stenciled, and over a faded "No Smoking" sign at that.

Early this year I made my third visit to the desert near Alamogordo, to the place that for some inexplicable reason was given the code name Trinity. Here, twenty years ago, I watched while the first atomic bomb was successfully tested in the greatest of secrecy that Monday morning, July 16, 1945, at 5:30 Mountain War Time.

As the sole official reporter chosen by the wartime heads of the Manhattan Project to record the event publicly, once the curtain of secrecy had been lifted, I stood on the slope of a hill, named Compania for the occasion, some twenty miles to the northwest of Ground Zero. With me was a group of scientists from the Los Alamos Laboratory, where the bomb had been made.

Standing now at Ground Zero my mind ran back to that moment when, one hundred feet above this spot, at the top of a steel tower, the atomic bomb was unleashed. It created a sunrise in the predawn such as the world had never seen, a great green

From *Esquire*, 63 (May, 1965), pp. 120–138. Reprinted by permission of Curtis Brown, Ltd. Copyright © 1965 by Esquire, Inc.

fireball climbing in a fraction of a second to a height of more than eight thousand feet, rising ever higher until it touched the clouds, lighting up earth and sky all around with a bright luminosity. Scientists in a blockhouse ten thousand yards to the south leaped about in a primitive dance of joy, their shouts lost in the long, deafening roar. Unsuspecting inhabitants in the little town of Carrizozo thirty miles east awoke with a start and thought the world was ending. Windows rattled in Gallup, New Mexico, two hundred and thirty-five miles to the northwest. In Amarillo, Texas, some four hundred and fifty miles east, a weird flash lit up the nighttime sky. And halfway around the world at the Potsdam Conference in Germany, President Truman was handed the coded message, "Babies satisfactorily born." Seven weeks later I returned to Alamogordo after I had watched the same model of the A-bomb devastate the city of Nagasaki. On that return visit I saw for the first time what the bomb had done to the desert. Over a radius of four hundred yards the ground had been depressed to a depth ranging from ten feet at the periphery to twenty-five feet in the center. All life within a mile, vegetable as well as animal, had been destroyed. There was not a rattlesnake left in the region, nor a blade of desert grass. The sand in the depression had been fused into a glasslike substance the color of jade, all of it radioactive. Eight hundred yards away a steel rigging tower weighing thirty-two tons had been turned into a twisted mass of wreckage. The one-hundred-foot-high steel tower at the top of which the bomb was exploded was completely vaporized. A herd of antelope that had been grazing several miles away had vanished. It was believed they had started on a mad dash for the wilds of Mexico. A number of cows at a similar distance developed grey spots from deposits of radioactive dust. These radioactive cows and their progeny became the nearest equivalent to "sacred cows" in the United States, being carefully studied for the effects of radiation.

With the approach of the twentieth anniversary of the test I succumbed to an irresistible urge once again to visit the spot that had marked the birth of a new age. And so one clear day I set out in an Army car on a one-hundred-fifty-mile journey from

El Paso, Texas, to the Trinity site. It now constitutes a small unused area at the northern end of the White Sands Missile Range. The range, which is at present the testing ground for missiles developed by the Army, Navy, Air Force and N.A.S.A., is forty miles wide and one hundred miles long. Trinity is eighty miles uprange, within the present ninety-mile impact area of the Missile Range.

Observation bunkers dot the flat desert floor at ten-mile and five-mile radii from Ground Zero. But most of these outposts are difficult to spot and some have given way to the elements; they are now brush-filled and half collapsed.

My first impression on arriving at the site in broad daylight was one of disillusion. The country is desolate and silent. A chain-link fence weaves irregularly about the blast area and is broken by a gate at the south end. A faded sign affixed to the fence evokes a ghostly echo of the tense enterprise that once took place within: "Dangerous Area, Keep Out, By Order of the War Department." The warning is repeated in Spanish. Beyond the padlocked gate, a small pocket in the center is all that remains of the blast's crater. Winds have shifted the sand, leveling and smoothing the ground over the years, and scrub vegetation scraggily covers the soil which twenty years ago glistened with the new-formed Trinitite. Only small bits of that greenish glass are left: what the weather didn't bury, scientists and souvenir hunters have carried off.

Just outside the fence, at the west, north and southeast perimeters, lie three large mounds of sand, partly covering what used to be instrument bunkers. They are concrete-sided and concrete-topped dugouts about six feet by twelve. The entrance to these structures is small, about three by four feet, and foot-thick concrete panels placed mazelike just inside the doorway gave protection against blowback. Deteriorated padding rims the doorways, and bolt studs indicate where tight-fitting covers for the entrance hatches used to be. But these doors are nowhere in sight.

Well inside the fence, forming a square nine yards on a side around Ground Zero, there remains the stubble of four reinforced concrete piers which were the feet of the hundred-foot detonation tower. Right after the test, these piers were about a foot high with iron rods projecting from them. The rods have been sawed off in the interests of science, and the weather has undertaken to wear down the concrete a bit more. A rusted generator at one side is left over from one of the public religious observations at the site held yearly on the Sunday nearest to the date of the explosion.

Of the little that remained to be seen, two remnants in addition to Ground Zero brought back particularly poignant memories. One of these was a crumbling stone ranch house two miles southwest of Ground Zero. It was in this completely abandoned and unidentified dwelling that the assembly of the plutonium core, heart of the atomic bomb, began on the night of Thursday, July 12, 1945. As I passed through the windowless, doorless, littered rooms, I could see once again the specialized teams, comprised of the top men in their respective fields, working feverishly to put together something they called a "gadget" which, if successful,* would mean the construction of the Ultimate Weapon. I could see my friend, Professor Robert F. Bacher, then at Cornell University, now at the California Institute of Technology, who was in charge of the assembly, standing there during an agonizing three minutes. The core, which had been machine-tooled to the finest precision, became tightly wedged after it had been partially inserted and would go no further. I could hear Dr. Bacher reassuring his group that time would solve the problem, and after a three-minute period that seemed eternal, the core glided gently into its proper place.

It was at 3:18 the following afternoon, Friday, July 13 (nobody paid attention to the fact that it was Friday the thirteenth), that Dr. Bacher and his team, known as the "G Engineers," brought the vital core to a white tent at the base of the hundred-foot steel tower at Ground Zero, where Commander Norris E. Bradbury, now Director of the Los Alamos Scientific Laboratory, was supervising the assembly of the non-nuclear components. Dr. J. Robert Oppenheimer, the scientific director of the project, anxiously looked on. Late that evening everything was in place except the detonating system. On Saturday morning, July 14, Commander Bradbury ordered the operator of a hoist to remove the tent and lift the assembled "gadget" to the galvanized-iron shed at the top of the tower.

It was then that the group headed by Dr. Kenneth Greisen, of Cornell University, installed the first and last detonators and the firing circuit. By five that afternoon the gadget was complete except for the final electrical connections that were not made until shortly before firing time the following Monday morning.

All these partly forgotten memories came fully alive again as I stood there amid the desolation and rubble in the old abandoned ranch house. Here, I thought to myself, should be one of the shrines of modern history, preserved as one of the landmarks of our time. It was here that the lives of possibly thousands of young Americans hung in the balance. That moment at the end of those seemingly endless three minutes signaled the gift of life to many who otherwise would have died if the war had to be prolonged even for a few days.

The second of the ruins that brought back even more poignant memories was the observation shelter ten thousand yards south of Ground Zero, and thus named S-10. It is a wooden structure, its walls reinforced by concrete buried under a massive layer of earth. This was the control center for the test. Here Dr. Oppenheimer ("Oppie" to his colleagues) and his field commander, Professor Kenneth T. Bainbridge of Harvard, issued the orders and synchronized the activities of the other sites at various points in the desert. Here the signal was given and a complex of mechanisms set in motion to detonate the bomb.

Here at forty-five seconds to zero young Dr. Joseph L. McKibben of the University of California, at a signal from Dr. Bainbridge, activated a master robot that set in motion a series of other robots. The timing device which alerted the complex system of instrumentation was designed by Dr. Donald F. Hornig, now Special Assistant to the President for Science and Technology.

From the moment the robot mechanism took over, the whole great complicated mass of intricate mechanisms was in operation without human control. However, Dr. Hornig was stationed at a reserve switch ready to stop the operation at an order from the field commander in case anything went wrong.

As I stood there in the deserted shelter I relived again those agony-filled hours that preceded the final moments. Somehow the sunlit desert was transformed into the starless cold night of twenty years ago. I once again saw the lightning flashes and heard the ominous peals of thunder. Once more I heard the voice of Professor Samuel K. Allison of the University of Chicago, assistant director at Los Alamos, intoning the countdown over the radio network, first at periodic five-minute intervals and the last ten seconds at intervals of one second that seemed to get more agonizing with each second that passed.

"Zero minus three seconds!" I heard Dr. Allison's voice as clearly as I heard it twenty years ago.

"Zero minus two seconds!"

"Zero minus one second!"

And then I remembered the voice, sounding as though it had come from above the clouds, shouting *"Now!"*

At that instant, as I recorded soon after that same morning, there rose from the bowels of the earth a light not of this world. Up it went, a great ball of fire about a mile in diameter, changing colors as it kept shooting upward, an elemental force freed from its bonds after being chained for billions of years.

I remembered the words of Dr. George B. Kistiakowsky, of Harvard, one of the leaders in the project who was present in the shelter. "This was the nearest thing to Doomsday that one could possibly imagine," he said to me later that morning. "I am sure that at the end of the world—in the last millisecond of the earth's existence, the last man will see something very similar to what we have seen this morning." It was the same Dr. Kistiakowsky who a few days earlier had bet Dr. Oppenheimer a month's salary against $10 that the gadget would work. Standing there in the deserted command shelter, I could hear him say: "Oppie, you owe me $10!"

Dr. Kistiakowsky was one of the optimists in the group. There were many who were still doubtful. Among the memories that came rushing back on my recent visit was a bit of doggerel that I had named the "Los Alamos Blues":

> From this crude lab that spawned the dud
> Their necks to Truman's ax uncurled
> Lo the embattled savants stood
> And fired the flop heard round the world.

Among the lighter episodes on my return this year was a visit
for the first time to Carrizozo, in 1945 a sleepy town of 1,500
souls. If the wind at the time of the blast had changed in an
easterly direction, there would have been a real danger that the
radioactive cloud might blanket the sleeping town and expose
its inhabitants to deadly fallout.

To prepare for this emergency, several hundred Army trucks,
manned with carefully briefed personnel, surrounded Carrizozo
during the night. At a radio signal they would have dashed into
the dark houses and carried the inhabitants to safety without
giving them time to dress or telling them the reason why.

To the present day none of the original inhabitants of Carrizozo, now a lively town, knows what surprise was in store for
them had the wind blown in their direction, though all of them
were indeed aroused from their slumbers by the blast. Those I
spoke to remember it clearly as the shattering explosion of a
bomb right over their roofs.

One of those so rudely awakened was fifty-eight-year-old Louis
Montoya, who now lives in the hamlet of Oscura, some fifteen
miles to the south of Carrizozo. It is a little ghost town in the
desert with a few scattered dwellings of some thirty inhabitants.
One of the houses bears the neon sign, "Atomic Bar." Louis
Montoya saw the blinding flash and heard the great roar that
followed. For a while he thought the world was coming to an
end. And when I told him that he and his family had narrowly
missed being carried away by the Army that morning, all he
could say was that he was glad it didn't happen.

The prevailing winds were favorable. The Carrizozoans could
return to sleep. Early one morning three weeks later the citizens
of Hiroshima would not be so fortunate. For the atomic bomb,
having been born in the desert, would move swiftly to leave two
horrid monuments to itself in the wreckage of Hiroshima and
Nagasaki. But all the platitudes of a "humble birthplace" apply.
Indeed, the babies were satisfactorily born, but in drab surroundings. To this day, the place is humble—and as a symbol
of the ironic simplicity of its birthplace an old, overturned privy
now lies outside the very blockhouse where the leading scientists of the day saw the bomb through its delivery.

Unseen in this landscape is the stark reality of what happened here. The slight depression at Ground Zero could have been a natural gully. The four concrete piers might have once supported a grain silo. The bunkers, for all their real significance, could have been storage huts. The old ranch house where the bomb was assembled looks indeed like an old ranch house. The few scattered pieces of the jadelike Trinitite that are still to be found look like ordinary stones. But here is where the truth lies, invisible to the naked eye. I picked up a piece of it and brought it to New York. The next day I went to see Dr. John H. Harley of the Health and Safety Laboratory of the Atomic Energy Commission in his offices in lower Manhattan and left the Trinitite with him. A week later I received this note from Dr. Harley:

"There is no doubt that the Trinitite is quite radioactive. The radioautographs which we exposed for more than four days give much more intense blackening than the usual fallout samples.

"The presence of strontium 90 as a major constituent was shown by beta analysis. The other expected major constituent, cesium 137, appears in the gamma spectrum. Two other gamma emitters, cobalt 60 and europium 152, also appear. The cobalt may result from activation of metal parts of the divide and it is possible that europium 152 is a low-yield fission product that appears here because of its relatively long half life (about twelve and a half years). This material has not been mentioned before and we expect to send a brief note to *Science* on its appearance."

After twenty years, Alamogordo stills bears the mark.

At the end of a conference on human genetics last year, a biologist rose to summarize the proceedings. "I have visions," he said, "of a future great clinic in which a person will have not one, but hundreds, of his proteins analyzed completely in short order. The results will be run through a computer, and a license to reproduce will then be issued on the basis of a passing grade

Genetics and the Survival of the Unfit

with respect to his (or her) genes." The prospective spouse would also have to be tested, he added, "but as my vision begins to assume the proportions of a nightmare I shall abstain from further speculation along these lines."

Eugenic proposals like this are commonplace at scientific meetings nowadays. After twenty years of ill repute, eugenics is again the subject of respectable scientific investigation. But while most eugenicists agree that eventually we will have to put together some kind of eugenic plan, they do not agree on two basic questions. First, will our descendants be feebler and less fit if we do not practice eugenic planning? Second, is eugenics really possible? Do techniques exist *at the present time* for improving the human race by means of selective breeding?

While opinion varies widely, there is a large group of scientists today who answer the first question affirmatively. Among its most eminent members are Linus Pauling, the eternal controversialist, and P. B. Medewar, Fellow of the Royal Society. Pauling has written several short articles about genetic deterioration, and Medewar, who like Pauling is a Nobel Prize winner, made it the subject of his lecture at the Mayo Centennial Symposium last year. The spokesman for the group is the geneticist and popular author Hermann Muller, another Nobel laureate. Muller has been predicting genetic disaster since 1935 and today, at seventy-five, he is still a persuasive and articulate prophet of doom.

The disaster which Muller fears is a result of gene mutations. These are small structural changes in the genes (he calls them "submicroscopic accidents") which are usually harmful to the organism. Because Muller believes that mutations are accumulating, he concludes that the human race is beginning to decline. In the end, the whole world will become a hospital, "and even the best of us will only be ambulatory patients in it."

This prospect has worried Muller for many years. But few scientists worried with him so long as the only gene mutations that occurred were spontaneous ones which could not be avoided. Then in 1945 the United States exploded three atomic bombs. Thereafter—because radiation is known to cause a large increase in the gene mutation rate—a number of scientists were converted to Muller's point of view. Seized of apocalyptic visions, geneticists by the hundreds rushed into their labs to study radiation effects. Others set off for Japan to find out if radiation really had increased the mutation rate and what its effects would be on children born after the bomb. Throughout the 1950s, the customary calm of scientific conventions was shattered by technical arguments about experimental results, by emotional discussions of nuclear testing and what we should adopt as an "acceptable level" of radiation fallout.

Tension has been further heightened by the more recent discovery that certain chemicals such as formaldehyde and boric acid can cause gene mutations, and that these chemicals are being incorporated into all sorts of manufactured products, from lipstick to cold-cereal packaging. Furthermore, doctors are learning how to arrest or cure a mounting number of hereditary diseases that are caused by mutant genes. In saving the victims of these maladies they are not, of course, increasing the mutation rate as does radiation or a chemical mutagen. They are, however —by scientific cunning—foiling nature's plan for eliminating mutants. As a result, defective genes that were once eliminated by the death of their carriers are now being maintained and passed on to future generations.

The newly "conquered" hereditary diseases are still rare and even their names are unfamiliar to most people. From a genetic standpoint however, the problem posed is the same as that involved in diabetes (which is also a hereditary disease although the exact method of inheritance is somewhat obscure). Doctors have been treating diabetes successfully since 1921, and the result of this treatment, like those now being developed for other hereditary diseases, is to increase the frequency of defective genes.

Before the discovery of insulin in 1921, all young diabetics died before they could grow up and reproduce. Their genes were thus removed from the pool. (Geneticists often refer to an imaginary pool which contains the genes of every living person). Since 1921 however, many child diabetics have survived, married, and produced children (although the incidence of stillbirth and miscarriage is high among them). The result has been an increase in the frequency of diabetic genes and a consequent increase in the incidence of diabetes. The precise effect is hard to measure since diabetes has also become more prevalent simply because people live longer. There is no doubt however that the survival of diabetic genes is contributing to the effect.

Another group of hereditary diseases for which doctors have lately developed tests and therapies are all fatal if untreated. One of these is Wilson's disease. In its victims a defective gene causes faulty copper metabolism, which leads in turn to insanity and death. However, if the disease is spotted early enough and correctly treated, the symptoms never develop. (The therapy consists of a simple prescription taken by mouth, and removal from the diet of foods with a high copper content such as oysters, chocolate, and nuts.) I talked with one expert, Dr. Herbert Scheinberg at Bronx Municipal Hospital in New York. He sees no reason why the youngsters who are now growing up under treatment for Wilson's disease should not be able to have children of their own one day. Thus his patients will in due course pass on their defective genes.

To be sure, many—perhaps most—of the babies now born with Wilson's disease are not surviving. But this is only because not all doctors as yet know how to test for the malady while it is still mild enough to be treated. However, legislation has been proposed in New York State to ensure that this test will be done on all children. Similar legislation is in committee to insure testing for galactosemia, another hereditary disease whose victims cannot digest sugar, especially milk sugar. A test is already

required by law for phenylketonuria—a blood disease that causes
idiocy (40 per cent of those untreated have IQs under 10.) The
law guarantees that babies who inherit phenylketonuria (PKU)
will be spotted early, treated, given a chance to grow up and
bear children of their own.

A Little Abnormality May Be a Good Thing

The prospect of gene mutations being increased by radiation
and chemicals, while at the same time science makes the victims of hereditary disease more fertile, has caused the Mullerian
faction of geneticists to close ranks and sound the cry of doom.
Another group of scientists, however, have questioned their conclusions. The latter, including Theodosius Dobzhansky at the
Rockefeller Institute in New York, are much less apprehensive
about an increase in mutation rate; nor do they believe that even
if all mutant, "abnormal" genes could be eliminated, the race
would become healthier and more fit. They are far more optimistic about our future than Muller's group because they have
placed their faith in a concept called "heterosis" which holds
that "defective" genes are not nearly as defective as they seem.

Because "heterosis" is a rallying cry in this controversy, I
made a deliberate effort to understand what it means. (Many
scientists are convinced that it is much too complex for the layman. A British biologist has even proposed to start a course in
genetics for members of the Cabinet and other interested politicians.)

Actually, the pertinent facts are not complex at all. One need
know only that chromosomes are threadlike structures in the
nucleus which determine the genetic characteristics of the cell.
The chromosomes themselves are differentiated into more or less
discrete regions called genes, which have genetically distinct
properties. Each chromosome has hundreds, perhaps thousands,
of genes, each of which has its own special position, or "locus,"
on the chromosome. (The chromosomes themselves come in
pairs; 46 chromosomes, 23 pairs.)

If we remember that for every trait we inherit *two* genes,

heterosis turns out to be a simple idea. It means that if both genes are exactly the same, the organism will be normal (a fitness of 1). If, however, a mutation takes place and one gene is slightly different from the other, the organism will be supernormal (with a fitness of 1.1 or even 1.5). Hence, the fortunate creature who carries two slightly different (*i.e.*, "polymorphic") genes enjoys what geneticists call "heterotic vigor."

The paradox of heterosis appears when we consider that a pair of mutant genes can cause serious diseases such as diabetes, cystic fibrosis, and the others I have mentioned earlier. (Almost all mutant genes are "recessive," which means that the disease does not appear unless we inherit *two* defective genes. Out of the four possible combinations, only Child Number 4 will have the disease.) Nevertheless, if the theory of heterosis is true, the person who carries one defective gene and one normal gene (like Children 2 and 3) is more fit than the person who struggles along with two normal genes.

At first glance, the theory seems highly unlikely. But studies of a disease called sickle-cell anemia have proved it can be true. Babies who inherit two sickle-cell genes have a severe case of anemia and usually die soon after birth. Doctors have found, however, that a single dose of the sickle-cell gene confers a specific kind of heterotic vigor on its carriers, namely, resistance to malarial infection. Thus wherever malaria is endemic, people who carry a single sickle-cell gene are fortunate. They live longer and have more children. This means, of course, that the gene is "selected for" in the course of evolution and that it spreads. The result of this evolutionary process can be clearly seen in Central Africa, where malaria is extremely common, and where the sickle-cell gene is carried by at least 20 per cent of the population.

Sickle-cell anemia is a marvelous topic for cocktail-party conversation (if one is drinking with geneticists) not only because it is the classic example of heterosis, but also because it illustrates the close relationship between proteins and genes.

Scientists had long suspected that genes are responsible for manufacturing proteins, but they could not be certain until Linus Pauling, who was studying sickle-cell anemia, demonstrated that a structurally deficient (*i.e.*, mutant) gene produces a structurally deficient molecule of protein. Pauling discovered that in sickle-cell anemia the hemoglobin protein is malformed, and that all the symptoms of the disease (including the peculiar, sickle-shaped red blood cells which give it its name) can be traced to this one "molecular" defect.

There is no doubt that heterosis explains the prevalence of the sickle-cell gene. It is also conceivable that "diabetic" genes have spread for a similar reason. Very possibly one "diabetic" gene (coupled with one normal gene) confers resistance against chronic malnutrition by altering the mechanism for digesting sugar. "Diabetic" genes would, according to this theory, have been particularly useful to cavemen who in the best of times ate in excess, and the rest of the time ate nearly nothing. According to one geneticist, a doctor practicing eight thousand years ago might have examined his patient and said, "You're doing just fine; just enough diabetes to keep you in the pink of condition."

Though the correlation between diabetes and resistance to malnutrition has not been proven, a large number of geneticists believe that the theory of heterosis applies to a great many, if not a majority, of genes. They believe that for any given locus on a chromosome there are two, or perhaps more, genes which vary slightly owing to some past mutation. These "polymorphic" genes, as they are called, are maintained in the population because of the "vigor" they bring.

Adherents to this theory are forced to a rather startling conclusion: if "defective" genes are taken out of the pool, then future generations will be less rather than more fit, since getting rid of all the defective genes would also eliminate the extra vigor that results from a single dose of a faulty gene. Hence, even if one could control marriage and reproduction it will never be possible to breed a super-race, free from hereditary disease.

One wants to know, of course, why such theories cannot be tested and one or another proved true. Either we are as a race declining, or we are not. Either defective genes are an advantage when present in a single dose, or they are not. Unfortunately, however, in the field of human genetics, facts are hard to find. It is difficult to measure the rate of spontaneous mutation, much less find out whether the rate is increasing because of radiation. It is hard to put together enough case histories for a given disease because many of them are so rare. And it is usually impossible to detect the people who carry a single defective gene in order to find out whether they really are more vigorous or not. *Two* recessive genes can be spotted because all the protein they produce is defective (like the defective hemoglobin in sickle-cell anemia) or because the protein they are supposed to produce is missing altogether (lack of a protein called phenylalanine hydroxylase produces PKU). But when only one gene is defective, its effects are often hidden by the activity of the other, normal gene.

Poetry, Politics, and Genes

Human beings are peculiar; when they are not sure that what they are saying is true, they say it louder and with greater conviction. This is a weakness which most scientists try to avoid. The genetic controversy, however, has moved some of its participants to an unusual lack of discretion. "It is clear," Sir Julian Huxley said recently, "that the general quality of the world's population is not very high, is beginning to deteriorate, and should and could be improved." In fact, it has not been proved that we are deteriorating and it is not at all clear that the means to improve us exist.

Predictably, the scientists most concerned about genetic deterioration are the same ones who believe improvement is possible if society will only adopt a eugenic plan. Herman Muller, who has worried longest and loudest about deterioration, is also the acknowledged spokesman for eugenic planning. Similarly, Muller's opponents in the deterioration controversy also argue that far too little is yet known to justify deliberate action. "It's not that improvement isn't possible," said one British physiologist of this school, "but I do not think we know much more about how to bring it about than Galileo or Newton knew about how to fly."

One essentially negative goal of the eugenicists is to prevent the spread of hereditary disease. To accomplish this they would forbid people who carry a dangerous dominant gene to have children. Those with two faulty but recessive genes, on the other hand, would be allowed to reproduce, as would healthy people carrying a single dose of the undesirable gene. However a man and woman who carry the *same* dangerous recessive gene would be barred from marrying each other. Thus a man with Wilson's disease could marry whomever he wants as long as she too does not carry the gene for Wilson's disease. Their children will carry the Wilson's gene but none of them would actually have the disease. In this fashion, hereditary diseases would be wiped out in a single generation—if this program were adopted.

However, eugenicists are notoriously vague on the question of implementation. At the Mayo Clinic Centennial proceedings last year, one of them—Peter Brian Medewar—was asked how he would put such a plan into effect. "Of course," he replied, "I do not propose to do it myself, rushing around and forbidding the banns." But, he added, there is no reason why "sensible" people could not be dissuaded from marrying if they know that one out of four of their children is likely to inherit a disease.

Actually, a positive eugenic program would require much more radical steps. Muller's program for example involves a total departure from our present ideas and conventions about marriage and children. Like all believers in positive eugenics, his great hope is that society will improve its genetic stock by adopting the techniques of animal husbandry and breeding only from the best sires and dams.

To this end, he has evolved a plan called AID, Artificial Insemination from Donors. He proposes that banks be established where the sperm of various extraordinary men will be stored. When a woman decides to have children, she will then choose sperm from the donor whose qualities she most admires. "How many women," Muller cried when he launched his plan in 1935, "would be eager and proud to bear and rear a child of Lenin or Darwin! Is it not obvious that restraint, rather than compulsion, would be called for?"

Because of this chance remark Muller has been taunted for years, even by his friends. For the fact is that choosing a sire from among many more or less celebrated men is fraught with complications. As one scientist put it to me, "The trouble with Muller's bank is that he's always having to take people out of it.

If it's not politics, it's something else." The latest reject, he mentioned, is Abraham Lincoln, who is now suspected of having had something called Marfan's syndrome (a hereditary condition characterized by excessively long fingers and a cardiac defect). Muller's own solution is to store the sperm for twenty years. In two decades, he thinks, "a bétter appraisal of the donors will be possible and personal biases and entanglements will fade away."

But Muller still finds little support for his plan. The real obstacle is that as yet we know desperately little about man's genetic endowment and about the interaction between genes and environment which shapes the final human product. Although man carries an estimated 20,000 pairs of genes, scientists know the function of only a very small fraction, 500 at most. They have still to discover how genes interact, and whether some combinations of genes are possible and others are not. There also is a great deal more to be learned about gene linkage and function before the results of a "breeding program" can be predicted with success.

J. B. S. Haldane tells a cautionary tale about positive genetics and directed breeding. It concerns a recessive gene which lowers resistance to tubercular infection. According to Haldane, both John Keats and Emily Brontë inherited a pair of these genes, and as a result they both died prematurely. But he also believes that the poetic and literary talent of both these geniuses was inherited and that it was carried by the same rare and "defective" genes which made them susceptible to TB. The moral—that defective genes are not always what they seem—should surely give pause to those who would tamper with genes without being sure of their function.

"Genetic Alert"

It is not easy to discover the function of any particular gene. They are too small to be seen with most microscopes and even under the electron microscope they all look exactly alike. Nor is there any chemical test which can distinguish between different ones. One way to study a gene is to investigate inherited traits (as Mendel studied the size and shape of generations of peas in the nineteenth century). A better way is to study the protein that a gene is responsible for making. If a geneticist finds that a protein (like sickle-cell hemoglobin) is inherited according to Mendelian law, he infers that a gene is responsible for the manufacture of hemoglobin and that a mutant form of the gene produces a defective molecule of hemoglobin.

Until recently geneticists have concentrated their efforts on small animals like fruit flies and mice. They also know a great deal about the genes of a red mold called *Neurospora crassa.* But human beings take so long to breed and are so hard to control that geneticists have only recently begun to investigate and catalogue man's genes.

This is now being done systematically and on a large scale by a group of doctors at the Albert Einstein College of Medicine, under the code name "Genetic Alert." With funds from the National Foundation for Neuromuscular Disease they have set up laboratory facilities at the Bronx Municipal Hospital in New York, Children's Hospital in Boston, St. Christopher's Hospital for Children in Philadelphia, and Stanford University Hospital in California. At these hospitals a sample of blood is taken from every well baby brought into the clinic and examined for a possible abnormality in each of three proteins. The results of these tests are read into a computer and then punched onto cards which are automatically filed.

If the tests show that a child does have an abnormal protein, then the doctors can start treatment early enough to prevent the onset of a hereditary disease (or at least to prevent its most serious symptoms). This is however only one of the goals of "Genetic Alert." The other objective is to accumulate information about human genes systematically, so that it can be used for future research. When this is done, a doctor who wants to investigate a certain hereditary condition will only have to push a button to collect the subjects for his study. The computer will type out the names of all the people previously tested by the hospital who inherited the gene that interests him. The information will also be used to make reliable estimates of gene frequencies and for complicated genetic studies called chromosome "mapping."

Hideous Memories

The purposes of "Genetic Alert" are both clinical—that is, to cure disease—and to advance genetic research. But the directors of the project have no interest in its eugenic implications. Still, these cannot be altogether ignored. If, for example, the project were expanded to cover every child born in the country, it could provide all the information needed to eliminate hereditary disease—which is the goal of negative eugenics.

Scientists do not agree that we should apply eugenic techniques to eliminate hereditary disease or attempt, on the positive side, to improve the human race. And few if any responsible political leaders are prepared even to discuss a question freighted with hideous memories of the "eugenics" of Hitler's Third Reich. Nonetheless, it seems inevitable that—as with the splitting of the atom—scientific progress in genetics will in the foreseeable future raise issues of public policy which scientists alone cannot resolve.

RACHEL CARSON

A Fable for Tomorrow

There was once a town in the heart of America where all life seemed to live in harmony with its surroundings. The town lay in the midst of a checkerboard of prosperous farms, with fields of grain and hillsides of orchards where, in spring, white clouds

The Silent Spring

of bloom drifted above the green fields. In autumn, oak and maple and birch set up a blaze of color that flamed and flickered across a backdrop of pines. Then foxes barked in the hills and deer silently crossed the fields, half hidden in the mists of the fall mornings.

Along the roads, laurel, viburnum and alder, great ferns and wildflowers delighted the traveler's eye through much of the year. Even in winter the roadsides were places of beauty, where countless birds came to feed on the berries and on the seed heads of the dried weeds rising above the snow. The countryside was, in fact, famous for the abundance and variety of its bird life, and when the flood of migrants was pouring through in spring and fall people traveled from great distances to observe them. Others came to fish the streams, which flowed clear and cold out of the hills and contained shady pools where trout lay. So it had been from the days many years ago when the first settlers raised their houses, sank their wells, and built their barns.

Then a strange blight crept over the area and everything began to change. Some evil spell had settled on the community: mysterious maladies swept the flocks of chickens; the cattle and sheep sickened and died. Everywhere was a shadow of death. The farmers spoke of much illness among their families. In the town the doctors had become more and more puzzled by new kinds of sickness appearing among their patients. There had been several sudden and unexplained deaths, not only among adults but even among children, who would be stricken suddenly while at play and die within a few hours.

There was a strange stillness. The birds, for example—where had they gone? Many people spoke of them, puzzled and disturbed. The feeding stations in the backyards were deserted. The few birds seen anywhere were moribund; they trembled violently and could not fly. It was a spring without voices. On the mornings that had once throbbed with the dawn chorus of robins, catbirds, doves, jays, wrens, and scores of other bird voices there was now no sound; only silence lay over the fields and woods and marsh.

On the farms the hens brooded, but no chicks hatched. The farmers complained that they were unable to raise any pigs— the litters were small and the young survived only a few days. The apple trees were coming into bloom but no bees droned among the blossoms, so there was no pollination and there would be no fruit.

The roadsides, once so attractive, were now lined with browned and withered vegetation as though swept by fire. These, too, were silent, deserted by all living things. Even the streams were now lifeless. Anglers no longer visited them, for all the fish had died.

In the gutters under the eaves and between the shingles of the roofs, a white granular powder still showed a few patches; some weeks before it had fallen like snow upon the roofs and the lawns, the fields and streams.

No witchcraft, no enemy action had silenced the rebirth of new life in this stricken world. The people had done it themselves.

This town does not actually exist, but it might easily have a thousand counterparts in America or elsewhere in the world. I know of no community that has experienced all the misfortunes I describe. Yet every one of these disasters has actually happened somewhere, and many real communities have already suffered a substantial number of them. A grim specter has crept upon us almost unnoticed, and this imagined tragedy may easily become a stark reality we all shall know.

What has already silenced the voices of spring in countless towns in America? This book is an attempt to explain.

*   *   *

Needless Havoc

As man proceeds toward his announced goal of the conquest of nature, he has written a depressing record of destruction, directed not only against the earth he inhabits but against the life that shares it with him. The history of the recent centuries has its black passages—the slaughter of the buffalo on the western plains, the massacre of the shorebirds by the market gunners, the near-extermination of the egrets for their plumage. Now, to these and others like them, we are adding a new chapter and a new kind of havoc—the direct killing of birds, mammals, fishes, and indeed practically every form of wildlife by chemical insecticides indiscriminately sprayed on the land.

Under the philosophy that now seems to guide our destinies, nothing must get in the way of the man with the spray gun. The incidental victims of his crusade against insects count as nothing; if robins, pheasants, raccoons, cats, or even livestock happen to inhabit the same bit of earth as the target insects and to be hit by the rain of insect-killing poisons no one must protest.

The citizen who wishes to make a fair judgment of the question of wildlife loss is today confronted with a dilemma. On the one hand conservationists and many wildlife biologists assert that the losses have been severe and in some cases even catastrophic. On the other hand the control agencies tend to deny flatly and categorically that such losses have occurred, or that they are of any importance if they have. Which view are we to accept?

The credibility of the witness is of first importance. The professional wildlife biologist on the scene is certainly best qualified to discover and interpret wildlife loss. The entomologist, whose specialty is insects, is not so qualified by training, and is not psychologically disposed to look for undesirable side effects of his control program. Yet it is the control men in state and federal governments—and of course the chemical manufacturers—who steadfastly deny the facts reported by the biologists and declare they see little evidence of harm to wildlife. Like the priest and the Levite in the biblical story, they choose to pass by on the other side and to see nothing. Even if we charitably explain their denials as due to the shortsightedness of the specialist and the man with an interest this does not mean we must accept them as qualified witnesses.

The best way to form our own judgment is to look at some of the major control programs and learn, from observers familiar with the ways of wildlife, and unbiased in favor of chemicals, just what has happened in the wake of a rain of poison falling from the skies into the world of wildlife.

To the bird watcher, the suburbanite who derives joy from birds in his garden, the hunter, the fisherman or the explorer of wild regions, anything that destroys the wildlife of an area for even a single year has deprived him of pleasure to which he has a legitimate right. This is a valid point of view. Even if, as has sometimes happened, some of the birds and mammals and fishes are able to re-establish themselves after a single spraying, a great and real harm has been done.

But such re-establishment is unlikely to happen. Spraying tends to be repetitive, and a single exposure from which the wildlife populations might have a chance to recover is a rarity. What usually results is a poisoned environment, a lethal trap in which not only the resident populations succumb but those who come in as migrants as well. The larger the area sprayed the more serious the harm, because no oases of safety remain. Now, in a decade marked by insect-control programs in which many thousands or even millions of acres are sprayed as a unit, a decade in which private and community spraying has also surged steadily upward, a record of destruction and death of American wildlife has accumulated. Let us look at some of these programs and see what has happened.

During the fall of 1959 some 27,000 acres in southeastern Michigan, including numerous suburbs of Detroit, were heavily dusted from the air with pellets of aldrin, one of the most dangerous of all the chlorinated hydrocarbons. The program was conducted by the Michigan Department of Agriculture with the cooperation of the United States Department of Agriculture; its announced purpose was control of the Japanese beetle.

Little need was shown for this drastic and dangerous action. On the contrary, Walter P. Nickell, one of the best-known and best-informed naturalists in the state, who spends much of his time in the field with long periods in southern Michigan every summer, declared: "For more than thirty years, to my direct knowledge, the Japanese beetle has been present in the city of Detroit in small numbers. The numbers have not shown any appreciable increase in all this lapse of years. I have yet to see a single Japanese beetle [in 1959] other than the few caught in Government catch traps in Detroit . . . Everything is being kept so secret that I have not yet been able to obtain any information whatsoever to the effect that they have increased in numbers."

An official release by the state agency merely declared that the beetle had "put in its appearance" in the areas designated for the aerial attack upon it. Despite the lack of justification the program was launched, with the state providing the manpower and supervising the operation, the federal government providing equipment and additional men, and the communities paying for the insecticide.

The Japanese beetle, an insect accidentally imported into the United States, was discovered in New Jersey in 1916, when a few shiny beetles of a metallic green color were seen in a nursery near Riverton. The beetles, at first unrecognized, were finally identified as a common inhabitant of the main islands of Japan. Apparently they had entered the United States on nursery stock imported before restrictions were established in 1912.

From its original point of entrance the Japanese beetle has spread rather widely throughout many of the states east of the Mississippi, where conditions of temperature and rainfall are suitable for it. Each year some outward movement beyond the existing boundaries of its distribution usually takes place. In the eastern areas where the beetles have been longest established, attempts have been made to set up natural controls. Where this has been done, the beetle populations have been kept at relatively low levels, as many records attest.

Despite the record of reasonable control in eastern areas, the midwestern states now on the fringe of the beetle's range have launched an attack worthy of the most deadly enemy instead of only a moderately destructive insect, employing the most dangerous chemicals distributed in a manner that exposes large numbers of people, their domestic animals, and all wildlife to the poison intended for the beetle. As a result these Japanese beetle programs have caused shocking destruction of animal life and have exposed human beings to undeniable hazard. Sections of Michigan, Kentucky, Iowa, Indiana, Illinois, and Missouri are all experiencing a rain of chemicals in the name of beetle control.

The Michigan spraying was one of the first large-scale attacks on the Japanese beetle from the air. The choice of aldrin, one of the deadliest of all chemicals, was not determined by any peculiar suitability for Japanese beetle control, but simply by the wish to save money—aldrin was the cheapest of the compounds available. While the state in its official release to the press acknowledged that aldrin is a "poison," it implied that no harm could come to human beings in the heavily populated areas to which the chemical was applied. (The official answer to the query "What precautions should I take?" was "For you, none.") An official of the Federal Aviation Agency was later quoted in the local press to the effect that "this is a safe operation" and a representative of the Detroit Department of Parks and Recreation added his assurance that "the dust is harmless to humans and will not hurt plants or pets." One must assume that none of these officials had consulted the published and readily available reports of the United States Public Health Service, the Fish and Wildlife Service, and other evidence of the extremely poisonous nature of aldrin.

Acting under the Michigan pest control law which allows the state to spray indiscriminately without notifying or gaining permission of individual landowners, the low-flying planes began to fly over the Detroit area. The city authorities and the Federal Aviation Agency were immediately besieged by calls from worried citizens. After receiving nearly 800 calls in a single hour, the police begged radio and television stations and newspapers to "tell the watchers what they were seeing and advise them it was safe," according to the Detroit *News*. The Federal Aviation

Agency's safety officer assured the public that "the planes are carefully supervised" and "are authorized to fly low." In a somewhat mistaken attempt to allay fears, he added that the planes had emergency valves that would allow them to dump their entire load instantaneously. This, fortunately, was not done, but as the planes went about their work the pellets of insecticide fell on beetles and humans alike, showers of "harmless" poison descending on people shopping or going to work and on children out from school for the lunch hour. Housewives swept the granules from porches and sidewalks, where they are said to have "looked like snow." As pointed out later by the Michigan Audubon Society, "In the spaces between shingles on roofs, in eaves-troughs, in the cracks in bark and twigs, the little white pellets of aldrin-and-clay, no bigger than a pin head, were lodged by the millions . . . When the snow and rain came, every puddle became a possible death potion."

Within a few days after the dusting operation, the Detroit Audubon Society began receiving calls about the birds. According to the Society's secretary, Mrs. Ann Boyes, "The first indication that the people were concerned about the spray was a call I received on Sunday morning from a woman who reported that coming home from church she saw an alarming number of dead and dying birds. The spraying there had been done on Thursday. She said there were no birds at all flying in the area, that she had found at least a dozen [dead] in her backyard and that the neighbors had found dead squirrels." All other calls received by Mrs. Boyes that day reported "a great many dead birds and no live ones . . . People who had maintained bird feeders said there were no birds at all at their feeders." Birds picked up in a dying condition showed the typical symptoms of insecticide poisoning—tremoring, loss of ability to fly, paralysis, convulsions.

Nor were birds the only forms of life immediately affected. A local veterinarian reported that his office was full of clients with dogs and cats that had suddenly sickened. Cats, who so meticulously groom their coats and lick their paws, seemed to be most affected. Their illness took the form of severe diarrhea, vomiting, and convulsions. The only advice the veterinarian could give his clients was not to let the animals out unnecessarily, or to wash the paws promptly if they did so. (But the chlorinated hydrocarbons cannot be washed even from fruits or vegetables, so little protection could be expected from this measure.)

Despite the insistence of the City-County Health Commissioner that the birds must have been killed by "some other kind of spraying" and that the outbreak of throat and chest irritations that followed the exposure to aldrin must have been due to "something else," the local Health Department received a constant stream of complaints. A prominent Detroit internist was called upon to treat four of his patients within an hour after they had been exposed while watching the planes at work. All had similar symptoms: nausea, vomiting, chills, fever, extreme fatigue, and coughing.

The Detroit experience has been repeated in many other communities as pressure has mounted to combat the Japanese beetle with chemicals. At Blue Island, Illinois, hundreds of dead and dying birds were picked up. Data collected by birdbanders here suggest that 80 per cent of the songbirds were sacrificed. In Joliet, Illinois, some 3000 acres were treated with heptachlor in 1959. According to reports from a local sportsmen's club, the bird population within the treated area was "virtually wiped out." Dead rabbits, muskrats, opossums, and fish were also found in numbers, and one of the local schools made the collection of insecticide-poisoned birds a science project.

Perhaps no community has suffered more for the sake of a beetleless world than Sheldon, in eastern Illinois, and adjacent areas in Iroquois County. In 1954 the United States Department of Agriculture and the Illinois Agriculture Department began a program to eradicate the Japanese beetle along the line of its advance into Illinois, holding out the hope, and indeed the assurance, that intensive spraying would destroy the populations of the invading insect. The first "eradication" took place that year, when dieldrin was applied to 1400 acres by air. Another 2600 acres were treated similarly in 1955, and the task was presumably considered complete. But more and more chemical treatments were called for, and by the end of 1961 some 131,000 acres had been covered. Even in the first years of the program it was apparent that heavy losses were occurring among wildlife and domestic animals. The chemical treatments were continued, nevertheless, without consultation with either the United States Fish and Wildlife Service or the Illinois Game Management Division. (In the spring of 1960, however, officials of the federal Department of Agriculture appeared before a congressional committee in opposition to a bill that would require just such prior consultation. They declared blandly that the bill was unnecessary because cooperation and consultation were "usual." These officials were quite unable to recall situations where cooperation had not taken place "at the Washington level." In the same hearings they stated clearly their unwillingness to consult with state fish and game departments.)

Although funds for chemical control came in never-ending streams, the biologists of the Illinois Natural History Survey who attempted to measure the damage to wildlife had to operate on a financial shoestring. A mere $1100 was available for the employment of a field assistant in 1954 and no special funds were provided in 1955. Despite these crippling difficulties, the biologists assembled facts that collectively paint a picture of almost unparalleled wildlife destruction—destruction that became obvious as soon as the program got under way.

Conditions were made to order for poisoning insect-eating birds, both in the poisons used and in the events set in motion by their application. In the early programs at Sheldon, dieldrin was applied at the rate of 3 pounds to the acre. To understand its effect on birds one need only remember that in laboratory experiments on quail dieldrin has proved to be about 50 times as poisonous as DDT. The poison spread over the landscape at Sheldon was therefore roughly equivalent to 150 pounds of DDT per acre! And this was a minimum, because there seems to have been some overlapping of treatments along field borders and in corners.

As the chemical penetrated the soil the poisoned beetle grubs crawled out on the surface of the ground, where they remained for some time before they died, attractive to insect-eating birds. Dead and dying insects of various species were conspicuous for about two weeks after the treatment. The effect on the bird populations could easily have been foretold. Brown thrashers, starlings, meadowlarks, grackles, and pheasants were virtually wiped out. Robins were "almost annihilated," according to the biologists' report. Dead earthworms had been seen in numbers after a gentle rain; probably the robins had fed on the poisoned worms. For other birds, too, the once beneficial rain had been changed, through the evil power of the poison introduced into their world, into an agent of destruction. Birds seen drinking and bathing in puddles left by rain a few days after the spraying were inevitably doomed.

The birds that survived may have been rendered sterile. Although a few nests were found in the treated area, a few with eggs, none contained young birds.

Among the mammals ground squirrels were virtually annihilated; their bodies were found in attitudes characteristic of violent death by poisoning. Dead muskrats were found in the treated areas, dead rabbits in the fields. The fox squirrel had been a relatively common animal in the town; after the spraying it was gone.

It was a rare farm in the Sheldon area that was blessed by the presence of a cat after the war on beetles was begun. Ninety per cent of all the farm cats fell victims to the dieldrin during the first season of spraying. This might have been predicted because of the black record of these poisons in other places. Cats are extremely sensitive to all insecticides and especially so, it seems, to dieldrin. In western Java in the course of the antimalarial program carried out by the World Health Organization, many cats are reported to have died. In central Java so many were killed that the price of a cat more than doubled. Similarly, the World Health Organization, spraying in Venezuela, is reported to have reduced cats to the status of a rare animal.

In Sheldon it was not only the wild creatures and the domestic companions that were sacrified in the campaign against an in-sect. Observations on several flocks of sheep and a herd of beef cattle are indicative of the poisoning and death that threatened livestock as well. The Natural History Survey report describes one of these episodes as follows:

> The sheep . . . were driven into a small, untreated blue-grass pasture across a gravel road from a field which had been treated with dieldrin spray on May 6. Evidently some spray had drifted across the road into the pasture, for the

sheep began to show symptoms of intoxication almost at once . . . They lost interest in food and displayed extreme restlessness, following the pasture fence around and around apparently searching for a way out . . . [They] refused to be driven, bleated almost continuously, and stood with their heads lowered; they were finally carried from the pasture . . . They displayed great desire for water. Two of the sheep were found dead in the stream passing through the pasture, and the remaining sheep were repeatedly driven out of the stream, several having to be dragged forcibly from the water. Three of the sheep eventually died; those remaining recovered to all outward appearances.

This, then, was the picture at the end of 1955. Although the chemical war went on in succeeding years, the trickle of research funds dried up completely. Requests for money for wildlife-insecticide research were included in annual budgets submitted to the Illinois legislature by the Natural History Survey, but were invariably among the first items to be eliminated. It was not until 1960 that money was somehow found to pay the expenses of one field assistant—to do work that could easily have occupied the time of four men.

The desolate picture of wildlife loss had changed little when the biologists resumed the studies broken off in 1955. In the meantime, the chemical had been changed to the even more toxic aldrin, *100 to 300 times* as toxic as DDT in tests on quail. By 1960, every species of wild mammal known to inhabit the area had suffered losses. It was even worse with the birds. In the small town of Donovan the robins had been wiped out, as had the grackles, starlings, and brown thrashers. These and many other birds were sharply reduced elsewhere. Pheasant hunters felt the effects of the beetle campaign sharply. The number of broods produced on treated lands fell off by some 50 per cent, and the number of young in a brood declined. Pheasant hunting, which had been good in these areas in former years, was virtually abandoned as unrewarding.

In spite of the enormous havoc that had been wrought in the name of eradicating the Japanese beetle, the treatment of more than 100,000 acres in Iroquois County over an eight-year period seems to have resulted in only temporary suppression of the insect, which continues its westward movement. The full extent of the toll that has been taken by this largely ineffective program may never be known, for the results measured by the Illinois biologists are a minimum figure. If the research program had been adequately financed to permit full coverage, the destruction revealed would have been even more appalling. But in the eight years of the program, only about $6000 was provided for biological field studies. Meanwhile the federal government had spent about $375,000 for control work and additional thousands had been provided by the state. The amount spent for research was therefore a small fraction of 1 per cent of the outlay for the chemical program.

These midwestern programs have been conducted in a spirit of crisis, as though the advance of the beetle presented an extreme peril justifying any means to combat it. This of course is a distortion of the facts, and if the communities that have endured these chemical drenchings had been familiar with the earlier history of the Japanese beetle in the United States they would surely have been less acquiescent.

The eastern states, which had the good fortune to sustain their beetle invasion in the days before the synthetic insecticides had been invented, have not only survived the invasion but have brought the insect under control by means that represented no threat whatever to other forms of life. There has been nothing comparable to the Detroit or Sheldon sprayings in the East. The effective methods there involved the bringing into play of natural forces of control which have the multiple advantages of permanence and environmental safety.

During the first dozen years after its entry into the United States, the beetle increased rapidly, free of the restraints that in its native land hold it in check. But by 1945 it had become a pest of only minor importance throughout much of the territory over which it had spread. Its decline was largely a consequence of the importation of parasitic insects from the Far East and of the establishment of disease organisms fatal to it.

Between 1920 and 1933, as a result of diligent searching throughout the native range of the beetle, some 34 species of predatory or parasitic insects had been imported from the Orient in an effort to establish natural control. Of these, five became well established in the eastern United States. The most effective and widely distributed is a parasitic wasp from Korea and China, *Tiphia vernalis*. The female *Tiphia*, finding a beetle grub in the soil, injects a paralyzing fluid and attaches a single egg to the undersurface of the grub. The young wasp, hatching as a larva, feeds on the paralyzed grub and destroys it. In some 25 years, colonies of *Tiphia* were introduced into 14 eastern states in a cooperative program of state and federal agencies. The wasp became widely established in this area and is generally credited by entomologists with an important role in bringing the beetle under control.

An even more important role has been played by a bacterial disease that affects beetles of the family to which the Japanese beetle belongs—the scarabaeids. It is a highly specific organism, attacking no other type of insects, harmless to earthworms, warm-blooded animals, and plants. The spores of the disease occur in soil. When ingested by a foraging beetle grub they multiply prodigiously in its blood, causing it to turn an abnormally white color, hence the popular name, "milky disease."

Milky disease was discovered in New Jersey in 1933. By 1938 it was rather widely prevalent in the older areas of Japanese beetle infestation. In 1939 a control program was launched, directed at speeding up the spread of the disease. No method had been developed for growing the disease organism in an artificial medium, but a satisfactory substitute was evolved; infected grubs are ground up, dried, and combined with chalk. In the standard mixture a gram of dust contains 100 million spores. Between 1939 and 1953 some 94,000 acres in 14 eastern states were treated in a cooperative federal-state program; other areas on federal lands were treated; and an unknown but extensive area was treated by private organizations or individuals. By 1945, milky spore disease was raging among the beetle populations of Connecticut, New York, New Jersey, Delaware, and Maryland. In some test areas infection of grubs had reached as high as 94 per cent. The distribution program was discontinued as a governmental enterprise in 1953 and production was taken over by a private laboratory, which continues to supply individuals, garden clubs, citizens' associations, and all others interested in beetle control.

The eastern areas where this program was carried out now

enjoy a high degree of natural protection from the beetle. The organism remains viable in the soil for years and therefore becomes to all intents and purposes permanently established, increasing in effectiveness, and being continuously spread by natural agencies.

Why, then, with this impressive record in the East, were the same procedures not tried in Illinois and the other midwestern states where the chemical battle of the beetles is now being waged with such fury?

We are told that inoculation with milky spore disease is "too expensive"—although no one found it so in the 14 eastern states in the 1940's. And by what sort of accounting was the "too expensive" judgment reached? Certainly not by any that assessed the true costs of the total destruction wrought by such programs as the Sheldon spraying. This judgment also ignores the fact that inoculation with the spores need be done only once; the first cost is the only cost.

We are told also that milky spore disease cannot be used on the periphery of the beetle's range because it can be established only where a large grub population is *already* present in the soil. Like many other statements in support of spraying, this one needs to be questioned. The bacterium that causes milky spore disease has been found to infect at least 40 other species of beetles which collectively have quite a wide distribution and would in all probability serve to establish the disease even where the Japanese beetle population is very small or nonexistent. Furthermore, because of the long viability of the spores in soil they can be introduced even in the complete absence of grubs, as on the fringe of the present beetle infestation, there to await the advancing population.

Those who want immediate results, at whatever cost, will doubtless continue to use chemicals against the beetle. So will those who favor the modern trend to built-in obsolescence, for chemical control is self-perpetuating, needing frequent and costly repetition.

On the other hand, those who are willing to wait an extra season or two for full results will turn to milky disease; they will be rewarded with lasting control that becomes more, rather than less effective with the passage of time.

An extensive program of research is under way in the United States Department of Agriculture laboratory at Peoria, Illinois, to find a way to culture the organism of milky disease on an artificial medium. This will greatly reduce its cost and should encourage its more extensive use. After years of work, some success has now been reported. When this "breakthrough" is thoroughly established perhaps some sanity and perspective will be restored to our dealings with the Japanese beetle, which at the peak of its depredations never justified the nightmare excesses of some of these midwestern programs.

Incidents like the eastern Illinois spraying raise a question that is not only scientific but moral. The question is whether any civilization can wage relentless war on life without destroying itself, and without losing the right to be called civilized.

These insecticides are not selective poisons; they do not single out the one species of which we desire to be rid. Each of them is used for the simple reason that it is a deadly poison. It therefore poisons all life with which it comes in contact: the cat beloved of some family, the farmer's cattle, the rabbit in the field, and the horned lark out of the sky. These creatures are innocent of any harm to man. Indeed, by their very existence they and their fellows make his life more pleasant. Yet he rewards them with a death that is not only sudden but horrible. Scientific observers at Sheldon described the symptoms of a meadowlark found near death: "Although it lacked muscular coordination and could not fly or stand, it continued to beat its wings and clutch with its toes while lying on its side. Its beak was held open and breathing was labored." Even more pitiful was the mute testimony of the dead ground squirrels, which "exhibited a characteristic attitude in death. The back was bowed, and the forelegs with the toes of the feet tightly clenched were drawn close to the thorax . . . The head and neck were outstretched and the mouth often contained dirt, suggesting that the dying animal had been biting at the ground."

By acquiescing in an act that can cause such suffering to a living creature, who among us is not diminished as a human being?

DON K. PRICE

The United States was founded at a time when philosophers were beginning to believe in the perfectibility of mankind. Ever since Benjamin Franklin and Thomas Jefferson, Americans have been inclined to put their faith in a combination of democracy and science as a sure formula for human progress.

Today that faith burns much less bright. Since the Second

Escape to the Endless Frontier

World War it has seemed to many, and especially to scientists, that the faith was dimmed by the mushroom cloud of the atomic bomb. The scientists who found themselves, to their great surprise, caught up in the political troubles of the contemporary world are tempted to blame their fate on their success in discovering nuclear fission: they see their tragedy, like that of Prometheus, as the result of seizing the secrets of the gods. But it seems more realistic to remind them that their own faith in inevitable progress had been dampened before Hiroshima—during the Great Depression or even before.

The earlier creed of progress had two main articles of faith, one relating to the progress of science, the other to the progress of society. The first was that men's desire for material benefits would lead society to support the advancement of science and technology, just as the profit motive would encourage the development of the economy. The second was the corollary that the advancement of science would lead society toward desirable purposes, including political freedom.

The depression gave the general public reason to doubt these beliefs, as many scientists and philosophers had already come to do. After economists and politicians lost their confidence that the individual profit motive would automatically guarantee economic progress, and that technological innovation would necessarily further social welfare, it became easier for the general pub-

Reprinted by permission of the publishers from Don K. Price, *The Scientific Estate*. Cambridge, Mass.: The Belknap Press of Harvard University Press, Copyright, 1965, by the President and Fellows of Harvard College.

lic to share the skepticism of scientists. The leaders of the scientific world, of course, had already come to understand that science makes progress less by the effort of inventors to find solutions for the practical problems of industry or government, than by the formulation of abstract theory and the search for basic knowledge. And they had much earlier given up their faith that science was certain to further either divine purpose or political progress.

At the end of the Second World War, the scientists' skepticism became a basis not for despair, but for vigorous action to guarantee the progress of science. Under the leadership of Vannevar Bush, the scientists undertook to teach the nation that basic research would not be produced automatically by the efforts of industry or government to apply science and technology to their own purposes, and that as a matter of policy the government should support basic research without regard to its application. The United States had been weak in basic science, and had had to rely on Europe for the fundamental knowledge that guided the development of the spectacular new weapons during the war. Now, knowing that "basic research is the pacemaker of technological progress," the United States must provide support from government funds for the advancement of fundamental science. This argument, presented to President Roosevelt by Dr. Bush in his famous report, *Science the Endless Frontier,* reversed the traditional policy of the United States in two ways: it persuaded universities and private research institutions that they had to ask the government for financial aid, and it persuaded the government that basic science, as well as applied research, deserved support.

But although the report abandoned the traditional faith in automatic progress with respect to science, and proposed deliberate governmental policies to encourage that progress, it did not undertake to deal with the second and more general aspect of the problem—progress in social and political affairs. The relation of science to political purposes was set aside with the assurance that the progress of science is essential to "our health, prosperity, and security as a nation," and the disclaimer that science alone would provide no panacea for social problems.

The Bush report thus dealt—as, of course, Dr. Bush was asked by the President to do—with only half of the total problem of science in its relation to politics. On that half of the problem, it taught its lesson well, and the electorate learned it thoroughly. The results can be graded, in a crude way, by looking at what Congress was persuaded science is worth to the taxpayer: we are spending more dollars today on research and development than the entire federal budget before Pearl Harbor. If the lesson was an incomplete one, no one should single out the scientists for blame. Dr. Bush was not asked by the President to revise our political philosophy, but only to present a plan for the support of science. It is curious, in retrospect, that the political questions were not raised, but the fault was not that of the scientists, but of the politicians and political scientists. There were, indeed, some arguments about such questions as how the officials should be appointed who were to make grants to scientists, and what the procedures should be for accounting and overhead payments. But these were applied details, and hardly anyone stopped to ask the fundamental question: how is science, with all its new power, to be related to our political purposes and values, and to our economic and constitutional system?

By ignoring this question, we have been trying to escape to science as an endless frontier, and to turn our backs on the more difficult problems that it has produced.

For more than a decade, this escape seemed a sound strategy for science. Plenty of money was being provided, although there were indeed some minor inconveniences, as well as some worries in principle, about the way in which basic research was subordinated to certain applied programs. But then it began to be clear, in two ways, that troubles were sure to arise in the relationship between science and politics. The first way has now become clear to everyone in practice; the second is more theoretical, and therefore more important, but less obvious.

The practical trouble has arisen because practical politicians came to doubt that the identity of purpose between government and the scientific community should be taken for granted. "Health, prosperity, and security"—it was an argument, in a more sophisticated form, that what's good for science is good for the nation. This is surely true, in a general sense, but it is no longer completely persuasive as unfriendly members of Congress

begin to look for conflicts of interest between the scientific com-
munty and the nation as a whole.

Conflicts of interest appear first in petty problems, such as
those of accounting for federal grants to universities. But then
they appear in graver problems, like the degree to which scientists as such should have a voice in policy decisions, or government should control the direction of research and the use of its
results. The simple reassurance that science is bound to be good
for you is not likely to be adequate, especially in view of the new
potentialities for both good and evil of the biological and social,
as well as the physical, sciences. Our popular worries about
intercontinental missiles and radiation fallout, in which our
alarm can be directed against an alien enemy, are bad enough.
But to these worries we have added the fear that scientists are
about to use chemistry to poison our crops and rivers, biology
to meddle with our heredity, and psychology to manipulate our
ideas and our personality.

So we are about to reach the point when both scientists and
politicians begin to worry not merely about specific issues, but
about the theoretical status of science in our political and constitutional system, and no longer rely on the assumption—which
was acceptable enough to the general public when Dr. Bush
presented his memorable report—that science and democracy
are natural allies. Especially since some scientists have never believed it: some have been profoundly suspicious of the American
version of democratic politics, rather preferring the status of science in the more conservative and traditional societies of Western Europe, and a few have been persuaded that science would
prosper better under some form of socialism.

But most scientists, of course, like most politicians, have not
thought very much about the problem at all. Indeed, any reasonable foreign observer would be obliged to conclude that we have
socialized our science at best in a fit of absence of mind, and at
worst with the purpose of subordinating it to the purposes of
military power.

Accordingly, the scientific community and the United States
generally are in even deeper trouble for their lack of a theory
of the politics of science, than for their failure to solve practical
problems of organization or policy. The nation that was born of

the first effort in history to marry scientific and political ideas—
the political heir of Franklin and Jefferson—is apt to speak of
the relationship of science and politics with an air of apology,
while throughout Asia and Africa the missionaries of Marxism
teach the developing intelligentsia that the Communist system
is the only approach to politics that is firmly grounded on the
scientific method.

The clearest example of this contrast, as it has percolated
down from the scholarly elite to the general public, may be found
in science fiction. This is a form of literature unwisely neglected
by students of politics. On something like the theory that if I
could write a nation's songs I would be glad to let someone else
write its laws, I am inclined to think that it is the space cadets
of the comic strips—and their fictional counterparts back to
Jules Verne or even Daedalus—who have fired our enthusiasm
for the race with the Russians to the moon. That enthusiasm is
certainly shared on both sides of the Iron Curtain. But with a
difference, and a difference that may be more important to the
future of our political system than the amount of money that we
spend on space exploration.

The difference is that the Soviet space cadet, in sharp contrast to his opposite number in Western science fiction, seems to
be very conscious not only that he is in a race for prestige or
power with another country, but that he has discovered the key
to the use of the scientific method in human affairs. This is the
materialist dialectic, which is supposed not merely to let the
Communist system make the best use of science in technical
matters, but to give the scientific intellect a generally dominant
role in the society of the future.

This notion began to appear in Soviet space fiction long before the first Sputnik. Forty years ago Aleksei Tolstoi, with some
technical help from the pioneering rocket engineer Tsiolkovski,
used a new propellant to put a heroic Red Army man on Mars,
where he proceeded to help organize a proletarian revolution
against a decadent Martian society. More recently, it has become even clearer that the Soviet conquest of space will be a
means of extending to the cosmos the spread of Marxist philosophy. Thus, as one space ship rushes through the void to its first
meeting with beings from another solar system, the hero reas-

sures his colleagues that sympathetic communication will surely be possible: "Thought, no matter where it is found, will inevitably be based on mathematical and dialectical logic." (Incidentally, the hero does not rely entirely on such spiritual comfort, for he goes on to issue tranquilizers to all hands on board.) And his comrade replies with a sententious expression of confidence that they will be congenial with the beings they are about to meet, since it is inevitable that on other worlds, as on the Earth, "humanity has been able to harness the forces of Nature on a cosmic scale only after reaching the highest stage of the communist society."

In the West, of course, the science fiction hero is a good deal less sure that science is about to bring the cosmos to a state of perfection. As Isaac Asimov has noted, most contemporary science fiction in America is not utopian, but anti-utopian. If the hero is not full of complexes from his infancy or frustrated by romantic difficulties, he is likely to be upset by the feeling that the social system in which he lives is not all it should be. The clear-eyed young hero in his space suit (like the clear-eyed cowboy or the earlier pioneers and pathfinders) is all too likely to be betrayed by selfishness or weakness in high places. Or in the more recent and more apocalyptic stories, the hero, if any, is likely to be struggling in a world that is about to be ruined, or has been ruined, by the inability of politicians to understand and control the powers released to mankind by modern science.

A generation ago, the popular utopias were mainly in the tradition of Edward Bellamy's *Looking Backward,* which in turn was still in the tradition of Francis Bacon's *New Atlantis:* the world remade to the heart's desire by the rationalism and the power of science. But today, the few scientific utopias are not calculated to inspire much hope for humanity. Even a Marxist scientist like J. D. Bernal finds some of them repulsive because "a lack of freedom consequent on perfect organization" leads to a society in which the "Utopian seems, notwithstanding his health, beauty, and affability, to partake too much of the robot and the prig." The anti-utopian theme, on the other hand, appears in serious pronouncements by scientists as well as in science fiction; even at meetings of scientific societies, speeches are likely to be made gloomily predicting disaster from our advance in scientific knowledge, and calling for a revival of something like traditional faith.

And if the utopias have changed, so have the horror stories. A generation or two ago the traditional symbol of political oppression had not changed since before the days of Thomas Jefferson: it was the rack of the Inquisition. If you were brought up on *Westward Ho!* and Browning's dramatic monologues, to say nothing of Jefferson and Macaulay and later political historians in the liberal tradition, you were likely to believe that the main historic threat to human freedom had been averted from the English-speaking world by the defeat of the Armada, and destroyed in America by the disestablishment of the church in Virginia. About all that was necessary to perfect the possibility of human freedom (one could learn from *Huckleberry Finn* or *Elmer Gantry*) was to destroy the last vestiges of enforced conformity in our society.

But within a few decades, the popular symbol of oppression had changed completely. The techniques of torture in *Westward Ho!* had been replaced by the more scientific methods of Orwell's *1984* or Zamyatin's *We*. A society founded on technology, rather than superstition, had become the most plausible system of tyranny.

The difference between the democratic and Communist camps in the popular attitude toward the political significance of science might be dismissed as the product of frivolous fiction if it did not also appear in the writings of eminent scientists. It is tempting to hope that the Soviet scientists are really dedicated only to their science, and eager to join in an international community with their Western colleagues. But it is hard to write off completely the official point of view, as expressed by Academician S. I. Vavilov, that Lenin had correctly comprehended the philosophical significance of science in general, and physics in particular, when he had "pointed out that the crisis in physics could be overcome by mastering the science of dialectical materialism. This provided a sure way for physics to surmount every kind of crisis and develop further." As a result, it is supposed to be the obligation of Soviet physicists to take the dialectic as their guide not only in their approach to politics and philosophy, but also to physics itself.

In practice, all the evidence suggests that this has very little to do with the way physicists actually work in their laboratories; if they make a few rhetorical gestures in the direction of political orthodoxy in an introductory paragraph of a scientific paper, they can write as they please on scientific subjects. But Marxist dialectic is still the orthodoxy; like other authoritarian orthodoxies, it cannot stamp out skepticism and cynicism, but it can stamp out open dissent.

The scientists of democratic nations, even if they are ardent anti-Communists, take no such confident view of the role of science in their political systems. Some of this pessimism comes out when leading scientists take to science fiction as a medium. Fred Hoyle, the Cambridge University astronomer, has his hero in *The Black Cloud* sum up the British political system thus: "Politicians at the top, then the military, and the real brains at the bottom . . . We're living in a society that contains a monstrous contradiction, modern in its technology but archaic in its social organization . . . We [scientists] do the thinking for an archaic crowd of nitwits and allow ourselves to be pushed around by 'em in the bargain." And the late Leo Szilard, University of Chicago physicist, seems to sum up his view of American politics when he has his delightful dolphins, who are surely the most engaging heroes in recent science fiction, tell why politicians fail to solve modern problems:

> Political issues were often complex, but they were rarely anywhere as deep as the scientific problems which had been solved . . . with amazing rapidity because they had been constantly exposed to discussion among scientists, and thus it appeared reasonable to expect that the solution of political problems could be greatly speeded up also if they were subjected to the *same kind* of discussion. The discussions of political problems by politicians were much less productive, because they differed in one important respect from the discussions of scientific problems by scientists: When a scientist says something, his colleagues must ask themselves only whether it is true. When a politician says something, his colleagues must first of all ask, "Why does he say it?"

The same themes come out when scientists undertake to write explicitly about the relation of science to politics. The difference that Dr. Szilard's dolphins noted between science and politics is indeed a major difference, and one that could be a starting point for a political theory. Why, indeed, do politicians, unlike scientists, have to worry about the unstated purposes of another politician, or another government? But a great many scientists do not like to follow up on the implications of that question. It is more satisfying to argue that the straightforward scientific approach of the scientist should replace the devious and prejudiced ways of politicians, and to wonder whether the scientific revolution has indeed not made obsolete the institutions of modern democracy, or at least the present way in which they are organized and managed.

Thus a federal research administrator may complain of the scientists' lack of influence by comparison with lawyers and politicians, and argue that the federal government should have a Secretary of Science to mobilize the nation's scientific resources and coordinate all its policies from a scientific point of view. Or a great German physicist and Nobel prize winner may summon his colleagues to international discussions of their difference in ideology, and to international cooperation to end the race in atomic armaments, arguing that they need to apply to politics the methods of thinking used successfully in physics—"to think out these problems, which have arisen out of our research, in our own simple realistic manner." And one of his colleagues in those international discussions, Dr. Eugene Rabinowitch, poses the central problem directly: "The capacity of the democratic, representative systems of government to cope with the problems raised by the scientific revolution is in question."

Dr. Szilard and Dr. Rabinowitch probably represent a distinct minority of American scientists, rather than the majority who are (or wish they were) consultants to corporations and members of Rotary Clubs, and who do not trouble their heads about political theory. But the question that this minority poses about the relation of representative government to the scientific revolution cannot be brushed off lightly. For the scientific revolution has changed not only the basic sciences themselves, but their consequent ability to produce new technology; it is this ability that has led to their new financial support by government, and changed the nature of military strategy and even of the economic and political system. It is accordingly very difficult, when speak-

ing of the social effects of science, to distinguish it from technology; even those who keep accounts on government expenditures for research and development admit that the distinction
they make between basic research and applied technology is
not a precise boundary. (I will try later to distinguish the roles of
science and technology a little more clearly, but at first I must
discuss some of their joint effects.)

The relationship of the scientific and technological revolution
to our system of representative government is a cogent question,
both in its own right and because it has been raised with such
urgency not only by those who seek to strengthen the political
influence of scientists, but by others who are worried about the
way in which such influence may be used.

During the early 1960's, it was a rare scientific meeting that
failed to discuss two pronouncements on the relation of science
to politics. The first was Sir Charles Snow's vivid story about the
wartime rivalry of Tizard and Lindemann as scientific advisers
to the British government. That "cautionary tale" warned us that
democracy was in danger from the great gulf in understanding
between the Two Cultures of science and the humanities, and
from any possible monopoly on scientific advice to high political
authority. The second was the farewell address of President
Eisenhower, warning the nation that its public policy might "become the captive of a scientific-technological elite."

It is easy to appreciate why President Eisenhower felt as
strongly as he did. His administration had started out to cut back
on expenditures for research and development, but had ended
by quadrupling them. This increase was by no means for defense
alone; during his eight years in office the Congress multiplied
the appropriations for the National Institutes of Health more
than ninefold, giving them each year more than he had recom-
mended. Science seemed clearly to be getting out of hand. It
was almost enough to make one try to apply to the budgeting
process the theory of Henry Adams that science, as it becomes
more abstract, increases in geometrical progression the physical
power that it produces.

The President's statement was a great shock to the scientists,
especially to those who had been working with the administration rather than criticizing it in the columns of the *Bulletin of*

the Atomic Scientists. President Eisenhower, indeed, quickly explained that he was not talking about science in general, but only those parts allied with military and industrial power. Nevertheless, to the typical American scientist who still believed that science had helped to liberate man from ancient tyrannies, it was disconcerting to be told by a conservative president that he had become a member of a new priesthood allied with military power.

Yet it had begun to seem evident to a great many administrators and politicians that science had become something very close to an *establishment,* in the old and proper sense of that word: a set of institutions supported by tax funds, but largely on faith, and without direct responsibility to political control. The terms under which this support is now given to science do not seem to many politicians to fit into the traditional ideas of Jeffersonian democracy.

From the point of view of scientists and university administrators, on the other hand, the growing dependence of science on government brings a great many problems, especially the danger of increasing government control over universities. It is hard to turn money down, but more and more scientific spokesmen are beginning to worry about the conditions that come with it. From the point of view of government, the sentiment in Congress now seems to be considerably more critical of the terms on which money is provided for scientific research. Edward Gibbon summed up the cynical eighteenth-century attitude toward a religious establishment by remarking that all religions were "considered by the people, as equally true; by the philosopher, as equally false; and by the magistrate, as equally useful." And now, it seems that all sciences are considered by their professors, as equally significant; by the politicians, as equally incomprehensible; and by the military, as equally expensive.

So we are beginning to observe in the Congressional attitude toward science some of the symptoms of friction between an establishment and a secular government. The symptoms showed up, for example, in Congressman L. H. Fountain's investigations of the National Institutes of Health, wherein he sought reform by uncovering abuses in the administration of the cloistered but tax-supported laboratories. And they showed up in Congressman Wright Patman's attacks on the tax-exempt foundations—institutions which by a modern kind of *mortmain* give science a range of political initiative outside the control of politics.

These attacks do not get at the main issues. They have so far been only a minor nuisance to scientific institutions, with an effect measured mainly in the time taken to fill out accounting forms. But they are a threat because they may reflect a more fundamental uneasiness in the intellectual as well as the political world. This is an uneasiness not merely about the terms of the financial relationship between government and science, but about the question whether the growing influence of science can be kept compatible with representative government. It is, in short, the same question asked by Dr. Rabinowitch—can democratic government cope with problems raised by the scientific revolution?—but from the opposite point of view.

These attitudes, as yet, may have very little to do with the way most American scientists think, either on or off duty, and practically nothing to do with the amount of money their laboratories get in government grants. They are only a small cloud on the intellectual and political horizon of the United States. But they correspond to a much greater intellectual disturbance, over the past century and a half, in Europe, where the political faith in the alliance of science and reason with free government that was characteristic of the Enlightenment gave way in the late nineteenth century to various forms of scholarly despair. In America, a faith in the political rationalism of the Enlightenment tended to persist in the political thinking of scientists, even after the depression shook their confidence in the inevitability of progress. Right up to the present, American scientists have shown singularly little interest in either the conservative political theorists who tell them that scientists cannot deal with basic values or solve the major human problems, or the radical theorists who tell them that science can do so if it will only join in a political system, like Marxism, that will give it real power over society.

Even the strongest critics of the government and its scientific policies—for example, many of the contributors to the *Bulletin of the Atomic Scientists*—are surprisingly traditional in their approach to the political system. They may question the capacity of our representative institutions to cope with the scientific revolution, but they tend to propose as remedies more international good will and cooperation, adequate scientific education of political leaders and the electorate, and unbiased scientific advice for members of Congress.

It is hard to quarrel with any of these ideas. But they are a little like the remedy that was most often proposed for corruption in government during the late nineteenth century: more good men should go into politics. That exhortation surely did some good, but probably less than the effort to adjust our political and economic institutions to the realities of the industrial revolution. That adjustment required a great many changes, by Congress and the judiciary and administrators, but it did not follow the prescriptions of any of the single-minded political prophets. It came instead from a new way of looking at the problem: we gave up thinking about politics merely in terms of the formal Constitutional system, which had been based on an analogy with Newtonian thought—a mechanistic system of checks and balances. In the latter part of the nineteenth century, students of politics (if they had not given up their interest in science) might have noted with interest a new analogy: as science penetrated the structure of the molecule, and identified its elements, politicians were becoming preoccupied with the elements of politics—with parties and economic classes and pressure groups—as well as its mechanistic Constitutional balances.

The scientific revolution in nuclear physics and in such fields as genetics is carrying us into a third stage of complexity. That revolution seems certain to have a more radical effect on our political institutions than did the industrial revolution, for a good many reasons. Let us note three of them.

1. *The scientific revolution is moving the public and private sectors closer together.*

During the industrial revolution, the most dynamic economic interests were more or less independent of the political system. They might depend on it, as many American corporations did by relying on tariff protection, and they might try with some success to control it, but they were not incorporated into the administrative system, they did not receive support from taxation, and the main directions of their new enterprise were controlled by their owners and managers. Today, our national policy assumes that a great deal of our new enterprise is likely to follow from technological developments financed by the government and directed in response to government policy; and many of our most dynamic industries are largely or entirely dependent on doing business with the government through a subordinate relationship that has little resemblance to the traditional market economy.

2. *The scientific revolution is bringing a new order of complexity into the administration of public affairs.*

The industrial revolution brought its complexities, and relied heavily on new forms of expertise, but it did not challenge the assumption that the owner or manager, even without scientific knowledge, was able to control the policies of a business. And the same general belief was fundamental to our governmental system: the key ideas, if not the lesser details, could be understood by the legislature and debated before the public, and thus controlled by a chain of public responsibility. In one sense this was never true; in another and more fundamental sense, I think it is still true. But it is much less apparently true today than it was, and a great many more people doubt it. The great issues of life and death, many people fear, are now so technically abstruse that they must be decided in secret by the few who have the ability to understand their scientific complexities. We were already worrying about the alleged predominance of the executive over the legislature; now we worry lest even our elected executives cannot really understand what they are doing, lest they are only a façade that conceals the power of the scientists—many of whom are not even full-time officials, but have a primary loyalty to some university or corporation—who really control the decisions. If (as I believe) this is not really true, it is nevertheless true that the scientific revolution has upset our popular ideas about the way in which policies are initiated and adopted, and in which politicians can control them and be held responsible for them. We have to reconsider our basic ideas about the processes of political responsibility.

3. *The scientific revolution is upsetting our system of checks and balances.*

From a moral or ethical point of view, the industrial revolution raised problems that were relatively simple. Everyone admitted that it was possible for economic interests to control politics, but the remedy seemed to be clear: regulate business to prevent abuses, and keep selfish business interests out of the political process. This seemed clearly the basic formula for dealing with the obvious conflict of the public interest with the special interests of business. And the formula of separation of business and government was analogous in a comforting way to the formula for the separation of church and state. A church that was not dependent on government support was able to provide an independent source of moral judgment which could help to control the ethical standards of our politics and our business. As the problems began to seem a bit complex for unaided theological opinion, the universities began to provide an additional source of more scientific, but equally independent, advice to the public on the basic value judgments that should govern our policies. This was the fundamental system of checks and balances within our society: the check on practical political affairs imposed by sources of utterly independent criticism, based on a system of values that was not corrupted by the political competition for wealth or power.

But the scientific revolution seems to threaten to destroy this safeguard in two ways: First, it has gradually weakened the moral authority of religious institutions by the critical skepticism that it has made predominant in Western intellectual life, most notably in the universities. Second, it has made the universities themselves financially dependent on government, and involved them deeply in the political process. Thus, after helping to disestablish churches and free most universities from ecclesiastical control, science has now made those universities dependent on a new form of establishment, in the guise of government grants, and allied them more closely with a military power that is capable of unlimited destruction.

These three developments make some of our traditional reactions—our automatic political reflexes—unreliable in dealing with our present problems. We are automatically against socialism, but we do not know how to deal with an extension of governmental power over the economy that technically leaves ownership in private hands. It is almost an instinct with us to distrust the political bosses who, by controlling the votes of the ignorant masses, seek personal profit or power without accepting official responsibility. But we do not know how to deal with irresponsible influence that comes from status in the highest sanhedrin of science, untainted by any desire for personal profit. And we are fanatically against the public support of any institutions that might impose religious values on public policy, but when the institutions of organized skepticism tell us what science believes or how much money science needs, we have no reliable procedure for questioning their infallibility, or even for criticizing their budgets.

Science has thus given our political evolution a reverse twist. It has brought us back to a set of political problems that we thought we had disposed of forever by simple Constitutional principles. These are the problems of dealing not only with territorial subdivisions of government, and not only with economic interests and classes, but also with various groups of citizens which are separated from each other by very different types of education and ways of thinking and sets of ideals. This was the problem of the medieval estates.

The three estates of the realm, whose customary privileges grew into constitutional functions, were the clergy, the nobility, and the burgesses—those who taught, those who fought, and those who bought and sold. In our impatience with privilege at the time of the American Revolution, we abolished the estates in our political system so thoroughly that we have almost forgotten what the word meant. To abolish the first estate, we disestablished the church and provided secular education through local governments. To abolish the second, we forbade titles of nobility, made the military subordinate to civil authority, and relied on a popular militia rather than a standing army. To abolish the third, we did away with property qualifications on voting and exalted freedom of contract and competition above legislative interference.

But now the results of scientific advance have been to require federal support of education and the appropriation of a tithe of the federal budget for research and development, to set up the most powerful and professional military force in history, and to make free competition a minor factor in the relationship to government of some of the major segments of the economy.

Thus we are left to face the second half of the problem which we were afraid to face during the depression, and tried to escape at the end of the Second World War: the necessity for discovering a new basis for relating our science to our political purposes. We learned half of our lesson from the scientists: the lesson that we could not have a first-rate scientific establishment if we did not understand that first-rate science depended on fundamental theoretical work and required the support of basic research for its own sake, and not merely as a by-product of applied science. Now the outlines of the second, or political, half of our problem are becoming more clear. Basic science as such became steadily more powerful as it freed itself from the constraints of values and purposes. As an institution in society, it had to free itself in an analogous way from subordination to the applied purposes of the industrial corporation or the government bureau or the military service. And in the unpredictability of its progress it challenges the old notion that in matters of public policy the scientist must be controlled completely by purposes defined by politicians. So we must face the possibility that science will no longer serve as a docile instrument toward purposes that are implicit in a system of automatic economic progress, or even toward purposes that are defined for scientists by business and political leaders. In short, we can no longer take it for granted that scientists will be "on tap but not on top."

Accordingly, we need to consider not only the practical relation of scientific institutions to the economy and the government, but also the theoretical relation of science to political values, and to the principles that are the foundation of the constitutional system. Only with the help of scientists can we deal with the great issues of war and peace, of the population explosion and its effects in the underdeveloped countries, or of the dangers to our environment from our technological advances not only in weaponry but also in civilian industry and agriculture. But before we are likely, as a nation, to let science help us solve such problems, we are sure to want to know the full terms of the bargain. For although some of the political reflexes that we have acquired by several centuries of constitutional experience may be out of date, one of the most automatic is still useful: we want to know not only whether some political pronouncement is true, but why the speaker said it, having a healthy suspicion that we need to know whose interests it would further, and what its effect would be on our capacity to govern ourselves, or at least to hold our governors responsible.

The scientific community in the United States is not an organized institution, or a group with definite boundaries. It is not a hierarchical establishment. But its existence as a loosely defined estate with a special function in our constitutional system is becoming apparent, and we would do well to assess its political significance. If we do, we may find that a deeper understanding of the basic relation of science to government will help us to give it the kind of support it needs for its own purposes, as well as use it more effectively for the practical ends of public policy. And if we are willing to renounce the utopian hope that science will solve our problems for us, we may find that science by its very nature is more congenial to the development of free political institutions than our anti-utopian prophets would have us believe.

Automation is said to have ancient beginnings. To be sure, the technology from which it stems goes back several centuries, at least. Automatic devices in the middle 18th century included a mechanical loom for the manufacture of figured silks; James Watt's steam engine utilized a fly-ball governor which controlled the speed at which his contrivance operated; and it has been

Man, Work and the Automated Feast

suggested that automation's basic concept—the linkage of machines—is evident in the detachable harpoon head of the Eskimo. Yet to assert that automation is simply the latest link in a great chain of industrial history obscures what is patently a new phenomenon. In the old days, industrial change developed through fission: division of labor was the key to progress and work was made available to a huge pool of unskilled persons who in the main had been forced to migrate from farm to city. Today, it is precisely these unskilled, together with semi-skilled and even some of management's people, who are displaced and poured back into the pool. Furthermore, automation represents a marked acceleration of change with so cumulative a force that this alone spells a profound difference from what went on before.

Automation is already moving with a rapidity that threatens to tear apart existing social and organizational structures; according to some observers, it will even alter the habits of thought that men have up to now prided themselves on. Such a prospect is perhaps not surprising when we consider the cataclysmic results of the 18th century's Industrial Revolution: the changes then were so swift as to constitute a whole new phenomenon. And Marx and Weber and Sombart had shown convincingly how human and social transformation accompanied technological transformation.

Now, new industrial functions, new economic forms, new work habits, and new social headaches are being created in ways

From *Commentary*, 34 (July, 1962), 9–19. Reprinted with permission of The American Jewish Congress and the author.

that signify a kind of dialectic leap. Even John Diebold, who claims to have invented the word "automation" and whose ebullient advocacy of computer technology has done much to spread the gospel, confesses: "I believe that [automation] marks a break with past trends, a qualitative departure from the more conventional advance of technology that began with jagged pieces of flint and progressed up to the steam engine."

Why is this so? Up to recent times, technology simply sought to substitute natural force for animal or human force. In the early days, primacy of place was given to windmills and waterfalls. Then came metallurgical discoveries; and the screw and the lathe made possible the machine, essentially a contrivance which man could watch in action. But man remained at the center of the whole business, essential to both operation and control, still more or less the maker and master of materials. With automation, man not only loses irrevocably his function as *homo faber;* he no longer even possesses the character of *animal laborans.* At best, he is a sometime supervisor of a flow process. Actual control is removed from him and given to an electronic contraption whose feedbacks and servomechanisms make it possible to produce goods and manipulate information in a continuous system, without human participation.

To realize what automation implies we must examine the kinds of machines employed and see what they do to people and organizations. Essentially, today's scientific upheaval comprises four aspects: the conversion of industrial materials into a flow; the setting of uniform standards so that output can be treated as a flow; the utilization of electronic computers with built-in feedbacks to enable the exercise of automatic control; and the application of new energy sources to the whole process. Thus, raw materials, which represent the "input" of an industry, must be handled without human hands, as in a modern meat-packing plant. Production, at one time a series of discrete steps, is completely integrated by means of transfer machines. In some cases, computers tied to cams or templates can make the producing machine follow a predetermined pattern with greater accuracy and sharper tolerances than were dreamed possible in the heyday of the skilled machinist. Computers, into which all sorts of complex information can be fed by "programmers," automatically correct errors. A wide range of goods is now produced in this startling manner—chemicals, automobiles, steel, glassware, electric bulbs, television sets, beverages, and drugs, to name a few. Factories are able to function 24 hours a day, 365 days a year, while manpower needs are reduced dramatically. And with the development of nuclear energy for industrial power, manufacturers no longer need to be near their source of raw materials; they can set up their plants closer to markets, or—if they are seeking to escape the union organizer—in the most isolated of places. Yet one industry necessarily must relate itself more intimately with the next; a seamless web envelops all the entrepreneurs and their works.

There is no lack of Panglossian attempt to assuage our concern. In the long run, we are told (who lives that long?), natural economic forces will work out the necessary adjustments. A shorter work week might stem from automation, suggest some experts; but at the thought that men might work less than the ordained forty hours a week, all kinds of people, from Secretary of Labor Arthur Goldberg down, immediately explode with great cries of anguish. Or we are told that human desires are insatiable: demand will grow, enough to reabsorb men displaced by machines—which calls to mind an apocryphal conversation between Henry Ford II and Walter Reuther. "How," said Ford, as he revealed his automatic factory, "are these machines going to pay you dues, Walter?" "How," replied Reuther, "will they buy your autos?"

We are assured that more jobs will be created by new industry, that higher skills will be required, that economic stability will be guaranteed by automation. There are pitifully few facts available to support these euphoric hopes. More likely a vast trauma awaits us all, to use Irving Howe's phrase. Then why automate? The underlying motives were exposed with unaccustomed bluntness in one of the trade journals recently when an automation advocate wrote: "[Machines] don't call in sick; they don't talk back; they work early and late and without overtime; they don't get tired; and last, but far from least, they don't line up at the cashier's window every week for a slice of the operating funds."

The automobile industry illustrates how an integrated set of machines can function. There the engine production line, for example, consists of a series of drilling, boring, and milling operations connected by transfer machines which move the engine blocks from one point to the next. Tolerances are checked automatically; if something is awry, the whole line is stopped by an electronic device. Or one can see an automatic assembly machine put the components of a television set on a printed board and then solder them into place. These are repetitive operations and their economic justification stems from the replacement market. There is not much of a style factor here and such model changes as do occur can be handled with relative ease. Yet even where variation in the product is essential, as in machine tools, the operation still can be made automatic.

The machine tool industry, mainly a congeries of small shops employing highly skilled labor, has notoriously resisted innovation. But since it is now so closely allied to Air Force and Space technology, it has been impelled willy-nilly by the needs of the armed forces to the adoption of newer techniques. Formerly, a human operator worked from blueprints, controlling his equipment with a variety of jigs and templates. To avoid waste, and perhaps because he was concerned with craftsmanship, he worked slowly. But now, all the variables can be "programmed" into computers, and with the technique known as "numerical control" these electronic brains direct the same cutting tools, handle the same jigs and templates once operated by the machinist. Most important of all, this sort of automation is economically feasible for small lots in which there are changes in product design.

The key here is feedback, the simplest case of which is the home thermostat turning a furnace on and off in order to maintain a constant room temperature. In essence, signals are sent from one part of the automated line to another, correcting errors, shifting power loads, or modifying the speed of the line. No human need adjust gauges or read thermometers or press buttons. Feedback or servomechanisms do a better control job than humans, especially when many elements are involved. Whereas the human eye can follow the motion of a gauge at about two cycles a second, a servomechanism does about 100 a second. Now, marry feedback to a computer and automation is complete. The computers, really giant adding machines and calculators, receive information from the gauges and thermometers, analyze the data, and then transmit new instructions to other gauges and instruments.

Computers, whose basic concept goes back to Blaise Pascal, were developed in their electronic form during World War II to help guns hit their targets more efficiently. There are two basic types—the analog and digital computer. The former operates . . . as . . . a kind of electronic slide rule able to apply higher mathematics to problems of rates of change in various flows. However fast it might have been, for the engineer, mathematician, and operations researcher it was not fast enough. So the digital computer was devised, a machine that employs the binary number system and consequently can only add and subtract. This is no impediment, for like an electronic abacus, the digital computer sends its impulses forward at an unbelievable speed, giving it a marked advantage over the analog machine. Moreover, digital computers have "memory" drums in which data can be stored for future use. The electrical pulses in a digital computer last less than one-millionth of a second. Information can be extracted from the memory drum in about ten-millionths of a second.

Of course, a considerable amount of human brain power is expended before the computer can be put to work. This is the science of programming. Instructions are written on a process sheet, then coded and entered on tape. That is, English is translated into machine language. The control unit of the system then "reads" the tape, gives forth with the appropriate electrical impulses, and sets the servomechanisms to work. One writer compared the operation to an old-fashioned player piano in which the punched holes in the roller actuate the hammers to bang out either the "Basin Street Blues" or a Beethoven sonata.

Lending a nightmarish quality to these developments is the current scientific talk about artificial intelligence. Machines, it is said, can be built to recognize certain patterns and can learn to plan simple tasks. While the computer may be something of a moron, awaiting instructions from a human Ph.D., the fact that an electrical contrivance can be made to learn anything is astonishing enough. If a heuristic or generalized solution is sufficient, then a thinking computer is no longer science fiction. Chess-playing machines are at least feasible; the only problem seems to be that they would have to review the outcomes of all possible plays and that might take centuries. Perhaps that is what makes them morons.

The names one often sees bandied about—PERT, ALGOL, COBOL, GECOM, SURE—are merely abbreviations for specific programming methods, each utilizing one or more computer installations constructed by Burroughs, Bendix, Rand, or IBM. PERT, for example—Program Evaluation and Review Technique —is based on the concept of a tree network with alternatives to be considered at each node of the tree. Since the computer works so much faster than the human mind and also uses stored information, it can review the accumulating cost of a flow process at each step and then direct the sequence of decisions along the critical or least-cost pathway. PERT originated in the Polaris Missile Project when it became essential to keep track of some 11,000 contractors and subcontractors. Again, military need provided the research motive. So complex can these matters become that the Defense Department had to work out a standardized pidgin English to coordinate programming.

It is sometimes said that the considerable investment in these systems precludes all but the largest firms from employing them. This is not so. Any number of consulting services are available for smaller concerns to meet data-processing needs, and some firms have set up cooperative research centers. Span, Inc. is one such co-op doing the bookkeeping for a number of insurance companies in Hartford; Tamcor maintains brokerage records in New York, and IBM, the biggest of them all, makes its equipment available to all comers through 70 locations around the country. In fact, the latter is now compiling tape libraries, dubbed by one journal "computer laundromats." Thus, the new technology is available to anyone who wants to make use of it.

All this must be worthwhile, for rental costs run from $12,000 a year up and outright purchase of computer equipment can cost millions. Some $2 billion has been invested in computers by private companies since 1950, and this does not include what the government has spent. It is estimated that by 1970 computer sales will hit $500 million a year or about 2½ times present outlays. When the Pennsylvania Railroad automated its Conway, Pa. yards, it expected to recoup its $34 million cost within three years. At Ford, 9 workers at 3 machines putting holes into crankshafts replaced 39 workers at 39 machines. A Philco plant reduced its work force by 25 per cent by using printed circuitry. A computer engineer once remarked that he could cut one man off the payroll for every $5,000 spent on automated equipment. And finally, the initial cost of installing a computer system, according to Wassily Leontief, comes to no more than 6 per cent of total plant investment. The value of the new technology seems undeniable.

By now "Detroit" automation is quite well known. Automatic machines, linked by transfer equipment move engine blocks through a complete manufacturing process, performing 530 precision cutting and drilling operations in 14½ minutes as compared to 9 hours in a conventional plant. The Chrysler Corporation's recent breakthrough on computer "balancing" of assembly lines, essentially a "combinatorial" problem, now defines each job so rigidly that little liberties like a worker's taking a few minutes out for a smoke become serious impediments to the smooth flow of cars. An automated power plant in Louisiana saved $175,000 in fuel, $100,000 in maintenance, $1.5 million in eliminating delays and mishaps, and $500,000 in labor. A Jones & Laughlin sheet-plate mill turns out strip at the speed of 7 miles an hour with no labor other than the supervision of engineers. Punch-card systems in a reversing roughing mill modify ingot shapes, and the computer even "remembers" what to do when the forms have to be changed. Foundry work, traditionally a hand operation, is now being tied to the computer. In petroleum and chemicals, the story is almost ancient: as far back as 1949 catalytic cracking plants were turning out 41,000 barrels a day with instruments and only a few workers to watch gauges. In a Texaco refinery the computer controls 26 flow rates, 72 temperatures, 3 pressure levels, and 3 gas combinations. General Electric uses segmented "automation," that is, batch production, for motors of varying models up to 30 horsepower.

Ribbon machines make 800 electric bulb blanks a minute, running without end, and requiring only one worker who stands by
to make an occasional adjustment.

Even in the office and retail store, one finds evidence of the
new technology. Although office work has expanded tremendously since 1910 (today 17 per cent of the labor force is found
in the office as compared to 5 per cent fifty years ago), it is
precisely the enormous quantity of paper work and routine operation that makes automation feasible here. Banks, utilities, insurance companies, and government bureaus have eagerly made
room for yards of the new equipment—so much faster is the
computer than the old-fashioned bookkeeper and clerk. As a
result, office work no longer is the growth industry it was—at
least in terms of jobs. One California firm, studied by Mrs. Ida
R. Hoos, put only two accounting operations on a computer and
promptly eliminated 300 out of 3,200 office jobs and drastically
altered the functions of some 980 others.

In retailing, automation starts with inventory and accounting
records. Sales data are transmitted to control centers where
billing, inventory, and credit information is stored. Bad credit
risks are automatically checked and information returned to the
sales clerk before the package can be wrapped. Sylvania and
IBM have been working on automatic check-out counters for
supermarkets—the number of cash registers would be reduced,
as well as the number of workers. Ferris wheels, conveyor belts,
chutes, and slides, all controlled by electronic computers, deliver
garments from receiving platforms to stockrooms and even return the merchandise to the ground floor if necessary. Eventually
we will pay our traffic penalties to a computer: in Illinois,
records of driver violations are stored in a computer and the
fines calculated by machine.

This, then, is the automated feast. Tasks are accomplished
with unimaginable speed. Decisions are made by coded instructions and errors quickly detected. Facts are stored and extracted
from memory drums. The machines learn and "perceive": they
analyze stock market conditions; establish rocket flight patterns
before the shot is fired into space; write television scripts that

compare favorably with what is now available; compose music; translate; and play games. They combine high technical competence with just enough of an I.Q. to keep them tractable. They do precisely the kind of work to which junior executives and semi-skilled employees are usually assigned.

No slur is intended here, for in addition to the ordinary worker it is the middle manager, the backbone of the average corporation, who will be most affected by automation. He has a bleak future indeed, when computers relay information to each other, do all the scheduling, and control manufacturing from inception to the point at which the product is packaged and rolled onto a box car. It is rather the archon of industry—as Edward Ziegler has dubbed him—who ultimately wins out, for with the elimination of both plant and office staff, this man at the very top gains even tighter control over the decision-making process. The sort of organizational looseness that prevailed prior to the advent of the computer is eliminated, and corporate structure becomes more formal, more "integrated," since with the computer there must be greater "cooperation." The number of links in the chain of command is reduced drastically; vice-presidents are soon out of a job. No less an authority than Herbert A. Simon of Carnegie Tech has said that by 1985 machines can dispense with all middle echelons in business. Production planning is handed over to the digital demon, while both the middle manager and the displaced worker drive taxicabs. The sociologist may very well ask, whither the American dream of status and success?

Quite often, the computer engineer tries to build his own empire within the corporation. Fresh to the ways of business life, he has unabashedly played havoc with established relations. He and his programmer cohorts, cutting across all divisions, have often ignored and undermined the authority of department heads and vice-presidents. Many middle management people in automated companies now report that they are awaiting the ax, or if more fortunate, retirement. Bright young men leave for non-automated firms, hoping to reach the top elsewhere before the computer catches up with them. Sometimes the new elite does lose out; it has not been unknown for a computer installation to be yanked as a result of corporate internecine warfare.

Usually though, archon and engineers are in complete accord. With the computer creating certain expectations, the firm must operate through a series of highly rigid sequences. Flexibility has been dispensed with, for the whole plant is now a single technical structure in which total performance must be "optimized." The engineer examines each step in the process solely in terms of efficiency—industrial logic of the most unremitting kind takes primacy of place. Under automation, the engineer or mathematician is *the* skilled man in the plant, while workers, those who remain and those who do not, are expected to adjust with equanimity to a situation for which they have had no responsibility. In fact, the engineer's attitude quite often is tough and hard, too much so for ordinary men: what the worker doesn't know, says he, won't hurt him. The scientists appreciate only "facts": the human problems of an industrial system frequently have little meaning for them. Unlike the organization men of the 50's, they are usually "inner directed," disturbers of the corporate peace, free-booters in pursuit of the idols of efficiency. Since the latter is measured by high profit and low cost, such scientific ruthlessness meets the approval of the archon. The latter really doesn't know what the scientist is doing: top management merely voices a faith based on payoff. Thus the programmer, who often assumes the aspect of a medieval alchemist, runs his own show, designing projects, cutting corporate red tape with abandon, and advising the industrial relations department that labor displacement is "none of your business." At best, the engineer can parrot some devotee of the conventional economic wisdom by repeating that automation creates new demand and new jobs, upgrades the worker and inspires everyone with its challenge. There must be a certain glory in the marvels of automation: but the men who once worked in the chemical plants, oil refineries, and steel mills are now out of sight and out of mind.

Between 1953 and 1960, a million and a half jobs disappeared. In one plant, studied by Floyd Mann of Michigan State University, automation reduced the work force by half. In the electrical industry, output increased 21 per cent between 1953 and 1961, while employment declined 10 per cent. There was a loss of 80,000 production jobs in steel during the decade of the

50's. In the shift from aircraft to missiles, 200,000 jobs went down the technological drain. For the 5-year period 1955–1960, production workers in automobile factories were down 21 per cent. All this displacement occurred in an affluent society that itself went through four postwar recessions each of which left behind an increasingly hard-core residue of unemployment— 3 per cent in 1951–53; 4 per cent in 1955–57; and 5 per cent in 1959–60.

Full employment for the next 10 years means creating 12 million new jobs—25,000 a week, or almost double the number of new openings in the 1947–57 decade. Extending the period to 1961, we find that output rose 65 per cent while the number of production and maintenance jobs declined. True, white collar workers increased 7 per cent, but now automation is making them just as insecure. If we assume that demand in the 60's will expand at the same rate as it did in 1947–57, then output by 1970 may very well be 50 per cent greater. However, if the present rate of productivity is maintained, then the number of required man-hours will have increased by 12 per cent, providing only 75 million jobs at the end of the decade. Thus, about 8 million persons, 10 per cent of the labor force, will have no work. And this is a moderate forecast, for should the secular growth rate fall below 3 per cent per annum, as is conceivable, output will have gone up about 40 per cent. Add to this the effects of automation, and the job increase by 1970 may be only 2 million, leaving a residue of perhaps 10 million persons without jobs.

Is this so weird a tale? The ever optimistic Bureau of Labor Statistics' chief, Ewan Clague, recently admitted to an Arden House conclave that 200,000 jobs a year would be lost through "disemployment by automation." He found that in 70 per cent of manufacturing industries such "disemployment" comprised four-fifths of the jobs lost. And his estimate did not include computer displacement among white collar workers.

The unions now know what automation can do to them. No matter how strong the security clause in a collective bargaining agreement, the serious drop in membership for most internationals is a harbinger of approaching catastrophe. Further, it is so much easier now for plants to escape to communities where unionism seems to represent little threat. And in such towns, management does not worry about a labor supply, for under automation what need is there for workers? There are also related problems for the unions: What happens to seniority? How about pension rights? Can traditional unionism with its roots in craft concepts cope with an industry whose shape has assumed the form of a process? Is the programmer a part of the bargaining unit? Or does his role in decision-making place him in management's ranks? And how effective is the strike when a handful of engineers can operate the whole works? This last question was answered in Port Arthur, Texas, where about 3,700 production workers walked off the job at an oil refinery, leaving 600 white collar employees and supervisors behind to run the plant at 65 per cent of capacity. One labor relations man was reported to have said: "Maybe they ought to have removed a couple of transistors."

Some have argued that the displaced can be directed to jobs in the service and white collar fields. What jobs? Automation, as we have already noted, has been moving into these fields in the last three years just as rapidly as elsewhere. In 1960, at the Census Bureau, 50 technicians plus a battery of computers did the work that it had taken over 4,000 statisticians to do in 1950. The little black code numbers now appearing on bank checks inform us that our accounts are debited, credited, and cleared by a scanning device hooked into a computer. It is poor consolation, moreover, to be told that employment adjustments will be made via the A & P route—attrition and pregnancy—for this is an admission that there really are no jobs for those who want to work.

The notion that all who have been displaced by machines will quickly find new employment is a cheerful thought, something like whistling while walking through a cemetery. Some years ago, such cheerfulness was quite common, even among labor leaders. Walter Reuther's early speeches all but embraced the computer, so high was the regard for technology, so powerful the belief in growth and progress. The Joint Economic Committee's 1955 report on automation urged laissez-faire, for no serious problems were envisioned. In the short space of seven years, hesitation and doubts have cropped up. There is no longer the ancient and well-regarded optimism that more machines mean expanded employment elsewhere or that automation will upgrade workers. It is evident, rather, that the new technology enforces a deterioration of skills for the great mass of workers and offers only the social junk pile for the unskilled and untutored.

What is the solution? Frankly, there is none, at least none of a definitive character. The numerous suggestions for dealing with the pressing problems that stem from automation are all piecemeal, pecking at a spot here and a point there. No amount of federal fiscal tinkering will meet the immediate needs of those who are attached to a dying industry. Economic growth, while essential, will not of itself put to work again the idle coal miner, ex-machinist, and troubled bookkeeper whose jobs have vanished like the first atom bomb tower. Administration economists believe that automated unemployment can be solved by turning on ordinary Keynesian tap valves: it's all a matter of failing effective demand, they assert. There seems little awareness in important circles that the American economy is undergoing deep-rooted and subtle structural changes and that it will take massive economic and social therapy to assuage the hurt.

The AFL-CIO has been advocating a series of measures, including meaningful retraining programs, especially for workers over forty, area redevelopment, better unemployment insurance, an improved national placement service, special help to relocate the "disemployed," higher pensions, and even shorter hours. But will we—American management, American unions, Congress, the administration—really expend the necessary hard thought? Don Michael doubts it, for it is unlikely, says he, that ". . . our style of pragmatic making-do and frantic crash programs can radically change in the next few years. . . ." It is hard to disagree.

Consider the retraining effort. A case of too little, if not too late, it is hardly a roaring success. In West Virginia, the federal pilot scheme plus the state's own 22-month-old program have been able to uncover new jobs for only half the 3,000 "graduates." Most of the others simply returned to the ranks of the unemployed. In Pennsylvania, 1,760 persons enrolled in retraining courses in 1957. Of these, 884 completed their re-education, 741 obtained new jobs. The state had a half million unemployed at the time.

Where private enterprise undertakes some corrective steps, it is usually found that a labor union had been doing the prodding, as in the meat-packing industry. Yet when 433 workers were laid off in Armour's Oklahoma City plant, only 60 could qualify for retraining and those who did secure new employment had to accept a lower rate of pay. Some firms are genuinely disturbed about the effects of automation. For example, U. S. Industries, a manufacturer of electronic equipment, and the machinists union have agreed upon a jointly managed fund to study the entire question. The company's president, John Snyder, at least acknowledges that each one of his machines sends 60 workers scurrying to the unemployment insurance offices. Incidentally, one of U. S. Industries' contributions is the invention of automatic equipment to train displaced workers for typing and similar tasks.

There have been other experiments in adjustment. Some take the form of liberal severance-pay allowances. One of the earliest such schemes, though not related to automation per se, was the famous 1936 Washington Agreement between the railroad companies and the unions. Displaced workers receive 60 per cent of their average pay as severance compensation for periods as long as five years whenever mergers occur. In cases of relocation, moving expenses are paid and losses resulting from forced sale of homes reimbursed. More recently, another generous plan was agreed upon by TWA and its navigators, who if replaced by automatic instruments will receive $25,000 plus $400 a month for three years as severance. In addition, the now foot-loose navigators will be given free lifetime travel passes on the airline. Thus they will have at least acquired mobility and will be able to search for jobs in all corners of the globe. Yet such measures offer no genuine solution: they are mere palliatives, for they fail to confront the fundamental question—what does a man do with his time, either during the temporary period of affluence, or when the windfall resources will have given out, or for that matter, even when he has not been detached from industry?

Not every arrangement exhibits a handsome concern for the displaced. In the coal fields a contemptible alliance between John L. Lewis and the operators has cast adrift almost 300,000 miners. The coal industry, caught between the grinders of competitive fuels and high operating costs, was thoroughly rundown by the mid-40's. Deciding not to worry any more about the unemployed at the pits, Lewis acquiesced in rapid technological change. Output per day rose from 6.4 tons in 1949 to 14.4 tons in 1961; one ton of coal now requires less than half the labor it did a decade ago. At the Paradise, Kentucky, coal field an automatic shovel larger than the Statue of Liberty strips 200 tons of material in one scoop. In Harvey Swados's words, Lewis decided to trust to time and mortality to resolve the problem of the unemployed. And so the coal industry no longer suffers from economic decay. With a return on investment of 7.5 per cent, it compares favorably with steel and oil. To hasten the day when his union can depend upon a healthy industry for its 40-cent per ton royalty, Lewis directed the mine workers to invest in sundry mine operations and even lent $35 million to Cyrus Eaton, whose interests include peace movements as well as coal. Of course, it would have been troublesome to apprise the membership of these transactions, so all the deals were carried through with great secrecy, only to be smoked out last year in a Tennessee lawsuit. At a recent convention of the union, an innocent delegate who suggested that perhaps something might be done for the unemployed was ". . . verbally torn to pieces by a buckshot charge of oratory from John L. Lewis himself." Declining dues are amply compensated for by investment returns in banks, mines, railroads, and power plants. Meanwhile, 300,000 miners continue to rot in the idle towns of Pennsylvania and West Virginia.

This sort of cooperation could set a strange trend if other unions were to adopt the Lewis formula. One that did is Harry Bridges's West Coast Longshoremen's International. Several years ago, the ILWU signed an agreement with the Shipping Association that was hailed as a reply to automation. Indeed, the retirement benefits are quite munificent and the pay scale was increased somewhat, but at the same time the employers were given the go-ahead signal to install a whole range of technological improvements which will virtually exclude entire blocs of workers not yet ready to retire. Moreover, the new work rules, extracted by the employers as a price for the higher pay and liberalized pensions, have intensified work loads on the docks virtually to the human breaking point.

Thus, one comes back to an immediate step, which though not by any means a "solution," nevertheless offers a practicable way for mitigating some of the effects of automation—the shorter work week. Mere mention of this is apt to send a shudder down the backs of administration economists and devotees of the conventional wisdom. Expressing their horror at the thought that man should have even more leisure than he now enjoys, the latter urge that a shorter work week means less production and higher costs. And in the present context of growthmanship, this is unthinkable. Arthur Goldberg, whose grasp of legal subtleties contrasts sharply with his simplistic formulations of economic issues, warned the International Ladies' Garment Workers' Union recently that fewer hours per week would ". . . impair adversely our present stable price structure [and] make our goods less competitive both at home and abroad. . . ." The enormous productive capacity of America's industry was conveniently forgotten, a capacity so enhanced by automation that it can more than compensate for the alleged loss of output. And this is to say nothing about the quality and content of contemporary "production"—that would require another essay. The point to observe now is the curious inner tension of an industrial system whose fundamental Puritan outlook demands an incessant, unremitting outpouring of goods (for what?) while at the same time it imposes dreary idleness and dismal futures on those to whom the cornucopia is directed. We may well ask, what is the feedback in this insane circle?

But to return to the shorter work week—a cursory review of its history would demonstrate how completely reasonable it is. Prior to 1860, the rule was dawn to dusk with as much as 72 hours as the weekly standard. Demands for a shorter span were met with the contention that 12 hours a day, 6 days a week had been divinely ordained in order to strengthen worker morality. Three decades later the work week had been shortened by 12 hours. In 1910, the average ranged from 51 to 55 hours, and at that time a work force of 34 million produced a Gross National Product of about $37 billion. The work week continued to shrink: in 1920, it was 48 hours; in 1929, 44 hours; and since 1946, 40 hours. By 1955, the labor force had almost doubled while GNP increased 10-fold as compared to 1910. And all the time the work week kept declining, about 13 hours in a 45-year span, or roughly 15 minutes a year.

Was anyone hurt? Did productivity lag? Has technology been impeded? The depression years aside, whatever unemployment did occur would have been unquestionably greater without the steady drop in hours. A continuation of this secular decline would cut back the normal work week by one hour every four years. According to one estimate, this might create about a million jobs a year which, together with the normal increase in job openings, could really begin to cut into the displacement caused by automation. When Harry van Arsdale of the New York electricians' union obtained a 5-hour day, he was savagely flayed for selfishness and lack of patriotism. Even the labor movement felt embarrassed. Arsdale insisted that he was only seeking to "spread the work." Now it seems, according to Theodore Kheel, the industry's arbitrator, that well over 1,000 new jobs will be made available as a result of the union's action.

What has happened in agriculture presents, in a sense, an object lesson we ought to heed. As W. H. Ferry remarked in a perceptive paper on affluence and plenty, the farm is technology's most notorious victory. Here abundance has become an economic catastrophe. So advanced is our agricultural establishment that even the 10 per cent of the labor force it now employs is too much. Farm output increased 77 per cent between 1910 and 1954, while land used for crops went up only 15 per cent. During the same period, labor on farms as measured by man-hours dropped over 30 per cent. This suggests an almost three-fold rise in productivity. According to the late John D. Black, a leading farm expert, the major element in this change unquestionably was the substitution of machine power for muscle power. Yet the economic and political thrust of our system is such that 70 to 80 per cent of the federal government's spending on agriculture goes to counteract the price impact of an ever accumulating surplus.

The parallel between farm and industry is startling. There is enough grain in storage to feed everyone from Maine to Hawaii, but some 50 million Americans, barely manage to subsist, even today. The steel industry functions at 65 per cent of capacity, or thereabouts, while thousands of able-bodied men are shoved aside by automation. Strategic curtailment of production is employed, like the farm parity program, to distort the genuine capacities of our economy. Technology, rather than man, becomes the central focus of existence, and at the same time that it destroys, for example, the belief in the family farm, it seemingly ought to compel a desiccated concept of resource allocation and optimum production to retire in favor of a philosophy of distribution. But we really have no adequate social theory to deal with the latter. The ideas of a Galbraith, a C. Wright Mills, a Paul Goodman, or a Harvey Swados deal only with aspects of the problem. We await to be told what is happening to us, what we need to do. And even then we shall not listen.

It is of course a common cliché that scientific advances have outrun our capacity to deal with them. Technology, the practical and material basis of life, has acquired a tidal force of its own which threatens to inundate human thought. Moreover, modern technology as evidenced by automation, manifests no orderly growth. Its leads and lags, its uneven development, create new power centers that result in unaccustomed strains. To be sure, this has happened before, but always at immense human cost. It is this that the high priests of automation fail to grasp, while those of us who are merely bystanders can only hope that society will eventually catch up with the engineers and scientists and archons of industry who see only a handsome profit in what the machine can do.

9

Literature

In literature, as elsewhere, the Sixties upended traditions. The particular tradition which the writers of the decade overthrew was that which demanded that serious subjects be treated seriously and trivial subjects lightly. Many of the young writers, having absorbed or developed a vision of human life as absurd, found the traditional demarcations between the serious and the light, the magnificent and the trivial, to be arbitrary and unreal. A world in which life is largely irrational and meaningless is a world in which tragedy and comedy are one. The tragedy of life in fact arises from the awareness that life is a farce, a vast cosmic joke. Thus the temper of the new literature was largely a mixture of tragedy and farce, popularized by the title *black humor*.

The perception dominated the age's view not only of contemporary literature but of the great works of the past. Thus Jan Kott's analysis of the "absurd" elements in *King Lear* is designed to show that play's thematic affinity with Samuel Beckett's *Endgame*. The ultimate effect of the mixing of the comic and the tragic is often profoundly pessimistic. That it need not always be so is suggested in the essays of John Barth and Philip Roth, both of whom affirm the possibility of transcending absurdity by the comic defiance of the individual.

433

BRUCE JAY FRIEDMAN

It is called "Black Humor" and I think I would have more luck
defining an elbow or a corned-beef sandwich. I am not, for one
thing, even sure it is black. It might be fuchsia or eggshell and
now that I look at the table of contents I think some of it is in
brown polka dots. My story, for example, is a brilliant midnight
blue with matching ruffles around the edges. I certainly know

Black Humor

what color it is since I did the coloring on this one myself and
did not bring in a decorator as is my usual custom.

I am not sure of very much and I think it is true of the writers
in this volume that they are not sure of very much either. They
have some pretty strong notions, however, and one of mine is
that the work under discussion, if not black, is some fairly dark-
hued color. The humor part of the definition is probably accurate
although I doubt that the writers here are bluff and hearty joke-
tellers who spend a lot of time at discotheques. Invite them all
to a party and you would probably find a great deal of brooding
and sulking. At no time during the evening would they circle
round the piano to sing hit tunes from Jerome Kern musicals.
I think there would be many furtive glances about the room,
each writer eyeing his neighbor suspiciously. One might suddenly fly through an open window, but only after carefully
checking to see that the drop was shallow. For all I know one
might seize another and cane him soundly about the shoulders
as George Washington did to irreverent newspaper editors. They
might all begin to cry, although I don't think so, for if there is a
despair in this work, it is a tough, resilient brand and might very
well end up in a Faulknerian horselaugh.

There would, in other words, be a certain resistance to the
idea of lumping together thirteen writers with thirteen separate,
completely private and unique visions, who in so many ways
have nothing at all to do with one another and would not know

or perhaps even understand one another's work if they tripped over it. And it is true that when you read through the work, it is, on the one hand, the separateness that strikes you as much as the similarity. You have storytellers in the old tradition here and you have others who will tell you to take your plot machinery and stick it in your ear. You have writers who know exactly what they are doing and others who do not have the faintest idea and are finding out in rather brilliant fashion as they go along. You have John Barth coming at you out of the late seventeenth century, J. P. Donleavy working his way through some insanely beautiful Irish song and Nabokov demoniacally using muscles no one else is blessed with. There is Thomas Pynchon appearing out of nowhere with a vision so contemporary it makes your nose bleed and there is Celine who reminds you that he thought all your thoughts, worked the same beat, was dumbfounded as many times a day as you are, long before you were born.

So you have thirteen separate writers who could not care less about one another and are certainly not going to attend any bi-monthly meetings to discuss policy and blackball new members. But there are some similarities, some stubborn echoes bouncing from one to the other, and I had better hurry up and outline them or else the anthology is over and everyone has to go home and nobody gets to make a buck.

You hear an awful lot about the "fading line between fantasy and reality" in the modern world and I had better put that in fast or else I am not going to get to do any more Forewords. So here it comes. I agree. There *is* a fading line between fantasy and reality, a very fading line, a goddamned, almost invisible line and you will find that notion riding through all of the selections in this volume. Then, too, if you are alive today, and stick your head out of doors now and then, you know that there is a nervousness, a tempo, a near-hysterical new beat in the air, a punishing isolation and loneliness of a strange, frenzied new kind. It is in the music and the talk and the films and the theater and it is in the prose style of Joe Heller and Terry Southern. You can find it in Gogol and Isaac Babel, too, and perhaps they saw it all coming. But that is another anthology.

These are fairly tangential considerations and what it really comes down to is *The New York Times*, which is the source and fountain and bible of black humor. The Secretary of State, solemnly reviewing the Vietnam crisis, suddenly begins to strangle on a wild gastronomical metaphor. Hanoi's support of the rebels, that's the "meat and potatoes issues." When we get to the root of that, then we can consider the salt and pepper issues. The bombing raids? Secondary stuff, just a lot of garlic and oregano talk, really, just a bunch of diversionary sweet basil and East Indian nutmeg baloney.

A ninety-year-old Negro sharecropper lady watches Ladybird Johnson—on a poverty-inspection tour—sweep up to her shack in a presidential limousine and says, "Ain't it wonderful." Fun-loving Tennessee students pelt each other with snowballs and suddenly scores are dead of heart attacks and gunshot wounds. A mid-flight heart-attack victim is removed from an airliner, suddenly slides from the stretcher and cracks her head on the runway. We bomb North Vietnam and nervously await the re-action of Red China, scourge of the Free World. Red China breaks her silence. The Imperialist dogs have behaved like ver-min and Communist China is not going to sit idly by. With all the fury and power of a frenzied 900-million populace behind her, Red China speaks.

"We are going," says Radio China, "to return you tit for tat."

You guess that it has always been this way, that Tolstoi must have had this unreal sensation when Napoleon came east. But then the police Urinary Squad swoops down and spears a high governmental official at the Y.M.C.A. trough; five hundred cap-tured Congo rebels are ushered into a stadium before their Free World captors. The ones who are booed have their heads blown off. Those with good acts who draw applause go free; Nehru sends troops rushing up to the India-China border "with orders to shout if necessary."

"How does it feel?" the TV boys ask Mrs. Malcolm X when her husband is assassinated. We send our planes off for nice, easy-going, not-too-tough bombing raids on North Vietnam. Sixteen U.S. officers in Germany fly through the night in Klansmen robes burning fiery crosses and are hauled before their commanding officer to be reprimanded for "poor judgment." It confirms your belief that a new, Jack Rubyesque chord of absurdity has been struck in the land, that there is a new mutative style of behavior afoot, one that can only be dealt with by a new, one-foot-in-the-asylum style of fiction.

If you are fond of pinning labels on generations, I wonder whether this one could not be called the surprise-proof generation. What might possibly surprise America? Another presidential assassination. Kidstuff. A thousand Red Chinese landing on the Lever Brothers building and marching toward Times Square. Hardly worth a yawn. Mike Todd suddenly showing up on the Johnny Carson show, not dead after all, involved in Broadway's greatest hoax. It's sort of expected.

What has happened is that the satirist has had his ground usurped by the newspaper reporter. The journalist, who, in the year 1964, must cover the ecumenical debate on whether Jews, on the one hand, are still to be known as Christ-killers, or, on the other hand are to be let off the hook, is certainly today's satirist. The novelist-satirist, with no real territory of his own to roam, has had to discover new land, invent a new currency, a new set of filters, has had to sail into darker waters somewhere out beyond satire and I think this is what is meant by black humor.

So you have Mrs. Liuzzo dead with a bullet in her brain, the federal government swinging into action because her "civil rights have been violated." The New York Police Department steps forth with a plan to keep Puerto Ricans from committing suicide in their cells: guards are to watch them like hawks now, running in to cut them down before they get their nooses rigged up. A news magazine says what's all the fuss about anyhow and describes one of our Vietnam gases as "fragrant-smelling," the implication being that if the little Red bastards weren't so sneaky, hiding in caves, we would not have to use gas in the first place. In one of our states, the penalty for fornication is six-to-seven years in prison. . . .

It may be said that the Black Humorist is a kind of literary Paul Revere, a fellow who unfreezes his mind, if only for a moment and says, ". . . what in hell is going on here? What do you mean, 35,000 Vietnam *advisers?*"

They say it is a critic's phrase, Black Humor, and that whatever it is, you can count on it to fizzle after a bit. And besides, don't these fellows just write about outcasts? Fags, junkies, hunchbacks, "preverts," Negroes, Jews, other assorted losers? What's that got to do with anything anyway? I think they may be wrong on that first count. I have a hunch Black Humor has probably always been around, always will be around, under some name or other, as long as there are disguises to be peeled back, as long as there are thoughts no one else cares to think. And as to the idea that these writers do not deal with "representative" types—it may be that you can govern by consensus, but you can't write anything distinctive by consensus. And it may be that if you are doing anything as high-minded as examining society, the very best way to go about it is by examining first its throw-aways, the ones who can't or won't keep in step (in step with what?). And who knows? Perhaps "bad" behavior of a certain kind is better than "good" behavior. The American Health Society claims that only 5% of syphilis is spread by prostitutes.

So there is a Black Humor, after all, although you wish they would call it something else or perhaps call it nothing and just know it is in the air. Especially since there is no single perfect example of it, the way you can produce a perfect Uppman cigar. What is true is that the serious and effective social critics—the novelists, film makers, playwrights, the Feiffer-Krassner-Bruce axis—are working through humor; there is also an awful lot of questioning these days, some of it despairing, bleary-eyed be-dazzled, some of it young, vigorous, outrageous. And a group of novelists, very often working obliquely, coming at you from somewhere in left field, throwing you some laughs to get you to lower your guard, have decided that the novel is the proper place to open every door, to follow every labyrinthian corridor to its source, to ask the final questions, turn over the last rock, to take a preposterous world by the throat and say okay, be preposter-ous, but also make damned sure you explain yourself.

It is a good time to be around, to ask some of the questions, to watch the action.

JOHN BARTH

I beseech the Muse to keep me from ever becoming a Black Humorist. Mind, I don't object to Black Humorists, in their place, but to be numbered with them inspires me to a kind of spiritual White Backlash. For one thing they are in their way *responsible*, like more conventional social satirists: they dramatize—and good for them!—the Madness of Contemporary

Muse, Spare Me

Society, of Modern Warfare, of Life with the Bomb, of What Have We Nowadays. But I say, Muse spare me (at the desk, I mean) from Social-Historical Responsibility, and in the last analysis from every other kind as well, except Artistic. Your teller of stories will likely be responsive to his time; he needn't be responsible to it. I'm not impressed by the apocalyptic character of the present age—nor is the age by my indifference!— though I note the fact, and will return to it. Joyce figured the writer as Dedalus, Mann as Faust; the best of the Black Humorists are good comical Amoses and Isaiahs.

My own favorite image in this line used to be Cassandra—a *laughing* Cassandra, of course—the darling of many another young writer convinced that he has unhappy truth by the tail, or on his back, and that no one's getting the message. Later, shorn of such vanity, I preferred an image out of Dante: the Florentine assassins alluded to in Canto XIX of the *Inferno*. Head-downwards in a hole and sentenced to be buried alive, the murderer postpones his fate by drawing out his confession to the attendant priest. The beauties of this image are its two nice paradoxes: the more sins he has to confess, the longer retribution is delayed, and since he has nothing to lose anyhow, he may well invent a few good ones to hold the priest's attention.

But as soon as his audience grants absolution, the wretch's mouth is stopped with earth: "Nothing fails like success," as Mr. Fiedler says of our popular novelists. Less satisfactory are the details that his audience is also captive, duty-bound to hear

From *Book Week*, September 26, 1965, The New York *World Journal Tribune*. Reprinted by permission of *Book Week*.

him out whether entertained or not; respite is granted only as
long as he talks, not as long as he amuses, and there's no real
stay of execution, only a hold in the countdown. Moreover, the
fact that his tale consists of fabricated or exaggerated misde-
meanors of his own, a perverse kind of authorial self-aggran-
dizement, while it may make the image apter yet for some novelists we know—assassins indeed of the characters they "draw
from life," as one draws a man to the gallows—does not, I hope,
apply to my own concoctions.

In any case, the image I'm lately fonder of—the aptest, sweet-
est, hauntingest, hopefullest I know for the storyteller—is
Scheherazade. The whole frame of those thousand nights and a
night speaks to my heart, directly and intimately—and in many
ways at once, personal and technical. The sultan Shahryar,
you remember, is so disenchanted with life in general and love
in particular that he marries a virgin every night and has her
killed in the morning; Scheherazade, who has "perused the
books, annals, and legends of preceding kings, and the stories,
examples and instances of by-gone men . . . antique races and
departed rulers," volunteers herself; the King "abates her vir-
ginity" (as if it were an intense condition!), whereafter, with
the prearranged assistance of her younger sister Dunyazad—
about whose role much might be said—Scheherazade beguiles
her deflowerer with a tale, artfully continued, involuted, compounded, and complicated through a thousand and one noc-
turnal installments, during the invention of which she also bears
three sons by her imperious audience. It is on behalf of these
offspring that, her inspiration spent at last, she begs for her life,
and the King grants her—in honor of her stories—the relative
tenure of formal marriage. Scheherazade's tales are published
(in 30 volumes) and their author lives happily with her hard-
earned family. But not ever after; only until they all are taken
by the Destroyer of Delights, whereafter, we're specifically told,
"their houses fell waste and their palaces lay in ruins . . . and
[other] kings inherited their riches"—including *The Thousand
and One Nights.*

My love affair with Scheherazade is an old and continuing
one. As an illiterate undergraduate I worked off part of my
tuition filing books in the Classics Library at Johns Hopkins,

which included the stacks of the Oriental Seminary. One was permitted to get lost for hours in that splendrous labyrinth and intoxicate, engorge oneself with *story*. Especially I became enamored of the great tale-cycles and collections: Somadeva's *Ocean of Story* in ten huge volumes, Burton's *Thousand Nights and a Night* in twelve, the *Panchatantra*, the *Gesta Romanorum*, the *Novellini*, and the *Pent- Hept-* and *Decameron*. If anything ever makes a writer out of me, it will be the digestion of that enormous surreptitious feast of narrative.

Most of those spellbinding liars I have forgotten, but never Scheherazade. Though the tales she tells aren't my favorites, she remains my favorite teller, and it is a heady paradox that this persistence, being the figure of her literal aim, thereby generates itself, and becomes the emblem as well of my figurative aspiration. When I think of my condition and my hope, Musewise, in the time between now and when I shall run out of ink or otherwise expire it is Scheherazade who comes to mind, for many reasons—not least of which is a technical interest in the ancient device of the framing-story, used more beautifully in the *Nights* than anywhere else I know. Chaucer's frame, for example, the pilgrimage to Canterbury, is an excellent if venerable ground-metaphor—but, having established it, he does nothing with it. Boccaccio's frame—ten wealthy young ladies and gentlemen amusing themselves with clever stories while the great post-Easter plague of 1348 lays waste the countryside—is more arresting for its apocalyptic nature, for the pretty rules with which the company replaces those of their literally dying society, for the hints of growing relationships between the *raconteurs* and *raconteuses* themselves, and for the occasional relevance of the tales to the tellers and to the general situation. On the other hand, the very complex serial frames of the *Ocean of Story*, for example, are full-fledged stories in themselves, but except for the marvelous (and surely fictitious) "history of the text" and the haunting title, they have no apparent meaningfulness beyond their immediate narrative interest.

The story of Scheherazade excels these others, it seems to me, in all respects. For one thing her tales are told at night: an inestimable advantage, for the whole conception, despite its humor, is darker, more magical and dreamish than Boccaccio's

or Chaucer's. Consider too the prerequisites for her taleteller-
hood: not only native endowment and mastery of the tradition,
but the sacrifice of her present personal maidenhead to her
auditor and absolute critic—whose pleasure, by the way, ferti-
lizes as well as spares her, and who finally rewards her (for
what they have in a manner of speaking created together) with
official distinctions which *he* will not take away (though her
productivity, it seems, ends with the award of tenure), but time
will.

Consider finally that in the years of her flourishing, her talent
is always on the line: not enough to have satisfied the old cynic
once, or twice; she's only as good as her next piece, Scehera-
zade; night by night it's publish or perish. Thus her situation is
no less apocalyptic in its way than the *Decameron's,* and perhaps
more pointed, even without regard to the interesting "public"
state of affairs: the King's epical despair and the ruin it's bringing his kingdom to. For though the death of one person is not
the death of a people, even mankind's demise will have to consist of each of our dyings; in this respect all apocalypses are
ultimately personal—an important fact, since it validates apocalyptic visions age after age despite the otherwise awkward circumstance that the world has, so far, persisted.

Even the detail that Scheherazade's stories are drawn from
the literal and legendary foretime I find arresting. It reminds
me that the eschewing of contemporaneous, "original" material
is a basic literary notion, by comparison to which its use is but
an occasional anomaly and current fad. Not only classical epic
and tragedy and Elizabethan and neo-classical drama, but virtually all folk and heroic narrative, both Eastern and Western,
follows Horace's advice: ". . . *safer shall the bard his pen
employ/With yore, to dramatize the Tale of Troy,/Than, ventur-
ing trackless regions to explore,/Delineate characters untouched
before."*

Joyce's Dedalus calls history a nightmare from which he's
trying to wake; some other writers have found it more a wet-
dream (and their readers, perhaps, a soporific). For me, also,
the past is a dream—but I laugh in my sleep. The use of historical or legendary material, especially in a farcical spirit, has
a number of technical virtues, among which are esthetic dis-

tance and the opportunity for counter-realism. Attacked with a long face, the historical muse is likely to give birth to costume romances, adult Westerns, tiresome allegories, and ponderous mythologizings; but she responds to a light-hearted approach. *Magic* is what chiefly saves Scheherazade's tales from these poor categories—a device we may hardly use today, for the realistic tradition and its accompanying cultural history are under our belts, for better or worse, and may not be ignored. They may, however, be come to terms with and got beyond, not by the use of farce alone, surely, but by farce inspired with passion—and with mystery, which, older than magic, still enwraps our lives as it does the whole queer universe. In passionate, mysterious farce, it seems to me, lies also the possibility of transcending categories more profound than Tragedy and Comedy: I mean the distinction between Tragedy and Mystery—or, if you like, tragicism and mysticism, the finest expressions respectively of the Western and Eastern spirits. No matter that the achievement of such a synthesis would want the talents of Scheherazade, Shakespeare, and Schopenhauer combined; it is a polestar that even a middling comic novelist may steer by, without mistaking it for his destination.

Like a parable of Kafka's or a great myth, the story of deflowered Scheherazade, yarning tirelessly through the dark hours to save her neck, corresponds to a number of things at once, and flashes meaning from all its facets. For me its rich dark circumstances, mixing the subtle and the coarse, the comic and the grim, the realistic and the fantastic, the apocalyptic and the hopeful, figure, among other things, both the estate of the fictioner in general and the particular endeavors and aspirations of this one, at least, who can wish nothing better than to spin like that vizier's excellent daughter, through what nights remain to him, tales within tales within tales, full-stored with "description and discourse and rare traits and anecdotes and moral instances and reminiscences . . . proverbs and parables, chronicles and pleasantries, quips and jests, stories and . . . dialogues and histories and elegies and other verses . . ." until he and his scribblings are fetched low by the Destroyer of Delights.

Several winters back, while I was living in Chicago, the city was shocked and mystified by the death of two teen-age girls. So far as I know the populace is mystified still; as for the shock, Chicago is Chicago, and one week's dismemberment fades into the next's. The victims this particular year were sisters. They went off one December night to see an Elvis Presley movie, for the

Writing American Fiction

sixth or seventh time we are told, and never came home. Ten days passed and fifteen and twenty, and then the whole bleak city, every street and alley, was being searched for the missing Grimes girls, Pattie and Babs. A girl friend had seen them at the movie, a group of boys had had a glimpse of them afterwards getting into a black Buick; another group said a green Chevy, and so on and so forth, until one day the snow melted and the unclothed bodies of the two girls were discovered in a roadside ditch in a forest preserve on the West Side of Chicago. The coroner said he didn't know the cause of death and then the newspapers took over. One paper, I forget which one, ran a drawing of the girls on the back page, in bobby socks and levis and babushkas; Pattie and Babs a foot tall, and in four colors, like Dixie Dugan on Sundays. The mother of the two girls wept herself right into the arms of a local newspaper lady, who apparently set up her typewriter on the Grimes's front porch and turned out a column a day, telling us that these had been good girls, hard-working girls, average girls, churchgoing girls, et cetera. Late in the evening one could watch television interviews featuring schoolmates and friends of the Grimes sisters: the teen-age girls look around, dying to giggle; the boys stiffen in their leather jackets. "Yeah, I knew Babs, yeah she was all right, yeah, she was popular. . . ." On and on until at last comes a confession. A Skid Row bum of thirty-five or so, a dishwasher, a prowler, a no-good named Benny Bedwell, admits to killing

From *Commentary*, 31 (March, 1961) 223–233. Reprinted from *Commentary* by permission; copyright © 1961 by the American Jewish Committee and the author.

both girls, after he and a pal had cohabited with them for several weeks in various flea-bitten hotels. Hearing the news, the mother weeps and cries and tells the newspaper lady that the man is a liar—her girls, she insists now, were murdered the night they went off to the movie. The coroner continues to maintain (with rumblings from the press) that the girls show no signs of having had sexual intercourse. Meanwhile, everybody in Chicago is buying four papers a day, and Benny Bedwell, having supplied the police with an hour-by-hour chronicle of his adventures, is tossed in jail. Two nuns, teachers of the girls at the school they attended, are sought out by the newspapermen. They are surrounded and questioned and finally one of the sisters explains all. "They were not exceptional girls," the sister says, "they had no hobbies." About this time, some good-natured soul digs up Mrs. Bedwell, Benny's mother, and a meeting is arranged between this old woman and the mother of the slain teen-agers. Their picture is taken together, two overweight, overworked American ladies, quite befuddled but sitting up straight for the photographers. Mrs. Bedwell apologizes for her Benny. She says, "I never thought any boy of mine would do a thing like that." Two weeks later, or maybe three, her boy is out on bail, sporting several lawyers and a new one-button roll suit. He is driven in a pink Cadillac to an out-of-town motel where he holds a press conference. Yes—he barely articulates—he is the victim of police brutality. No, he is not a murderer; a degenerate maybe, but even that is going out the window. He is changing his life —he is going to become a carpenter (a carpenter!) for the Salvation Army, his lawyers say. Immediately, Benny is asked to sing (he plays the guitar) in a Chicago night spot for two thousand dollars a week, or is it ten thousand? I forget. What I remember is that suddenly there is a thought that comes flashing into the mind of the spectator, or newspaper reader: is this all Public Relations? But of course not—two girls are dead. At any rate, a song begins to catch on in Chicago, "The Benny Bedwell Blues." Another newspaper launches a weekly contest: "How Do You Think the Grimes Girls Were Murdered?" and a prize is given for the best answer (in the opinion of the judges). And now the money begins; donations, hundreds of them, start pouring in to Mrs. Grimes from all over the city and the state.

For what? From whom? Most contributions are anonymous. Just money, thousands and thousands of dollars—the *Sun-Times* keeps us informed of the grand total. Ten thousand, twelve thousand, fifteen thousand. Mrs. Grimes sets about refinishing and redecorating her house. A strange man steps forward, by the name of Shultz or Schwartz—I don't really remember, but he is in the appliance business and he presents Mrs. Grimes with a whole new kitchen. Mrs. Grimes, beside herself with appreciation and joy, turns to her surviving daughter and says, "Imagine me in that kitchen!" Finally the poor woman goes out and buys two parakeets (or maybe another Mr. Shultz presented them as a gift); one parakeet she calls "Babs," the other, "Pattie." At just about this point, Benny Bedwell, doubtless having barely learned to hammer a nail in straight, is extradited to Florida on the charge of having raped a twelve-year-old girl there. Shortly thereafter I left Chicago myself, and so far as I know, though Mrs. Grimes hasn't her two girls, she has a brand new dishwasher and two small birds.

And what is the moral of so long a story? Simply this: that the American writer in the middle of the 20th century has his hands full in trying to understand, and then describe, and then make *credible* much of the American reality. It stupefies, it sickens, it infuriates, and finally it is even a kind of embarrassment to one's own meager imagination. The actuality is continually outdoing our talents, and the culture tosses up figures almost daily that are the envy of any novelist.

*　　*　　*

The daily newspapers then fill one with wonder and awe: is it possible? is it happening? And of course with sickness and despair. The fixes, the scandals, the insanities, the treacheries, the idiocies, the lies, the pieties, the noise . . . . Recently, in *Commentary*, Benjamin DeMott wrote that the "deeply lodged suspicion of the times [is] namely, that events and individuals are unreal, and that power to alter the course of the age, of my life and your life, is actually vested nowhere." There seems to be, said DeMott, a kind of "universal descent into unreality." The other night—to give a benign example of the descent—my wife turned on the radio and heard the announcer offering a series of cash prizes for the three best television plays of five minutes' duration written by children. At such moments it is difficult to find one's way around the kitchen; certainly few days go by when incidents far less benign fail to remind us of what DeMott is talking about. When Edmund Wilson says that after reading *Life* magazine he feels that he does not belong to the country depicted there, that he does not live in that country, I think I understand what he means.

However, for a writer of fiction to feel that he does not really live in the country in which he lives—as represented by *Life* or by what he experiences when he steps out his front door—must certainly seem a serious occupational impediment. For what will be his subject? His landscape? It is the tug of reality, its mystery and magnetism, that leads one into the writing of fiction—what then when one is not mystified, but stupefied? not drawn but repelled? It would seem that what we might get would be a high proportion of historical novels or contemporary satire—or perhaps just nothing. No books. Yet the fact is that almost weekly one finds on the best-seller list another novel which is set in Mamaroneck or New York City or Washington, with people moving through a world of dishwashers and TV sets and advertising agencies and Senatorial investigations. It all *looks* as though the writers are still turning out books about our world. There is *Cash McCall* and *The Man in the Gray Flannel Suit* and *Marjorie Morningstar* and *The Enemy Camp* and *Advise and Consent,* and so on. But what is crucial, of course, is that these books aren't very good. Not that these writers aren't sufficiently horrified with the landscape to suit me—quite the contrary. They are generally full of concern for the world about them; finally, however, they just don't seem able to imagine the corruptions and vulgarities and treacheries of American public life any more profoundly than they can imagine human character —that is, the country's private life. All issues are generally solvable, which indicates that they are not so much wonder-struck or horror-struck or even plain struck by a state of civilization, as they are provoked by some topical controversy. "Controversial" is a common word in the critical language of this literature as it is, say, in the language of the TV producer. But it is clear that though one may refer to a "problem" as being controversial, one does not usually speak of a state of civilization as controversial, or a state of the soul.

It is hardly news that in best-sellerdom we frequently wind up with the hero coming to terms and settling down in Scarsdale, or wherever, knowing himself. And on Broadway, in the third act, someone says, "Look, why don't you just love each other?" and the protagonist, throwing his hand to his forehead, cries, "Oh God, why didn't I think of that!" and before the bulldozing action of love, all else collapses—verisimilitude, truth, and interest. It is like "Dover Beach" ending happily for Matthew Arnold, and for us, because the poet is standing at the window with a woman who understands him. If the investigation of our times and the impact of these times upon human personality were to become the sole property of Wouk, Weidman, Sloan Wilson, Cameron Hawley, and the theatrical *amor-vincit-omnia* boys it would indeed be unfortunate, for it would be somewhat like leaving sex to the pornographers, where again there is more to what is happening than first meets the eye.

And of course the times have not yet been left completely to lesser minds and talents. There is Norman Mailer. And he is an interesting example, I think, of one in whom our era has provoked such a magnificent disgust that dealing with it in fiction has almost come to seem, for him, beside the point. He has become an actor in the cultural drama, the difficulty of which, I should guess, is that it leaves one with considerably less time to be a writer. For instance, to defy the Civil Defense authorities and their H-bomb drills, you have to take off a morning from the typewriter and go down and stand outside of City Hall; then if you're lucky and they toss you in jail, you have to give up an evening at home and your next morning's work as well. To defy Mike Wallace, or challenge his principle-less aggression, or simply use him or straighten him out, you must first go on the program—there's one night shot. Then you may well spend the next two weeks (I am speaking from memory) disliking yourself for having gone, and then two more writing an article (or a confession to a gentle friend) in which you attempt to explain

why you did it and what it was like. "It's the age of the slob,"
says a character in William Styron's new novel. "If we don't
watch out they're going to drag us under. . . ." And the drag-
ging under, as we see, takes numerous forms. We get, for instance, from Mailer a book like *Advertisements for Myself*, a
chronicle for the most part of why I did it and what it was like
—and who I have it in for: life as a substitute for fiction. An
infuriating, self-indulgent, boisterous, mean book, not much
worse than most advertising we have to put up with, I think—
but also, taken as a whole, a curiously moving book, moving in
its revelation of the connection between one writer and the times
that have given rise to him, in the revelation of a despair so
great that the man who bears it, or is borne by it, seems for the
time being—out of either choice or necessity—to have given up
on making an imaginative assault upon the American experience, and has become instead the champion of a kind of public
revenge. Unfortunately, however, what one is champion of one
day, one may wind up victim of the next; that is everybody's
risk. Once having written *Advertisements for Myself*, I don't see
that you can write it again. Mr. Mailer probably now finds himself in the unenviable position of having to put up or shut up.
Who knows—maybe it's where he wanted to be. My own feeling
is that times are tough for a writer when he takes to writing
letters to his newspaper rather than those complicated, disguised
letters to himself, which are stories.

The last is not meant to be a sententious, or a condescending
remark, or even a generous one. However one suspects Mailer's
style or his reasons, one sympathizes with the impulse that leads
him to be—or to want to be—a critic, a reporter, a sociologist,
a journalist, a figure, or even Mayor of New York. For what is
particularly tough about the times is writing about them, as a
serious novelist or storyteller. Much has been made, much of it
by the writers themselves, of the fact that the American writer
has no status and no respect and no audience: the news I wish
to bear is of a loss more central to the task itself, a loss of subject; or if not a loss, if to say that is, romantically and inexactly
and defensively, an attempt to place most of the responsibility
outside the writer for what may finally be nothing more than the
absence of genius in our times—then let me say a voluntary

withdrawal of interest by the writer of fiction from some of the grander social and political phenomena of our times.

Of course there have been writers who have tried to meet these phenomena head on. It seems to me I have read several books or stories in the past few years in which one character or another starts to talk about "The Bomb," and the conversation generally leaves me feeling half convinced, and in some extreme instances, even with a certain amount of sympathy for fall-out; it is like people in college novels having long talks about what kind of generation they are. But what then? What can the writer do with so much of the American reality as it is? Is the only other possibility to be Gregory Corso and thumb your nose at the whole thing? The attitude of the Beats (if such a phrase has meaning) is not in certain ways without appeal. The whole thing is a kind of joke. America, ha-ha. The only trouble is that such a position doesn't put very much distance between Beatdom and its sworn enemy, best-sellerdom—not much more, at any rate, than what it takes to get from one side of a nickel to the other: for what is America, ha-ha, but the simple reverse of America, hoo-ray?

It is possible that I have exaggerated both the serious writer's response to our cultural predicament, and his inability or unwillingness to deal with it imaginatively. There seems to me little, in the end, to be used as proof for an assertion having to do with the psychology of a nation's writers, outside, that is, of their books themselves. So, with this particular assertion, the argument may appear to be somewhat compromised in that the evidence to be submitted is not so much the books that have been written, but the ones that have been left unwritten and unfinished, and those that have not even been considered worthy of the attempt. Which is not to say that there have not been certain literary signs, certain obsessions and innovations and concerns, to be found in the novels of our best writers, supporting the notion that the world we have been given, the society and the community, has ceased to be as suitable or as manageable a subject for the novelist as it once may have been.

Let me begin with some words about the man who, by reputation at least, is *the* writer of the age. The response of college students to the works of J. D. Salinger should indicate to us that perhaps he, more than anyone else, has not turned his back on the times, but instead, has managed to put his finger on what is most significant in the struggle going on today between the self (all selves, not just the writer's) and the culture. *The Catcher in the Rye* and the recent stories in the *New Yorker* having to do with the Glass family surely take place in the social here and now. But what about the self, what about the hero? This question seems to me of particular interest here, for in Salinger more than in most of his contemporaries, there has been an increasing desire of late to place the figure of the writer himself directly in the reader's line of vision, so that there is an equation, finally, between the insights of the narrator as, say, brother to Seymour Glass, and as a man who is a writer by profession. And what of Salinger's heroes? Well, Holden Caulfield, we discover, winds up in an expensive sanitarium. And Seymour Glass commits suicide finally, but prior to that he is the apple of his brother's eye—and why? He has learned to live in this world—but how? By not living in it. By kissing the soles of little girls' feet and throwing rocks at the head of his sweetheart. He is a saint, clearly. But since madness is undesirable and sainthood, for most of us, out of the question, the problem of how to live *in* this world is by no means answered; unless the answer is that one cannot. The only advice we seem to get from Salinger is to be charming on the way to the loony bin. Of course, Salinger is under no burden to supply us, writers or readers, with advice, though I must admit that I find myself growing more and more curious about this professional writer, Buddy Glass, and how *he* manages to coast through this particular life in the arms of sanity.

It is not Buddy Glass, though, in whom I do not finally believe, but Seymour himself. Seymour is as unreal to me as his world, in all its endless and marvelous detail, is decidedly credible. I am touched by the lovingness that is attributed to him, as one is touched by so many of the gestures and attitudes in Salinger, but this lovingness, in its totality and otherworldliness, becomes for me in the end an attitude of the writer's, a cry of desperation, even a program, more than an expression of character. If

we forgive this lapse, it is, I think, because we understand the
depth of the despairing.

There is, too, in Salinger the suggestion that mysticism is a
possible road to salvation; at least some of his characters respond well to an intensified, emotional religious belief. Now my
own involvement with Zen is slight, but as I understand it in
Salinger, the deeper we go into this world, the further we can
get away from it. If you contemplate a potato long enough, it
stops being a potato in the usual sense; unfortunately, though,
it is the usual sense that we have to deal with from day to day.
For all the loving handling of the world's objects, for all the
reverence of life and feeling, there seems to me, in the Glass
family stories as in *The Catcher*, a spurning of life as it is lived
in this world, in this reality—this place and time is seen as
unworthy of those few precious people who have been set down
in it only to be maddened and destroyed.

A spurning of our world—though of a much different order
—seems to occur in another of our most talented writers, Ber-
nard Malamud. Even, one recalls, when Malamud writes a book
about baseball, a book called *The Natural*, it is not baseball as
it is played in Yankee Stadium, but a wild, wacky baseball,
where a player who is instructed to knock the cover off the ball
promptly steps up to the plate and knocks it off; the batter
swings and the inner hard string core of the ball goes looping
out to centerfield, where the confused fielder commences to
tangle himself in the unwinding sphere; then the shortstop runs
out, and with his teeth, bites the center-fielder and the ball free
from one another. Though *The Natural* is not Malamud's most
successful, nor his most significant book, it is at any rate our
introduction to his world, which has a kind of historical relationship to our own, but is by no means a replica of it. By historical I mean that there are really things called baseball players
and really things called Jews, but there much of the similarity
ends. The Jews of *The Magic Barrel* and the Jews of *The Assistant*, I have reason to suspect, are not the Jews of New York City
or Chicago. They are a kind of invention, a metaphor to stand
for certain human possibilities and certain human promises, and

I find myself further inclined to believe this when I read of a statement attributed to Malamud which goes, "All men are Jews." In fact we know this is not so; even the men who are Jews aren't sure they're Jews. But Malamud, as a writer of fiction, has not shown specific interest in the anxieties and dilemmas and corruptions of the modern American Jew, the Jew we think of as characteristic of our times; rather, his people live in a timeless depression and a placeless Lower East Side; their society is not affluent, their predicament not cultural. I am not saying—one cannot, of Malamud—that he has spurned life or an examination of the difficulties of being human. What it is to be human, to be humane, is his subject: connection, indebtedness, responsibility, these are his moral concerns. What I do mean to point out is that he does not—or has not yet—found the contemporary scene a proper or sufficient backdrop for his tales of heartlessness and heartache, of suffering and regeneration.

Now Malamud and Salinger do not speak, think, or feel for all writers, and yet their fictional response to the world about them —what they choose to mention, what they choose to avoid—is of interest to me on the simple grounds that they are two of our best. Surely there are other writers around, and capable ones too, who have not taken the particular roads that these two have; however, even with some of these others, I wonder if we may not be witnessing a response to the times, perhaps not so dramatic as in Salinger and Malamud, but a response nevertheless.

Let us take up the matter of prose style. Why is everybody so bouncy all of a sudden? Those who have been reading in the works of Saul Bellow, Herbert Gold, Arthur Granit, Thomas Berger, Grace Paley, and others will know to what I am referring. Writing recently in the *Hudson Review,* Harvey Swados said that he saw developing "a nervous muscular prose perfectly suited to the exigencies of an age which seems at once appalling and ridiculous. These are metropolitan writers, most of them are Jewish, and they are specialists in a kind of prose-poetry that often depends for its effectiveness as much on how it is ordered, or how it looks on the printed page, as it does on what it is expressing. This is risky writing, . . ." Swados added, and perhaps it is in its very riskiness that we can discover some kind of explanation for it. I should like to compare two short descriptive passages, one from Bellow's *The Adventures of Augie March,* the other from Gold's new novel, *Therefore Be Bold,* in the hope that the differences revealed will be educational.

As has been pointed out by numerous people before me, the language of *Augie March* is one that combines a literary complexity with a conversational ease, a language that joins the idiom of the academy with the idiom of the streets (not all streets—certain streets); the style is special, private, and energetic, and though occasionally unwieldy and indulgent, it generally, I believe, serves the narrative, and serves it brilliantly. Here for instance is a description of Grandma Lausch:

> With the [cigarette] holder in her dark little gums between which all her guile, malice, and command issued, she had her best inspirations of strategy. She was as wrinkled as an old paper bag, an autocrat, hard-shelled and jesuitical, a pouncy old hawk of a Bolshevik, her small ribboned gray feet immobile on the shoekit and stool Simon had made in the manual-training class, dingy old wool Winnie [the dog] whose bad smell filled the flat on the cushion beside her. If wit and discontent don't necessarily go together, it wasn't from the old woman that I learned it.

Herbert Gold's language has also been special, private, and energetic. One will notice in the following passage from *Therefore Be Bold* that here too the writer begins by recognizing a physical similarity between the character described and some unlikely object, and from there, as in Bellow's Grandma Lausch passage attempts to move into a deeper, characterological description, to wind up, via the body, making a discovery about the soul. The character described is named Chuck Hastings.

> In some respects he resembled a mummy—the shriveled yellow skin, the hand and head too large for a wasted body, the bottomless eye sockets of thought beyond the Nile. But his agile Adam's apple and point-making finger made him less the Styx-swimmer dog-paddling toward Coptic limbos than a high school intellectual intimidating the navel-eyed little girl.

First I must say that the grammar itself has me baffled: ". . . bottomless eye sockets of thought beyond the Nile." Is the

thought beyond the Nile, or are the eye sockets? What does it
mean to be beyond the Nile anyway? The a-grammaticality of
the sentence has little in common with the ironic inversion with
which Bellow's description begins: "With the holder in her dark
little gums between which all her guile, malice, and command
issued. . . ." Bellow goes on to describe Grandma Lausch as "an
autocrat," "hard-shelled," "jesuitical," "a pouncy old hawk of a
Bolshevik"—imaginative terms certainly, but toughminded,
exact, and not exhibitionistic. Of Gold's Chuck Hastings however, we learn, "His agile Adam's-apple and point-making finger
made him less the Styx-swimmer dog-paddling toward Coptic
limbos, etc. . . ." Is this language in the service of the narrative,
or a kind of literary regression in the service of the ego? In a
recent review of *Therefore Be Bold*, Granville Hicks quoted this
very paragraph in praise of Gold's style. "This is high-pitched,"
Mr. Hicks admitted, "but the point is that Gold keeps it up and
keeps it up." I take it that Mr. Hicks's sexual pun is not deliberate; nevertheless, it should remind us all that showmanship
and passion are not, and never have been, one and the same.
What we have here, it seems to me, is not so much stamina or
good spirits, but reality taking a backseat to personality—and
not the personality of the character described, but of the writer
who is doing the describing. Bellow's description seems to arise
out of a firm conviction on the part of the writer about the
character: Grandma Lausch IS. Behind the description of Chuck
Hastings there seems to me the conviction—or the desire for us
to be convinced—of something else: Herbert Gold IS. I am! I am!
In short: look at me, I'm writing.

Because Gold's work serves my purposes, let me say a word or
two more about him. He is surely one of our most productive and
most respected novelists, and yet he has begun to seem to me a
writer in competition with his own fiction. Which is more interesting—my life or my work? His new book of stories, *Love
and Like,* is not over when we have finished reading the last
narrative. Instead we go on to read several more pages in which
the author explains why and how he came to write each of the
preceding stories. At the end of *Therefore Be Bold* we are given
a long listing of the various cities in which Gold worked on this
book, and the dates during which he was living or visiting in

them. It is all very interesting if one is involved in tracing lost mail, but the point to be noted here is that how the fiction has come to be written is supposed to be nearly as interesting as what is written. Don't forget, ladies and gentlemen, that behind each and every story you have read here tonight is—me. For all Gold's delight with the things of this world—and I think that his prose, at its best, is the expression of that delight—there is also a good deal of delight in the work of his own hand. And, I think, with the hand itself.

Using a writer for one's own purposes is of course to be unfair to him (nearly as unfair as the gambit that admits to being unfair); I confess to this, however, and don't intend to hang a man for one crime. Nevertheless, Gold's extravagant prose, his confessional tone (the article about divorce; then the several prefaces and appendices about his own divorce—my ex-wife says this about me, etc.: then finally the story about divorce)—all of this seems to have meaning to me in terms of this separation I tried to describe earlier, the not-so friendly relationship between the writer and the culture. In fact, it is paradoxical really, that the very prose style which, I take it, is supposed to jolt and surprise us, and thereby produce a new and sharper vision, turns back upon itself, and the real world is in fact veiled from us by this elaborate and self-conscious language-making. I suppose that in a way one can think of it as a sympathetic, or kinetic, response to the clamor and din of our mass culture, an attempt to beat the vulgar world at its own game. I am even willing to entertain this possibility. But it comes down finally to the same thing: not so much an attempt to understand the self, as to assert it.

I must say that I am not trying to sell selflessness. Rather, I am suggesting that this nervous muscular prose that Swados talks about may perhaps have to do with the unfriendliness between the self of the writer and the realities of the culture. The prose suits the age, Swados suggests, and I wonder if it does not suit it, in part, because it rejects it. The writer pushes before our eyes—it is in the very ordering of our sentences—personality, in all its separateness and specialness. Of course the mystery of personality is nothing less than the writer's ultimate concern;

and certainly when the muscular prose is revelatory of character
—as in *Augie March*—then it is to be appreciated; at its worst,
however, as a form of literary onanism, it seriously curtails the
fictional possibilities, and may perhaps be thought of, and sym-
pathetically so, as a symptom of the writer's loss of the community as subject.

True, the bouncy style can be understood in other ways as
well. It is not surprising that most of these writers Swados sees
as its practitioners are Jewish. When writers who do not feel
much of a connection to Lord Chesterfield begin to realize that
they are under no real obligation to try and write like that distinguished old stylist, they are quite likely to go out and be
bouncy. Also, there is the matter of the spoken language which
these writers have heard, as our statesmen might put it, in the
schools, in the homes, in the churches and the synagogues; I
should even say that when the bouncy style is not an attempt to
dazzle the reader, or one's self, but to incorporate into written
prose the rhythms, the excitements, the nuances and emphases
of urban speech, or immigrant speech, the result can sometimes
be a language of new and rich emotional subtleties, with a kind
of back-handed grace and irony all its own, as say the language
of Mrs. Paley's book of stories, *The Little Disturbances of
Man*.

There is one more point to be made about bounciness, and
that is that it is an expression of pleasure. One cannot deny that
there is that in it. However, a question arises: if the world is as
crooked and unreal as I think it is becoming, day by day; if one
feels less and less power in the fact of this unreality, day by day;
if the inevitable end is destruction, if not of all life, then of much
that is valuable and civilized in life—then why in God's name is
the writer pleased? Why don't all of our fictional heroes wind up
in institutions like Holden Caulfield, or suicides like Seymour
Glass? Why is it, in fact, that so many of our fictional heroes—
not just the heroes of Wouk and Weidman, but of Bellow, Gold,
Styron, and others—wind up affirming life? For surely the air is
thick these days with affirmation, and though we shall doubtless
get this year our annual editorial from *Life* calling for affirmative
novels, the plain and simple fact is that more and more books by
serious writers seem to end on a note of celebration. Not just the

tone is bouncy, but the moral is bouncy too. In *The Optimist,*
another novel of Gold's, the hero, having taken his lumps, cries
out at the conclusion, "More. More. More! More! More!" This is
the book's last line. Curtis Harnack's novel, *The World of an Ancient Hand,* ends with the hero filled with "rapture and hope" and
saying aloud, "I believe in God." And Saul Bellow's *Henderson
the Rain King* is a book which is given over to celebrating the regeneration of a man's heart, feelings, blood, and general health.
Of course it is of crucial importance, I think, that the regeneration of Henderson takes place in a world that is thoroughly and
wholly imagined, *but does not really exist;* that is, it is not a
part of that reality which we all read about and worry over—
this is not the tumultuous Africa of the newspapers and the
United Nations discussions that Eugene Henderson visits. There
is nothing here of nationalism or riots or *apartheid.* But then,
why should there be? There is the world, but there is also the
self. And the self, when the writer turns upon it all his attention
and talent, is revealed to be a remarkable thing. First off, it exists,
it's real. *I am,* the self cries, and then, taking a nice long look,
it adds, *and I am beautiful.*

At the conclusion of Bellow's book, the hero, Eugene Henderson, a big, sloppy millionaire, is returning to America, coming
home from a trip to Africa where he has been plague-fighter,
lion-tamer, and rainmaker; he is bringing back with him a real
lion. Aboard the plane he befriends a small Persian boy, whose
language he cannot understand. Still, when the plane lands at
Newfoundland, Henderson takes the child in his arms and goes
out onto the field. And then:

> Laps and laps I galloped around the shining and riveted
> body of the plane, behind the fuel trucks. Dark faces were
> looking from within. The great, beautiful propellers were
> still, all four of them. I guess I felt it was my turn now to
> move, and so went running—leaping, leaping, pounding,
> and tingling over the pure white lining of the gray Arctic
> silence.

And so we leave Henderson, a very happy man. Where? In the
Arctic. This picture has stayed with me since I read the book a
year or so ago: of a man who finds energy and joy in an imagined Africa, and celebrates it on an unpeopled, icebound
vastness.

Earlier I quoted from Styron's new novel, *Set This House on Fire*. Now Styron's book, like Bellow's, is also the story of the regeneration of a man, and too of an American who leaves his own country and goes abroad for a while to live. But where Henderson's world is removed from our own, not about riots or nationalism, Kinsolving, Styron's hero, inhabits a planet we immediately recognize. The book is drenched in details that twenty years from now will surely require footnotes to be thoroughly understood. The hero of the book is an American painter who has taken his family to live in a small town on the Amalfi coast. Cass Kinsolving detests America, and himself to boot. Throughout most of the book he is taunted and tempted and disgraced by Mason Flagg, a fellow countryman, rich, boyish, naive, licentious, indecent, and finally, cruel and stupid. Kinsolving, by way of his attachment to Flagg, spends most of the book choosing between living and dying, and at one point, in a language and tone that are characteristic, he says this, concerning his expatriation:

> the man I had come to Europe to escape [why he's] the man in all the car advertisements, you know, the young guy waving there—he looks so beautiful and educated and everything, and he's got it *made*, Penn State and a blonde there, and a smile as big as a billboard. And he's going places. I mean electronics. Politics. What they call communication. Advertising. Saleshood. Outer space. God only knows. And he's as ignorant as an Albanian peasant.

However, at the end of the book, for all his disgust with what the American public life does to a man's private life, Kinsolving, like Henderson, has come back to America, having opted for existence. But the America that we find him in seems to me to be the America of his childhood, and, if only in a metaphoric way, of all our childhoods: he tells his story while he fishes from a boat in a Carolina stream. The affirmation at the conclusion is not as go-getting as Gold's "More! More!" nor as sublime as Harnack's, "I believe in God," nor as joyous as Henderson's romp on the Newfoundland airfield. "I wish I could tell you that I had found some belief, some rock . . ." Kinsolving says, "but to be truthful, you see, I can only tell you this: that as for being and nothingness, the only thing I did know was that to choose be-

tween them was simply to choose being . . ." Being. Living. Not
where one lives or with whom one lives—but that one lives.

And now, alas, what does all of this add up to? It would certainly be to oversimplify the art of fiction, and the complex relationship between a man and his times, to ignore the crucial
matters of individual talent, history, and character, to say that
Bellow's book, or Styron's, or even Herbert Gold's prose style,
arise naturally out of our distressing cultural and political predicament. However, that our communal predicament is a distressing one, is a fact that weighs upon the writer no less, and
perhaps even more, than his neighbor—for to the writer the
community is, properly, both his subject and his audience. And
it may be that when the predicament produces in the writer not
only feelings of disgust, rage, and melancholy, but impotence,
too, he is apt to lose heart and finally, like his neighbor, turn to
other matters, or to other worlds; or to the self, which may, in a
variety of ways, become his subject, or even the impulse for his
technique. What I have tried to point out is that the sheer fact
of self, the vision of self as inviolable, powerful, and nervy, self
as the only real thing in an unreal environment, that that vision
has given to some writers joy, solace, and muscle. Certainly to
have come through a holocaust in one piece, to have survived, is
nothing to be made light of, and it is for that reason, say, that
Styron's hero manages to engage our sympathies right down to
the end. However, when survival itself becomes one's *raison
d'être*, when one cannot choose but be ascetic, when the self can
only be celebrated as it is excluded from society, or as it is exercised and admired in a fantastic one, we then, I think, do not
have much reason to be cheery. Finally there is for me something
hollow and unconvincing about Henderson up there on top of the
world dancing around that airplane. Consequently, it is not with
this image that I should like to conclude, but instead with the
image that Ralph Ellison gives to us of his hero at the end of
Invisible Man. For here too the hero is left with the simple stark
fact of himself. He is as alone as a man can be. Not that he
hasn't gone out into the world; he has gone out into it, and out
into it, and out into it—but at the end he chooses to go underground, to live there and to wait. And it does not seem to him
a cause for celebration either.

Since the end of the eighteenth century no dramatist has had a greater impact on European drama than Shakespeare. But the theatres in which Shakespeare's plays have been produced were in turn influenced by contemporary plays. Shakespeare has been a living influence in so far as contemporary plays, through which his dramas were interpreted, were a living force themselves.

King Lear or Endgame

When Shakespeare is dull and dead on the stage, it means that not only the theatre but also the plays written in that particular period are dead. This is one of the reasons why Shakespeare's universality has never dated.

The book devoted to "Shakespeare and the new drama" has not yet been written. Perhaps it is too early for such a book to appear. But it is odd how often the word "Shakespearean" is uttered when one speaks about Brecht, Dürrenmatt, or Beckett. These three names stand, of course, for three different kinds of theatrical vision, and the word "Shakespearean" means something different in relation to each of them. It may be invoked to compare with Dürrenmatt's full-bloodedness, sharpness, lack of cohesion, and stylistic confusion; with Brecht's epic quality; or with Beckett's new *Theatrum mundi*. But every one of these three kinds of drama and theatre has more similarities to Shakespeare and medieval morality plays than to nineteenth-century drama, whether romantic, or naturalistic. Only in this sense can the new theatre be called anti-theatre.

A striking feature of the new theatre is its grotesque quality. Despite appearances to the contrary, this new grotesque has not replaced the old drama and the comedy of manners.

* * *

Grotesque exists in a tragic world. Both the tragic and the grotesque vision of the world are composed as it were of the same elements. In a tragic and grotesque world, situations are imposed, compulsory and inescapable. Freedom of choice and decision are part of this compulsory situation, in which both the tragic hero and the grotesque actor must always lose their struggle against the absolute. The downfall of the tragic hero is a confirmation and recognition of the absolute; whereas the downfall of the grotesque actor means mockery of the absolute and its desecration. The absolute is transformed into a blind mechanism, a kind of automaton. Mockery is directed not only at the tormentor, but also at the victim who believed in the tormentor's justice, raising him to the level of the absolute. The victim has consecrated his tormentor by recognizing himself as victim.

In the final instance tragedy is an appraisal of human fate, a measure of the absolute. The grotesque is a criticism of the absolute in the name of frail human experience. That is why tragedy brings catharsis, while grotesque offers no consolation whatsoever. "Tragedy," wrote Gorgias of Leontium, "is a swindle in which the swindler is more just than the swindled, and the swindled wiser than the swindler." One may travesty this aphorism by saying that grotesque is a swindle in which the swindled is more just than the swindler, and the swindler wiser than the swindled. Claire Zachanassian in Dürrenmatt's *Visit* is wiser than Anton Schill, but he is more just than she is. Schill's death, like Polonius's death in *Hamlet*, is grotesque. Neither Schill, nor the inhabitants of Güllen are tragic heroes. The old lady with her artificial breasts, teeth and limbs is not a goddess; she hardly even exists, she might almost have been invented. Schill and the people of Güllen find themselves in a situation in which there is no room for tragedy, but only for grotesque. "Comedy," writes Ionesco in his *Expérience du théâtre*, "is a feeling of absurdity, and seems more hopeless than tragedy; comedy allows no way out of a given situation."

The tragic and the grotesque worlds are closed, and there is no escape from them. In the tragic world this compulsory situation has been imposed in turn by the Gods, Fate, the Christian God, Nature, and History that has been endowed with reason and inevitability.

On the other side, opposed to this arrangement, there was

always man. If Nature was the absolute, man was unnatural. If man was natural, the absolute was represented by Grace, without which there was no salvation. In the world of the grotesque, downfall cannot be justified by, or blamed on, the absolute. The absolute is not endowed with any ultimate reasons; it is stronger, and that is all. The absolute is absurd. Maybe that is why the grotesque often makes use of the concept of a mechanism which has been put in motion and cannot be stopped. Various kinds of impersonal and hostile mechanisms have taken the place of God, Nature and History, found in the old tragedy. The notion of absurd mechanism is probably the last metaphysical concept remaining in modern grotesque. But this absurd mechanism is not transcendental any more in relation to man, or at any rate to mankind. It is a trap set by man himself into which he has fallen.

The scene of tragedy has mostly been a natural landscape. Raging nature witnessed man's downfall, or—as in *King Lear*—played an active part in the action. Modern grotesque usually takes place in the midst of civilization. Nature has evaporated from it almost completely. Man is confined to a room and surrounded by inanimate objects. But objects have now been raised to the status of symbols of human fate, or situation, and perform a similar function to that played in Shakespeare by forest, storm, or eclipse of the sun. Even Sartre's hell is just a vast hotel consisting of rooms and corridors, beyond which there are more rooms and more corridors. This hell "behind closed doors" does not need any metaphysical aids.

Ionesco's hell is arranged on similar lines. A new tenant moves into an empty flat. Furniture is brought in. There is more and more furniture. Furniture surrounds the tenant on all sides. He is surrounded already by four wardrobes but more are brought in. He has been closed in by furniture. He can no longer be seen. He has been brought down to the level of inanimate objects and has become an object himself.

In Beckett's *Endgame* there is a room with a wheelchair and two dustbins. A picture hangs face to the wall. There is also a staircase, a telescope and a whistle. All that remains of nature is sand in the dustbins, a flea, and the part of man that belongs to nature: his body.

HAMM
Nature has forgotten us.
CLOV
There's no more nature.
HAMM
No more nature! You exaggerate.
CLOV
In the vicinity.
HAMM
But we breathe, we change! We lose our hair, our
teeth! Our bloom! Our ideals!
CLOV
Then she hasn't forgotten us.

(p. 16)[1]

It can easily be shown how, in the new theatre, tragic situations become grotesque. Such a classic situation of tragedy is the necessity of making a choice between opposing values. Antigone is doomed to choose between human and divine order; between Creon's demands, and those of the absolute. The tragedy lies in the very principle of choice by which one of the values must be annihilated. The cruelty of the absolute lies in demanding such a choice and in imposing a situation which excludes the possibility of a compromise, and where one of the alternatives is death. The absolute is greedy and demands everything; the hero's death is its confirmation.

The tragic situation becomes grotesque when both alternatives of the choice imposed are absurd, irrelevant or compromising. The hero has to play, even if there is no game. Every move is bad, but he cannot throw down his cards. To throw down the cards would also be a bad move.

It is this situation that Dürrenmatt's Romulus finds himself in. He is the last emperor of a crumbling empire. He will not alter the course of history. History has made a fool of him. He can either die in a spectacular fashion, or lie on his bed and wait to be butchered. He can surrender, compose speeches, or

---

[1] All quotations from Beckett are given in the author's own translation. Page references in quotations from *Endgame* and *Act Without Words* apply to the Faber & Faber edition of 1958.

commit suicide. In his position as the last Roman emperor, every
one of these solutions is compromising and ridiculous. History
has turned Romulus into a clown, and yet demands that he treat
her seriously. Romulus has only one good move to make: consciously to accept the part of a clown and play it to the end. He
can breed chickens. In this way the historical inevitability will
have been made a fool of. The absolute will have been
flouted.

Antigone is a tragedy of choice, *Oedipus* a tragedy of "unmerited guilt" and destiny. The gods loyally warn the protagonist
that fate has destined him to be a patricide and his own mother's
husband. The hero has full freedom of decision and action. The
gods do not interfere; they just watch and wait until he makes a
mistake. Then they punish him. The gods are just, and punish
the hero for a crime he has indeed committed, and only after he
has committed it. But the protagonist had to commit a crime.
Oedipus wanted to cheat fate, but did not and could not escape
it. He fell into a trap, made his mistake, killed his father and
married his mother. What is to happen will happen.

The tragedy of Oedipus may, perhaps, be posed as a problem
belonging to the theory of game. The game is just, i.e., at the
outset both partners must have the same chances of losing or
winning, and both must play according to the same rules. In its
game with Oedipus fate does not invoke the help of the gods,
does not change the laws of nature. Fate wins its game without
recourse to miracles.

The game must be just, but at the same time must be so arranged that the same party always wins; so that Oedipus always
loses.

Let us imagine an electronic computer, which plays chess and
calculates any number of moves in advance. A man must play
chess with an electronic computer, cannot leave or break the
game, and has to lose the game. His defeat is just, because it is
effected according to the rules of the game; he loses because he
has made a mistake. But he could not have won.

A man losing the chess game with an electronic computer,
whom he himself has fed with combinatorial analysis and rules,
whom he himself has "taught" to play, is not a tragic hero any
more. If he plays that chess game from the moment he was born

until he dies, and if he has to lose, he will at most be the hero of a tragi-grotesque. All that is left of tragedy, is the concept of "unmerited guilt," the inevitable defeat, and unavoidable mistake. But the absolute has ceased to exist. It has been replaced by the absurdity of the human situation.

The absurdity does not consist in the fact that man-made mechanisms are in certain conditions stronger, and even wiser, than he. The absurdity consists in the fact that they create a compulsory situation by forcing him to a game in which the probability of his total defeat constantly increases. The Christian view of the end of the world, with the Last Judgement and its segregation of the just and the unjust, is pathetic. The end of the world caused by the big bomb is spectacular, but grotesque just the same. Such an end of the world is intellectually unacceptable, whether to Christians or to Marxists. It would be a silly ending.

The comparison between fate's game with Oedipus, and a game of chess with an electronic computer, is not precise enough. An automatic device to play chess, even if it could compute any number of moves, need not win all the time. It would simply more often win than lose. But among automatic devices that really exist one could find a much better example. There is a machine for a game similar to tossing coins for "heads or tails." I put a coin on the table the way I like, with "heads" or "tails" on top. The machine does not see the coin, but it is to make out how I have put it. If it gives the right answer, it wins. I inform the machine whether it has given the right answer. I put the coin again, and so on. After a time the machine begins to win by giving the right answers more and more often. It has memorized and learned my system; it has deciphered me as it were. It foresees that after three "heads" I will put two "tails." I change the system, and play using a different method. The blind machine learns this one too, and begins to win again. I am endowed with free will and have the freedom of choice. I can put "heads" or "tails." But in the end, like Oedipus, I must lose the game.

There is a move by which I do not lose. I do not put the coin on the table, I do not choose. I simply toss it. I have given up the system, and left matters to chance. Now the machine and I have even chances. The possibility of win and loss, of "heads" or "tails" is the same. It amounts to fifty-fifty. The machine wanted me to treat it seriously, to play rationally with it, using a system, a method. But I do not want to. It is I who have now seen through the machine's method.

The machine stands for fate, which acts on the principle of the law of averages. In order to have even chances with fate I must become fate myself; I must chance my luck; act with a fifty-fifty chance. A man who, when playing with the machine, gives up his free will and freedom of choice, adopts an attitude to fate similar to that which Dürrenmatt's Romulus adopted with regard to historical necessity. Instead of putting the coin with "heads" on top a hundred times in succession, or "heads" and "tails" in turn, or two "tails" after ten "heads," he would just toss the coin up. That kind of man most certainly is not a tragic hero. He has adopted a clownish attitude to fate. Romulus is such a man.

In modern tragedy fate, gods and nature have been replaced by history. History is the only frame of reference, the final authority to accept or reject the validity of human actions. It is unavoidable and realizes its ultimate aims; it is objective "reason," as well as objective "progress." In this scheme of things history is a theatre with actors, but without an audience. No one watches the performance, for everybody is taking part. The script of this grand spectacle has been composed in advance and includes a necessary epilogue, which will explain everything. But, as in the *commedia dell'arte,* the text has not been written down. The actors improvise and only some of them foresee correctly what will happen in the following acts. In this particular theatre the scene changes with the actors; they are constantly setting it up and pulling it down again.

Actors are often wrong, but their mistakes have been foreseen by the scenario. One might even say that mistakes are the basis of the script, and that it is thanks to them that the action unfolds. History contains both the past and the future. Actors from previous scenes keep coming back, repeating old conflicts, and want to play parts that are long since over. They needlessly prolong the performance and have to be removed from the stage.

They arrived too late. Other actors have arrived too early and start performing a scene from the next act, without noticing that the stage is not yet ready for them. They want to speed up the performance, but this cannot be done: every act has to be performed in its proper order. Those who arrive too early are also removed from the stage.

It is these parts that nineteenth-century philosophy and literature considered tragic. For Hegel the tragic heroes of history were those who came too late. Their reasons were noble but onesided. They had been correct in the previous era, in the preceding act. If they continue to insist on them, they must be crushed by history. La Vendée was for Hegel an example of historical tragedy. Count Henry in Krasiński's *Undivine Comedy* is a Hegelian tragic hero.

Those who came too early, striving in vain to speed up the course of history, are also history's tragic heroes. Their reasons, too, are one-sided; they will become valid only at the next historical phase, in the succeeding act. They failed to understand that freedom is only the conscious recognition of necessity. Consequently they were annihilated by historical necessity, which solves only those problems that are capable of solution. The Paris commune is an example of this kind of historical tragedy. Pancrace in *Undivine Comedy* is a tragic hero of history thus conceived.

The grotesque mocks the historical absolute, as it has mocked the absolutes of gods, nature and destiny. It does so by means of the so-called "barrel of laughs," a popular feature of any funfair: a score or more people try to keep their balance while the upturned barrel revolves round its axis. One can only keep one's balance by moving on the bottom of the barrel in the opposite direction to, and with the same speed as, its movement. This is not at all easy. Those who move too fast or too slow in relation to the barrel's movement are bound to fall. The barrel brings them up, then they roll downwards trying desperately to cling to the moving floor. The more violent their gestures and their grip on the walls, the more difficult it is for them to get up, and the funnier they look.

The barrel is put in motion by a motor, which is transcendental in relation to it. However, one may easily imagine a barrel that is set in motion by the people inside it: by those who manage to preserve their balance and those who fall over. A barrel like this would be immanent. Its movements would, of course, be variable: sometimes it would revolve in one direction, sometimes in the other. It would be even more difficult to preserve one's balance in a barrel like this: one would have to change step all the time, move forward and backward, faster or slower. In such an immanent barrel many more people would fall over. But neither those who fall because they move too fast, nor those who fall because they move too slow, are tragic heroes. They are just grotesque. They will be grotesque even if there is no way out of this immanent barrel. The social mechanism shown in most of Adamov's plays is very much like the barrel of laughs.

The world of tragedy and the world of grotesque have a similar structure. Grotesque takes over the themes of tragedy and poses the same fundamental questions. Only its answers are different. This dipute about the tragic and grotesque interpretations of human fate reflects the everlasting conflict of two philosophies and two ways of thinking; of two opposing attitudes defined by the Polish philosopher Leszek Kolakowski as the irreconcilable antagonism between the priest and the clown. Between tragedy and grotesque there is the same conflict for or against such notions as eschatology, belief in the absolute, hope for the ultimate solution of the contradiction between the moral order and every-day practice. Tragedy is the theatre of priests, grotesque is the theatre of clowns.

This conflict between two philosophies and two types of theatre becomes particularly acute in times of great upheavals. When established values have been overthrown, and there is no appeal, to God, Nature, or History, from the tortures inflicted by the cruel world, the clown becomes the central figure in the theatre. He accompanies the exiled trio—the king, the nobleman and his son—on their cruel wanderings through the cold endless night which has fallen on the world; through the "cold night" which, as in Shakespeare's *King Lear,* "will turn us all to fools and madmen."

II

After his eyes have been gouged out, Gloucester wants to throw himself over the cliffs of Dover into the sea. He is led by his own son, who feigns madness. Both have reached the depths of human suffering; the top of "the pyramid of suffering," as Juliusz Slowacki has described *King Lear*. But on the stage there are just two actors, one playing a blind man, the other playing a man who plays a madman. They walk together.

GLOUCESTER
When shall I come to th' top of that same hill?
EDGAR
You do climb up it now. Look how we labour.
GLOUCESTER
Methinks the ground is even.
EDGAR
                         Horrible steep.
Hark, do you hear the sea?
GLOUCESTER
                              No, truly.
(IV, 6)

It is easy to imagine this scene. The text itself provides stage directions. Edgar is supporting Gloucester; he lifts his feet high pretending to walk uphill. Gloucester, too, lifts his feet, as if expecting the ground to rise, but underneath his foot there is only air. This entire scene is written for a very definite type of theatre, namely pantomime.

This pantomime only makes sense if enacted on a flat and level stage.

Edgar feigns madness, but in doing so he must adopt the right gestures. In its theatrical expression this is a scene in which a madman leads a blind man and talks him into believing in a non-existing mountain. In another moment a landscape will be sketched in. Shakespeare often creates a landscape on an empty stage. A few words, and the diffused, soft afternoon light at the Globe changes into night, evening, or morning. But no other

Shakespearean landscape is so exact, precise and clear as this one. It is like a Breughel painting thick with people, objects and events. A little human figure hanging halfway down the cliff is gathering samphire. Fishermen walking on the beach are like mice. A ship seems a little boat, a boat is floating like a buoy.

It is this abyss of Shakespeare's imagination that Slowacki makes the hero of his *Kordian* look into:

> Come! Here, on the top stand still. Your head will whirl,
> When you cast your eyes on the abyss below your feet.
> Crows flying there half-way no bigger are than beetles.
> And there, too, someone is toiling, gathering weed.
> He looks no bigger than a human head.
> And there on the beach the fishermen seem like ants . . .

This veristic and perspective landscape created on an empty stage is not meant to serve as part of the decor, or to replace the non-existent settings. Slowacki understood perfectly the dramatic purpose of this scene:

> Oh, Shakespeare! Spirit! You have built a mountain
> Higher than that created by God.
> For you have talked of an abyss to a man blind . . .

The landscape is now just a score for the pantomime. Gloucester and Edgar have reached the top of the cliff. The landscape is now below them.

> Give me your hand. You are now within a foot
> Of th' extreme verge. For all beneath the moon
> Would I not leap upright.
>
> > (*King Lear*, IV, 6)

In Shakespeare's time the actors probably put their feet forward through a small balustrade above the apron-stage, immediately over the heads of the "groundlings." But we are not concerned here with an historical reconstruction of the Elizabethan stage. It is the presence and importance of the mime that is significant. Shakespeare is stubborn. Gloucester has already jumped over the precipice. Both actors are at the foot of a non-existent cliff. The same landscape is now above them. The mime continues.

GLOUCESTER
But have I fall'n, or no?
EDGAR
From the dread summit of this chalky bourn.
Look up a-height. The shrill-gorg'd lark so far
Cannot be seen or heard. Do but look up.

(IV, 6)

The mime creates a scenic area: the top and bottom of the cliff, the precipice. Shakespeare makes use of all the means of anti-illusionist theatre in order to create a most realistic and concrete landscape. A landscape which is only a blind man's illusion. There is perspective in it, light, men and things, even sounds. From the height of the cliff the sea cannot be heard, but there is mention of its roar. From the foot of the cliff the lark cannot be heard, but there is mention of its song. In this landscape sounds are present by their very absence: the silence is filled with them, just as the empty stage is filled with the mountain.

The scene of the suicidal leap is also a mime. Gloucester kneels in a last prayer and then, in accordance with tradition of the play's English performances, falls over. He is now at the bottom of the cliff. But there was no height; it was an illusion. Gloucester knelt down on an empty stage, fell over and got up. At this point disillusion follows.

The non-existent cliff is not meant just to deceive the blind man. For a short while we, too, believed in this landscape and in the mime. The meaning of this parable is not easy to define. But one thing is clear: this type of parable is not to be thought of outside the theatre, or rather outside a certain kind of theatre. In narrative prose Edgar could, of course, lead the blind Gloucester to the cliffs of Dover, let him jump down from a stone and make him believe that he was jumping from the top of a cliff. But he might just as well lead him a day's journey away from the castle and make him jump from a stone on any heap of sand. In film and in prose there is only the choice between a real stone lying in the sand and an equally real jump from the top of a chalk cliff into the sea. One cannot transpose Gloucester's suicide attempt to the screen, unless one were to film a stage performance. But in the naturalistic, or even stylized theatre, with the precipice painted or projected onto a screen, Shakespeare's parable would be completely obliterated.

The stage must be empty. On it a suicide, or rather its symbol, has been performed. Mime is the performance of symbols. In Ionesco's *Le tueur sans gages* the Architect, who is at the same time the commissioner of police, shows Berenger round the *Cité Radieuse*. On an empty stage Berenger sniffs at non-existent flowers and taps non-existent walls. The Radiant City exists and does not exist, or rather it has existed always and everywhere. And that is why it is so terrifying. Similarly, the Shakespearean precipice at Dover exists and does not exist. It is the abyss, waiting all the time. The abyss, into which one can jump, is everywhere.

By a few words of dialogue Shakespeare often turned the platform stage, the inner stage, or the gallery into a London street, a forest, a palace, a ship, or a castle battlement. But these were always real places of action. Townspeople gathered outside the Tower, lovers wandered through the forest, Brutus murdered Caesar in the Forum. The white precipice at Dover performs a different function. Gloucester does not jump from the top of the cliff, or from a stone. For once, in *King Lear*, Shakespeare shows the paradox of pure theatre. It is the same theatrical paradox that Ionesco uses in his *Le tueur sans gages*.

In the naturalistic theatre one can perform a murder scene, or a scene of terror. The shot may be fired from a revolver or a toy pistol. But in the mime there is no difference between a revolver and a toy pistol: in fact neither exists. Like death, the shot is only a performance, a parable, a symbol.

Gloucester, falling over on flat, even boards, plays a scene from a great morality play. He is no longer a court dignitary whose eyes have been gouged out because he showed mercy to the banished king. The action is no longer confined to Elizabethan or Celtic England. Gloucester is Everyman, and the stage becomes the medieval *Theatrum Mundi*. A Biblical parable is now enacted; the one about the rich man who became a beggar, and the blind man who recovered his inner sight when he lost his eyes. Everyman begins his wanderings through the world. In medieval mystery plays also the stage was empty, but in the background there were four mansions, four gates representing Earth, Purgatory, Heaven and Hell. In *King Lear* the stage is empty throughout: there is nothing, except the cruel earth, where man goes on his journey from the cradle to the grave. The theme of *King Lear* is an enquiry into the meaning of this journey, into the existence or non-existence of Heaven and Hell.

From the middle of Act II to the end of Act IV, Shakespeare takes up a Biblical theme. But this new *Book of Job* or a new Dantean *Inferno* was written towards the close of the Renaissance. In Shakespeare's play there is neither Christian Heaven, nor the heaven predicted and believed in by humanists. *King Lear* makes a tragic mockery of all eschatologies: of the heaven promised on earth, and the Heaven promised after death; in fact—of both Christian and secular theodicies; of cosmogony and of the rational view of history; of the gods and the good nature, of man made in "image and likeness." In *King Lear* both the medieval and the Renaissance orders of established values disintegrate. All that remains at the end of this gigantic pantomime, is the earth—empty and bleeding. On this earth, through which tempest has passed leaving only stones, the King, the Fool, the Blind Man and the Madman carry on their distracted dialogue.

LIONEL ABEL

For Merry Abel, 1940–1964, in memoriam

Our Estimate of Writers with the "Tragic Sense"

We set a particular value on those writers of plays, sometimes of novels—who give expression to what has been called the "tragic sense of life." Do we overvalue them? The truth is, I think, that

Is There a Tragic Sense of Life?

we value them in a very special way. For we see demonstrated in their works the possibility of viewing life other than with optimism or pessimism: and for ourselves, when we reflect, the only possible choice lies with one or the other of these extremes. So that it is not only the art of the writer of tragedy we admire, but some special insight, which we feel that without his aid we are denied, and can only achieve through his intervention, but which he—for that is our assumption—enjoys by some peculiar privilege of rare wisdom, or intelligence, or some yet more mysterious endowment. He seems more *philosophic* than other writers of equal art or scope, so that by a kind of tacit consent philosophers have honored the authors of tragedy as the most *philosophical* of writers. In this estimate of the writer of tragedy I think there is a misunderstanding of his very special achievement, hence also a misunderstanding of what he achieves— namely, tragedy. If we correctly think out what we are right to admire the author of tragedy for, we can correct some wrong notions of what tragedy is.

Our Dissatisfaction with Optimism and Pessimism

Now it should be clear why optimism as an attitude toward life cannot satisfy us. It should be clear, too, that our dissatisfaction with it is mainly *intellectual*. For we are quite naturally optimistic insofar as we are active beings, living in time and planning the future which our very life structure requires us to think of as being capable of yielding to our purposes. But when we reflect, when we remember "Things said and done long years ago," and also the things we did not say or do, as well as those said and done by others, we cannot but realize that there are a great many negative facts. Only a few of these, and there are a great many of them, would be enough to invalidate any optimistic hypothesis that the world as it is can be truthfully described as *good*. Instances of such negative facts may be remote or local; the unjust sentence passed on Socrates, or the example raised by André Malraux at a Congress of Soviet writers during the 30's, of a man run over by a trolley car.* Such negative facts are able to render void all optimistic *generalizations* about the world, just as a few tiny facts which remain obdurate to explanation are sufficient to refute a whole scientific theory accounting for a multitude of others. So those who live by optimistic beliefs are like bad scientists, clinging, despite the evidence, to refuted theories.

But what about the negative facts? Do they at least justify pessimism? Not as a hypothesis, not as a generalized view. For the negative facts comprise merely one set of facts, and the world is such that no one set of facts is able to speak for it. Alas for the heartbreak of the defeated and the dead! If we do not straightaway share their fate—we are forced to think of something else.

---

* The reply made to Malraux was that the Soviet authorities would see to it that accidents of that sort decreased annually. The argument of the Soviet writers was for optimism, to them obligatory; the greater relative safety of future generations would more than make up for the absolute harm which had befallen a single man.

The Russian thinker Shestov—I will not call him a philosopher—repeated again and again in his writings that the injustice done to Socrates was a fact he could not endure. He thought, too, that a fact of this sort should make us suspicious of any facts we ordinarily think of as positive. But even if the positive facts were far fewer than the negative they could still not justify our electing for pessimism. (For Schopenhauer a preponderance of negative facts did justify pessimism; his argument lacks subtlety.) The positive facts remain, and they prevent us from resolving without artificiality in favor of a pessimistic view. A very few positive facts can make pessimism unacceptable. This is illustrated, I think, in the Biblical story of Abraham's debate with God when He was intent on destroying the wicked cities of Sodom and Gomorrah. Abraham argued that if there were even ten good men in those cities, the Lord's proposed action would be unjust. And God finally conceded Abraham to be the better philosopher, admitting that if there were even fewer than ten good men in Sodom and Gomorrah, His pessimism about the two cities would be unjustified, notwithstanding all the wicked in them.

That the positive facts stand in the way of a resolve for pessimism is not in any sense an argument for being optimistic. Far from it! It is a sad fact indeed that sadness is no closer than lightness of spirit to the very heart of things.

What argues for optimism is that it is required by our life structure. If we plan to be optimistic, then at least we are not contradicting ourselves; but if we plan to be pessimistic—and since we live in time, to be pessimistic means to plan to be pessimistic—then we are contradicting ourselves; we are placing our trust in the view that things will be untrustworthy; we are reasoning that Failure cannot fail, and so, in a sense, can be depended upon. Then, too, except in cases of present or permanent distress, optimism is natural and spontaneous, while pessimism is inevitably theatrical. Life requires optimism; but optimism leaves out of account and quite disregards pain, frustration, and death; such disregard is, of course, intellectually shallow. So we are back with our dilemma: we can be optimists or pessimists; but can we *want* to be either?

The Tragic Sense

And the remedy is a fantastic one: it is a vision of the irremedi-
able. We go to the theater to see a tragedy. We see human
action in the clearest light the mind can cast on it, and behold,
we see the human person at his best. We do not disregard pain
or frustration or death; in fact, we give them our whole attention, and they do not make us pessimistic, they give us joy. As
Aristotle said, we are relieved of pity and terror—the very emotions pessimism would yield to and optimism would avoid. We
see life tragically; we have for the duration of the play at least,
and perhaps for some time afterward, the tragic sense. Would
that it were more lasting!

Can we make it so? Can we not make permanent the view of
life we enjoyed in the theater and in recollection afterward for
however short a time? Can we not acquire or develop a sense of
life such as the playwright himself must have had? Of course
we cannot be Sophocles, Shakespeare, or Racine. The question
then is: can the tragic sense be acquired without the special
genius of the writer of tragedy, and if so, how?

Why We Cannot Acquire the Tragic Sense

Suppose, though—for I think this true—that what we call the
tragic sense does not form part of the playwright's genius and
does not involve superior capacities of mind. Then it must be the
result of experience. Of what experience? The answer to this
question is obvious, we should have thought of it immediately;
the experience which leads to the tragic sense of life is the
experience of tragedy; it is by undergoing tragedy that one
arrives at the tragic sense. Or rather, the word "arrives" is misleading here, for one does not acquire or develop the tragic
sense, it is not realized but imposed; one never possesses it; one
has to be possessed by it.

We cannot add the tragic sense to our present sense of life,
be that present sense optimistic or pessimistic. And without our

present sense we have neither terms nor criteria with which to decide whether the tragic sense is worth what it will cost us. And from this it follows that no reason can ever be given for recommending the tragic sense, however good or great a thing the tragic sense may be.

Mr. Herbert J. Muller in a recent book, *The Spirit of Tragedy*, has had the temerity to urge on us the acquisition of the tragic sense for reasons which he himself does not deny are frankly utilitarian. He writes: "We might not continue to get along as a free open society without more of the tragic sense of life." I think the error he has fallen into is expressed in his use of the word "more." If we had *some* of the tragic sense of life, then perhaps we could get still *more* of it, but it would not be the drastic thing it is if that were the way it could be come by. The prospect we would face, if we had not just "more" of the tragic sense, but enough of it to have it, would be one of all or nothing.

So we cannot urge the tragic sense on ourselves or on others. To try to attain it or to recommend it is comical and self-refuting, tragedy being real only when unavoidable. There would be no such thing as tragedy if a tragic fate could be rationally chosen.

The Writer of Tragedy and the Philosopher

But what about the writer of tragedy? Must he not possess the tragic sense of life since he is able to make it available to us at least for the time we spend under his spell? Is there not reason for thinking that the writer of tragedy must have a more permanent relation to the tragic view than those who receive it from him? Does he have a special philosophy, a tragic philosophy if you please, permanently his and which, through his art, he is able to share with us in some small measure?

I do not think the writer of tragedy has to have any view of life drastically different from our own. Supposing he were a philosopher, what difference would that make? He could not by means of philosophy resolve the question of optimism or pessimism, which we, who are not philosophers, face. For philoso-

phies are also either optimistic or pessimistic. (Some philosophies are neutral, but this last attitude is finally subsumed under
pessimism. Neutrality to life really means pessimism about it.)

And when the vision of a writer of tragedy is stated philosophically it is always converted (I submit, necessarily) into a
form of optimism or of pessimism. I shall give two examples.
The first is taken from Matthew Arnold's famous poem, "Dover
Beach." Arnold, looking out at the sea from Dover Beach and
hearing in the cadence of the waves the "eternal note of sadness," thinks of Sophocles:

> Sophocles long ago
> Heard it on the Aegean, and it brought
> Into his mind the turbid ebb and flow
> Of human misery. . . .

And the image of Sophocles hearing the note of "human misery"
leads Arnold to this pessimistic declaration:

> Ah, love, let us be true
> To one another! for the world, which seems
> To be before us like a land of dreams,
> So various, so beautiful, so new,
> Hath really neither joy, nor love, nor light,
> Nor certitude, nor peace, nor help for pain;

The view of life expressed here is not one that I, or any one else,
could derive from seeing a performance of *Oedipus, Oedipus at
Colonus,* or *Antigone.* Perhaps Sophocles had such thoughts
when he looked at the Aegean, but these are not the thoughts we
think when witnessing his tragedies. And from the reports about
Sophocles by his contemporaries, we are scarcely justified in
calling to mind an individual contemplating human misery.
The tragic poet was said to have been charming, gracious,
genial, and with no better opinions about politics or life than
other cultivated Athenians.

The wonderful Spanish writer and thinker Miguel de Unamuno, who is actually responsible for the phrase "the tragic
sense of life," trying to state this "tragic sense" as a philosophical
attitude, converts it, I think, into a refined and pleasing, though
somber, form of optimism. Unamuno's tragic sense is even a
misnomer; there is little that is tragic about it, for he is not urg-
ing us to set something above life; rather what he does urge us

to set above life is nothing more than life, immortal life, the immortality of the soul, on which immortality he asks us to gamble the existence we are certain of. That this violently optimistic Christianity should attract us with its death-splashed Spanish cloak is due, of course, to our obscure recognition, even if we have not thought the matter through, that optimism presented simply as optimism would offer us only what we are well acquainted and dissatisfied with.

A novel and, I think, quite wrong view that thought, even philosophic thought, can have and has had a tragic cast is presented by Lucien Goldmann in his much-praised book on Pascal and Racine, Le Dieu Caché ("The Hidden God"). According to Goldmann, there are certain philosophers whose thought can be characterized as tragic. He cites as instances Pascal and Kant. Why is their thought tragic? Because, says Goldmann, it expresses the conflict in them between alternative and exclusive world views, the world view of mathematical science and the world view of revealed religion. But surely no character on the stage would be convincing in the tragic hero's part if his torment were due to nothing more drastic than his inability to choose between or mediate conflicting views. In fact, Kant and Pascal did both. What I mean is this: Kant opted for religion in his metaphysics and for science in his epistemology. And I think Pascal did the same in his distinction between l'esprit géométrique and l'esprit de finesse (reasoning of the mind and reasoning of the heart).

I submit that it is not through any particular philosophy that the tragic writer is able to give expression to his tragic sense of life, although this tragic sense does have for us, the audience, a virtue which has been called philosophic. Then is it by art alone that the writer of tragedy affects us as he does?

The Writer of Tragedy without the Philosopher

The very great probability is, I suggest, that the writer of tragedy is no more endowed with a tragic sense of life than are we to whom he makes it available. By which I mean that he, too, in his regular experience of life is condemned to the same unsatisfactory choice between optimism and pessimism that we are, and that only in the act of writing tragedy, only by making the tragic view available to us, is he himself enabled to envisage life in its terms. His creation then is a communion with us, in the experiencing of a view of things which we could not have without him, but which he in turn can only have insofar as he is capable of extending it to us.

Why could we not have the tragic sense without the *written* tragedy? Let us consider this point from a somewhat different angle. There is something we could have without the help of art, and which many people may confuse with the tragic sense, namely, the feeling of a *pessimism that is justified*. This is all we can get from the lesser masters of the art of tragedy, from Euripides and Webster at their best, and from Shakespeare in his unsuccessful tragedies such as *Troilus and Cressida, Coriolanus, Julius Caesar*, and *King Lear*. Moreover, it is not this which makes them tragic. When Richard in Shakespeare's *Richard II* complains of the vulnerability of kings—

> . . . for within the hollow crown
> That rounds the mortal temples of a king
> Keeps Death his court; and there the antic sits . . .
> Allowing him a breath, a little scene . . .
> . . . and humour'd thus,
> Comes at the last, and with a little pin
> Bores through his castle wall, and farewell King!

he gives expression to a pessimism which in view of his situation he is certainly justified in feeling. And the greatness of the verse penetrates Richard's feeling completely; what he says seems all the more inevitable because said in lines of such power. Who can be secure if the best protected of men, the king, is not? It is to be noted that a negative fact, in this instance death, armed with so mean and trivial an instrument as a pin, is seen as rendering meaningless the highest state a man can aspire to, that of kingliness. Later in the play Richard will say that man

> . . . who but man is
> With nothing shall be pleased till he be eased
> By being nothing.

The feeling expressed here of life's meaninglessness we may all
have felt, indeed must have felt, at some time or other and with
some measure of poetry too, for such feelings provide a verbal
talent all by themselves. We would not need the art of tragedy
to acquaint us with such a judgment of life nor even with the
necessity to pronounce it consummately.

A judgment of life similar in its pessimism to Richard's and
equally justified is uttered by Macbeth:

> Life's but a walking shadow, a poor player,
> That struts and frets his hour upon the stage
> And then is heard no more. It is a tale
> Told by an idiot, full of sound and fury,
> Signifying nothing.

This judgment, too, we could form for ourselves without either
the experience of tragedy or Shakespeare's art. But what we
could not get without actual or invented tragedy is the experience of resolution when nothing can follow from resolve, a resolution beyond optimism or pessimism, hope or despair. This we
get from Macbeth's great words:

> Though Birnam Wood be come to Dunsinane
> And thou opposed, being not of woman born,
> Yet will I try the last.

Richard's speech about the death of kings is a protest against
the weakness and impotence of the most highly placed. Macbeth's lines of resolution express a much more complicated feeling, one in which are allied, to use Heidegger's terms, utter
impotence and super power. Richard's lines about the death of
kings, justifying pessimism, point to the negative fact, death,
which renders optimistic notions of life invalid even for a king.
Macbeth's lines of resolution refer to no negative facts at all,
nor to anything common in human experience, not even to the
common experience of kings, but exclusively to the withdrawal
of their aid from him by those metaphysical beings, the witches,
who had for a time supported him. Macbeth's lines are thrilling;
Richard's are merely sad. What has to be explained is why Macbeth's lines thrill us, and why he had to pass through the experience of tragedy in order to be able to utter them. The weakness
of Richard is evident, so is Macbeth's. But whence comes Macbeth's power?

What Is Tragedy?

In tragedy, it is not the negative facts, rendering optimism invalid, which cause ultimate misfortune. Such negative facts as commonly threaten all of us are even converted in the mechanism of tragedy into positive goods. Blindness is an evil; yet Oedipus deliberately blinds himself. Death we would think is to be avoided at all costs; yet Antigone elects to die and denies her sister Ismene the same privilege. Ajax, when told that if he spends the day in his tent he will be allowed to live, deliberately leaves his tent and falls on his sword. In the tragic universe the negative facts of experience are finally unimportant. What might lead us in ordinary life to be pessimistic is never the cause of tragedy.

What is the cause, then, of tragedy? It is the opposition, as Hegel affirmed, of two conflicting goods. Tragedy is never caused by what is unambiguously evil. It is the sheerly positive in conflict with the sheerly positive that destroys the tragic protagonist. In the Greek world it was the collision of the values of the family with those of the state. For these contrary values, as Aeschylus and Sophocles understood them, could not be held to with equal fidelity in any superior experience of life. The superior man would inevitably violate the one or the other.[1] Perhaps it may be said that while this may have been true of the ancient Greek world, it was not true of the Shakespearian world. For in what sense can the witches who incite Macbeth to kill Duncan be called sheerly positive? In what sense can they be called representatives of the good? Are they not an expression of unmitigated evil?

If they were, *Macbeth* would not be a tragedy. It would be a

---

[1] It may be asked: Why is a collision of values different from a collision of world views? But a collision of views, even if we call them world views, takes place within *consciousness* and not within the *world*. Values such as the family and the state are not merely values; they are valued realities. I should like to point out here that one of the most interesting insights of Martin Heidegger—much more interesting than his remarks about anguish and guilt, which have become part of current twaddle—is his judgment that world views imply the absence of a world rather than a world's enduring presence. Tragedy takes place in a world, not in a consciousness which is uncertain as to what the world is.

melodrama, and Macbeth's story would merely be that of a villain defeated. But once again: in what sense can the witches be said to represent the good? In this sense: the witches in *Macbeth* are the only dramatic expression of the metaphysical. Duncan, the reigning king, is presented as kingly, just, morally upright. But Macbeth and Banquo are the characters in the play who have direct contact with the representatives of the metaphysical —that is to say, the witches. Now in *Macbeth* the metaphysical does not coincide with the moral, but is at odds with it; yet both are to be valued. Since the justification for kingship was finally metaphysical—the Elizabethans believed in the divine right of kings as opposed to any merely moral right to kingship—how could an immoral deed of murder to attain kingship, when metaphysical forces (in this case, the witches) seemed to support that deed, be thought of as evil? And, in fact, we never feel Macbeth is evil. We think of him as suffering, suffering because he has violated moral values he cannot deny, in support of values neither he nor Shakespeare's age could think criticizable in moral terms. As in the Greek tragedies, we have in *Macbeth* good pitted against good, and the protagonist is the victim of their collision. What is dreadful, then, is never the mere negative facts ordinary experience fears. It is the good which is dreaded and has to be dreaded. Søren Kierkegaard, peculiarly sensitive to these matters, summed up what, I think, can be called the experience of tragedy when he said in his acute analysis of dread that it is fundamentally dread of the good.

What Has the Writer of Tragedy Seen?

So the tragic writer has to have seen some collision of good with good in order to have been able to arrange the events he describes into a tragedy. Was he predisposed to see some such collision of good with good? Not, I should say, if it were not there to be seen, even if only he saw it. For can we want to see what it is undesirable to see? Some of us may, out of ambition or perversity, but not the writer of a proper tragedy. He sees what it is undesirable to see, without desiring to see it. This is one of the things we admire him for. To be sure, there are others. But in any case, what must be understood here is that the object of his vision was given by his age or epoch, and not created by him alone. The collision of good with good which he witnessed had then to be given him along with others to see; his part was to take what he saw, and what others may have seen, and fashion it into tragedy.

Thus the tragic view, properly understood, means to have seen the necessity for tragedy, to have recognized it rather than to have created it. That the tragic vision results from a direct act of seeing, and not from the holding of any particular view, or from any predilection for interpreting reality tragically, is something we must understand in order to evaluate that vision and judge it for its true worth. Just as in the tragedy he is going to write, the dramatist will set forth a sequence of events whose connections are necessary, so he himself can only be stirred to set forth such a sequence of events by the sight of a fatality that was thrust upon his view, and which was necessarily, not accidentally, there before him.

Once again: what did he see? A collision of good with good. Is it desirable that such a collision come within our view? Not in life. No. Nobody can genuinely say that he wants to see a tragedy enacted anywhere but on the stage. For it is a misfortune to a society or to a culture if its main values contradict one another. On the other hand, tragedy, that art which expresses the collision and not the harmony of such values, is in itself a positive aesthetic good. But this good, this aesthetic good, is achieved through an appropriate description of the ultimate in human misfortune: that men's values should contradict rather than support one another.

Once Again "The Tragic Thinker"

Perhaps it is right to say of the writer of tragedy that his thought, since it had to be equal to what he saw—what he saw was tragedy—is a kind of "tragic thinking." But this can only

mean that the writer of tragedy has not permitted any philosophy or ideology to impede or obstruct his vision. But what about
those thinkers who have been called "tragic," as for instance
Pascal? As I indicated before, I think the term "tragic" when
used to designate the thought of anyone not the writer of a
tragedy is always wrongly used. Nonetheless, there are in Pascal's *Pensées* many dramatic characterizations of experience
which give us a kind of thrill comparable to the kind we get
from tragedy. My contention is that in the case of such *Pensées,*
Pascal has merely created an abstract replica of the kind of
collision of values we find embodied with ever so much more
concreteness in tragic poetry. Here is one of the most famous
of Pascal's thoughts:

> Man is but a reed, the feeblest of Nature's growth, but he
> is a thinking reed. There is no need for the whole universe
> to take up arms to crush him; a breath, a drop of water, may
> prove fatal. But were the universe to kill him, he would still
> be more noble than his slayers: for man knows that he is
> crushed, but the universe does not know that it crushes him.

Now I think what we have here is an imitation in conceptual
terms of the kind of event set forth in a real tragedy. It is to be
noted that Pascal begins by saying men can be destroyed by a
drop of water or a breath; but he chooses not to continue the
thought that men can be destroyed by such small means. The
drop of water, the breath, are tiny facts: acting negatively, they
would be of no interest in tragedy. So in Pascal's thought they
are expanded—in possibility, of course—into the universe. From
the breath, the drop of water, Pascal goes to the whole universe
which he imagines in the act of overwhelming a man. Even
then, says Pascal, the man would be nobler than his slayer. But
in any case, the slayer would be noble, being the universe.
Insofar as Pascal's thought here may strike one as tragic, I
should say that the event he has described was modeled on that
structure of events always present in a true tragedy. For he who
is destroyed in a true tragedy is always destroyed by something
of worth. The drop of water, the breath may be thought of, as I
said before, as tiny facts behaving negatively, but which Pascal

had finally to forget about and obscure from his view in order to make a true judgment of man's nobility in misfortune.

What We Should Admire in the Writer of Tragedy

Let us turn from the "tragic thinker" to the writer of tragedy. Why do we admire him? Not for his philosophy, for he has none. If he does hold to one in his personal life, this is not pertinent to his achievement or to our judgment of it. Nor are we required to think of him as a master of experience, as wiser or more deeply human than ourselves. Let us admire him for his art; we should recognize, though, that what he gives us goes far beyond what art generally or regularly gives. And let us admire him for his luck, too, at having been given by his age the opportunity to see in his mind's eye certain paradigm instances of human adversity. Does not Pushkin say that the day after the flooding of Petrograd, "*Khostov, poet, favorite of the heavens, already sang in verses never to die the griefs of Neva's shores*"? [2]

Moreover, the effort the writer of tragedy makes has to be immense. He has seen the collision of the main values of his age or culture; he has seen the non-meaning of meanings. Now the mind naturally seeks for meanings; the writer of tragedy has to deny and reverse this process in the very movement with which he yields to it.

His interest is, of course, an aesthetic one. May I speak for just one moment from a professional point of view? When you have written a play you are faced with this problem: what does this play mean? If it is meaningless, it is uninteresting. Suppose it does have a meaning, though. This is scarcely better. For have you not then reduced the action in your play to the illustration of an idea? Now illustrative art is scarcely better for many of us today than is meaningless art. Here the idea of tragedy exerts its fascination. For it is the kind of idea that attains to its truth only when represented in the work itself: the play, the tragedy. We

[2] From Pushkin's poem *The Bronze Horseman* in Edmund Wilson's translation.

are much more clear about what tragedy is when we see a tragedy enacted than when we try to reason about tragedy.

And let us not forget that what the writer of tragedy gives, he himself gets in the very act of giving: communion with us in a privileged view of human adversity. We admire him then for what he has seen and what he makes us see, a world where the highest values collide and in which we know we could not live. We recognize this when the curtain comes down and we do not know where to go. We have to become optimists or pessimists again in order to think of going home.

10

The Sense of the Future

The future always eludes us and no prophecy makes any real sense. What is offered here is not prophecy in the ordinary sense. Each of the contributors to this section has had a profound effect on the Sixties. Marshall McLuhan taught us that in an electronic environment "the medium is the message." Michael Harrington made poverty first famous and then almost fashionable. That was not his intention, but as he points out in *The Accidental Century* we are only partially determined by our conscious intentions. Pierre Teilhard de Chardin is the most prophetic of those who have not only a message for the Sixties, but a sense of what might be beyond. A century after Darwin, Teilhard de Chardin has reminded us that evolution is not yet finished nor will it be finished until the human species is.

Teilhard also sums up a theme in McLuhan and Harrington. In *The Phenomenon of Man* and *The Future of Man* he argues that further evolution will take place in terms of a heightened consciousness. In short, the more man becomes man, the more aware of himself and his humanity he becomes. McLuhan and Harrington address themselves to the social implications of the evolutionary drives discernible in the Sixties.

The only sense of the future we have is the sense of its uncertainty. The implicit uncertainty in McLuhan, Teilhard, and Harrington is whether the evolutionary processes through which man is now passing will affirm his tenuous hold on his humanity or destroy what we know as the human.

From the neolithic age men had been engaged in creating technological extensions of their bodies in various fragmented and specialist forms, whether of script, or wheel, or housing, or money. These extensions serve to amplify, but also to fragment, human powers and faculties in order to store and to expedite knowledge and materials and processes. Naturally, such ampli-

Culture and Technology

fications of human powers greatly enlarge the means and incentives to violence and foster the enlargement of bureaucracy and enterprise alike. The break with the neolithic age came with electromagnetism and its derivative technologies. The electronic age is distinct from any other age in having extended the human nervous system itself in a group of external technologies. The numerous extensions of hands and feet in the various forms of spindles and wheels and roads now begin to yield to the circuit and the loop 'where the hand of man never set foot.' The immediate extensions of our nervous system by telegraph and telephone and radio and television not only usher us into a period when the codifying and moving of information supersede all other tasks in scope and in the creation of wealth, but they involve us totally in one another's lives. The extensions of our nerves and senses as they constitute a new man-made environment also require a wholly new kind of understanding of the sensory materials of this new environment and of the learning processes to which they are so deeply related.

One of the discoveries of Baudelaire and his followers concerned the means of relating the creative process in poetry to the stages of apprehension of human knowledge. Since Baudelaire, art has become coextensive with discovery and knowledge in every sphere of action and at every possible stage of human development. The gap between art and technology has now ceased to exist. As we become cognizant of our art and technology as immediate extensions of ourselves, we have also acquired

From *The Times Literary Supplement*, August 6th, 1964. Reprinted by permission of *The Times Literary Supplement*, London.

the responsibility of heeding the psychic and social consequences of such extensions. It is now many years since Mr. Eliot pointed to the effects of the internal combustion engine on poetic rhythms. Many forms of technology far more potent than the internal combustion engine have been assimilated to the rhythms of art and poetry and social life since that time.

With the extension of the nervous system in electric technology, information not only moves in much greater quantity than ever before, but at very much greater speed than ever before. Paradoxically, the acceleration of information movement restores us to the habit of mythical and inclusive perception. Whereas data were previously fragmented by earlier forms of codifying information, the electric circuit has restored us to the world of pattern recognition and to an understanding of the life of forms which had been denied to all but the artists of the now receding mechanical age. Our main concern today is with the patterns of the learning process itself, patterns which we can now see to be correlative with the processes of creativity. In the world of the organization of work, the electric revolution means the end of jobs. That is, electric circuitry eliminates the fragmentation and specialization of the work processes which created the "job" type of work in the Renaissance and after. The elimination of the job in the work process means a return to the depth involvement in role-playing formerly associated only with arts and crafts. But now in the Age of Information the work process and the learning process become interfused. Automation is "learning a living."

Precisely the same kind of a revolution is taking place in the world of learning as in the world of work. Numerous Centres such as the Centre for Culture and Technology at the University of Toronto have recently come into existence. They are the response not so much to a theory as to a need and even to a pressure. It has long been known that in graduate studies a research student crosses departmental boundaries as a matter of course. As access to all kinds of information becomes swifter, so does involvement in the patterns of every type of information. As an example, the Centre for Culture and Technology which exists by cross-appointments within the University of Toronto, is concerned to establish ways of quantifying the psychic and social consequences of every type of technology. It is natural that the extensions of our senses technologically should have a direct effect upon the sensory usage and preferences of any community. Many of these effects are quite incompatible with the continuance of older values. Once a sensory typology has been established for a given population, therefore, it is possible to predict the effect on that sensory typology of any given new artefact such as the motor car, or television. That is to say, it becomes possible to control or to avoid kinds of innovation that are destructive of such established values as we prefer to retain. A large measure of personal and social autonomy thus becomes possible across the entire spectrum of culture and technology, much in the way that we now have the means of thermostatic control of the thermal environment. A full understanding of the sensory typology of cultures on one hand, and the sensory order and impact of art and technology on the other hand, affords the possibility of a human environment sensorially programmed for the maximal use of the human powers of learning.

TEILHARD DE CHARDIN

It is the fundamental paradox of Nature as we see it now that its universal plasticity seems suddenly to have hardened. Like an ocean-wave caught in a snapshot, or a torrent of lava stiffened by cooling, the mountains and living things of the earth wear the aspect, to those who study them, of a powerful momentum that has become petrified. Nature seen at a distance appears to

The Future of Man

be malleable and in motion; but seek to lay hands on it, to deflect by force even the least of Life's directions, and you will encounter nothing but absolute rigidity, an unshakably stubborn refusal to depart from the pre-ordained path.

But let us note that this present rigidity of Nature does not, as some people believe, in any way lessen the certainty of its past mobility. What we regard as the fixity of present organisms may be simply a state of very slow movement, or of rest between spells of movement. It is true that we have not yet succeeded in shaping life to our requirements in the laboratory; but who has shaped or witnessed the shaping of a geological stratum? The rock which we seek to compress crumbles because we work too fast or with over-small fragments. Calcareous matter, if it is to be made malleable, needs to be embedded in a vast mass, and perhaps its reshaping is a process of immense slowness. If we have not seen the upward thrust of mountain ranges it is because their rise was accomplished either in widely spaced jerks or with so slow a rhythm that since the coming of Man nothing of the kind has happened, or at least nothing that has been perceptible to us. Why should not Life, too, be mobile only in great masses, or through the slow action of time, or in brief stages? Who can positively affirm that at this moment, although we perceive nothing, new forms are not taking shape in the contours of the earth and of Life? . . .

The plasticity of Nature in the past is an undeniable fact; its present rigidity is less capable of scientific proof. If we had to choose between a total process of evolution and a state of complete fixity, that is to say between two absolutes—everything incessantly in motion, or everything forever immovable—we should be bound to choose the first. But there is a third possible hypothesis, namely that everything was at one time fluid but is now irrevocably fixed. It is this third alternative that I wish to examine and dismiss.

The hypothesis of a definitive halt in terrestrial evolution is, to my mind, suggested less by the apparently unchanging nature of present forms than by a certain general aspect of the world coinciding with this appearance of cessation. It is most striking that the morphological change of living creatures seems to have slowed down at the precise moment when Thought appeared on earth. If we relate this coincidence to the fact that the only general line taken by biological evolution has been in the direction of the largest brain—broadly speaking, of the highest state of consciousness—we are compelled to wonder whether the true fundamental impulse underlying the growth of animal forces has not been the need to know and to think; and whether, when this overriding impulse eventually found its outlet in the human species, the effect was not to produce an abrupt diminution of "vital pressure" in the other branches of the Tree of Life. This would explain the fact that "evolving Life," from the end of the Tertiary Period, has been confined to the little group of higher primates. We know of many forms that have disappeared since the Oligocene, but of no genuinely new species other than the anthropoids. This again may be explained by the extreme brevity of the Miocene as compared with other geological periods. But does it not lead us to surmise that the "phyla" possessing higher psychic attributes have absorbed all the forces at Life's disposal?

If we are to find a definitive answer to the question of the entitative progress of the Universe we must do so by adopting the least favourable position—that is to say, by envisaging a world whose evolutionary capacity is *concentrated upon* and *confined to* the human soul. The question of whether the Universe is still developing then becomes a matter of deciding

whether the human spirit is still in process of evolution. To this
I reply unhesitatingly, "Yes, it is." The nature of Man is in the
full flood of entitative change. But to grasp this it is necessary
(a) not to overlook the *biological* (morphogenic) value of moral
action, and (b) to accept the organic nature of individual relationships. We shall then see that a vast evolutionary process is in
ceaseless operation around us, but that it is situated within the
sphere of consciousness (and collective consciousness).

What is the difference between ourselves, citizens of the
twentieth century, and the earliest human beings whose soul is
not entirely hidden from us? In what respects may we consider
ourselves their superiors and more advanced than they?

Organically speaking, the faculties of those remote forebears
were probably the equal of our own. By the middle of the last
Ice Age, at the latest, human groups had attained to the expression of aesthetic powers calling for intelligence and sensibility
developed to a point which we have not surpassed. To all appearance the ultimate perfection of the human *element* was achieved
many thousands of years ago, which is to say that the individual
instrument of thought and action may be considered to have
been finalised. But there is fortunately another dimension in
which variation and growth are still possible, and in which we
continue to evolve.

The great superiority over Primitive Man which we have
acquired and which will be enhanced by our descendants in a
degree perhaps undreamed-of by ourselves, is in the realm of
self-knowledge; in our growing capacity to situate ourselves in
space and time, to the point of becoming conscious of our place
and responsibility in relation to the Universe.

Surmounting in turn the illusions of terrestrial flatness, im-
mobility and autocentricity, we have taken the unhopeful surface of the earth and "rolled it like a little ball"; we have set it on
a course among the stars; we have grasped the fact that it is no
more than a grain of cosmic dust; and we have discovered that
a process without limit has brought into being the realms of
substance and essence. Our fathers supposed themselves to go
back no further than yesterday, each man containing within
himself the ultimate value of his existence. They held them-

selves to be confined within the limits of their years on earth
and their corporeal frame. We have blown asunder this narrow
compass and those beliefs. At once humbled and ennobled by
our discoveries, we are gradually coming to see ourselves as a
part of vast and continuing processes; as though awakening
from a dream, we are beginning to realise that our nobility consists in serving, like intelligent atoms, the work proceeding in
the Universe. We have discovered that there is a Whole, of which
we are the elements. We have found the world in our own souls.

What does this conquest signify? Does it merely denote the
establishment, in worldly terms, of an idealised system of logical, extrinsic relationships? Is it no more than an intellectual
luxury, as is commonly supposed—the mere satisfaction of
curiosity? No. The consciousness which we are gradually acquiring of our physical relationship with all parts of the Universe
represents a genuine enlarging of our separate personalities.
It is truly a progressive realisation of the universality of the
things surrounding each of us. And it means that in the domain
external to our flesh our *real and whole body* is continuing to
take shape.

That is in no way a 'sentimental' affirmation.

The proof that the growing co-extension of our soul and the
world, through the consciousness of our relationship with all
things, is not simply a matter of logic or idealisation, but is part
of an organic process, the natural outcome of the impulse which
caused the germination of life and the growth of the brain—
the proof is that it expresses itself in a *specific evolution of the
moral value of our actions* (that is to say, by the modification
of what is most living within us).

No doubt it is true that the scope of individual human action,
as commonly envisaged in the abstract theory of moral and
meritorious acts, is not greatly enhanced by the growth of
human knowledge. Inasmuch as the will-power of contemporary
man is not in itself more vigorous or unswerving than that of a
Plato or an Augustine, and individual moral perfection is still
to be measured by steadfastness in pursuance of the known good
(and therefore relative) we cannot claim as *individuals* to be
more moral or saintly than our fathers.

Yet this must be said, to our own honour and that of those

who have toiled to make us what we are: that between the behaviour of men in the first century AD and our own, the difference is as great, or greater, than that between the behaviour of a fifteen-year-old boy and a man of forty. Why is this so? Because, owing to the progress of science and of thought, our actions today, whether for good or ill, proceed from an incomparably higher point of departure than those of the men who paved the way for us towards enlightenment. When Plato acted it was probably in the belief that his freedom to act could only affect a small fragment of the world, narrowly circumscribed in space and time; but the man of today acts in the knowledge that the choice he makes will have its repercussions through countless centuries and upon countless human beings. He feels in himself the responsibilities and the power of an entire Universe. Progress has not caused the *action of Man* (Man himself) to change in each separate individual; but because of it the action of *human nature* (Mankind) has acquired, in every thinking man, a fullness that is wholly new. Moreover, how are we to compare or contrast our acts with those of Plato or Augustine? All such acts are linked, and Plato and Augustine are still expressing, through me, the whole extent of their personalities. There is a kind of human action that gradually matures through a multitude of human acts. The human monad has long been constituted. What is now proceeding is the animation (assimilation) of the Universe by that monad; that is to say, the realisation of a *consummated human Thought*.

There are philosophers who, accepting this progressive animation of the concrete by the power of thought, of Matter by Spirit, seek to build upon it the hope of a terrestrial liberation, as though the soul becomes mistress of all determinisms and inertias, may someday be capable of overcoming harsh probability and vanquishing suffering and evil here on earth. Alas, it is a forlorn hope: for it seems certain that any outward upheaval or internal renovation which might suffice to transform the Universe as it is could only be a kind of death—death of the individual, death of the race, death of the Cosmos. A more realistic and more Christian view shows us Earth evolving towards a state in which Man, having come into the full possession of his sphere of action, his strength, his maturity and his unity, will at last have become an adult being; and having reached this apogee of his responsibility and freedom, holding in his hands all his future and all his past, will make the choice between arrogant autonomy and loving excentration.

This will be the final choice: revolt or adoration of a world.[1] And then, by an act which will summarise the toil of centuries, by this act (finally and for the first time completely human) justice will ensue and all things be renewed.

The truth can now be seen: Progress is not what the popular mind looks for, finding with exasperation that it never comes. Progress is not immediate ease, well-being and peace. It is not rest. It is not even, directly, virtue. Essentially Progress is a *force,* and the most dangerous of forces. It is the Consciousness of all that is and all that can be. Though it may encounter every kind of prejudice and resentment, this must be asserted because it is the truth: to *be* more is in the first place to *know* more.

Hence the mysterious attraction which, regardless of all setbacks and *a priori* condemnations, has drawn men irresistibly towards science as to the source of Life. Stronger than every obstacle and counter-argument is the instinct which tells us that, to be faithful to Life, we must *know;* we must know more and still more; we must tirelessly and unceasingly search for Something, we know not what, which will appear in the end to those who have penetrated to the very heart of reality.

I maintain that it is possible, by following this road, to find substantial reasons for belief in Progress.

The world of human thought today presents a very remarkable spectacle, if we choose to take note of it. Joined in an inexplicable unifying movement men who are utterly opposed in education and in faith find themselves brought together, intermingled, in their common passion for a double truth; namely, that there exists a physical Unity of beings, and that they themselves are living and active parts of it. It is as though a new and formidable mountain chain had arisen in the landscape of the

---

[1] My purpose is not to show that a *necessary* or *infallible* line of progress exists, but simply to establish that, *for Mankind as a whole,* a way of progress is offered and awaits us, analogous to that which the individual cannot reject without falling into sin and damnation.

soul, causing ancient categories to be reshuffled and uniting higgledy-piggledy on every slope the friends and enemies of yesterday: on one side the inflexible and sterile vision of a Universe composed of unalterable, juxtaposed parts, and on the other side the ardour, the faith, the contagion of a living truth emerging from all action and exercise of will. Here we have a group of men joined simply by the weight of the past and their resolve to defend it; there a gathering of neophytes confident of their truth and strong in their mutual understanding, which they feel to be final and complete.

There seem to be only two kinds of mind left; and—it is a disturbing thought—all natural mystical power and all human religious impulse seem to be concentrated on one side. What does this mean?

There are people who will claim that it is no more than a mode, a momentary ripple of the spirit—at the most the passing exaggeration of a force that has always contributed to the balance of human thinking. But I believe we must look for something more. This impulse which in our time is so irresistibly attracting all open minds towards a philosophy that comprises at once a theoretical system, a rule of action, a religion and a presentiment, heralds and denotes, in my view, the effective, physical fulfilment of all living beings.

We have said that progress is designed to enable considered action to proceed from the will-power of mankind, a wholly human exercise of choice. But this natural conclusion of the vital effort, as we can now see, is not to be regarded as something consummated separately in the secret heart of the individual. If we are to perceive and measure the extent of Progress we must look resolutely beyond the individual viewpoint. It is Mankind as a whole, collective humanity, which is called upon to perform the definitive act whereby the total force of terrestrial evolution will be released and flourish; an act in which the full consciousness of each individual man will be sustained by that of every other man, not only the living but the dead. And so it follows that the *opus humanum* laboriously and gradually achieved within us by the growth of knowledge and in the face of evil, is something quite other than an act of higher morality: it is a living organism. We cannot distinctly view its progress because the organism encloses us, and to know a thing synthetically one has to be in control of it. Yet is there any part of ourselves which does not glow and responsively vibrate with the measure of our growth?

We need only to look about us at the multitude of disjointed forces neutralising each other and losing themselves in the confusion of human society—the huge realities (broad currents of love or hatred animating peoples and classes) which represent the *power of awareness* but have not yet found a consciousness sufficiently vast to encompass them all. We need only recall those moments in time of war when, wrested out of ourselves by the force of a collective passion, we have a sense of rising to a higher level of human existence. All these spiritual reserves, guessed at and faintly apprehended, what are they but the sure evidence that creation is still on the move, but that we are not yet capable of expressing all the natural grandeur of the human mission?

MICHAEL HARRINGTON

There is only one condition in which we can imagine managers not needing subordinates, and masters not needing slaves. This condition would be that each (inanimate) instrument could do its own work, at the word of command or by intelligent anticipation, like the statues of Daedalus or the tripods made by Hephaestus, of which Homer relates that

The Statues of Daedalus

Of their own motion they entered the conclave of
    Gods on Olympus
as if a shuttle should weave of itself, and a plectrum should
do its own harp playing.
                Aristotle, *The Politics*, 1253b

In the middle of the twentieth century, the statues of Daedalus, that "cunning craftsman" of Greek legend, are beginning to dance in the West.

Automation (i.e., self-correcting machines that feed back information and adjust themselves) and cybernation (i.e., making the automated machines capable of responding to a near infinity of contingencies by hooking them up to computers) possess the scientific capacity to accomplish the ancient myth.

As a result, the abolition of work, as Western man has defined the term, has become a technological possibility.

Aristotle understood that such a development would have the most profound consequences. His reference to the statues of Daedalus comes in the course of a defense of slavery. He realized that their discovery would shatter his own "natural" law: Managers would no longer need subordinates, masters could dispense with slaves. This is, happily, one of the options now open to technological man. But there are other, more complex and disturbing, possibilities if the statues of Daedalus are indeed coming to life in the twentieth century.

504

The modern West distinguished itself from other cultures by its Faustian assault upon reality, its relentless ambition to remake the very world. In the matter of a few hundred years, this drive created an industrial civilization and a standard of living that became the envy, and model, of the entire globe. It also deeply marked the ethic, the religious values, the psychology, and social system of Europe and America. If the statues of Daedalus have indeed been found, it is clear that the moment signals the decadence of much that passed as wisdom and morality for hundreds of years. Ironically, the triumph of Faustian man could mean his suicide. For what will Faust do if, as Paul Valéry once suggested, the world is to become "finished"? Or, to put the issue in American terms, if there are no more frontiers?

Such a happening is clearly in the far distance, though not so far as to be out of historical eyesight. Closer to the present, there are even now less ultimate, but extremely profound, results of the fact that work in the West is already being redefined.

The certitude that man must labor by the sweat of his brow was a weary, but consoling, knowledge. The machines are now lifting this burden from human shoulders and, in the doing, corrupting the central Western ethic of work. The stern necessities that drove Europe and America to secular greatness are disappearing. In their place, there is a bewildering freedom. Thus, the machines are not simply a technological fact but the stuff of a spiritual crisis as well.

Then, there is another effect upon the inner man of the West. As Sigmund Freud understood it, work was essential both to society and to the self. At his most pessimistic, in *The Future of an Illusion* and *Civilization and Its Discontents,* Freud argued that civilization itself was based upon the repression of instinctual gratification, demanding that the individual sacrifice himself to the discipline and needs of the collective, to a large extent through hard labor. The majority, Freud said, were lazy and indolent. Without work and its attendant coercion, society would fall apart.

More positively, Freud believed that work was a means of linking man to reality and thus therapeutic. But taking either his dark or his optimistic theory, the disappearance of work could be a social and individual catastrophe, a psychological revolution.

Finally, that other recent Western giant, Karl Marx, argued that the coming of automation would destroy the very rationality of the Western capitalist system itself. Only, he said, in a society in which the exploitation of labor was the essential element in creating commodities could economic rewards and values be measured in terms of how much productive work a man did. Once machines and the practical application of science become the true source of wealth, he concluded, capitalism is a dangerous, unworkable anachronism.

In each of these cases, and in many others, the same irony appears. The West, which more than any other part of the globe learned to cope with starvation and gradually to conquer it, faces the distinct possibility that abundance—its long-dreamed utopia, its Cockaigne—will be the decadence of some of its most cherished values and that it will take more ingenuity to live with freedom than it did to subsist under necessity.

I

The contemporary statues of Daedalus can be described quite prosaically. With so many apocalypses depending on their dance, it is well to start *sotto voce*, empirically, statistically.

In a series of American Government documents in 1964, and most particularly in the Report of the Senate Subcommittee on Employment and Manpower, some trends of automation and cybernation were noted. Among them were changes in the increase of productivity per man-hour, an important shift in the quality of manpower needs, and chronic, high levels of unemployment.

Taken by themselves, these transformations were regarded as serious enough by the Senate Subcommittee to merit the title of a "manpower revolution." They demonstrate that at this very moment, without too many people noticing, the nature of work is being redefined. The figures do not yet show that work as it has been known is actually being abolished, but they certainly suggest this possibility in the middle historical distance.

The evidence presented here is exclusively American. There are considerable differences between Europe and the United States in this regard, most notably in the widespread acceptance of national planning on the Continent. Yet, there is every reason to believe that the Old World will soon experience the troubles of the New. The consumer boom that took place in the United States right after the war did not occur in Europe until the mid-fifties and is still in progress. That has provided a favorable context for the new technology. Once this trend plays itself out, there is no reason to believe that Europe can avoid the revolutionary consequences of its technology. These figures suggest, then, not simply the American, but the European, future and, as industrialization proceeds around the globe, the fate of the world.

The American statues of Daedalus are visible in the prosaic statistics on the increase in output per man-hour in the private economy.

Between 1909 and 1962, American industry increased the worker's output by 2.4 percent a year. But then, this five-decade trend conceals a most significant shift. From 1909 to 1947, the productivity gain was only 2 percent a year. But between 1958 and 1963, productivity per manhour went up 3.1 percent a year, and between 1960 and 1963, 3.6 percent a year. And it was, of course, in this period of accelerated productivity growth in the fifties and early sixties that automation and cybernation began to emerge as an important factor in the American economy.

Translate these gross quantities into some of their significant details. In 1964, ten men could produce as many automobile motor blocks as 400 men in 1954; two workers could make a thousand radios a day, a job that required 200 a few years before; 14 operators were tending the glass-blowing machines that manufactured 90 percent of all the glass bulbs in the United States of America. During the fifties, Bell Telephone increased its volume by 50 percent and its work force by only 10 percent.

This same trend also illumines an economic paradox: the coexistence, in the late fifties and early sixties, of prosperity and chronic unemployment. More unskilled and semiskilled jobs in

private manufacture were destroyed than created, and joblessness persisted at over 5 percent of the work force despite the
prosperity (this 5-percent figure is an understatement; it does
not count those driven out of the labor market, possibly a million
and a half workers, nor the underemployed; a "true" estimate
of involuntary idleness would be in the neighborhood of 9 percent). At the same time, the machines were the source of enormous profit, and thus there was a deformed "prosperity," benign
for corporations, malignant for millions of workers.

Curiously enough, this process stands out in even starker relief
in American agriculture. There, productivity increases have recently hit a prodigious 6 percent a year. One result has been to
cut the postwar farming population from 14 percent of the
population to 7 percent. And even this statistic conceals the
radical character of the change. Farming supports a tremendous
amount of underemployment and hidden unemployment. A third
of the American agricultural producers do not market crops but
merely eke out an impoverished, miserable subsistence for
themselves.

In short, less than 5 percent of the American people are able
to produce more food than they can profitably sell to the other
95 percent under the present system. In order to satisfy these
politically powerful farmers, the Government now pays them
between $4 and $5 billion a year in subsidies. Here, then, is an
anticipation of one of the strange logics of abundance: that
American agriculture is so capable of plenty that nonproduction
must be publicly supported. (The extreme irrationality of re-
warding the rich farmer and penalizing the poor is not a deduction from technology but a conscious, and reactionary, political choice; yet the fundamental problem is there in any context.)

In private manufacturing, the decline in jobs has not been as
spectacular as on the farm, but the trend is clearly present.
Between 1957 and 1963, for instance, wage and salary employment in the nonagricultural, goods-producing sector dropped by
300,000 jobs—despite substantial increases in output, new products, and even new industries. In the ten years before this
period, from 1947 to 1957, employment in the same sector had
gone up at the rate of 250,000 new jobs a year.

In short, American industry broke through a technological barrier somewhere in the mid-fifties. Cybernation made it possible to expand production and contract the work force. Less labor produced more goods. Even so, the president of a corporation making automated equipment, John Snyder, remarked that his equipment was only at a "primitive" level, that an accentuation of the process was imminent.

At first, the new technology was most dramatically successful in reducing unskilled and semiskilled industrial jobs. But as time went on, other occupations began to be affected. In the financial services industry, machines took over more and more office work; transportation employment dropped; the increase in retail sales work slowed down (the automated department store will soon appear in the United States: machines will take orders, package goods, notify inventory of the sale, and keep instantaneous financial accounts).

But employment did grow in this period. And the areas where growth did take place indicate a significant change in the quality and meaning of work.

The largest single increase in jobs took place on the public payrolls, mainly through the hiring of teachers to handle the postwar baby boom. This category alone accounted for one-third of the new jobs in wage and salary employment, or 300,000 new places annually. Close behind was the personal service industry —hospitals, private schools, colleges and private social welfare organizations, hostelries—with 250,000 additional jobs each year. As *The Wall Street Journal* noted in October, 1964, during the previous year there had been more new jobs for schoolteachers than for production workers.

So it was that in this time the most easily cybernated positions, routine, repetitive factory functions, declined; that the simpler office tasks declined or leveled off; that retail employment slowed down; and that real increases were achieved in those areas, such as teaching and hospitals, which required the human care of human beings. Given the revolutionary character of American technology, this pattern is likely to become even more accelerated in the immediate future. Even menial, miserably paid work, like much of that of migrant field hands, can be taken over by machines (and, with savage irony, probably will, not out of compassion for those who bend and stoop in the fields, but because those workers will finally enforce minimal standards of decency for themselves and thus make it cheaper to enslave a machine than a man).

The striking aspect of this new pattern is that the job increases are in areas that are not "productive" in the lay sense of the term. Teaching and nursing do not make manufactured goods, or even help distribute them. The idea that the human care of human beings is an *economically* significant undertaking is a fairly new one. It was this significant change in American working life that led the Senate Subcommittee to speak of a "manpower revolution."

All of this takes place as a process, not as a sudden, definitive transformation. Millions of Americans still labor in fields and on assembly lines. But, as one scholarly vocabulary puts it, the trend is clearly away from primary employments like agriculture, to the secondary functions of industry, to the tertiary of services, and now to a fourth level of training and human care. At each point, work is receding from the direct confrontation of man and nature. And, as time goes on, it is possible to conceive the abolition of entire sectors of economic activity, most obviously that of the factory worker.

Without even looking into the middle distance, however, these new patterns have already posed some massive social problems in American society.

One of the effects of automation and cybernation is to increase the skill "mix" in manufacturing. An airplane plant organized by the United Automobile Workers during World War II had 85 percent of its work force in organizable (blue-collar, generally speaking) occupations. By the sixties, that figure had been reduced to 35 percent, and the rest of the plant was filled with highly trained engineers and other management personnel. In a 1964 Department of Labor study of 3,440 plants, 11 percent had progressed to advanced stages of automation, and, of these, 84.1 percent had reported that their skill requirements had risen.

Left to itself, this trend could create a large increase in involuntary joblessness as a by-product of abundance.

In the decade of the 1960's, according to the Government, 26 million new workers were entering the labor market. Of these, 7.6 million would be without high-school diplomas, 2.3 million without a grade-school education. At the same time, as Secretary of Labor Wirtz remarked, machines were being built with automated skills beyond the human reach of a high-school graduate. As a result, there were 730,000 youthful unemployed by October, 1963 (the figures neared a million in 1964), 350,000 young people were neither at school or work (and thus not "in the labor market" and not certified in the unemployment figures), and one million in the same age group were in what the Administration called "dead-end" jobs. Indeed, in the Selective Service examinations, fully a quarter of the young American males were declared unfit for military service by virtue of not being able to read up to seventh-grade levels.

For these young people—perhaps a third of their generation —the advance of American ingenuity is a catastrophe. Given their lack of skill and training, they are systematically misfitted for the economy which they are entering. Their future holds out chronic unemployment at worst, or at best laboring at tasks that are so menial they are beneath the dignity and education of machines. Part of their plight is already expressed in the explosive social conditions in the slums, the rise of juvenile delinquency, adult crime, and aimless violence.

Yet, under the American corporate system there are limits to this process. On the one hand, business can eliminate jobs in order to cheapen cost and maximize profit; on the other hand, it cannot abolish the consumer buying power needed to purchase the goods it produces, and this is still largely guaranteed through employment. Such a contradiction can, as will be seen, be resolved in many ways, not the least of them the transformation of the system itself. At this point, a few of the immediate American responses are relevant.

One answer, that of the Democratic Administrations of the sixties (theoretically stated by the Council of Economic Advisers) was to hold that technological unemployment was simply a temporary phenomenon. If money could be pumped into the economy by a cut in taxes, that would increase aggregate effective demand and make it profitable to put people to work (the same tax cut, however, included a corporate bonus that could well be utilized to cybernate). In addition, the patchwork of

American social insurance, welfare, and relief schemes was seen as adequate to handle those who fell out of the economy altogether. As the preceding analysis should make clear, this view simply does not meet the radical character of contemporary technological change.

A second response was somewhat more profound, involving redefinitions of work. In the discussion of the Senate Subcommittee on Employment and Manpower, there were demands for an expansion of the public sector in fulfilling the nation's unmet needs for housing, hospitals, schools, and transportation systems. While clearly leaving the corporate basis of the economy intact, this would amount to a modest political allocation of economic resources on the basis of social need. In addition, the Subcommittee urged the extension of universal free public education to two years beyond high school and Government support for those workers who were retired from the economy some years before they were eligible for Social Security.

Behind these suggestions were the beginnings of new ideas. First, they recognize that the public sector—where social personal services must be provided—takes on a new significance. Secondly, there is the emphasis on education and the recognition that it is probably no longer possible to train a young person for a lifetime skill, but necessary to give him a liberal education that would prepare him to change his skill several times according to the demands of technology. Thirdly, there is the advocacy of curtailing the working life of the citizen: through a later entry into the work force after prolonged education, and through an earlier exit by retirement. All of these ideas involve the intimation of new social principles: the importance of the public service sector of the economy; the recognition that going to school is an economically productive function; the realization that not working, for the young and the old, is becoming a social necessity.

These are only some of the changes which the reality of American life in the sixties has made into questions for discussion (there are also, of course, proposals to shorten the workweek itself to thirty hours). They indicate that a profound transformation in the character of work is taking place even now.

But more than that, they point in the not-too-distant future to the appearance of the statues of Daedalus. The almost totally cybernated production of commodities and routine office services is not merely technologically possible; it is now probable.

In all of this, traditional wisdoms are being turned topsy-turvy. In a statement which would have been incomprehensible to the starving man of the past, John R. Bunting, a vice-president of the Federal Reserve Bank of Philadelphia, said in 1964, "I think on balance that the American economic system is threatened more by abundance than by scarcity."

And, well to the Left of Bunting on the political spectrum, the British scholar, Richard M. Titmuss, an important adviser to the Labor Party, wrote in the same year, "If the first phase of the so-called (industrial) revolution was to force men to work, the phase we are now entering may be to force many men not to work."

To a mankind which has been engaged in a grim struggle with hunger since the beginning of time, the idea that men would be forced not to work would, at first glance, seem a salvation. That could well be the case—so long as it is understood that this salvation would simultaneously portend the decadence of some of the most fundamental economic, ethical, and even religious assumptions of Western life. It would therefore require a tremendous burst of freedom and imagination to fill up the void left by the disappearance of starvation.

II

The capitalist West was built, in R. H. Tawney's phrase, by "practical ascetics."

This is to say that the West made hard labor into an ethical dictate, a guarantee of personal worth and even a path to God. In 1900, as remarked earlier, Henry Adams contrasted the Virgin, as the spiritual principle of the medieval age, and the dynamo, the god of force presiding over the new industrialism. Forty years later, in keeping with Adams' own law of the acceleration of history, the dynamo, a source of energy, was ceding its Olympian position to the computer and its "intelligent antici-

pation." And just as the dynamo counterposed its social philosophy to the Virgin's theology, so the statues of Daedalus, the
cybernated machines, mark the end of the practicality of asceticism.

The thesis that work took on a metaphysical and even theological significance under Western capitalism is, of course, most
identified with Max Weber's provocative study of the Protestant
ethic. In Puritanism, Weber wrote, "The premiums were placed
upon 'proving' oneself before God in the sense of attaining salvation—which is found in *all* Puritan denominations—and 'proving' oneself before men in the sense of socially holding one's
own within the Puritan sects. Both aspects were mutually supplementary and operated in the same direction: they helped to
deliver the 'spirit' of modern capitalism, its specific *ethos:* the
ethos of the modern *bourgeois middle classes.*"

Weber's analysis of the importance of the Calvinist idea of a
"calling" to the rise of capitalism has been widely disputed.
Some economic historians like Henri Pirenne have claimed to
trace the capitalist spirit well back into the Middle Ages before
the Reformation (and Marx once admitted in a letter to being
puzzled as to why capitalism had not developed in Rome at the
time of Christ, all of its preconditions having been fulfilled).
Yet whatever the specific weight of the Protestant ethic in *determining* the rise of capitalism, there is little doubt that its distinctive spirit was part of the event. If Puritanism was not god-
father to capitalism, then it was godson. As cause or effect, the
ethical and religious importance of hard work became a constituent principle of the capitalist West.

Indeed, in the past four or five centuries, it was precisely this
practical asceticism that drove the West to the most extraordinary material achievement history has known. Where Eastern
philosophy, for instance, would accept reality as an illusion or a
fate, and the cycles of suffering and starvation as events to be
ignored or endured, the West was remaking the world. (Yeats
understood this point when he limited tragedy, "the heroic cry,"
to the West.) In the mid-twentieth century, one of the great
problems of the developing nations, with their feudal and tribal
heritages, is to find a cultural basis for this Western attitude.

R. H. Tawney was a friendly critic of Weber's (some of their ideas converged). He stated the theological aspect of the work ethic this way: "For since conduct and action, though availing nothing to attain the free gift of salvation, are a proof that the gift has been accorded, what is rejected as means is resumed as a consequence and the Puritan flings himself into practical activities with the daemonic energy of one who, all doubts allayed, is conscious that he is a sealed and chosen vessel. Called by God to labor in his vineyard, he has within himself a principle at once of energy and order, which makes him irresistible both in war and in the struggle of commerce."

Tawney was writing of the origins of capitalism. Over time, the spirit which he described became less mystical, more secular, yet it persisted. Thorstein Veblen's *Theory of the Leisure Class* is primarily a description of the American *nouveau riche* of the late nineteenth century. It chronicles an ethic of conspicuous consumption that is almost the exact opposite of the Protestant spirit. Yet even in this setting, he told of the continuing thrust of the earlier idea.

"The substantial canons of the leisure class scheme of life," Veblen wrote, "are conspicuous waste of time and substance and a withdrawal from the industrial process; while the particular aptitudes here in question [essentially the Protestant ethic] assert themselves, on the economic side, in a deprecation of waste and of a futile manner of life, and in an impulse to participation or in identification with the life process, whether it be on the economic side or in any other of its phases or aspects."

Veblen's leisure class did exist (even if more complexly than he imagined). In Europe, the aristocratic tradition of regarding work and commerce as degrading persisted even under capitalism. And those who actually did the back-breaking toil hardly regarded their daily toil as a spiritual value. "Certainly the workers in Hogarth's Gin Alley," Daniel Bell has written, "or the people whom Melville's Redburn saw in the Liverpool slums, were little concerned with the scourging hand of God. What drove them to work was hunger, and much of the early movements of social protest can only be understood with that fact in mind."

But then, Western capitalism has not been aristocratic, proletarian, or leisured. It has been the bourgeois economic order. Without reducing all of its complexity to a single historic strand, one can say that it was dominated by the ethic, and even religion, of work. To this day, the West believes that a man establishes his worth in the eyes of his neighbor, and even before God, through industry and drudgery and saving. In its most acutely American form, as the poet William Carlos Williams once observed, this attitude asserts itself in the conversational opening, "What do you do?" This question follows immediately upon an exchange of names between strangers, it establishes much of the substance of their talk, it is the quickest means of identification. One is, it implies, what one does. One is one's work.

What, then, would happen if technology rendered work and the work ethic decadent?

Bread and circuses are an obvious, but hardly affirmative, substitute. In a series of Italian films of Antonioni and Fellini, there is a depiction of the empty, orgiastic lives of the leisure and celebrity class. They are tormented by their free time. Significantly, each of these movies contains a scene in which an anguished protagonist looks longingly upon the vitality of working-class or peasant life, admiring its muscularity or simplicity. These particular cases are examples of what Empson defined as the "pastoral" theme in literature and art (the romantic courtier sings of the rustic swain; the middle-class novelist or movie director celebrates the noble proletarian). But they could also be the intimation of a possible nostalgia in the technological future. Will people then turn back to yearn for the working present and the even more hardworking past?

Were it possible to build a society on the principles of bread and circuses, the event would signify the decadence of central Western values. But it is doubtful whether such a society could exist at all. Here, Ortega's inaccurate charge against the twentieth century might apply to the twenty-first. The very existence of technological abundance presupposes a high level of science and skill, at least on the part of the minority. A social order based upon orgy would destroy its own effortless prosperity by failing to reproduce its technological genius. (In terms of myth, Cockaigne, where there is only consumption, is impossible;

utopia, which recognizes some form of work, is still conceivable.)

There is another possible principle of the society that has eliminated work as it is now known: totalitarianism. In the past, hunger has been at least as important for the maintenance of order as for the fomenting of revolution. Out of necessity, millions "voluntarily" chose brutal toil in order to survive. If this indirect discipline were abolished, it might be replaced by the dictatorship of the programmers, of those who decide what decisions the machines will make. Indeed, a society split between the highly educated and sophisticated few on the one side, and the passive, consuming mass on the other, could hardly be democratic, since dialogue between the rulers and ruled would be impossible. Were this to happen, it would confirm the worst fears of sociologists like Weber and Mills that the functional rationalization of life necessarily leads to the loss of substantive rationality for the majority of individuals.

Some of the positive options of a cybernated culture will be discussed shortly, others in the next chapter. For now, it is clear that the West is already approaching the decadence of the work ethic. Thomas Malthus said, "If our benevolence be indiscriminate . . . we shall raise the worthless above the worthy; we shall encourage indolence and check industry; and in the most marked manner subtract from the sum of human happiness. . . . The laws of nature say with Saint Paul, 'If a man will not work, neither shall he eat.' "

That law of nature, so basic to the recent history of the West, is now being abolished by machines. In 1964, the President of the United States intimated the new era when, in announcing the enactment of a cut in taxes, he urged Americans to spend and consume as a patriotic duty. Paradoxically, this decadence of the Protestant ethic comes at the very moment when it has finally conquered the world. As Sebastian de Grazia has pointed out, the UNESCO Declaration of Human Rights announces, "Everyone has the right to work."

So it is that at that point in history at which the Western work ethic is finally in sight of subverting almost every remnant of tribalism, feudalism, and aristocracy on the globe, it ceases to be a practical guide for the culture that gave it birth.

III

Sigmund Freud made two basic arguments for the necessity of work. With the coming of abundance, one of them will become obsolete and the other will constitute the most fundamental challenge of the future.

Freud's first analysis of the need for work rests upon a conservative view of the industrial masses and the assumption of scarcity as a fundamental condition of human life. "The masses," he wrote in *The Future of an Illusion,* "are lazy and unintelligent; they have no love for instinctual renunciation and they are not to be convinced by argument of its inevitability; and the individuals composing them support one another in giving free rein to their indiscipline. It is only through the influence of individuals who can set an example and whom the masses recognize as their leaders that they can be induced to perform the work and undergo the renunciations on which the existence of civilization depends. . . .

"To put it briefly," Freud continues, "there are two widespread characteristics which are responsible for the fact that the regulation of civilization can only be maintained by a certain degree of coercion—namely, that men are not spontaneously fond of work and that arguments are of no avail against their passions."

Thus coercion, Freud makes clear, is essentially conservative in character. It aims "not only at affecting a certain distribution of wealth but at maintaining that distribution; indeed [it has] to protect everything that contributes to the conquest of nature and the production of wealth against men's hostile impulses." At the same time, this fact revolutionizes the majority. "In such conditions, an internalization of the cultural prohibitions among the suppressed people is not to be expected. On the contrary, they are not prepared to acknowledge their prohibitions, they are bent on destroying the culture itself, and possibly even on doing away with the postulates on which it is based."

In part, this analysis is that of a conservative mind, and was wrong on the day it was made. For Freud, it was the very nature of the masses to shirk work. Yet, as he himself was to recognize in *Civilization and Its Discontents,* the work to which these people were driven was degrading and unfree. Under such circumstances, it is realism, and not laziness, to detest work. When those same masses saw real choices, they were anything but indolent. At great personal sacrifice, even of life itself, they organized a mighty and disciplined labor and socialist movement and contributed to the very reshaping of Western society.

With all his marvelous depth and a candor that shook a culture, Freud never fully escaped from the prejudices of a Viennese bourgeois.

The second element in Freud's analysis is much less capricious. He understood that culture had "not got beyond a point at which the satisfaction of one portion of its participants depends upon the suppression of another, and perhaps larger, portion . . ." Here, his social psychology is based on understanding that economic scarcity is a massive determinant of societal structure and the individual self. His point is historical, and not rooted in any assumptions about the "natural" habits of the mass.

But events are now destroying the historical conditions that gave Freud his context. As noted before, there are already Government proposals in the United States for contracting the individual's working life through a late entry into, and early withdrawal from, the labor force. And in a time of cybernating technology, the coercive power of the Government under the neo-Keynesian ethic insists that the masses gratify their desires. The consequences of such developments for the Freudian perspective are momentous.

Insofar as Freud's deep pessimism (most poignantly put in *Civilization and Its Discontents*) rests upon the assumption of economic scarcity, then abundance makes a psychic liberation possible. Freud had said that man becomes more neurotic as society becomes more complex. The more sophisticated the collective life, he argued, the more pervasive is the denial of instinctual gratification, for increasing renunciation is required to maintain such a vast community. In this tragic thesis, there is something pathological about progress.

But if onerous work would no longer be necessary to the collective, then what function is there for coercion and repression? Under such conditions, the recent socialist interpretations of Freud by Herbert Marcuse and Norman Brown would become orthodox deductions from the master's premises. However, the matter is complicated because Freud, living through one world war, the rise of fascism, and the coming of the Second World War, also located an aggressive instinct in man's deepest self. If such a destructiveness is a "natural" human condition, then the elimination of scarcity would not mean the end of coercion but its irrational persistence. Then repression, having lost its economic function, would not express historical necessity but a basic human depravity. One hopes that Freud's dark thesis was an overgeneralization of post-1914 Europe in all of its violence. The possibility remains that it was not.

In any case, Freud's social psychology of work will be rendered obsolete if abundance, as threatened, does indeed come. Given the decadence of some of the basic assumptions of the Western psyche, the question will then be, what forms of repression or liberation will follow upon the event?

And it is here that Freud's second, and positive, argument on work becomes extremely relevant. "Laying stress upon the importance of work," he wrote in *Civilization and Its Discontents*, "has a greater effect than any other technique of living in the direction of binding the individual more closely to reality; in his work, he is at least attached to a part of reality, the human community. Work is no less valuable for the opportunity it and the human relations connected with it provide for a very considerable discharge of libidinal component impulses, narcissistic, aggressive and even erotic, than because it is indispensable for subsistence and justifies existence in society. The daily work of earning a livelihood affords particular satisfaction when it has been selected by free choice, i.e. when through sublimation it enables use to be made of existing inclinations, of instinctual impulses that have retained their strength, or are more intense than usual for constitutional reasons. And yet as a path to happiness, work is not valued very highly by men. They do not run after it as they do after other opportunities of gratification. The great majority work only when forced by necessity, and this natural human aversion to work gives rise to the most difficult social problems."

In the last few sentences on the "natural human aversion to work," Freud is once again the Viennese bourgeois. His own definition of therapeutic, i.e., freely chosen, work has been denied the overwhelming majority of men in history. The only kind of work they have known is that imposed upon them in a struggle for survival. Abundance could completely change this situation. If all routine and repetitive chores can be done by machines, man can be freed for activity of his own choosing.

Freud's really profound point here is that such activity would still be necessary, even if not for subsistence. Work, he says, does not merely discharge narcissistic and aggressive impulses; it can, when freely chosen, even be erotic, a "path to happiness." There is, Freud would say with scientific rigor, a labor of love. In it, man is united with reality and his fellowman, thus discovering some of his deepest satisfactions. And conversely, a man without any work at all would be shallow and sick and his narcissism, aggressiveness, and erotic energy could express themselves in subhuman and antisocial form.

In this psychological analysis of the meaning of work, one glimpses the extraordinary ambiguity of the present moment. Abundance could be the prelude to bread and circuses. A degrading leisure would be society's substitute for a degrading work. Some of these possibilities have already been outlined. On the other hand, there could.be a new kind of leisure and a new kind of work, or more precisely, a range of activities that would partake of the nature of both leisure and work.

This latter development will not simply happen. If the decision is left to technology in its present context, then the first, and grim, possibility is more likely. A society with a cybernated revolution and a conservative mentality is not going to make new definitions of leisure and work. It is much simpler, and in keeping with the current wisdom, to vulgarize the neo-Keynesian ethic and to provide a market for the products of machines by simply injecting quantities of money into the economy, without any planning for the use of this productivity. Such a course would be defended in the name of allowing the individual freedom of choice. In reality, it would tend to constrict that freedom to its basest and most commercial options.

But on the other side there are enormous possibilities. Activities which are now regarded as hobbies, like photography, gardening, and fishing, could be seen as important human occupations in a society where machines did all the drudgery. So could the practice of the arts, of scientific research, of politics and education. To the Athenians, these latter employments were indeed the truly human work of man. But the Greek ideal rested, as Aristotle made so clear in the *Politics*, upon the degradation of the slaves. That fatal immorality of the Aristotelian scheme is no longer necessary—as Aristotle himself realized when he said that the appearance of the statues of Daedalus would obviate the need for slaves. The machine slaves, the modern statues of Daedalus, are now coming into existence. Their appearance makes the Freudian notion of the labor of love a possible choice, not simply for an elite, but for all mankind.

This variant requires the active and conscious intervention of man. Such a radical departure from present certitudes will take an act of the social imagination as fundamental as the one which, in the Neolithic Revolution, established the basis for society itself. But here again, in either case, some of the most obvious assumptions of the contemporary psychology are turned into illusions.

And the ambiguity is, one does not yet know whether these developments simply portend a decadence—or both a decadence and a marvelous birth.

IV

In some notes which he never fully expanded, Karl Marx predicted that automation and cybernation would destroy the very basis of the capitalist system itself.

The analysis appears in *The Outline of the Critique of Political Economy* (*Grundrisse Der Kritik Der Politischen Oekonomie*), some "rough notes" dating from the late 1850's which have never been translated into English. In later years, Marx refined the vocabulary and argument of his outline but, to my knowledge, never returned to his remarkable anticipation of the statues of Daedalus. The intimations of 1857 and 1858 became the more prosaic theories of the change in the organic composition of capital (the substitution of machines for men) and the consequent tendency for the rate of profit to fall. Neither of these ideas is relevant here. The insights of the original notes, however, are utterly contemporary in the age of cybernation which began approximately one hundred years after Marx wrote.

These references are not made to document a historical curiosity, nor even to vindicate Marx as a seer. They are put forth because his words contain so much present truth.

Marx did not, of course, use terms like automation or cybernation, both of recent coinage. Yet he was unmistakably talking about these phenomena. "As large scale industry develops," he wrote, "the creation of real wealth depends less and less upon labor time and the quantity of labor expended, and more upon the might of the machines [*Agentien*] set in motion during labor time. The powerful effectiveness of these machines bears no relationship to the labor time which it cost to produce them. Their power, rather, derives from the general level of science and the progress of technology . . ."

Then Marx, in some remarkably prophetic phrases, notes how this changes the very character of work. "Man's labor no longer appears as incorporated in [*eingeschlossen*] the production process. Rather, the worker relates himself to production as a supervisor and regulator [*Wachter und Regulator*] . . . He watches over the production process rather than being its chief agent." Clearly, Marx did not have mystical, advance knowledge of inventions that were to take place after his death. But just as he derived the tendency of capital to concentrate in larger and larger units from the limited evidence on hand in the mid-nineteenth century, so also did he understand the direction of large-scale production, science, and technology.

Actually, the factory in which the worker became "supervisor and regulator" was not built until 1939, when Standard Oil of New Jersey and the M. W. Kellogg Company erected the first fluid-catalytic crackers. Today, in such plants, the work cycle is leisurely (a man repeats his routine only four times a day in one typical case, as compared to the assembly line on which he might perform the same task several times in the course of a minute). Since the complex system does most of the work by itself, management is content to have the workers "watch over the production process" and even loaf openly. In such factories, the main function of the work force is to be ready when the costly machines break down.

This development, Marx continues, means that the very basis of wealth has been transformed. Now, "neither the actual labor expended by man, nor the length of time during which he works, is the great pillar of production and wealth. That pillar is now the appropriation of man's own universal productivity." And, a little later Marx comments that this demonstrates "the degree to which society's general store of knowledge has become the main factor in increasing productivity."

For Marx, this eventuality does not simply transform the character of work and the source of wealth. It reveals a basic contradiction of the capitalist system itself.

In its earlier stages, Marx argues, capitalism was based upon the fact that riches were derived from poverty. The labor—and suffering—of the great mass was the source of surplus production (that is to say, after the capitalist deducted from his output the cost of paying his workers, that output, produced by those workers, was still much larger than what they received, directly or indirectly, in pay). This surplus constituted the profit of the few, and it was either reinvested to begin the process anew or consumed in luxuries for the few. There was thus a conflict between the demands of the people for more consumer's goods and the money to buy them and those of the entrepreneur for more producer's goods and profits (in another form, this contradiction is constantly plaguing the developing countries of the world today). But as production became more and more sophisticated, as it depended less and less upon the exploitation of brute labor and more upon the application of science to technology, this conflict no longer was necessary. An ever larger part of production can be devoted to new machines without sacrificing the immediate enjoyment of the producers.

Up to this point, Marx's argument resembles Freud's analysis of the way in which the collective represses the instinctual gratification of the many in order to forward the common good as defined, and enjoyed, by the few. It might even win the support of some of the more educated celebrants of the corporation who would be willing to admit that capitalism vastly increased the productive basis of society while simultaneously raising the standard of living. But Marx, of course, went well beyond this point.

"On the one hand," he says, "capital uses every power of science and nature . . . to make the creation of riches independent of the labor time spent in production." The great stimulus to replacing men with machines is to cheapen the cost of production and to maximize profit. "But on the other hand," he continues, "capital measures this growing and achieved social power of production in terms of labor time . . ." As a producer, the capitalist wishes to reduce the number of workers to cheapen costs; but as a seller, he looks to an expanding work force as the source of a growing market able to buy his goods. But once technology demonstrates itself capable of restricting employment while creating abundance, the system breaks down.

In simplified terms, Marx's insight could be illustrated by a (probably imaginary) conversation of the 1950's in America. Henry Ford III was said to have shown Walter Reuther of the United Automobile Workers a completely automated engine block plant. Pointing to the assembly line, on which there were no workers, the corporate chief taunted the trade unionist, "How will you organize workers here?" To which Reuther is said to have replied, "And what workers here will buy your cars?"

In a more complex case, Daniel Bell (who is a sympathetic, but determined, critic of Marx) tells of how the new technology has perhaps already outmoded the old labor-time system of production accounting. "Most important perhaps, there may be an end, too, to the measurement of work. Modern industry began not with the factory but with the measurement of work. *When the worth of the product was defined in production units, the worth of the worker was similarly gauged.* Under the unit concept, the time-study engineers calculated that a worker could produce more units for more money. This was the assumption of the wage-incentive schemes (which actually are output-incentive schemes) and the engineering morality of a 'fair day's pay for a fair day's work.'

"But under automation, with continuous flow, *a worker's worth can no longer be evaluated in production units.* Hence, output-incentive plans, with their involved measurement techniques, may vanish. In their place, as Adam Arbuzzi foretells, may arise a new work morality. Work will be defined not in terms of a 'one best way,' not by the slide rule and the stopwatch, not in terms of fractioned time or units of production, but on the basis of planning and organizing and the continuously smooth functioning of the operation" (emphasis added).

Bell has an important point. In the cybernated factory where the machine, whose production- and tending-cost stands in little relation to its ability to produce goods, is the main source of wealth, how can the worker's worth be evaluated in production units? When the amount of human muscle expended in making an item was an essential element of its value, both the muscle and the product could be computed in terms of labor time (the wages of the muscle and the price of the product). But if that is no longer the case, how can income, the right to consume, be tied to a labor time that is less and less relevant?

As a result of this contradiction, Marx held, "the laboring mass must consume its own surplus product." This consumption is not a grudging necessity of diverting scarce resources to keeping the body and soul of the work force together. It is a precondition of the functioning of the economy, for the people must have the capacity to consume what is made or else there will be overproduction and the crisis of glut. In a moderate form, this notion has become a basic principle of neo-Keynesian economics, recognized by the Western labor movement and the welfare state governments of most of the advanced countries. But it does not stop there.

Under such conditions, Marx concluded, "It is then no longer labor time but disposable time which is the measure of wealth." Now, precisely in order to expand productivity, there must be a vast expansion of consumption. Leisure, which robbed society of resources in a time of scarcity, goads society into activity in a time of abundance.

In short, from Marx's point of view, the decadence of the old principles of scarcity would mark a decisive moment in the liberation of man. Production would no longer rest upon the hard, sweaty labor of the mass but rather upon free time and enjoyment. Where Malthus feared that raising up the poor would degrade the worth and dignity of the few, the modern technological economy of abundance must be frightened of the exact opposite: that not abolishing poverty will destroy prosperity.

Marx's description of the change in the nature of work is now beginning to take place in the West. In the automated factory, the worker is indeed one who "watches over" the production process rather than being its chief agent. His theory that increasing consumption would become an economic necessity has been modestly recognized within the welfare state as a practical reform but not as a revolutionary principle of a new life. As technology takes over more and more occupations, as the working day, week, year, and life are contracted, his ultimate prophecy could come true: that it is the economic responsibility of the citizen to be free, leisured, to develop his own individual bents and proclivities, to consume, not simply manufactured goods, but freedom itself.

And yet, paradoxically, Marx did not realize one possible consequence of his own vision of cybernation and automation. He had assumed that a working-class revolution would transform the ownership of large-scale industry before the process which he described had reached its ultimate limits. The decadence of capitalism under conditions of abundance was not simply a decadence, since the system had created the historical agency for resolving its contradictions in a new way: the proletariat. The humane possibilities of the new development would be made practical by a social class, by those who had learned how to live joyously in the future out of the sufferings and miseries of the past.

But what if the working class in the Marxist sense is abolished before, or simultaneously with, the emergence of the fatal capitalist contradictions of abundance? That now seems quite possible.

V

When Aristotle imagined the statues of Daedalus, he drew one main conclusion from their discovery: that there would no longer be any necessity for slavery and subordination.

Here I suggest that the situation is more complex than the Greek philosopher imagined. Abundance has not really yet arrived in the West, but its possibility—and the abolition of work as it has traditionally been defined in Europe and America—is within the range of commonsensible speculation. Even within the most prosaic Government statistics, one can note that the statues of Daedalus have begun to dance in our midst.

The coming of abundance will unquestionably mean a decadence. Much of the social wisdom of scarcity, that is to say much of man's history, will become irrelevant to the future.

What will replace the conviction that it is through arduous, unfree labor that man realizes himself? A void? Bread and circuses? The dictatorship of the programmers? Or new definitions of freely chosen work, work as creativity, the labor of love?

Will the ending of the economic compulsion to work allow each individual to discover reality in his own way and thus obviate the whole system of social discipline required by the struggle against scarcity? Or will it simply strip away all the extraneous historical guises from the innate destructiveness of man?

Will cybernation force the West to some kind of social humanity, providing practical reasons for making social and personal development the end of collective life? Or will the infinitely capable machines create surplus products and surplus people?

The options are of an extreme range, more so than Aristotle thought. Abundance could actually produce new slaveries, new subordinations. Or, as John Maynard Keynes once said, under such conditions, ". . . we shall be able to rid ourselves of many of the pseudo-moral principles which have hag-ridden us for 200 years, by which we have exalted some of the most distasteful of human qualities into the position of the highest virtues."